THE BOOK OF THE
PIANO

THE BOOK OF THE
PIANO

Edited by Dominic Gill

A PHAIDON BOOK

CORNELL UNIVERSITY PRESS
ITHACA, NEW YORK

The usual acknowledgements, insufficient but heartfelt, to my wife, to friends, to colleagues, to librarians—without whose help this book would certainly have been possible, but far more difficult and less of a pleasure, to edit and write. Special thanks must go to Paul Snelgrove for his tireless and expert help with the illustrations and Index; and to Bryce Morrison, for his work on the Discography.

Frontispiece: Portrait of the artist's daughter at the piano by O. A. de Sequiera, *c.* 1822

First published 1981 by Cornell University Press.

Designed by Paul Watkins
Picture research by Paul Snelgrove

International Standard Book Number 0-8014-1399-0
Library of Congress Catalog Card Number 80-69990

Filmset in England by
BAS Printers Limited, Over Wallop, Hampshire

Printed in Spain by Heraclio Fournier S.A.Vitoria

Contents

Preface

If the name did not carry such unlooked-for associ-ations, and if the task were not patently impossible to achieve in the space of 100,000 words, this book might have been called *The Complete Book of the Piano*. Comprehensiveness, at any rate, has been a guideline from the start; and the other guideline has been balance. *The Book of the Piano* covers, or touches on, nearly every aspect of the piano, its history, its repertoire, its makers and performers, from the earliest times to the present day. But to have been led down too many side-tracks and byways, however fascinating, would have meant missing out too much of central importance; to have attempted to list every name and every fact would have resulted in a cumbersome and unreadable *catalogue raisonné*.

There are therefore certain conscious omissions: chief among them any investigation of the role of the chameleon piano as an orchestral and concerto instrument—a huge topic which, to be adequately represented, would call for a book half as long again. There are others too, which have been the subject of many difficult decisions, appraisals and reappraisals: in any book of this scope, some reader will find some favourite fact or favourite name left out. But few, I hope. A glance at the Index, as well as the Contents Page, will show just how comprehensive the book remains.

The Discography is another matter. There the selection has been unavoidably, and unashamedly, subjective: the reader is directed to the explanatory note at the head of the list. It has been a general policy, so that *The Book of the Piano* shall be accessible to those unable to read music, only to include music examples which also make a general visual point. The exception is Charles Rosen's chapter on 'The Romantic Pedal', where examples from autograph and printed scores are essential accompaniment to the text: but even here, readers unfamiliar with musical notation should be able to follow quite clearly the line of the argument.

The ambiguous term 'fortepiano', sometimes used to denote an early piano, but just as often used (and by some manufacturers still used today) as a synonym for 'piano' or 'pianoforte', has been intentionally sup-pressed to avoid confusion. A piano is a pianoforte is a piano, early or late. Dates of birth or death are often included in the text when they help to clarify the historical perspective or argument. But in the Index most proper names are dated—so the Index may also be used as a handy reference source for dates alone. The Glossary and Bibliography are short guides: to reading, and to further reading.

The Chronology of Pianists, like the Discography, makes no claim to completeness. But there has been a consistency, as well as a kind of poetry, involved in the choice all the same. The history of the piano is also the history of many hundreds of pianists of the first rank: great artists, justly esteemed, who have made an important and original contribution to the story of music. This book could not possibly list them all. But within that rank there is also a body of pianists which it may seem almost invidious to identify—but which stands out nonetheless: the magicians of the first rank, those pianists who force us (even against our will) to make a further division between greatness and genius; not just the many pianists who have together forged a tradition, but the pianists without whom it is impossible to imagine a piano tradition at all. There will be argument as to whether one name or other in the list should have appeared there; but there are, I think, no notable omissions—except of composer-pianists like Chopin and Liszt, who are treated separately in the main text; and of some early names from the pre-recording age— Kalkbrenner, Moscheles and Thalberg come im-mediately to mind—whose quality is by now almost impossible to estimate.

Opposite: A duet of clavichord and flute: anonymous German watercolour, *c.* 1750.

PROLOGUE

The piano is the nearest that civilized Western man has come, in five thousand years, to creating the universal musical instrument. Its full name, the Pianoforte, acknowledges only one of its qualities, and one which it shares with most other means of musical sound-production: the ability to make music both *piano* and *forte*, quiet and loud. The name sounds like a truism: a violin, a harp or a trumpet, after all, can do the same. And yet that very quality, obvious as it may be, is also the key to the piano's historical success, and to its eventual supremacy. The piano is capable of producing loud and soft sounds: but much more important is the fact that its sounds can be *very* loud or *very* soft. It can lend discreet support to the shyest chamber soloist, and it can hold its own (and better) against the forces of a full symphony orchestra in the largest concert hall. It is the range, the extent, the capacity of the piano in every one of its many capabilities that make it unique.

The story begins in Italy, but reaches its first important turning point in the Germanies of the early eighteenth century. From then onwards, it branches out into the whole of the Western world—and beyond. The direct ancestors of the piano, the clavichord and the harpsichord, emerged in Europe together at roughly the same time (the former perhaps beating the latter by a short head) in the later part of the fourteenth century—sophisticated, key-operated successors to the plucked lyre and harp and to the hammer-struck dulcimer, which in some form or other had existed in every part of the civilized world since the dawn of history.

The harpsichord was traditionally larger, grander, more expensive and desirable than the clavichord, and it was so for one reason alone—the voice of its long plucked strings was strong and resonant. It was the instrument best adapted to social gatherings and public functions; it could not easily be overwhelmed in ensemble; there was a magnificence and a glitter to the harpsichord's sound. It had only one serious drawback, which for many years was no drawback at all: because of the peculiar construction of its plucking mechanism, no variation of finger pressure on the harpsichord's key, gentle or fierce, sudden or slow, had the slightest effect on the loudness of the resulting note. Achieving greater or lesser volume meant pulling out or pushing in (like an organist) 'stops' or levers for different registers, thereby adding or subtracting extra sets of strings. Contrasts, either between the two or more keyboards of the larger harpsichords, or between alternating registers on the same keyboard, were a matter of different 'blocks' of volume or timbre juxtaposed or superimposed.

Four lyres: (from left to right) Grecian; Roman from a coin
of Nero; lyre of Timotheus; lyre from a Jewish shekel of
Simon Maccabaeus.

Grand and exciting polyphonic effect, which was the
principal concern, could easily be achieved; but subtle
shading of texture and dynamic, in any case much less of
a concern, was impossible.

The strings of the little clavichord, on the other hand,
were struck, not plucked (see p. 17): and its far simpler
mechanism was capable of producing—within very
narrow limits, as we shall see—just those subtle
dynamic modulations that the harpsichord was not. Its
voice was tiny: at the loudest no louder than a large
harpsichord's *pianissimo*. Its role was similarly humble:
for more than two hundred years it was known as 'the
poor man's Clavier'. It briefly gained in popularity
during the seventeenth century, but only because its
cheapness and compactness made it, perforce, attractive
to the reduced middle classes during the poverty-
stricken decades after the Thirty Years War (1618–48).

Quite suddenly, after a quarter of a millennium, the
clavichord's fortunes were reversed by a shift in the
cultural climate. With the rise in the early eighteenth
century, encouraged by the new Pietism, of the cult of
Empfindung or 'feeling', the humble instrument came to
be regarded—in historical terms almost overnight—as
essentially superior to, more 'spiritual', more 'soulful'
than the harpsichord. In its delicate voice, after so many
generations of the harpsichord's 'lisp and rustle', the
eighteenth-century listener discovered not merely a new
palette of expressive colouring but what seemed to be
the chief element of the expressive power of music
itself—the ability, in common with the human voice, to
match with its rise and fall of volume the rise and fall of
the emotions of the human heart. 'Feelings' did not shift
mechanically in jerks like stops or registers; they swelled
and faded, throbbed and pulsed. A *crescendo* was more
than just an exciting and pleasurable increase in volume

and stridency: it *expressed* a mounting anxiety, a
sharpening desire. A *diminuendo* was more than a fading
away: it was a relaxation, a resignation—'something
that has been somewhere', a leaving, a yielding, a
nostalgia, a relief.

No one at the time declared, in the language of the
modern acoustics technician, that 'the intensity [or
amplitude of vibration] of a tone is as much an organic
part of that tone as its pitch [frequency] or duration'.
But in so many other words, the primacy of the
principles of *arte modulatoria*—the art of singing—was
just as firmly established. As early as 1713, the musician
and composer (and friend and colleague of Handel)
Johann Mattheson of Hamburg was moved to write in
his *Das Neu-Eröffnete Orchester*:

Overtures, sonatas, toccatas, suites and the like are brought
out best and cleanest on a good clavichord, upon which one
can express the art of singing much more intelligently, with
sustaining and softening, than upon the *always alike* and
strongly resonant harpsichords and spinets. If anyone wishes
to hear a delicate hand and a pure style, let him lead his
candidate to a neat clavichord . . .

Another property, unique to the clavichord, made it
still more attractive as an 'expressive' instrument, and
still more akin to the voice. As noted in the following
chapter, when the clavichord's key was depressed, the
metal hammer, or 'tangent', of its striking mechanism
remained in contact with the string. If the finger,
without letting up the key, then rocked up and down
upon it, alternately releasing and renewing the pressure,
the note would pulse with a vibrato not unlike that made
by string-instrument players on their finger-boards.
The Germans called this effect *Bebung*—literally,
'quavering'. And as Arthur Loesser suggests in his book
Men, Women and Pianos:

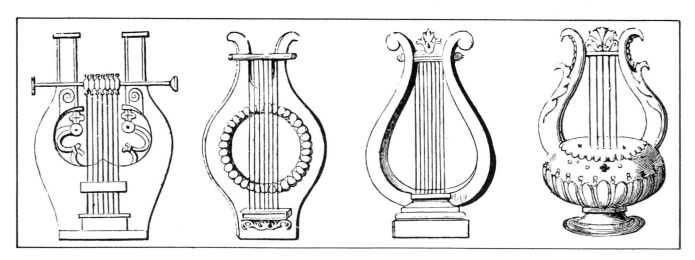

What a potent engine of 'feeling' this little movement could be! The throbbing heart, the panting breast, the trembling lip, the quivering voice—all this physiognomy of emotion could seem to be in the *Bebung*. Amateurs overdid it especially, to judge from the warnings issued in the instruction books of the period.

By the middle of the eighteenth century the clavichord had overtaken the harpsichord in popularity and esteem. By 1768, Johann Adam Hiller of Leipzig could claim with confidence in his weekly periodical '*Wöchentliche Nachrichten und Anmerkungen die Musik betreffend*' ('Weekly News and Comments concerning Music') that:

... the most acceptable and best-known instrument among music-lovers now seems to be the Clavier [clavichord]; therefore the quantity of things that has been written, printed and engraved for it exceeds everything that music can show for itself in other fields ...

Yet for all its new-found expressive advantages, the clavichord had disadvantages too. The gentle sound of the *sanft klagendes Clavier*—'poor in intensity of tone, yet so supple in its poverty'—could be drowned easily by almost any other instrument, including the voice; even alone, it could barely compete with the acoustic of a middle-sized drawing-room, much less that of a princely salon. It was the most intimate of instruments, 'the thrilling confidant of solitude', ideally suited to the *empfindsame* soul, the private, solitary muse. The little metal tangent performed a double, but contradictory, function: it struck the note, soft or loud, but then, still touching the string, muffled and damped it as well.

The clavichord's rise to eminence, in the space of hardly more than a generation, was remarkably fast; but its reign was brief—for it came at the very time when the new fashion of concert-going had already begun to gain a powerful momentum among the middle classes, especially in Germany. The clavichord could speak quietly, and with the greatest eloquence, of innermost feelings; but it most notably lacked any kind of public voice. During the previous century, it had not been uncommon for small groups of music lovers in the larger German towns to meet informally in taverns or private houses to play, discuss and listen to music. But the new class of *Kenner und Liebhaber*—'connoisseurs and amateurs' (see also pp. 44 and 223)—of the early eighteenth century was a more potent and widespread force. The wealthier burghers of Frankfurt founded their own *Collegium musicum* under the direction of Georg Philipp Telemann as early as 1716, and those of Hamburg another, under the direction of the same master, five years later. By the 1750s, Berlin's 'Music

Exercising Society' had become so popular that it was forced to move to the City of Paris Hotel, and to print admission tickets to cope with the demand for seats. In 1743, the 'Great Concert' was founded in Leipzig: and this concert-giving society, too, eventually moved to larger premises in the Clothiers' House—the *Gewandhaus*—to become one of the world's first, and still today one of the most celebrated, public musical institutions. Though the clavichord clung successfully to its solitary, domestic role for some years to come, in the public arena its sweet whisper was out in the cold.

The social and cultural climate of the early eighteenth century could not have been riper or more ready to receive the pianoforte. It could sing with the same subtly modulated art as the clavichord (only the *Bebung* was lost, and not all were sad to see that go); but its greater volume—at first roughly comparable with the harpsichord's, but soon far exceeding it—also gave the piano the power of public oratory. Its tonal range was flexible enough to be scaled down to the drawing-room, where it was still better suited than the clavichord to be home accompanist, and incapable of being subdued by even the most ardent vocal *Gefühlsduselei*. But in the concert hall it reigned supreme, quickly ousting the old-fashioned, rattle-toned harpsichord and taking a central place on the public platform that the meek clavichord had never dared to claim. Here, at last, was an instrument which magnified all of the expressive capabilities of the clavichord thrillingly larger than life-size.

In the late 1720s, Gottfried Silbermann made his first pianos in Dresden. By the late 1750s the new instruments were firmly established in Germany; by the 1770s they were all the rage. On 28 December 1777—the year in which Sébastien Erard built his first piano in Paris—Anna Maria Mozart wrote to her husband Leopold during a two months' stopover in Mannheim (the eventual destination was Paris) with the latest news of their young son's career:

Wolfgang is highly regarded everywhere; but here he plays very differently from the way he does in Salzburg, because here they have pianos everywhere—and he knows how to handle them so incomparably that nobody has ever heard the like ...

But the young Mozart had already been converted. Two months before the stop in Mannheim, he had been to the workshop of the instrument maker Johann Andreas Stein in Augsburg, arriving incognito in the hope of giving the old man a surprise. A surprise it was: 'Oh, he cried, and embraced me!' Mozart wrote later to his father, 'He crossed himself, made faces, and in brief

Egyptian harp and harpist: after a wall-painting in the
Tomb of the Kings, Thebes.

was very well contented . . .' Mozart was also greatly
impressed by the new instruments (see p. 240); nor
could he resist the chance when it came of another
tease—and Stein's reaction to it, as Mozart describes in
another letter, shows just how far, in three quarters of a
century, the Expressionist pendulum had swung.

When I said to Mr Stein that I would like to play his organ,
because the organ is my passion, he was much amazed, and
said, 'What? A man like you, such a great Clavierist, wants to
play an instrument on which no tenderness, no expression, no
piano and *forte* can take place, but which always goes the
same?' 'All that means nothing; in my ears and eyes the organ
is still king of the instruments!'—and Stein replied, 'Well,
that's all right with me!'

But all that, as it turned out, meant nothing: Mozart
spent the greater part of his stay in Augsburg in Stein's
workshop playing, not the king of instruments, but all
the pianofortes he could lay his hands on. From that
time, the piano was his chosen keyboard instrument—
just as it was to be the central, chosen instrument of
every succeeding musical generation.

In all its functions, the piano answered to a musical
need. It was the Chameleon of Music—indeed, for two
centuries, it prescribed and shaped the very ways in

which Western music itself was conceived. Its keyboard
became a workplace. Composers from Haydn to
Stravinsky (and including both of these) as often as not
wrote their music, for whatever combination, *at* the
piano. Schumann believed in theory that the composer
should compose away from the keyboard—although he
himself, to his chagrin, never could. For two centuries,
music was pitches, tuned in well-tempered sequence,
twelve semitones to the octave, in the mind's eye neatly
divided into clusters of white and black.

The piano was soloist, accompanist, ensemble-
partner, orchestral instrument, orchestra and gramophone. The pianist could play his own repertoire,
also everyone else's; pick out a simple monody, or
thunder (in powerfully authentic arrangement) a
symphony. He could play not merely two or three notes
at once, like the player of the violin, mouth-organ,
cimbalom or guitar, but a dozen notes together by the
double handful, and hold many more than a dozen (with
the aid of the sustaining pedal) in impressive resonance.

He eventually commanded not merely the extent of
the male and female voices combined—but a great way
beyond in either direction, down to the lowest notes of
the contrabass tuba, and up to the highest reaches of the
piccolo, encompassing in eight octaves only fourteen
tones less than the entire human-audible range. Nor did
he control merely two or three contrasting timbres, but a
huge palette of tone-colours to parallel (and often
conjure with uncanny exactness) the sounds of many
other, wholly dissimilar instruments—the crack of a
drum, the plangent voice of the oboe, the full tenor of
the cello: and most remarkable of all for a percussion
instrument, even to some degree the *cantabile* (if not the
infinitely subtle gradation) of the human voice.

In more recent years, some of the functions of the
piano have been eclipsed: by the gramophone especially, and by the portable tape-recorder and radio;
and by the age of electronics, which has introduced
composers to a new world of combinations and colours
and to computer techniques of control that are simpler
and quicker, and far more flexible, than ten fingers on
nearly one hundred keys. The piano has been dethroned
as an idol; but it is not obsolete, nor likely to become so.
The vast body of great music written for it is not likely to
lose its appeal, nor performances of that music their
magic. And still it remains the one instrument in our
culture of infinite resource for the player of genius, on
which the player of only moderate talent can achieve,
within a relatively short space of time, a plausible,
beautiful and satisfying result—the Chameleon of
Music: the universal instrument.

Flute and dulcimer: from a 16th-century tapestry in the
Musée de Cluny.

'The public voice of the harpsichord'—*Le Concert:* engraving
after a drawing by Augustin de Saint-Aubin, late 18th
century.

Below: *Young Woman Playing a Clavichord*: painting from the workshop of Jan Sanders van Hemessen, Flemish, 16th century.
Bottom: Diagram of a clavichord from the important French work on musical instruments, the *Book of Universal Harmony* by Marin Mersenne, published in 1636.

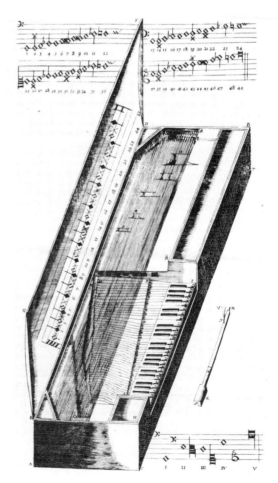

View of a modern piano, showing the four principal component parts: the action, the case, the soundboard, and the cast iron frame which carries the strings.

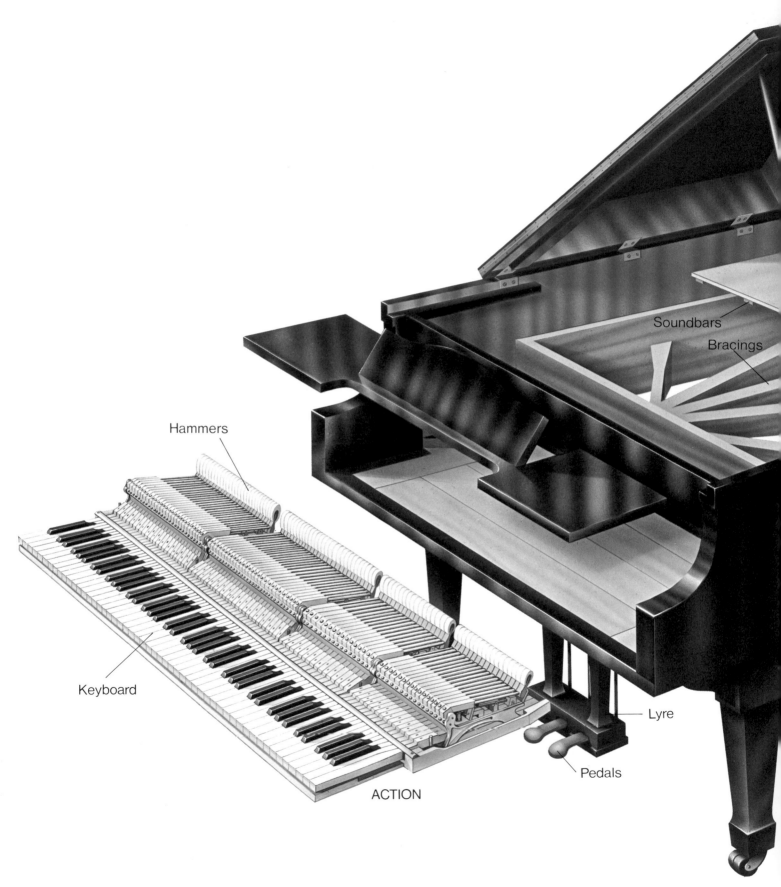

Soundbars

Bracings

Hammers

Keyboard

Lyre

Pedals

ACTION

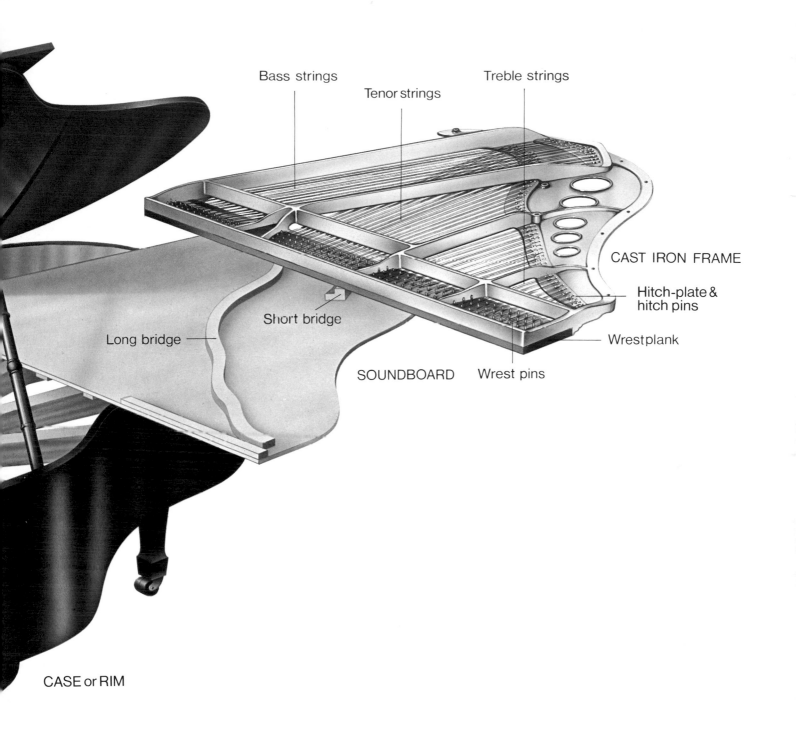

Bass strings

Tenor strings

Treble strings

CAST IRON FRAME

Hitch-plate & hitch pins

Wrestplank

Wrest pins

SOUNDBOARD

Short bridge

Long bridge

CASE or RIM

THE ANATOMY OF THE PIANO

Left: Primitive musical bow from South Africa.
Below: Two-manual harpsichord by J. Kirkman, 1773.
Bottom: Fretted, double-strung clavichord by an unknown maker: German, 18th century. The seemingly erratic spacing of the keys is necessary because some pairs of keys must strike the same strings.

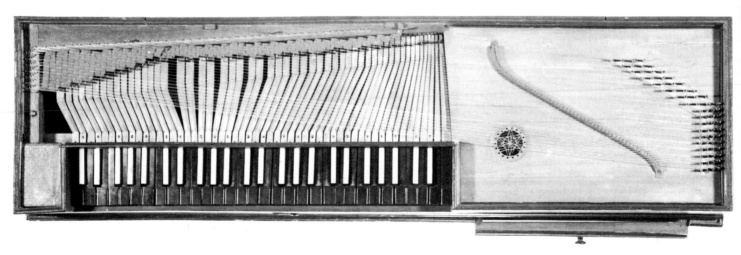

Man's first stringed instrument perhaps was the hunting bow—the bow-string could be plucked or struck, and the mouth used as a resonator. Through the ages the stretched string has continued to be one of the major means of generating a musical sound, set in vibration by a bow of hair, plucked by the fingers or a hard plectrum, or struck with hammers, each method of vibrating (or 'exciting') the string forming the central mechanical element of separate groups or families of musical instruments.

When the keyboard first came to be applied to stringed instruments late in the fourteenth century, only two of these methods were pressed into use. In the harpsichord, the strings of an instrument somewhat like a psaltery were each provided with a plucking mechanism operated by the key levers. The clavichord on the other hand made use of a small slip of metal fixed directly in the far end of the key lever; this *tangent* struck the string and remained in contact with it while the key remained depressed. The tangent also defined the actual 'speaking length' of the string, and thus its pitch, according to the precise spot at which it struck: therefore the same string, struck by different tangents, could serve to produce two, or even more, different pitches (though not simultaneously).

For all its virtues, the clavichord was unable to compete with the harpsichord in one important characteristic—loudness. Since the tangent strikes the string at one end (a nodal point) it can impart only a tiny amount of energy to it, and so the clavichord's volume of sound can never equal the full tone of the harpsichord.

Unexpectedly it was only at the beginning of the eighteenth century that an ancient instrument called the dulcimer was noticed by an inventive harpsichord maker who saw that it could be fitted with a keyboard-operated mechanism. The strings of the dulcimer are struck not by tangents, but with hammers held in the hands of the player. The fundamental difference between the two methods of sounding the strings is that the hammers (unlike the tangents, which remain in contact with the strings as long as the keys are depressed) are allowed to bounce off the strings after the blow, so leaving the strings free to vibrate and the sound to ring on.

A musically inclined inventor, given the problem of constructing a dulcimer operated by a keyboard, would find himself confronted by a number of problems. It is a simple matter to place a row of hinged hammers beneath a series of stretched strings, and to transmit the motive force required to throw a hammer against a string from the key lever to that hammer. This transmission mechanism, which in the simplest actions consists of a metal rod provided with a leather head, is called the *jack*.

A complication arises, however, since the jack having pushed the hammer upward must then be disengaged from it, to allow the hammer to fall back, leaving the string to vibrate freely. This action is called the *escapement*. If the hammer does not escape, then it may be pressed against the string and so prevent the string from vibrating. The note is then said to be *blocked*.

A second difficulty arises out of the great advantage the hammer mechanism has over a plectrum: the ability to produce degrees of loudness and softness varying with the velocity at which the hammer head is travelling when it strikes the string. A key depressed slowly (gently) will in turn cause the hammer to travel slowly, and produce a much softer tone than a key that is depressed rapidly to give a loud tone. The velocity at which a string must be struck to produce even a soft tone, however, is considerably greater than the speed at which a key itself can easily move, and so our inventor must design a mechanism which gears up the movements of the key. This may be done by placing an intermediate *lever* between the hammer and the jack. The free end of the lever acts directly on the hammer, but the jack acts on the lever at a point much closer to its fulcrum, so both the distance and velocity at which the hammer travels are greatly increased.

A hammer travelling at high speed poses another problem for our inventor, for it is likely to rebound from the string with such force that it will bounce from the hammer-rest to strike the string a second time. To prevent this, a pad of soft leather is made to move forward as the key is depressed to catch the hammer as it falls back from the string. Only when the key is released does the pad move back to release the hammer. This device is the *check*.

A wooden shaft passes between each pair of strings, carrying a strip of soft leather or felt which rests on them and prevents their vibration. When the note is struck, the key lifts the leather from the strings and they are free to sound; when the key is released, the shaft falls back and the strings are silenced once again. This is the *damper*.

With two hundred and eighty years of accumulated experience of the piano and its music behind us, it is easy to state that these are the basic requirements of a refined piano action designed to respond reliably and with sensitivity to the player's hands. However, let us for a moment go back to the beginning of the eighteenth century: since the skill of an inventor lies as much in his ability to define and describe problems as to solve them,

Below: A lavishly decorated Italian harpsichord, *c.* 1710.
Opposite above: The earliest surviving piano by
Bartolommeo Cristofori, 1720.
Opposite below: Harpsichord by John Broadwood and
Burkat Shudi, 1770, showing the Venetian Swell open. This
device, similar to the organ swell, was an attempt to give
the harpsichord greater dynamic variety and range.

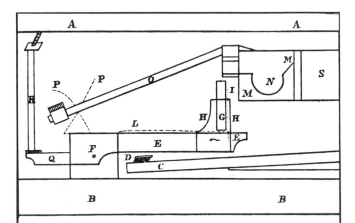

Cristofori's piano action after Scipione Maffei, from *The Pianoforte: Its Origins, Progress and Construction* by E. Rimbault, published in 1860.

and given none of our historical hindsight and no preconceived notion of the potential of the idea, we can use the word 'genius' to describe the man whose mind conceived not only the complex series of requirements of the instrument, but who also constructed the mechanism which solved these problems with the elegance of a Euclidean proof.

The genius was Bartolommeo Cristofori (1655–1731), keeper of harpsichords and spinets at the Florentine court of Prince Ferdinand de' Medici (see p. 237), and his invention was described in 1711 by Scipione Maffei in a Venetian quarterly journal:

Everyone who enjoys music knows that one of the principal sources from which those skilled in this art derive the secret of especially delighting their listeners is the alternation of soft and loud. This may come either in a theme and its response, or it may be when the tone is artfully allowed to diminish little by little, and then at one stroke made to return to full vigour. . . .

Now of all this diversity and variation in tone . . . the harpsichord is entirely deprived, and one might have considered it the vainest of fancies to propose constructing one in such a manner as to have this gift. Such a bold invention, nevertheless, has been no less cleverly thought out than executed, in Florence, by Mr. Bartolommeo Christofali [*sic*] . . . a harpsichord player.

Maffei included a description of Cristofori's instrument and a diagram of the action. Happily, three of these earliest pianos have survived, and give us a clearer idea of the complexity and details of the action than this rather primitive diagram. The *clavicembalo col piano e forte* remained in obscurity in Italy; but the fertile seed had been planted, and Maffei's treatise was translated into German and included in a collection of musical essays edited by Johann Mattheson and published in Dresden in 1725. Without doubt this translation was known to the outstandingly skilful organ-builder Gottfried Silbermann, known for his eccentric behaviour as well as superlative craftsmanship. The novelty, and perhaps even the complexity, of Cristofori's idea must have appealed to him, for he had made two pianofortes by 1730. It is probable that the conservative J. S. Bach saw these instruments on his visit to Dresden in 1736. His criticism is said to have been sharp—weak tone in the treble and difficult to play—and the deeply wounded Silbermann to have destroyed the instruments with an axe! But the idea must have remained in his mind, for he persisted in his experiments and by the end of the decade had produced instruments regarded as completely successful, whose special qualities began to pass into the general musical currency of the day.

The construction of these early German pianos is so

EXPLANATION OF THE DIAGRAM.

A. String.

B. Frame of the key-board.

C. The key or first lever, which at its extremity raises the second lever.

D. The block on the first lever by which it acts.

E. The second lever, on each side of which is a jawbone-shaped piece to support the little tongue or hopper.

F. The pivot of the second lever.

G. The moveable tongue (hopper), which, being raised by the second lever (E), forces the hammer upwards.

H. The jawbone-shaped pieces between which the hopper is pivoted.

I. The strong brass wire pressed together at the top, which keeps the hopper in its place.

L. The spring of brass wire that goes under the hopper and holds it pressed firmly against the wire which is behind it.

M. The receiver, in which all the buts of the hammers rest.

N. The circular part of the hammers, which rests in the receiver.

O. The hammer, which, when pressed upwards by the hopper, strikes the string with the leather on its top.

P. The strings of silk, crossed, on which the stems, or shanks, of the hammers rest.

Q. The end of the second lever (E), which becomes lowered by the act of striking the key.

R. The dampers, which are lowered when the key is touched, leaving the string free to vibrate, and then returning to their places, stop the sound.

S. Part of the frame to strengthen the receiver.

Grand piano by Gottfried Silbermann, *c.* 1745. This one of three Silbermann pianos belonging to Frederick the Great that survived into this century.

close to that of Cristofori that it seems probable that Silbermann had actually seen one of Cristofori's instruments, and did not base his design merely on Maffei's writing. But what is beyond doubt is that Silbermann's work, supported by the leading musicians and theorists of the day, served to disseminate Cristofori's work throughout Europe—even to the point that Silbermann was for many years regarded as the inventor of the piano!

Sadly, it was the effect of a terrible and devastating war, not merely enthusiasm for the instrument, which brought the piano its sudden popularity. In 1756 the Seven Years' War began, scattering the piano-builders of Saxony across Europe. One group fled their country and found refuge in London, working at first with established harpsichord makers. Several, however, ultimately set up their own workshops to make the 'new instrument', which until then had been virtually unknown in England.

The pianos they built were not at first in the form of harpsichords, but smaller, more modest instruments in the form of rectangular clavichords, with the keys placed on one of the longer sides, and with an action that was notably inferior to Cristofori's. Early in the eighteenth century, musical taste was developing its preoccupation with the expressive possibilities of contrasts and gradations of loudness of tone. At the same time that Cristofori made his leap into the future, others also sensed the new ideas in the air and made their own

experiments in designing actions which would provide the harpsichord with *piano e forte.*

Jean Marius in 1716 submitted designs for four hammer-harpsichords to the Académie des Sciences. The first of these re-invents the clavichord, very little known in France; but the others are true piano actions. In each case the key lever acted directly on to a hinged hammer, or thrust a rectangular slip of wood with a metal rod projecting from one side against the string. In the absence of an escapement, to ensure that the hammer was in free flight at the moment of impact with the string, a large amount of free play (known as *lost motion*) was incorporated in the action to ensure freedom from blocking. On the other hand the absence of any means of gearing up the hammer-velocity made control, particularly of soft tones, excessively difficult.

Another important experimenter was Christopher Schröter of Dresden who, in 1717 at the age of only eighteen, had a model made demonstrating the feasibility of a hammer action. This, too, possessed no escapement but had the advantage of an intermediate lever which increased the velocity of the hinged hammer. Like Marius's work, this idea also fell into obscurity, but later in life Schröter complained that others had passed his invention off as their own.

The first pianos built in London around 1765 incorporated such actions as these. Johann Zumpe, the foremost piano maker amongst the group of immigrant Saxons, used small, leather-covered hammers pivoted from a fixed *rail* by a leather hinge. A leather-covered metal jack, screwed directly into the key lever, hit (or *attacked*) the hammer near to the fulcrum formed by the hinge. To avoid blocking, about one quarter of an inch of free flight was allowed for the hammer head when the key had been fully depressed—but without an escapement the danger of the hammer rebounding to re-strike the string was very great.

The dampers consisted of a series of wooden levers placed above the strings, hinged to the back of the case, each carrying a small piece of soft leather pressed downwards by a spring of whalebone. A rod or *sticker*, operated on by the end of the key lever, raised the damper from the strings. Fitted into the case to the left of the keyboard were two or more stop-knobs of the kind familiar on harpsichords. These operated devices which lifted the dampers in groups from the strings, either treble or bass, or both together. Freed from the restriction of the dampers, the strings could then continue to vibrate after the release of the keys, and widely spaced chords and arpeggios could be sustained. This effect, found also in Silbermann's pianos, must

Opposite top: Detail of the interior of a square piano by Zumpe, 1767, showing the hammers pivoted from a fixed rail and (bottom left) exterior view of the same piano.
Centre: Perhaps Broadwood's first square piano—made in 1774 before he began the commercial production of square pianos in 1783.
Bottom right: Grand piano by Americus Backers, 1772.

Below: Detail of a square piano by Johannes Pohlmann, c. 1780, showing the stops or hand-levers to the left of the keyboard.

have struck Londoners used to the precise clarity of the harpsichord as a seductive novelty. The third stop-knob operated a 'buff' stop which pressed a thin strip of leather against the ends of the strings to produce a soft, muted *pizzicato* effect.

These 'square' or 'small' pianos, perfectly adapted to English taste in furniture, took London by storm and were manufactured in quantity there by many instrument-makers. Zumpe himself sought for no great improvement in his basic action, although he did introduce an intermediate lever between the jack and hammer.

John Broadwood, an apprentice of Burkat Shudi the Swiss harpsichord maker resident in London, and later a partner in Shudi's business, began the construction of square pianos in 1783. His patented design rationalized certain details of the layout of the instrument, and introduced a much improved damper placed *under* the strings and held firmly against them by a counterweight. The mechanical principle of the action remained the same as that of Zumpe.

The Cristofori/Silbermann action, which must have been perfectly familiar to the Saxon craftsmen working in London, was rejected because of its mechanical complexity and consequent expense. Initially there could have been no great demand for improvement, since the English, unfamiliar with the 'new' piano and the technique of playing it, were persuaded to ignore its defects, so charmed were they by its sound. This tendency towards simplification is a constant feature of the evolution of the piano—for every significant development or improvement, it is usually possible to detect a contrary movement involving a rejection of that advance, usually dictated by commercial interests.

In 1786, however, John Geib patented an action derived from Silbermann's, having an easily regulated escapement (the *grasshopper* or *hopper*) acting on an intermediate lever, but lacking the check. This patent was immediately adapted and fitted to English square pianos in a form that became remarkably standardized, and continued in use until the 1860s, only the check being added to these later instruments. Zumpe's lever damper with its fragile spring was also displaced by an improved mechanism: a small wooden head fitted with soft cloth was mounted on a wire crank raised by the movement of the keylever, the damper returning to rest by gravity, the return spring being eliminated.

The large piano or grand in the shape of a harpsichord was at first neglected in England—and again an immigrant was responsible for its introduction. Showing an admirable adaptability to English working

methods, the Dutchman Americus Backers designed an instrument in about 1770 based on the construction of the contemporary English harpsichord. The action, although ultimately derived from Silbermann, dispensed with the intermediate lever but had a refined escapement mechanism acting as near as possible to the pivot of the hammer, and a very efficient check. The overdamper was glued to a slip of wood like a harpsichord jack, and lifted by the keylever.

The handstops of Silbermann's and Zumpe's pianos were now replaced by pedals, that on the right lifting all the dampers together, while the left pedal was made to shift the entire keyboard and action together to the right so that the hammers could strike only one or two strings to a note at will, instead of the usual three—this shifting pedal became known in consequence as the *una corda* (one string), today sometimes called the 'soft pedal' (see also p. 27).

This English action was gradually improved by the

Erard Frères grand piano, 1801: front and side views.

combined efforts of Backers, Broadwood and Robert Stodart (a 'gentleman apprentice' of Broadwood's), and became the standard action fitted to English grand pianos until the middle of the nineteenth century, by which time it had become obsolete.

For all its very real virtues, the English action was criticized for its heaviness of touch and its slowness of repetition. A player accustomed only to the harpsichord or clavichord would indeed find the touch uncomfortably heavy; but the difficulty was not so much a matter of weight as of *depth* of touch, combined with the necessity of allowing the key to return fully to rest (for the re-engagement of the hopper) before the note could be sounded again.

In France the pianos of Zumpe and his school enjoyed a considerable vogue, and this led to the construction of very similar instruments in Paris workshops, mainly by an immigrant population. In 1768 the 16-year-old Sebastian Erhard arrived in Paris from Strasbourg to be apprenticed to a harpsichord maker. In

The hammer and strings of the note middle-C from five different instruments, showing their relative dimensions. The earliest pianos were light wooden structures with thin strings struck by light hammers—Cristofori's were made from a coil of stiff paper covered with one layer of leather.

As instruments gradually grew more powerful and were more heavily built, so thicker strings were used and the hammers made larger and heavier. The felt hammers of the modern piano were first used in place of leather in 1826.

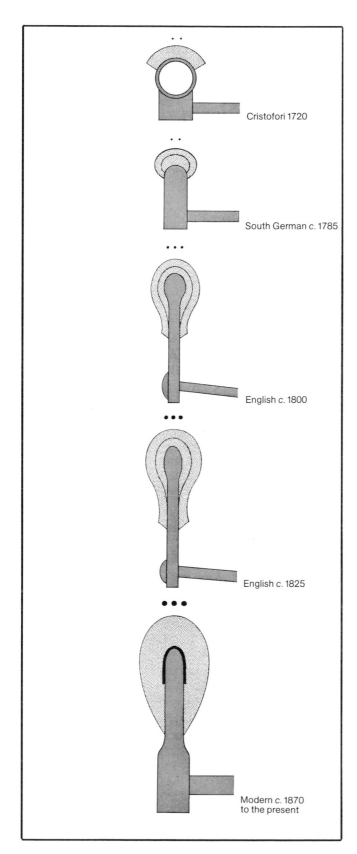

Cristofori 1720

South German c. 1785

English c. 1800

English c. 1825

Modern c. 1870 to the present

1777, his name now Sébastien Erard, he built his first piano, which drew attention to his extraordinary skills. He was joined in that year by his brother Jean-Baptiste, and together they founded a firm that was to become one of the finest in Europe.

In 1796 or 1797 the first Erard grand piano was built in Paris, based closely on contemporary English models, and fitted with a Backers-type single escapement action differing from its model only in the extreme refinement of every detail. The usual criticism of heaviness of touch was levelled at these instruments; but in 1808 or 1809 Sébastien produced a grand piano that was not only smaller and more graceful in appearance than his earlier pianos, but was fitted with an action containing a remarkable improvement. The essence of the new action was that after the moment of escapement, the hammer did not return to rest but fell back only a short distance to remain under the control of the key while this remained depressed. It was possible to strike the strings repeatedly without the necessity of allowing the key to rise to its full extent. Rapid repetition of notes and complex figurations became much easier to execute; but the main advantage of the action lay in its lightness and responsiveness, although it was prone to excessive wear.

In 1822 the most famous of all piano actions was patented by the Erard brothers: the *double escapement action*. The purpose of the mechanism was the same as that of 1808, but while showing its descent from the Cristofori/Silbermann action, the function of each of its separate parts was worked out with still greater insight and ingenuity. Again the hammer did not fall back completely after its initial escapement, but returned to rest simultaneously on a check piece and a sprung, oblique lever which retained the hammer close to the strings. If the key was then raised slightly, the check released the hammer and it could be propelled against the strings once more, the movement of the key being transmitted to the hammer not by the hopper, but via the oblique lever. The action was noted at once for its remarkable lightness, flexibility and reliability; and its significance cannot be exaggerated, since with only small modifications of detail it became the action to be fitted to the modern grand piano.

In the history of the grand piano the advantages of gravity-operated overdampers were not so clearly appreciated as the superiority of up-striking to down-striking hammer mechanisms. In his earliest pianos, Erard had chosen the conventional overdampers of the English piano, but in his action of 1822 he opted for an underdamper, which his firm continued to use even until near the end of the nineteenth century. The effect

Below: Andreas Stein piano of the 1770s, made in the Augsburg workshop.
Bottom: Interior view of an upright piano by C. Ehrlich, *c.* 1820, showing six pedals to operate the following effects: bassoon, mute, *pianissimo*, *piano*, *una corda*, drums and bells.

of this type of damper was to eliminate rapidly the fundamental and lower harmonics of the vibrating strings, but to leave sounding a shimmer of upper harmonics: a special tonal effect much admired at the time, which deliberately reproduced the effect of the very light dampers of early English grand pianos. (Interestingly enough, contemporary Viennese pianos by contrast were notable for the very reverse effect—a great precision of damping, without any trace of harmonic shimmer, the sound of the note being instantly cut off when the key was released.)

Until the 1820s the customary material used for covering the hammers was soft but resilient leather, usually deerskin. This material was perfectly suited to the thin strings and light construction of pianos until this time; but as musical taste changed and pianos grew in power, a new material was sought to give a rounder, fuller, and less clearly defined tone. The perfect material was found by Jean-Henri Pape, a German-born Paris builder who delighted in constructing pianos of bewildering mechanical complexity. Pape patented hammer-covers of hard felt of carefully graduated thickness throughout the compass. The advantages of the innovation were universally appreciated, and within a short time felt-covered hammers were used by all piano builders. Felt has remained the standard material to the present day.

In the eighteenth century, the search for a simplification of Cristofori's action produced an alternative solution to that of the Saxon, English and French builders. This is the action known as the *Prellmechanik*, which originated in Germany, although the exact date of its introduction is not known. In its simplest form, the hammer is mounted not on a fixed rail but on the key itself, the head towards the player and pivoted in a fork or *Kapsel*. When the key is depressed, a projection of the hammer-shank beyond the pivot point strikes an overhead rail or ledge and the hammer is flicked up to strike the strings. Johann Andreas Stein, a pupil of Silbermann, is credited with improving this simple action by replacing the over-rail with individual hopper-like escapement levers for each note. Towards the end of the century a simple but highly effective check mechanism was fitted to the action.

The pianos fitted with this German action (later referred to as the *Viennese action*) normally had a greater clarity of tone, though somewhat less power, than English and French instruments. The Viennese school of builders flourished until the middle of the nineteenth century, when the individuality of their instruments was absorbed by the modern piano. It was possible

Modern upright piano.   Modern upright piano action.

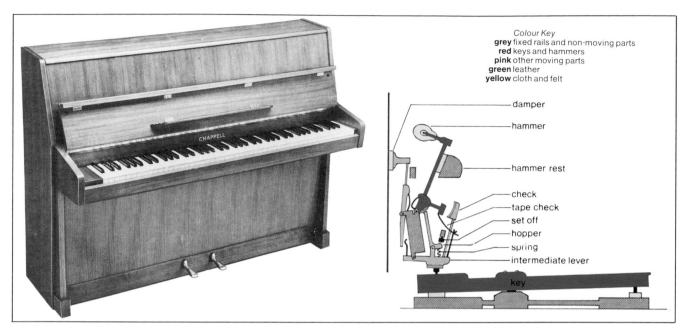

Colour Key
grey fixed rails and non-moving parts
red keys and hammers
pink other moving parts
green leather
yellow cloth and felt

— damper
— hammer
— hammer rest
— check
— tape check
— set off
— hopper
— spring
— intermediate lever
key

nonetheless, even as late as the early years of the present century, to obtain conventional pianos fitted with the Viennese action identical in mechanical principles (if enlarged in scale) to those early Stein actions played by Mozart in 1777 (see pp. 9–10).

Mechanisms (or 'stops') for modifying the tone were fitted to both large and small pianos from the beginning of their history. The device that is still considered an essential component of the instrument is the sustaining pedal, which lifts the dampers from the strings, leaving them free to vibrate even when the keys have been released. Initially this device was controlled by hand-operated stops, frequently lifting only the treble or bass dampers according to the performer's choice. The hands had to be lifted from the keyboard to operate the mechanism, which could thus function only to give broad colouristic effects. As the potential of the sustaining device was realized, a more convenient way of controlling it became desirable. On South German pianos this was first achieved by knee-controlled levers, and later in all pianos by means of a pedal, often misnamed the *forte*-pedal or 'loud pedal'. In this form it has survived to the present day. The possibility of lifting only sections of the dampers rather than the whole set is found in English and Viennese pianos even after 1820, but thereafter this refinement was generally forgotten in Europe, though it still remains in widespread use on North American upright pianos to this day (see also p. 170).

Hand knobs, knee levers and pedals controlled all the following effects which have been built into pianos in the past either for their genuine musical usefulness or because their novelty was irresistible.

Una corda: by shifting the entire action frame, the hammers strike only one or two strings to a note, instead of three. Now limited to the modern grand piano, where its effect is strictly speaking '*due corde*', producing a softer, more ethereal tone.
Moderator, celeste: a layer of soft cloth or leather is interposed between hammers and strings to give a sweet, singing and muted quality. Much used in Viennese pianos but little known in England until the device came to be fitted occasionally to inexpensive modern upright pianos.
Buff, jeu de luth: a narrow strip of soft leather is pressed against the strings to give a dry, soft tone of little sustaining power.
Bassoon: a roll of paper and silk is laid over the bass strings, the resultant buzzing tone being supposed to imitate the wind instrument.
Cembalo stop: an alternative to the bassoon stop in which small leathered weights are made to rest on the strings to imitate the tone of the harpsichord; found on some modern pianos.
Turkish Music, Janizary Musik: a pedal operates a drumstick striking the underside of the soundboard, a set of tuned bells, and exceptionally a 'cymbal crash' consisting of a strip of brass foil striking the bass strings.
Sostenuto: a third, 'middle' pedal (acting quite independently of the sustaining pedal) fitted to some modern grand pianos, particularly Steinways, whereby the damper of any note whose key is already depressed may be made to remain raised until the pedal is released (see also p. 170).

The upright piano, so commonplace today, was not always so: only occasional attempts had been made to construct pianos standing vertically in the style of the clavicytherium until William Stodart introduced his

Upright grand piano by John Broadwood, *c.* 1815. The front is normally covered by a curtained door (removed in this picture).

upright grand in 1795. This was a full-size grand piano placed vertically on a stand of four legs, tail uppermost, with the normally short treble cheek extended to the full height of the instrument, the whole enclosed by silk-lined doors (see p. 243). The illusion of a tall bookcase or desk was complete, since the space between the curved bentside and the side of the piano was filled with bookshelves!

The fashion for such impressive instruments lasted for little more than thirty years, by which time both English and Continental builders had commenced the construction of more practical and compact instruments of great ingenuity of design. Matthias Müller of Vienna and John Isaac Hawkins of London (later of Philadelphia) both independently built vertical pianos at the turn of the century in which the strings were made to pass behind the keyboard to the floor; here the layout of the upright grand (with the wrestplank placed immediately above the keys and the tail uppermost) is inverted, so that the tail is placed at floor level. The action, which in the earlier forms was made to strike from behind, now had to be placed in front of the strings. In England an adaptation of the Geib action was used in these 'cabinet' pianos, the intermediate lever acting not directly on the hammers, but communicating its movement to them via a sticker, which was sometimes of incredible length.

The great height (over eight feet) of the largest of these upright grand and cabinet pianos was reason enough for instrument builders to continue to experiment with the construction of much smaller pianos, and in England the 'cottage piano', a miniature cabinet piano, became popular after 1820—although the length of its bass strings (which run vertically from top to bottom) was limited by the height of the case, and its tone in consequence lacked weight and sonority. As early as 1802 Thomas Loud placed the bass strings diagonally across the soundboard, running from top left to bottom right, and so achieved both the possibility of longer bass strings and an even more compact case. This important idea was developed by many Continental builders, especially by Pape in Paris, whose 'console' pianos incorporated many innovations of design and mechanics. In London Robert Wornum's main contribution to the early upright piano was the development of an action derived from the English grand action and having a tape check—a device which ensures the rapid return of the hammer from the string after impact, without the use of a return spring. With some improvement, this action continues to be fitted to all modern upright pianos.

Below: The evolution of the keyboard compass (or range) from 1700 to the present.

Bottom: Console piano by Jean Henri Pape, 1844.

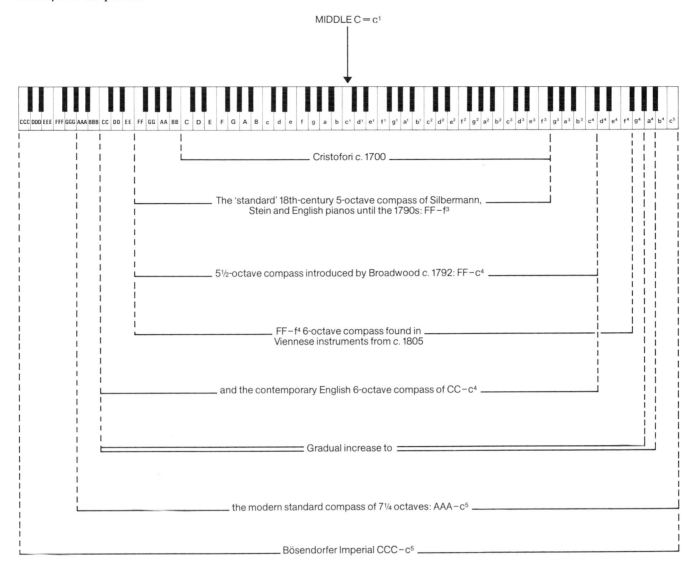

MIDDLE C = c¹

| CCC | DDD | EEE | FFF | GGG | AAA | BBB | CC | DD | EE | FF | GG | AA | BB | C | D | E | F | G | A | B | c | d | e | f | g | a | b | c¹ | d¹ | e¹ | f¹ | g¹ | a¹ | b¹ | c² | d² | e² | f² | g² | a² | b² | c³ | d³ | e³ | f³ | g³ | a³ | b³ | c⁴ | d⁴ | e⁴ | f⁴ | g⁴ | a⁴ | b⁴ | c⁵ |

Cristofori *c.* 1700

The 'standard' 18th-century 5-octave compass of Silbermann, Stein and English pianos until the 1790s: FF–f³

5½-octave compass introduced by Broadwood *c.* 1792: FF–c⁴

FF–f⁴ 6-octave compass found in Viennese instruments from *c.* 1805

and the contemporary English 6-octave compass of CC–c⁴

Gradual increase to

the modern standard compass of 7¼ octaves: AAA–c⁵

Bösendorfer Imperial CCC–c⁵

Throughout the history of the piano, there has been a steady increase in its power and dynamic range. At the same time its compass has steadily increased from the 4½-octave compass of Cristofori to the present standard 7¼ octaves (AAA–c^5)—although the compass of the instrument has never at any stage been entirely standardized, and enlargement has proceeded by a series of steps, each serving for a time before being superseded. The earliest range of C–f^3 rapidly changed to FF–f^3, and this remained current until the last decade of the eighteenth century. In the 1790s Broadwood was prevailed upon by Dussek to introduce pianos of extended range. From 1792 the compass of FF–c^4 became standard in England, but these pianos with the 'additional keys' were soon supplanted by those having six octaves, CC–c^4.

Viennese and German pianos during this same period underwent a similar development from five octaves, first to 5½ and then to six, but in this case the further extension was limited to the treble to give a range of

Evolution of the action, and principle places of development.

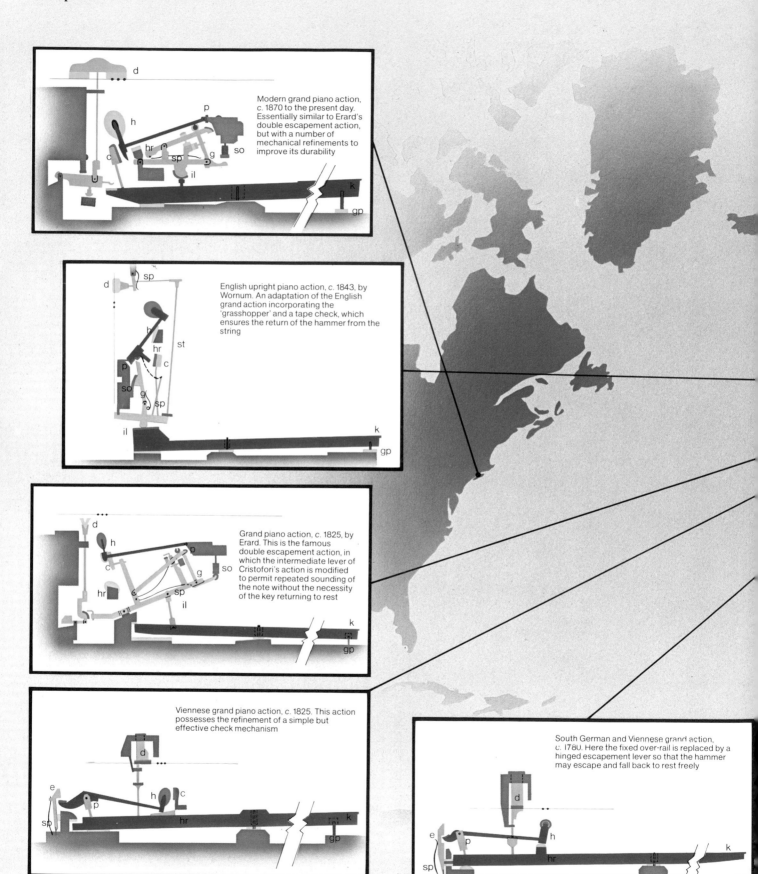

Modern grand piano action, *c.* 1870 to the present day. Essentially similar to Erard's double escapement action, but with a number of mechanical refinements to improve its durability

English upright piano action, *c.* 1843, by Wornum. An adaptation of the English grand action incorporating the 'grasshopper' and a tape check, which ensures the return of the hammer from the string

Grand piano action, *c.* 1825, by Erard. This is the famous double escapement action, in which the intermediate lever of Cristofori's action is modified to permit repeated sounding of the note without the necessity of the key returning to rest

Viennese grand piano action, *c.* 1825. This action possesses the refinement of a simple but effective check mechanism

South German and Viennese grand action, *c.* 1780. Here the fixed over-rail is replaced by a hinged escapement lever so that the hammer may escape and fall back to rest freely

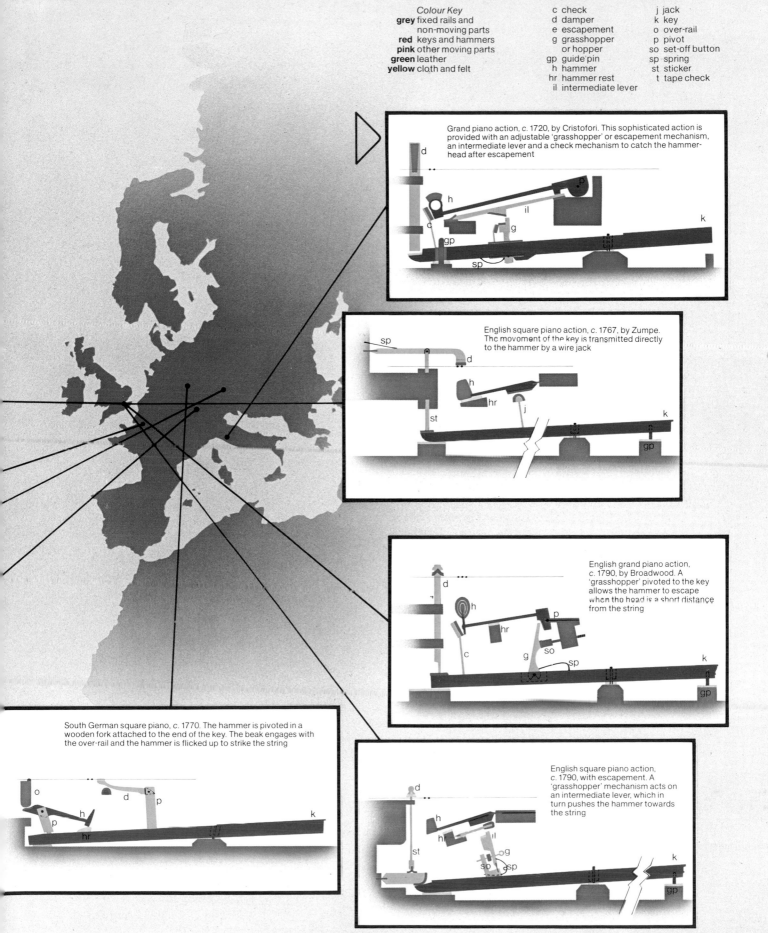

grey fixed rails and
non-moving parts
red keys and hammers
pink other moving parts
green leather
yellow cloth and felt

c check
d damper
e escapement
g grasshopper
or hopper
gp guide pin
h hammer
hr hammer rest
il intermediate lever

j jack
k key
o over-rail
p pivot
so set-off button
sp spring
st sticker
t tape check

Grand piano action, *c.* 1720, by Cristofori. This sophisticated action is provided with an adjustable 'grasshopper' or escapement mechanism, an intermediate lever and a check mechanism to catch the hammer-head after escapement

English square piano action, *c.* 1767, by Zumpe. The movement of the key is transmitted directly to the hammer by a wire jack

English grand piano action, *c.* 1790, by Broadwood. A 'grasshopper' pivoted to the key allows the hammer to escape when the head is a short distance from the string

South German square piano, *c.* 1770. The hammer is pivoted in a wooden fork attached to the end of the key. The beak engages with the over-rail and the hammer is flicked up to strike the string

English square piano action, *c.* 1790, with escapement. A 'grasshopper' mechanism acts on an intermediate lever, which in turn pushes the hammer towards the string

$FF–f^4$. Unusual compasses commonly appeared: small for inexpensive domestic instruments and very large when a builder sought to impress with novelty. In 1844 Pape introduced an eight-octave piano with a range from $FFF–f^5$! Today the largest compass available is that of the Imperial model of Bösendorfer, which extends from $CCC–c^5$, also eight octaves.

The stretched strings of a harpsichord or piano impose a considerable stress on the frame of the instrument; but the thin strings of the family of plucked instruments are matched by a light body-structure well able to support the relatively low tensions required. It is not surprising that the Italian Cristofori should have made use of the basic structural approach of the Italian harpsichord for his pianos; one of his discoveries, however, was that, to give a satisfactory tone, the piano must be fitted with stiffer and thicker strings than would be suitable for a quill action. Flexibility of a piano string must also be strictly controlled: for if a hammer displaces a string excessively at the moment of impact not only will there be a serious 'detuning' effect due to a momentary increase in tension and consequent rise in pitch, but the hammer might remain in contact with the string for longer than one half cycle of its vibration, and damping would occur. As a result, Cristofori had to increase the thickness and strength of every part of the wooden frame to resist the greater tension of the strings.

The pianos made in the tradition established by Stein in Germany also owed much to the design of Italian harpsichords—a thick *baseboard* supporting a system of *stretchers* and *buttresses*, which in turn transmitted the stress of the strings from the *hitchrail* to the baseboard. The *wrestplank* was of conventional type, but to allow the action to be removed from the case, a *sledge* supporting the action in its correct relationship with the strings is first removed like a drawer. The action then drops to baseboard level, and can then be withdrawn.

Eighteenth-century English grand pianos, with their different origins, had frames derived from contemporary harpsichords. Here it is the case or rim itself, stoutly constructed of oak, cross-braced with pine beneath the soundboard and with only a thin baseboard, that supports the stress of the strings. Square pianos followed the design of their own older prototype, the clavichord. Again a strong and heavy baseboard and case supported the stress of the strings transmitted by the hitchrail and the wrestplank.

As the power, dynamic range and compass of the piano increased, the mass of the strings themselves had to be increased to deal with the greater energy imparted to them by ever larger and heavier hammers, and the ever greater onslaughts of the new generation of keyboard virtuosos. The working load of the strings was as a result also proportionally increased—and so stronger frames had to be devised to support the greater tension.

Eighteenth-century grands had commonly made use of some form of bracing across the action gap between the unsupported part of the wrestplank and the rest of the frame. In England these were always of metal although the rest of the frame was made entirely of wood. When John Isaac Hawkins made his first cabinet piano in 1800, his design not only eliminated the action gap (the chief Achilles heel of all early grand pianos) but also made use of a brilliantly conceived iron frame. This invention was not immediately taken up, but the general anxiety of builders for the stability of the instrument prompted a series of experiments in the use of iron reinforcement. John Broadwood made his own first experiments in 1808, but it was not until the 1820s that short iron braces were introduced at the treble end of the instrument as standard practice. Simultaneously iron *hitch-plates* were fitted to square pianos, and experiments made with entire iron frames fitted within the case under the soundboard. (It was about this time that the underside of grand pianos began to be left open— that is, without a baseboard underneath the soundboard.)

The principal defect of all these methods of reinforcement was the difficulty of transferring the stress from the metal parts to the wooden components of the structure without the various plates, screws and brackets tearing and crushing the wood at the small areas of contact where very high stresses were inevitably experienced. This problem was partially overcome by a stream of designs for metal frames introduced after 1820, some composed of a series of tubular braces, others incorporating continuous metal hitch-plates, still others with metal reinforcement of the wrestplank. Serious weaknesses still remained, however, at those points where the metal parts were bolted together, and where stress was transmitted to the wooden frame.

A complete solution was found in America: in 1825 Alpheus Babcock fitted a continuous cast iron ring frame, incorporating the hitch-plate, to a square piano. This was followed in 1833 by an improved frame designed by Conrad Meyer using Babcock's principle of a single continuous casting, and Jonas Chickering of Boston was the first to fit such a frame to a grand piano in 1843.

This complete cast iron frame which alone supports the tension of the strings without transferring it to the wooden frame was not at first universally adopted. A

Below left: Modern Bösendorfer Imperial concert grand with 8-octave compass *CCC-c⁵*. The bottom notes *CCC-GGG* are under a removable wooden flap.
Below right: Grand piano by William Stodart, 1835, showing the metal tubes used to strengthen the frame.

Bottom: Modern Russian upright piano—the middle pedal operates a 'practice mute', which can be locked into position to mute the sound when quiet practice is desired.

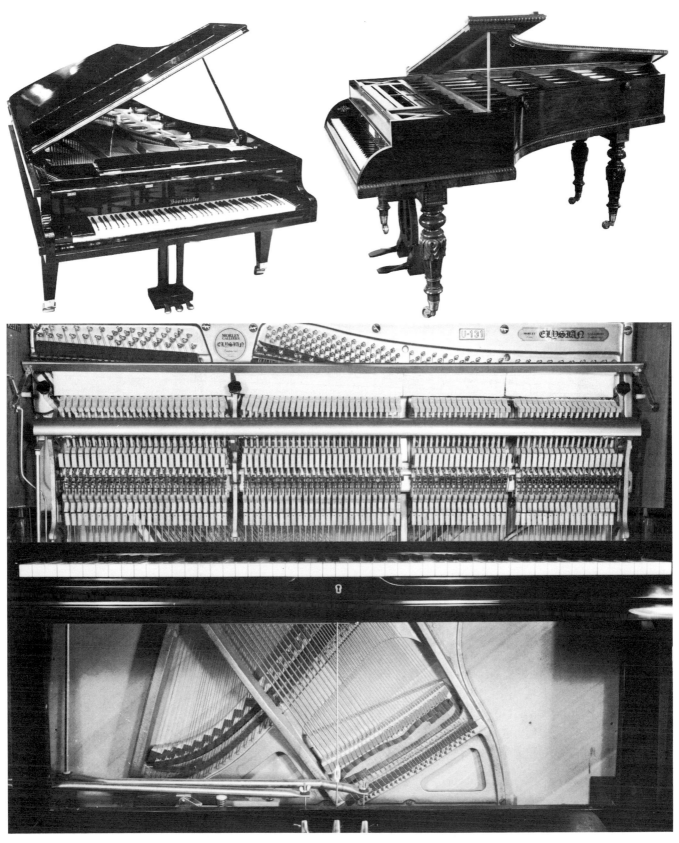

'Portable Grand Pianoforte' by John Isaac Hawkins, *c.* 1803 (below) and nameboard of the same piano (right).

Opposite top: Babcock square piano, *c.* 1835, showing the tubular metal frame.
Opposite centre: Square piano by Jonas Chickering, 1850, showing its single continuous cast iron frame.
Opposite bottom left: Top view of a Steinway grand piano, 1857, with parallel stringing.
Opposite bottom right: Modern Bösendorfer grand piano.

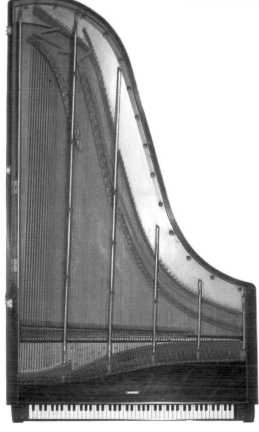

A sequence of frames—the stress-bearing structure of the piano—from Cristofori's delicate wooden model to the modern instrument, where the stress of the strings is taken entirely by a cast iron frame. Iron reinforcement, shown in black in these diagrams, was introduced in the last quarter of the eighteenth century and used to an increasing extent in English and French instruments for the next hundred years. Viennese builders were more conservative, believing that iron-work spoilt the tone of their instruments.

a The early 18th-century frame, used by Cristofori and Silbermann, built entirely from wood

b English, late 18th-century. Still built from wood, but some iron reinforcement has been fitted across the action gap to help resist the tension of the strings

c English and French, c. 1825. The heavy wooden frame and rim receive additional support from iron braces fitted above the strings at the treble end

d English and French, c. 1850. The high tension of thicker strings made necessary the introduction of additional iron bracing

e Modern frame from c. 1870 to the present. The tension of the strings is now supported entirely by a cast iron frame

I South German and Viennese, late 18th-century. The iron reinforcement of this wooden frame is limited to a single iron brace connecting the wrestplank to the rest of the structure

II Viennese, c. 1825. The principle of construction remains the same as that of the earlier Viennese frame, but all parts are made much heavier

tendency to distrust the use of iron in any part of a musical instrument prolonged the survival of relatively light composite frames in the pianos of some European builders until late in the nineteenth century, and in Vienna delayed the introduction of any kind of iron bracing to the magnificent pianos produced there until about 1845. Eventually the need for the greatest possible stability led to the cast iron frame's universal adoption, first in America and finally in Europe.

Overstringing or cross-stringing was another idea that had first occurred in Europe, but was only put to proper advantage in America. The seed had been sown in those little cabinet pianos whose strings were laid out diagonally to increase the length of the strings in the bass. Experiments in England in 1831, and also by Pape in Paris, passed the bass strings diagonally *over* the rest of the string band laid out in a more conventional manner. The particular advantages of this system were not at first appreciated. However, the prevailing fashion in America was not for the grand or the upright, but for the square piano, and these were developed into instruments of immense power, sonority—and size.

The square piano had retained the basic layout of the clavichord, the strings running parallel to the *bridge* and *soundboard* on the right. It was now realized that the excessive crowding of the strings could be relieved by dividing the bridge and fanning the strings, with those of the bass register passing over the tenor strings to one or more separate sections of the bridge. In 1855 Henry Steinway in New York combined the overstrung scaling with a cast iron frame, so achieving a remarkable advance towards the mid-nineteenth-century ideal of a full, round, 'organ-like' tone. The final step towards the modern piano was taken in 1859 with Steinway's patent for a grand piano which also combined the cast iron frame with overstringing. The overwhelming success of these instruments led ultimately to the universal acceptance of the American system.

As the greater convenience of domestic upright pianos compared with their large square cousins was recognized, they too came to be constructed by the same method, and Steinway began their large-scale manufacture early in the 1870s. The modern upright piano was established.

The soundboard of a piano is a thin, flexible wooden diaphragm glued at its edges to the wooden frame, and with the bridge attached to its upper surface. If the strings stretched above it had no contact with the bridge, the displacement of the surrounding air caused by the motion of their small surface area would also be very small, and the resulting sound almost inaudible. By

Below right: The soundboard, a thin membrane of wood which transmits the vibration of the strings to the surrounding air. In these diagrams, the bridges over which the strings pass are shown in black. Glued to the underside of the soundboard is a more or less elaborate system of 'soundbars', which serve to strengthen the soundboard, thus resisting the down-bearing of the stretched strings, and also to transmit the vibrations as rapidly as possible to every part of the board.

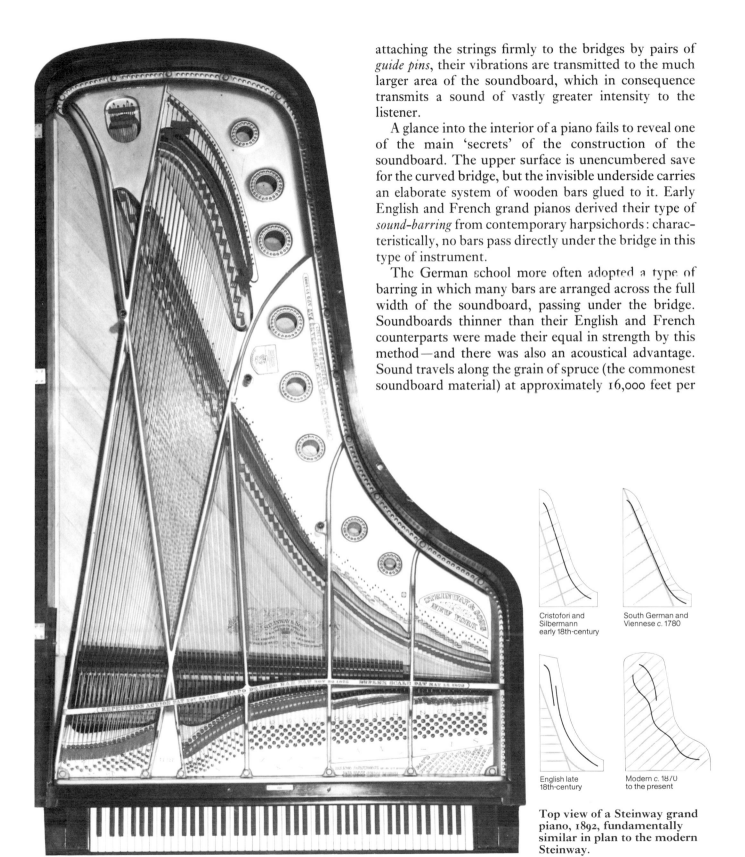

Cristofori and Silbermann early 18th-century

South German and Viennese c. 1780

English late 18th-century

Modern c. 1870 to the present

Top view of a Steinway grand piano, 1892, fundamentally similar in plan to the modern Steinway.

attaching the strings firmly to the bridges by pairs of *guide pins*, their vibrations are transmitted to the much larger area of the soundboard, which in consequence transmits a sound of vastly greater intensity to the listener.

A glance into the interior of a piano fails to reveal one of the main 'secrets' of the construction of the soundboard. The upper surface is unencumbered save for the curved bridge, but the invisible underside carries an elaborate system of wooden bars glued to it. Early English and French grand pianos derived their type of *sound-barring* from contemporary harpsichords: characteristically, no bars pass directly under the bridge in this type of instrument.

The German school more often adopted a type of barring in which many bars are arranged across the full width of the soundboard, passing under the bridge. Soundboards thinner than their English and French counterparts were made their equal in strength by this method—and there was also an acoustical advantage. Sound travels along the grain of spruce (the commonest soundboard material) at approximately 16,000 feet per second, but only one quarter of this speed *across* the grain. Since the soundbars in German instruments were glued with their grain direction at right-angles to the grain of the soundboard itself, rapid transmission of the sound waves in all directions to every part of the soundboard was easily achieved. This method of barring gradually became widely accepted, and is applied to all types of modern piano.

The familiar graceful curve of the bridge is not arbitrarily chosen, but dictated by the basic physical laws of stretched strings. First, the frequency of vibration of a string is in inverse proportion to its length—as it is lengthened it vibrates more slowly and so produces a lower note. For every fall of pitch of one octave, the length of the strings must, theoretically, be doubled, and the resulting bridge would have a parabolic curve.

But a practical musical instrument must have a limit to its length, and so a second law comes into play: when strings have the same length and tension, their frequency is in inverse proportion to their mass. By choosing a convenient length for the lowest string of the piano, and applying this second law by proportionately increasing the mass of the strings as they descend from treble to bass, it is possible to compress the theoretical curve of the bridge without a loss of tone quality.

There is, however, a danger that the stiffness of the thickened strings in the bass of the piano will be so great that their flexibility will be impaired and their tone inferior. This factor was appreciated by the early piano builders, who strung the bottom octave or so of their instruments with brass wire, which is inherently more flexible than the steel used for the rest of the compass. Brass, however, being denser than steel, has the disadvantage of requiring a higher tension to bring it to pitch. John Broadwood was the first to resolve this problem in 1788 by dividing the bridge into two sections, the shorter carrying the brass strings. This clever idea of a bridge divided into two parts was later to become the key to the development of overstrung pianos.

As the working tension of the strings increased greatly throughout the nineteenth century, brass came to be replaced by fabricated strings made from a thin and flexible steel core, increased in mass by one or two tightly wound coverings of copper wire. These *overspun* strings were first applied to the relatively short bass strings of square pianos in the eighteenth century, and have since become universal for the basses of all pianos.

Compared to the thick steel strings of the modern piano, early instruments were strung with mere threads.

The search for greater power, and the resulting increase in the mass of the strings, introduces us to a third law of stretched strings: the frequency of vibration of a string is in proportion to the *square root of its tension*. At once we can see why the construction of the modern piano must be so substantial and strong, for with the tension of each plain steel string standing as high as 160 pounds, the tension carried by the frame may be as great as thirty tons. Conversely, a thinly strung piano by Stein with a tension of approximately sixteen pounds on each of its steel strings needs only a very light structure.

A great number of factors affect the tone quality of a piano—every detail of the construction contributes to it in some way; but one of the most important factors was again first understood and applied by John Broadwood. This is the choice of the precise point at which the hammer strikes the string. The sound of the vibrating string is a compound of a fundamental frequency with a series of upper partials or overtones with their vibration rates in the ratio $1:2:3:4$ and so on. Of the lower overtones, all save the seventh and ninth will blend pleasantly with the fundamental. The formation of these dissonant harmonics can be discouraged, however, if the string is struck at a point about one eighth of its length from the wrestplank bridge. Although this method of controlling the tone quality was not universally adopted at first, the nineteenth-century taste for sweet roundness of tone gradually ensured the acceptance of the idea, which is now an invariable component of piano design.

In two hundred and seventy years of history the piano has reached a series of peaks of perfection, each one a summit perfectly adapted to the musical requirements of its own time, serving composers and performers alike as the chosen medium for, and inspiration of, some of the greatest music that we possess. As music changed, so too did the instrument, drawing on developing technology and industrial practice until the process of evolution led to the modern piano in 1859. Nothing that has come after that date can match the achievement of the thousands of craftsmen who transformed the pianos of the mid-eighteenth century into the iron grands of a hundred years later. The piano's real course of development was then run, and its history since has been one of refinement and consolidation rather than innovation. Even eyes accustomed to modern pianos cannot cease to wonder at the skill with which Cristofori perceived the nature and the problems of the new instrument more than two and a half centuries ago, and going straight to the heart of the matter, brought forth his brilliant invention.

THE CLASSICAL PIANO

He is the father, we are the children
Mozart, of C. P. E. Bach

*Whoever knows me thoroughly must discover
that I owe a great deal to Emanuel Bach*
Haydn, reported by Greisinger

You will receive the spirit of Mozart from the hands of Haydn
Count Waldstein to Beethoven

*I have only a few samples of Emanuel Bach's compositions
for the keyboard; and yet some of them should certainly
be in the possession of every true artist*
Beethoven

Johann Sebastian Bach.

Premonition

On 7 May 1747, Johann Sebastian Bach visited his son
Carl Philipp Emanuel at the court of Frederick the Great
in Potsdam. It is often recalled that, in deference to J. S.
Bach's reputation as a great composer and keyboard
player of the old school, Frederick the Great did him the
honour of asking him to improvise a fugue: first one in
three parts, and later one in six.

It is less often mentioned that the instrument on
which the first task was performed was a piano—one of
the new instruments which Frederick had acquired from
Gottfried Silbermann. J. S. Bach was well aware of
Silbermann's work; he had criticized his instruments
fiercely when they were in an early state of development
during the 1730s (see also p. 20), and subsequently
took a great interest in their progress; it appears that he
even acquired the rights to sell the pianos as sole agent in
Leipzig. And the supposedly conservative Bach was
most responsive to the special qualities of these new
keyboard instruments. The three-part fugue that he
improvised for Frederick the Great probably formed the
basis of the *ricercar* that opens the *Musical Offering* (a
homage to the King composed during the summer of
1747 and on sale by September of that year). Though its
subject, provided by the King, is conventionally
Baroque, the episodic working-out owes much to the
idiom of the piano. Flourishes of expressive triplets,
languishing chromatic runs, winding pairs of thirds: all
these were features of the 'advanced' keyboard style of
the time; they could have been performed on the
harpsichord or clavichord. But these figurations come
into their own only on the piano. Here variety of touch
and dynamic (impossible to achieve on the harpsichord)
could be combined with demonstrativeness and power
(impossible on the intimate clavichord). Bach's *ricercar
à 3* is one of the first pieces of piano music.

Problems

As the second half of the eighteenth century began, the
piano provided one focus, one centre of attention, for the
radical changes in musical language which we associate
with the development of the Classical style. The changes
were not, of course, confined to keyboard music. But in
the orchestra, no new instruments were needed to bear
the weight of a change of idiom. The absolute
dependence on a continuo bass line and a melody line
(consistent throughout the Baroque period, from the
earliest Italian monodies onwards) disappeared; after a
period in which harmonic and contrapuntal movement
was drastically simplified, the inner parts of the
orchestral texture began to assume a new importance.
The change was similar in chamber music—from the
treble-and-bass idiom, represented at its height by the
trio sonatas of Corelli and Handel, to the string quartets
of Haydn, in which the viola gradually took an equal
part in the discourse.

Yet the idea of continuous development implied in
these descriptions is false. The two fixed worlds of
'Baroque' and 'Classical' were never as stable as they
seem to us now. J. S. Bach's music was not confined to
one style, but looked forward to the new concern for
'inner feeling'; Haydn and Mozart were both thought of
in their time as too 'romantic' to meet the demands of
true Classicism. And between that pair of concepts,
which dominate so much of our musical thinking today,
there was a ferment of styles—adventurous, backward-
looking, regional, national, private, public—whose
variety and substance make nonsense of any claim to a
continuous line of development through this period.

So how to define 'the Classical piano'? If its music
was already being composed by J. S. Bach, it can
scarcely be said to be the preserve of the high Classicists,
Haydn, Mozart and Beethoven. Is it defined by a

Domenico Scarlatti: engraving by Joseph Weger.

particular musical style? Scarcely, for Mozart wrote a Handelian suite for piano; Beethoven included fugues in his greatest sonatas; whereas C. P. E. Bach continued to insist that some of his most piano-like music was for the clavichord. Other composers (who wished to ensure a wide circulation for their publications) made no distinction between piano and harpsichord on the title-pages of their works.

Is the Classical piano defined by the idea of contrast, of a range of different emotions integrated into one piece in a way that would have been thought impossible in the Baroque era? The late Baroque shows many examples of just such contrasts: the quartet of conflicting emotions in Handel's last oratorio *Jephtha*; the dialogues in Bach's cantatas, where two voices sing simultaneously in different styles. And the Classical period is full of sonata movements, especially by Haydn, in which contrast between themes is non-existent; in the music of Mozart, too, the subtle play of moods often makes 'contrast' a far too forceful word to use. (Where, for example, is it in the first movement of the B flat sonata K.333?)

Is the Classical piano defined by a particular form, by the use of the sonata principle? This too is dangerous ground. It has been said often enough that 'sonata form' was invented only after its death. The rationalization which nineteenth-century analysts made of sonata form—an organized sequence of first subject, transition, second subject, closing theme, development, and recapitulation, each with its 'proper' key—provides a handy terminology, but one which does not stand up if it is applied carefully to the actual sonata movements of Haydn, Mozart and Beethoven. The reason so many nineteenth-century sonata movements are so boring, it has been well observed, is that they conform so precisely to the notional plan of the sonata. The greatest eighteenth-century composers had no such conscious plan in mind: the sonata principle was a constantly developing idea within which experimentation and adventure took place. I think that it is going too far even to suggest that sonata form provided a set of fixed expectations for the educated listener, which the inventions of a great composer could then contradict. The eighteenth-century listener surely cannot have acquired any detailed expectations of first subjects, bridge passages and the rest before Haydn in the 1770s began to contradict them.

The Classical piano, then, can be conceived only in terms of the repertoire current during its lifetime. No one style, no single technique of composition, will help us define its range. The Classical piano simply reflects—and partly itself creates—the changes in the sense and sensibility of musical language after 1750. This summary account will concentrate on the peaks of the repertory, Haydn, Mozart and Beethoven, while also considering the important background to the work of these composers provided by C. P. E. Bach, J. C. Bach, and Clementi. (Those interested in the masters alone should read the penetrating discussion by Charles Rosen in his *The Classical Style*; those interested in the full range of Classical keyboard composition should read William Newman's compendious treatment, *The Sonata in the Classic Era*. This chapter is indebted to both.)

The Evolving Sonata

One factor which *is* crucial to the new musical languages which developed through the second half of the eighteenth century is the notion of tonality as a dramatic element of composition: the idea that the relationship between keys can be a force in the organization of a movement. However, we cannot say that even this is a deciding characteristic of *piano* music, for it makes its first appearance in sonatas which were

41

undoubtedly conceived for the harpsichord. It was in the works of Domenico Scarlatti (1685–1757), who was born in Italy but spent much of his life in Spain, that key relationships began to influence the structure of the sonata. The two-part form of his sonatas (a set of which was published in England in 1738) is not substantially different from that of a binary dance-movement in many a Baroque suite: the music starts in the tonic and concludes its first half in the dominant; it then starts from the dominant and returns to the tonic.

But in many of Scarlatti's marvellous pieces there is a loosening of the thematic treatment at the start of the second half, a kind of development (though often wholly new material is used); and at the end of the piece there is a definite return to the material which ends the first part. There need be no restatement of the opening material in the second half, but often there is. Thus a balance is established between the first part, the 'exposition' of what may be a very varied group of themes, and the second part, with its elements of development and recapitulation. The twin signposts—arrival in a new key at the end of the first half, and arrival in the home key using the same material at the end of the second half—are the essence of the form. This does not constitute anything like the sophistication of sonata form as later analysts understood it; but it provided a starting point.

Variants of this binary-form sonata type found favour with several Italian composers who began to produce sonatas around the same time as Scarlatti. G. B. Platti wrote pieces which also owe much to the typical Baroque forms of the *sonata da camera* (a suite of dances) and *sonata da chiesa* (slow-fast-slow-fast with fugal treatment in the fast movements)—but his music is filled with the cheerful, direct spirit of the *opera buffa*. Platti's op.1 sonatas appeared in 1742, the same year as C. P. E. Bach's first published set. Baldassare Galuppi was praised for one of his toccatas in a famous poem of Browning's, but ironically none of them survives. It is his sonatas which are his claim to fame: vivid pieces in a variety of new and old forms, always using a full range of virtuoso keyboard technique. Walsh published two sets of his pieces in London in 1756 and 1759. Domenico Paradisi (Paradics) is also remembered for a popular Toccata which has crept into many anthologies. He was one of a group of composers who settled in London (where his sonatas were published in 1754), making the city an important centre of developing keyboard styles.

The First Master
In 1742, before his father came to Potsdam and showed how a Silbermann piano could be used, Carl Philipp Emanuel Bach published his first set of sonatas. The younger Bach said as late as 1753 that the clavichord was preferable to the piano because piano touch was so difficult to master. But his two sonata sets, the 'Prussian' of 1742 and the 'Württemberg' of 1744, are nevertheless of great importance in the development of the Classical piano style. The quotations at the head of this chapter show how much the three great masters of the Classical era said they owed to C. P. E. Bach. In the intense, almost sickly world of North German expressionism which dominated literature and music there in the 1740s and 1750s, C. P. E. Bach evolved a personal style which had immense implications for the future. From the first bars of his first 'Prussian' sonata, he shows how adventurous he is prepared to be: there are sudden pauses, violent changes of dynamics, and (in the slow movement) passages which look and sound like operatic recitative. In all these early sonatas, it is the slow movements which are most striking. The second of the set is broken up by rests, chromatic lines, and sudden alternations between *forte* and *piano*. By the second group of sonatas, these innovations have reached the first movements: the A flat sonata (no. 2 of this set) has *ritardandi* and tempo changes in the manner of a free fantasia.

These innovations clearly had their roots in the search for 'inner feeling' which preoccupied North German artists of the period. But they showed, too, how the regular structure of a piece of music could be disintegrated without destroying its form—a lesson which Beethoven was to learn from C. P. E. Bach. Later commentators, while praising C. P. E. Bach's influence, have deprecated his excesses, declaring for example that his 'paradoxes' are the 'too-easy surprises of a style in which anything can happen'. This does less than justice to the formal inventions of C. P. E. Bach's keyboard sonatas. The criticism may be true of his extraordinary free fantasias, which found their proper effect, we may suspect, only when performed by the composer himself with that passion and involvement which Burney described—'drops of effervescence distilling from his countenance'.

But the sonatas are another matter. Here C. P. E. Bach does succeed in integrating the oddest twists and turns into one composition. Newman wrote that 'one is impressed above all by the extraordinary diversity and breadth of styles, by the originality and force of the ideas, and by the authority and skill with which these are executed.' C. P. E. Bach's eccentricities are all placed within a framework of balance; only Haydn and Beethoven were to surpass him in the control they

Six Sonatas by Joseph Haydn 'for the clavichord or pianoforte'. This edition of Haydn's sonatas (Hob. 35–9 and 20) was the seventh music publication of the celebrated Viennese house of Artaria (1769–1932) and their first original Haydn publication.

exerted over that balance. Nor was C. P. E. Bach unable to write in an easy, flowing style, as he shows in some of the sonatas which appear in his set 'with varied reprises' of 1760, or in the two later sets of 1761 and 1763.

By this time C. P. E. Bach had become convinced of the claims of the piano. In the second part of his important treatise the *Essay on the True Art of Playing Keyboard Instruments*, published in 1762, he admitted that the instrument was now equal in importance to the clavichord—and moreover discussed it with the assumption that his readers would know what he was writing about. In fact, the piano had already overtaken the clavichord, at least in public performance. Technical improvements such as escapement action and damping mechanisms, combined with the sophisticated craftsmanship of makers such as Stein (see also p. 240), made the piano a completely acceptable instrument. And during the following few years, it was to make appearances in the concert rooms of the world's important musical centres for the first time. The *concerts spirituels* in Paris made use of the instrument in 1768, and in June of the same year a newspaper advertisement announced an appearance by Johann Christian Bach playing the piano in London. Eve Badura-Skoda has also recently discovered an important reference to the piano's use in Viennese concerts of this period.

C. P. E. Bach was quick to respond to these developments, and in his later sonatas, published alongside rondos and fantasias in six volumes 'for connoisseurs and amateurs' in 1779, '80, '81, '83, '85 and '87, he gathered together works he had written since 1758. There are many passages here which require a large-scale gradation of tone and expressive inflection (parallel to the small-scale gradation of the clavichord music) and clearly demand a piano. By the time of the fifth set of these pieces, he could write a movement such as the *Largo* in E flat from the fifth sonata of the set, in which ethereal chord sequences in the treble register show themselves as piano music *par excellence*, incapable of realization on any other keyboard instrument, looking forward as far as the second subject of the first movement of Beethoven's 'Waldstein' sonata. And alongside these sonatas are the extraordinary visions of the *Fantasias*, and the consummate skill of the *Rondos*: a wonderfully rich collection which constitutes the first major corpus of music for the Classical piano.

Haydn

The inspiration of C. P. E. Bach stands behind much of Haydn's keyboard writing; for that we have the evidence of the composer himself, who played and studied Bach's op.2 sonatas eagerly. But behind Haydn's earliest pieces for the piano there are other influences, too. Chief among them is that of the early composers of symphonies in Vienna, many of whom also wrote keyboard music. Georg Christoph Wagenseil (1715–77) is the most distinguished—the teacher of the Empress Maria Theresa, and a link between the High Baroque style of Fux and Muffat and the new generation of pre-Classical symphonists. His keyboard sonatas (some published in London with 'accompaniment' for other instruments) are often called 'divertimenti', a practice Haydn followed in his early works. But they are nonetheless clearly sonatas, in which the basic principles of key contrast and recapitulation can be found. His bass lines often lack interest (one commentator castigated his works as examples of the German *'sonata col pum pum'*), but the importance of rhythmic shapes rather than melodies in the principal movements is a feature that Haydn was later to develop with great skill. Georg Matthias Monn (1717–50), who composed the first four-movement symphony in 1740 (an early, isolated example), wrote an eclectic group of about fourteen keyboard sonatas essaying a great diversity of styles and formal designs, which Haydn surely knew. His brother Johann Christoph Monn wrote even more brilliantly, with features of the keyboard style we associate with Scarlatti: hand-crossings, double thirds and wide leaps.

These twin influences, the open, emotionally simplistic world of the early Vienna symphonists and the dark, introverted, experimental world of C.P.E. Bach, made for an extremely interesting combination in the keyboard music of Joseph Haydn. It is important to remember that Haydn himself was not a keyboard player of virtuoso qualities: piano works assume less importance in his output than in that of either Mozart (though for Mozart the pre-eminent form was the concerto, not the sonata) or of Beethoven. But Haydn wrote piano works for his pupils and patrons, and the dedications of the music are one good guide to their intended style. Many of his sonatas have probably been lost: fragmentary works, together with the beginnings of six lost works which Haydn listed in his own thematic catalogue, bring the total in the authoritative Christa Landon edition to fifty-two. (Landon's numbering, from the Vienna Urtext Edition, is used here. The earlier Päsler numberings from the incomplete Breitkopf & Härtel edition, which Hoboken followed in his catalogue, still also widely used, are added in brackets.)

The first nineteen piano sonatas, which are grouped together as having been written before 1766, are by and large innocent two- and three-movement pieces which still show, in their lively conversational exchanges and shifts of register, the influence of the harpsichord—and in many cases sound just as well on that instrument. They are dominated by dance forms and by themes that sound orchestral in texture—certainly they are not vocal, as anyone who tried to sing the leaping arpeggios in the finale of the C major sonata Landon no. 6 (Päsler no. 10) would find. But none of these early keyboard works is wholly predictable, and in the later sonatas of the group Haydn's powerful originality can already be heard. No. 11 (2) has some jagged themes in the first movement and a decorated *Largo* full of the expressive filigree writing of C.P.E. Bach. Quite often in these works there is a minuet and *trio*, the latter quirkily original: that of no. 12 is made up entirely of sighing syncopations, while the *trio* of no. 13 (a cheerful G major work) builds a little oscillating figure over a chromatic bass line to a climax which subsides over an aching harmonic sequence that Mozart was often to use. It is noticeable that the writing is sometimes reminiscent of the symphony or the string quartet: the finale of the E major sonata no. 15 (13) could be from either, until the Alberti figurations take over. Here, too, is the distinctive alternation between major and minor modes which Haydn was to employ so wittily in his later music.

Around 1767 the scale of Haydn's sonatas suddenly enlarges, and the break with the harpsichord is firmly established. The sonata in D no. 30 (19), which Robbins Landon believes to bear a direct imprint of C.P.E. Bach's sonata op. 2 no. 3, is notable for a sparkling finale; while the A flat sonata no. 31 (46) has a remarkable first movement full of Bachian sextuplets, pauses and unaccompanied lines, an expressive D flat *Adagio*, and a *buffo* finale. In all of this group of sonatas light-hearted major-mode and deeply felt minor-mode

movements are juxtaposed—a feature also of the symphonies and string quartets of this new creative period.

The beautifully worked G minor sonata no. 32 (44) has an opening *Moderato* in which the pathos of the North Germans finds new strength and resolution. The C minor sonata no. 33 (20) is an even more powerful work which shows how Haydn used the evolving sonata scheme for his own ends. The grave opening subject leads to a strongly contrasting theme—a modulatory sequence which leads through an unaccompanied treble line without a break into a new lyrical theme in the relative major. This gathers strength in a rising chromatic passage, and dies away in an *adagio* cadenza ending. A *forte* bass chord slams the music back into E flat for a group of closing themes—which refer back, however, to the second lyrical theme.

One of the closing themes then provides the main material for development, which works up to a pounding climax (based on the accompaniment, not on the theme!). The contrasting modulatory sequence returns briefly, but with brilliant ingenuity it leads only to the recapitulation of the opening subject in the tonic. Then a passing idea from the development (putting the first subject *under* its accompanying octaves) is briefly and dramatically developed, leading to a complete recapitulation of the 'second subject', *adagio* cadenza, and closing themes.

After a masterpiece like this movement, the following sonatas sound a little more pallid. They were all gathered together for publication in groups of six: nos. 36–41 (21–6) were written in 1773 and published by Joseph Kurzbock in the following year with a dedication to Prince Nicolaus Esterházy. These unpretentious works include singing slow movements (the *Adagio* from no. 38 (23) in F minor) and a little trick minuet and *trio* (each of whose halves are mirror images) such as the Prince would have loved. What Haydn described as 6 *Sonaten von Anno 776*, nos. 42–7 (27–32), were published by Hummel in 1778. Here again Haydn seems intent on retaining a lightness of touch, and often writes minuet movements. This does not however preclude the weird humour of the F major sonata no. 44 (29) with its angular subjects, clashing semitones, jokey alternations between major and minor intervals, and an extraordinary chord sequence at the start of its development (C minor, A flat major, diminished seventh, G minor, A major dominant seventh, D minor . . .). The B minor sonata no. 47 (32) is also very fine, with a thrilling monothematic finale built from a terse repeated-note figure which the development treats in canon—a

Autograph of the opening of Haydn's last piano sonata, composed in London in 1794 and published by Artaria in Vienna in 1798.

complexity resolved at the end of the sonata by a statement of the theme in unison, in three octaves.

Then come five sonatas nos. 48–52 (35–9), which were published with the earlier C minor sonata no. 33 (20) in 1780 by Artaria and later by Hummel. They are dedicated to the von Auenbrugger sisters, and contain the very popular D major sonata no. 50 (37), with its racy first movement full of busy figuration, and an almost Baroque slow movement, heavily dotted, *largo e sostenuto*. If this collection should seem to mark a regression from the rich and inventive sonatas of around 1770, we should recall Charles Rosen's comment that 'we misunderstand the Haydn sonatas written before 1780 if we interpret them as examples of a still undeveloped style—it was the pianists who were not yet developed.' It would be wrong, however, to apply the

same judgment to the three sonatas for Princess Marie Esterházy, nos. 54, 55, 56 (40, 41, 42), for these are full of masterstrokes which Haydn must surely have expected the pianist to appreciate: the lilting variation-type first movement of no. 54, and its furious *Presto* with a development quite unrelated to what has gone before; the subtle harmonic twists of no. 55, with its last movement in string quartet texture.

The isolated sonata no. 53 was published in London in 1784, and has an unusual and attractive first movement in triple time. (Sonata no. 57 is a problematic work whose authenticity has not been fully established.) No. 58, on the other hand, is a mature work, highly original in the double-variation structure of its first movement (as unpredictable as anything of C. P. E. Bach's), which Haydn contributed to a 'musical pot-

Johann Christian Bach: painting by Thomas Gainsborough, *c.* 1776.

a remarkable, and perfectly viable, 'orchestral' effect of the kind that Beethoven was to employ much more radically four years later in the first movement of his 'Moonlight' sonata op. 27 no. 2 (see also pp. 110–11).

The piano writing in these final sonatas is grand and virtuoso: Haydn sets no restrictions on his style. The D major sonata no. 61 is far more concentrated than the flamboyant C major. Themes in octaves, strong *sforzandi* and dynamic changes show Haydn's late piano manner at its most fully developed. There are only two movements, both in D major; the finale is a triple-time *presto*, with accents continually falling on the wrong beats. The last sonata, in E flat, has been splendidly analysed by Tovey, who shows how the unprecedented modulations and transitions of the first movement help to prepare the plan of the whole sonata—a move into E major shortly before the return to E flat is paralleled by the unexpected move to the same key for the whole of the slow movement. In this *Adagio* the violent contrasts and elaborations are an entirely new version of C. P. E. Bach's keyboard style. There could be no clearer indication of Haydn's debt to Emanuel Bach than this sonata—and no clearer demonstration of the ways in which Haydn transcended his model. Only in one of his non-sonata works for piano did he ever achieve greater depth: the intimate set of Variations in F minor, composed on an intricate double-variation plan, which ranks among his most personal and affecting compositions in any medium.

Vienna and Paris

Before Haydn and Mozart met, their styles were poles apart. If the Viennese symphonists and C. P. E. Bach were the foundations of Haydn's style, it was the Mannheim symphonists and another of Bach's sons, Johann Christian, who formed the background to Mozart's idiom. True, Mozart knew and respected C. P. E. Bach's music, but its influence is not strongly felt until the later years. One of Bach's sonatas is among the set of various works by other composers which Mozart rewrote as keyboard concertos early in his life; the composers of the remainder of the set are an interesting indication of early influences. There is music by Raupach, Eckhardt and Schobert—the latter two fashionable composers in Paris during the late 1760s, whose music was also published in London; they captured the ease and grace of the *galant* style, whose main exponent was the younger member of the Bach family, Johann Christian. As a child, Mozart had come to know J. C. Bach well, and had improvised and played pianistic games with him on an early trip to London in

pourri' collected by the publisher Breitkopf & Härtel No. 59 was composed for Marianne von Genzinger, for whom its introverted slow movement was especially intended: Haydn said it had a special, unexplained significance.

The last three sonatas, nos. 60–2 (50–2), were composed in London in 1794 for the fine pianist Therese Jansen, wife of the engraver Bartolozzi. Oliver Strunk has surmised that they were written as a set, in reverse order. The C major sonata no. 60 (50) contains two intriguing passages in which Haydn directs the performer to 'open pedal' for the duration of two and four whole bars respectively in the first movement. Some authorities believe this to be the *una corda* pedal (see p. 27); others have suggested that Haydn may indeed have intended the sustaining pedal to be used to produce

Title-page of Johann Christian Bach's Six Sonatas.

1763. Leopold Mozart had held up Christian's elegance as an encouragement to his son to write in a popular style: 'What is slight can still be great, if it is written in a natural, flowing and easy style ... Did Bach lower himself by such work? Not at all ...'

J. C. Bach

Johann Christian Bach had settled in London in 1762, where he produced a large number of sonatas in the fashionable forms of the day: 'accompanied' keyboard sonatas, in which flute or violin duetted with the harpsichord or piano; keyboard music for four hands; and solo keyboard sonatas. The first publications in the last category coincide with Christian Bach's first appearance as a concert pianist in London. His 1768 set (op. 5) and his set of 1779 (op. 17) show clearly the idiom that endeared him to the London public: the themes are decorous, the accompaniments often routine, and the contrasts between the first and second subjects never so forceful as to disconcert the listener — the principle of 'good taste' is fundamental. He preferred to string together a sequence of melodies in his first section, and then repeat some of them in sequential patterns during the second section — development is often too strong a word for such procedures. Sometimes unrelated figuration forms the main part of the development, and the return to the main themes is compressed.

If this description sounds condescending, it must be said that it could well be applied to several of Mozart's own sonata movements; but Mozart was also concerned to add to his music a quality of tension which J. C. Bach seems deliberately to have avoided. Several of the latter's sonatas are in two movements, most in three,

with a varied repertory of finale types: minuets, rondos, variations. Just occasionally, as in the well-known but exceptional D major sonata op. 5 no. 2, and in the duet sonatas, he aims at a fuller orchestral sonority. (Mozart also adopts this approach in his early piano duet sonatas, which were written for public display rather than for private pleasure.) In the music of C. P. E. Bach we saw the piano supplant the clavichord as an expressive instrument; in that of J. C. Bach the piano supplants the harpsichord as a vehicle for public brilliance.

Mozart

Mozart's earliest piano works have to be seen against the background of the infant prodigy's tours, and the influence of his father Leopold. Occasionally there are passages of original and striking music, but most often these early pieces, simple and neatly worked, aim no higher than to make a pleasing public effect.

What is surprising about his oeuvre of published sonatas is its size. Mozart, unlike Haydn, was a performer on the piano; yet he left far fewer and less significant mature sonatas than Haydn, clearly considering the piano concerto a more suitable vehicle for his genius. When Mozart played alone, usually as an encore to a concerto performance, he improvised, performed variation sets and free-ranging fantasies. If he played sonatas in public, they were even then often partly improvised or not yet committed to paper in their final form. The C major sonata K.309 was, according to the composer, a product of just such a situation. While playing in Augsburg, he performed 'all of a sudden a magnificent sonata in C major out of my head, and a rondo to finish up with' (letter of 23 October 1777). This work was written down at Mannheim.

It is conceivable that, when he wrote K. 279–84 in Munich, early in 1775, Mozart had already seen Haydn's 1773 set of sonatas. The music of these early sonatas has a quality of virtuoso display announced by the opening flourishes of the first three, K. 279, 280 and 281. Several of the first movements sound like orchestral reductions: the D major sonata K. 284 (the last of the set) captures the mood of J. C. Bach's in the same key. This work continues with a *Rondeau en Polonaise* and a theme and variations — just the sort of public *divertissement* which Bach showed Mozart how to devise.

The finest sonata of Mozart's earlier period is the tempestuous A minor K. 310, probably finished in 1778. This untypical work perhaps owes something to Mozart's new-found enthusiasm for the pianos of Stein, about which he wrote ecstatically in October 1777 (see

p. 240). Once heard played on an early piano, the opening of the A minor sonata can be difficult to accept on a modern instrument; Arthur Hutchings does not exaggerate when he writes that this passage 'cannot easily sound well on a fine modern piano', for without the most careful attention the repeated chords of the left hand tend to muddy the sonority of the treble line. The same is true of the wonderfully expressive slow movement, where the trills in the bass line need the 'buzz' and clarity of the early piano, free from the rich range of overtones of a modern instrument, to make their full effect against the clash of the triplets in the treble register. The sonata as a whole shows Mozart at his most titanic: are we to deduce from the powerful opening of a G minor sonata (K. 312), which was left unfinished, that the mood was unpopular with the public of the day?

There is certainly a strong contrast between this work and the next sonatas, which Alan Tyson now dates between 1781 and 1783. The C major K. 330 and the A major K. 331 sound as if they were designed first and foremost to be popular: there is a beautiful F minor episode in the slow movement of the first, and a lovely set of variations preceding a minuet and the famous *Rondo alla turca* in the second, but little else that is arresting. The F major sonata K. 332 and the later B flat sonata K. 333 are more important, and both of them excellent guides to Mozart's highly original deployment of sonata principles. In the first movement of the F

major work, traditional lines of development are almost entirely eschewed in favour of a delicious succession of contrasting material. Consider the opening sequence: a flowing rising theme, a contrasted dotted-rhythm figure, a new, leaping theme in D minor (which sounds like development already) that takes us through diminished sevenths into C minor, A flat and G and thence to C major: a quiet, innocent theme. So this is the second subject! It takes off, however, into a brooding chord sequence whose sudden *fortes* and *pianos* knock the triple-time rhythm into duple time, then lead through winding thirds to another new tune, which is whisked away into an assertive closing theme. The development proper consists of a new tranquil theme, and a repetition of the chord sequence, this time leading towards the home key. The tensions of this movement are derived from sources quite different from those which 'ought' to be found in sonata form.

The B flat sonata K. 333 shows the style of J. C. Bach raised to its highest level. There is little contrast between any of the themes in the first movement; the accompaniment is unobtrusive, ordinary. But the succession of melodies is so perfectly organized that the slightest intensification in the development (a leap of an octave and a fifth on to a syncopated accent) is enough to point home the climax of the movement. The slow movement in E flat has one of the most remarkable twists in all Mozart's music at the start of its second section—a chromatic dissonance at the beginning of the

49

Below: Mozart's grand piano, made by Anton Walter, Vienna, c. 1780. This instrument, formerly fitted with a large sustaining pedal, was transported from the Schulerstrasse to the venues of Mozart's many Vienna concerts early in 1785.

Below: Detail of an unfinished portrait of Mozart in 1782–3: painting by Joseph Lange.
Bottom: Mozart plays at the Prince's court. *Thé à l'anglaise* by N. B. Ollivier.

Mozart as a child: painting by Joseph Siffrède Duplessis.

Mozart as a child: painting by Joseph Siffrède Duplessis.

Part of the sonata in B flat K.570 (1789). The attestation of authenticity is signed by Mozart's widow Constanze.

bar, shifting the music into D flat major and thence to F minor, reducing it to no more than a pulsating bass note and a wandering treble line, as it gropingly finds its way back to the comfort of A flat major.

If dramatic contrast seems to some extent to have been abandoned in these works in favour of greater continuity, it returns with new strength in the C minor sonata K. 457, written in Vienna in October 1784 (and prefaced in publication by the C minor *Fantasia*, for which see below). The double question-and-answer structure of its opening, which firmly establishes tonic and dominant in our ears, is precisely that found at the start of the 'Jupiter' symphony. The tone is assertive, violent; but the second group of themes, sung both above and below a quiet accompaniment, is calmness itself. The slow movement shows Mozart's pianistic style at its most elaborate, full of *piano* and *forte* contrasts: a remarkable example of his ability to forge purposeful and expressive music from Rococo decorativeness. The finale is one of his most irregular structures, juxtaposing a quiet but agitated syncopated theme with a wild repeated-note figure over pounding chords; at one point the formal pattern of the music, as in the finale of the wind Serenade in the same key, seems to disintegrate completely.

The F major sonata of 1788 (K. 533) was not finished; its intricate, imitative first movement sits oddly beside the innocent little *Rondo* of 1786 (K. 494) with which it was published. Relevant to any discussion of sonata form is the little sonata for beginners in C major, which dates from June 1788: for all its regularity, it recapitulates the first subject in the 'wrong' key. (Mozart was obviously not intending to teach his pupils late nineteenth-century sonata form; in fact, recapitulations starting in the sub-dominant were not uncommon in the eighteenth century.) The two last sonatas are in B flat, K. 570, and D, K. 576. The first uses a favourite Mozartian device to start the development section in the opening movement: a modulatory repeat of the cadential chords. The imitative complications of the D major sonata's first movement are developed in a torrent of rushing semiquavers; more striking still is the beautifully worked finale in sonata-rondo form, with solo-tutti contrasts and an immensely extrovert virtuosity.

The finest achievements of Mozart's piano music, however, are not these solo sonatas. The four-hand works include a sonata in F major (K. 497) which is as great a work as he wrote in any medium; and the G major variations for piano duet (K. 501) are more subtle

Autograph of part of the first of Clementi's three piano sonatas op. 10.

and eloquent than any of the variations for solo piano. Among the smaller solo piano works, are some outstanding pieces: frankly experimental miniatures like the Minuet in D of around 1786 (K. 355) with its astonishing reharmonization of the theme, and its unprepared, clashing dissonances; the contrapuntal Gigue in G (K.594) with its nearly atonal theme. Finest of all are the fantasia-like pieces in which Mozart reveals most fully his debt to C. P. E. Bach: the dramatic C minor *Fantasia* (K. 475); and the less demonstrative but no less powerful B minor *Adagio* (K. 540) and A minor *Rondo* (K. 511), in which Mozart captures a sense of deathly resignation and grief. They are among the most personal utterances of the Classical period.

Clementi

The three great masters of the Classical piano belong not to one era but to two. Beethoven's first published set of sonatas appeared only after Haydn's last; Mozart was already dead. The only important composer for the piano who spans this gap is Muzio Clementi, and his influence on the developing language of the piano was crucial. As with many secondary creative figures, that influence has been exaggerated (even to the extent of presenting Clementi as the source of most of

Beethoven's thematic ideas); this has obscured his real contribution, which was the development of the first idiomatic pianoforte style. Clementi's genius was for success, and that he achieved over a long and profitable lifetime spent in the capitals of the world. He spent much of his life in London, where he wrote and played and published some eighty keyboard sonatas, as well as numerous accompanied sonatas and an important book, *An Introduction to the Art of playing on the Forte Piano*, published in 1801. Mozart, with typical bluntness, despised him and his music: 'everyone who either hears [his sonatas] or plays them must feel that as compositions they are worthless . . . he had not the slightest expression or taste, still less, feeling . . .' These sentiments were the result of Mozart's famous 'contest' with Clementi in Vienna at the Imperial court on 24 December 1781; Clementi was wise (and courteous) enough to praise Mozart's playing highly, though he seems to have had the worst of the musical battle.

Before the achievement of C. P. E. Bach was acknowledged, Clementi was sometimes referred to as the 'inventor' of piano music. Such a label was always arguable, but we still encounter it today: 'Not only the first genuine piano sonatas ever composed but the first genuine piano music of any kind', writes Harold

Below: Muzio Clementi.

Opposite: Ludwig van Beethoven in 1815: painting by W. J. Mähler.

Truscott in *The Beethoven Companion* of Clementi's op. 2 sonatas published in 1779. It is true that the C major sonata op. 2 no. 2, which he quotes, is conceived wholly in terms of the piano—although Clementi's priority in this field may be disputed. But far more important is the quality of the music, which is frankly crude. Many of his later works are much more imaginative; a new lyricism appears in the sonatas of around 1790. Clementi's use of sonata form is never rigid: his first-movement structures have a freedom which comes from his unwillingness to abandon any thematic idea before its possibilities have been exhausted. Newman held that 'this discursiveness must not be dismissed peremptorily as a fault . . . Clementi must be allowed many pages of delectable length.' He wrote many sonatas up to 1804 (op. 41), and then there was a break of fifteen years before the mature, partly programmatic sonatas of op. 46 and op. 50, of which no. 2, called *Didone abbandonata*, is perhaps the best known. Clementi did indeed contribute to a musical language which exploited the new sounds of the piano, and his free-ranging imagination provided a stimulus to Beethoven's far more penetrating mind. His sonorities find many echoes in Beethoven's sonatas, but there essentially the resemblances end.

Beethoven

Beethoven stands alone. There are, of course, strong influences in his early music, not only of Clementi, but also of Dussek, Haydn and C. P. E. Bach, and these can readily be discerned in the early sonatas (WoO 47 and 51), which overlap with Haydn's output. But with the very first theme of his first published sonata, op. 2 no. 1, Beethoven asserts his individuality. We may notice its resemblance to a Mannheim symphonic theme, to a C. P. E. Bach sonata in the same key, or even (somewhat fancifully) to the finale of Mozart's fortieth symphony. Beethoven, however, treats it as a wholly original idea, developing it during the first sixteen bars with characteristic terseness. The three sonatas of op. 2 bear a dedication to Haydn; but the only work in the set which owes a significant debt to its dedicatee is the C major sonata, whose perky first movement and flashy finale both capture something of Haydn's spirit, though in a more jerky formal framework than Haydn himself might have used.

Beethoven's sonata in E flat op. 7 appeared in 1797, and in it we can recognize some of the fundamental qualities of his style. Musical material is pared down to its essentials: the opening theme is no more than an E flat chord, yet the power which that pattern accumulates in the development section is impressive. The C minor sonata op. 10 no. 1 owes something to Mozart's in the same key; its finale is recalled in Beethoven's first movement. But the violence of the contrasts is more akin to C. P. E. Bach's writing than to Mozart's. Similarly quirky is the F major sonata op. 10 no. 2, with its brilliant jump into D major in the development, and its manic finale which has the mood of that in Beethoven's first symphony. The real deepening in all these early sonatas can be heard in the slow movements: intensely sustained, often with little harmonic movement but overlaid with elaborate melodic lines, they look towards a new musical language that was only to be fully realized in the last sonatas.

The climax of the pre-1800 sonatas comes with the 'Pathétique' op. 13, in which the quasi-orchestral slow introduction once more broadens the scope of the musical argument—especially since its material twice interrupts the tumultuous course of the first *Allegro* (where Clementi's empty octave rumblings at last find real musical meaning). Though the rondo which follows the sublimely simple song of the *Andante* is quiet, it is also menacingly assertive.

Up to this point, Beethoven had experimented freely with form within the movements of the sonata: his constant desire to seek alternatives to the dominant key

Facsimile of a letter from Beethoven to Thomas
Broadwood, February 1818, thanking Broadwood for the
new piano he had just received.

'God knows why my piano music makes the worst
impression on me, especially when it is badly played,'
scribbled Beethoven in his notebook in 1804. Perhaps he
was dissatisfied with superficial performances of his new
and original works; he also said to Krumpholz at this
time that he wanted to compose in 'a new manner'. Yet
the op. 28 sonata, which preceded these comments, is a
fine example of Beethoven breathing new life into old
forms (here, the drone bass of eighteenth-century
pastoral tradition). The three sonatas of op. 31 revert to
a still more traditional plan. The D minor sonata no. 2
seems to look further back, to C. P.E. Bach, in the
pauses and recitatives which interrupt its hectic course.
In op. 31 no. 3, Beethoven achieves a new equilibrium,
surprising in a work which dates from the same year as
his despairing 'Heiligenstadt Testament': what could be
more consonant than this sonata's opening dissonance?

The 'Waldstein' sonata of 1804, op. 53, is often seen
as the culmination of the middle period of piano sonatas.
But more significantly, it looks forward to the late style
in several ways. The scale of the piano writing is
enlarged: perhaps Beethoven was influenced by the new
Erard piano, which had arrived from Paris the previous
year. Certainly he seems consciously to exploit the
Erard's new range of sounds in the treble register, both
in the luminous second subject of the first movement
and in the finale's theme. The widely-spaced textures of
the sonata also suggest a newly resourceful instrument
stimulating an ever more adventurous imagination—the
chords in the bass (whose notes would have been quite
distinct on this piano), answered by wisps of melody
high in the treble. Then the structure of each movement
is expanded, so much indeed that the original slow
movement was discarded as too long—it is now known
separately as the *Andante favori*. It is no coincidence
that the sketches for the 'Waldstein' are in the same
notebook as those for the 'Eroica' symphony. Finally,
there are the technical anticipations of the late style: the
use of trills to sustain a musical argument, a new
bareness in the imitative textures.

These innovations are intensified in the '*Appassionata*' sonata op. 57. Only ten years separate this work
from Beethoven's op. 2, yet an entirely new manner of
musical speech has been developed, in which the
extremes of the keyboard and extremes of dynamic and
rhythmic contrast are constantly exploited. Beethoven
seems able to disrupt any conventional tonal scheme
without destroying the organization of the whole (he
uses the key of A flat minor at the end of the exposition,
and later a disconcerting pedal C over which the F
minor opening is recapitulated).

as the secondary focus of his first movements is already
evident, for example, although throughout the opp. 14,
22 and 26 sonatas he preserves the conventional
movement plan. In the two op. 27 sonatas, however, he
attempts something quite different, welding together all
the movements to produce in each case a '*sonata quasi
una fantasia*' that captures something of the improvised
quality of earlier fantasias while retaining the contrasts
of the sonata movements. Op. 27 no. 1 moves with
deceptive ease from its calm chordal opening, through
its more violent C major central section, to the scherzo-
like 'second movement' in bare two-part writing. Here
what starts as a Haydnesque joke about misplaced
accents turns into a full-scale Beethovenian struggle
between syncopated, legato arpeggios and regular,
staccato ones. A brief *Adagio* follows at once, and then a
huge and furious *Allegro*, which carries all the weight
usually associated with the first movement of a sonata.
The same newly-placed point of tension and emphasis
occurs in the 'Moonlight', op. 27 no. 2, whose famous
opening movement is no more than a gentle prelude;
only a minuet and *trio* intervene before an extended
Presto agitato provides the sonata's main argument.

Life mask of Beethoven, 1812.

Five more years separate the 'Waldstein' and 'Appassionata' sonatas from 'Das Lebewohl' (op. 81a) and the G major op. 79 (designed as a *sonata facile* for pupils). Op. 81a is untypical, a programmatic sonata in the special tradition of the 'characteristic piece', to which the 'Pastoral' symphony also belongs. It depicts departure, absence and return, and was inspired by Archduke Rudolph's leaving Vienna in May 1809. Together with op. 90, it shows Beethoven gradually approaching the style of the late sonatas, a journey which is nearly achieved in op. 101. The first movement of this sonata, and the last of op. 90, both draw from a serene, melodious melody the most wide-ranging consequences: the conflicts which arise in op. 101 are quelled only by a sonata form movement with a development in the form of a fugue—that most characteristic feature of Beethoven's late style. In op. 101, too, movement form is practically disintegrated: memories of the first movement return to interrupt the transition from the *Adagio* to the finale.

The '*Hammerklavier*' op. 106, mighty as it is, forms a diversion in the progress to Beethoven's final sonatas, for its grand design, extrapolated on the largest possible scale, is formally conventional. Beethoven here attempts the apotheosis of the 'display' sonata, using all the technical aspects of his late style but also recalling many moments of his earlier works—the interrupted recitative, the song-like solemnity of the *Adagio* (which reaches back to the earliest published sonatas). Beethoven's struggle, of life-and-death proportions, here takes place on the public platform. Something of the same feeling of ultimate enlargement dominates the 'Diabelli' Variations, in which the language of the late style again serves a fundamentally virtuoso concept— there had been no larger set of variations since the 'Goldberg' Variations of J. S. Bach.

The remaining piano sonatas turn inwards. Of opp. 109, 110 and 111 it would be foolish here to attempt to explain the emotional significance. In the context of Classical piano style, their importance lies in their unprecedented compression of form and individual utterance of language. The first movement of op. 109 presents two ideas, as a sonata is supposed to—but they are entirely different, even in tempo, and are placed side by side; no fusion takes place in the course of the movement. In op. 110 the opening theme seems no more than a lyrical introduction to a 'second subject' which in its turn lasts only seven bars: as the music here drifts apart, treble and bass are momentarily separated by no less than four and a half octaves. In the two fiercely contrasted movements of op. 111 we sense that

sonata form has been reduced to a single pair of components: question and answer, activity and repose. There is no need for a 'final' movement to resolve the tension.

The other formal aspects of these last sonatas are familiar to us, yet they too are transformed almost out of recognition. The final variations of op. 109 not only explore but also completely dissolve the theme. The final fugue of op. 110 starts in A flat as a resolution of a recitative and *arioso dolente*, but it is interrupted by the return of the aria, and is then transformed into G major before being overwhelmed by cadenza-like semi-quavers. The fugue is vanquished, but its subject is finally heard above the figuration in triumph. There is no such triumph in the *adagio* variation movement of op. 111. Nor do the variations actually vary the theme in the usual way; they take it apart, expanding its slow harmonic motion so that in the rhapsodic trills and figurations of the final pages it has a continuous movement which attains, paradoxically, complete stillness. In the final cadence, all the music is simultaneously concentrated into one tiny moment and prolonged into timelessness. Even if this had not been the last bar of Beethoven's last piano sonata, it would have represented the last possible development of his style. Other composers would have to begin again, or take refuge in pale imitation.

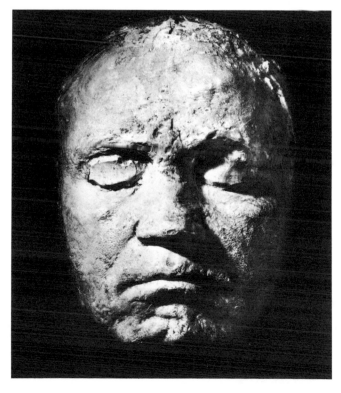

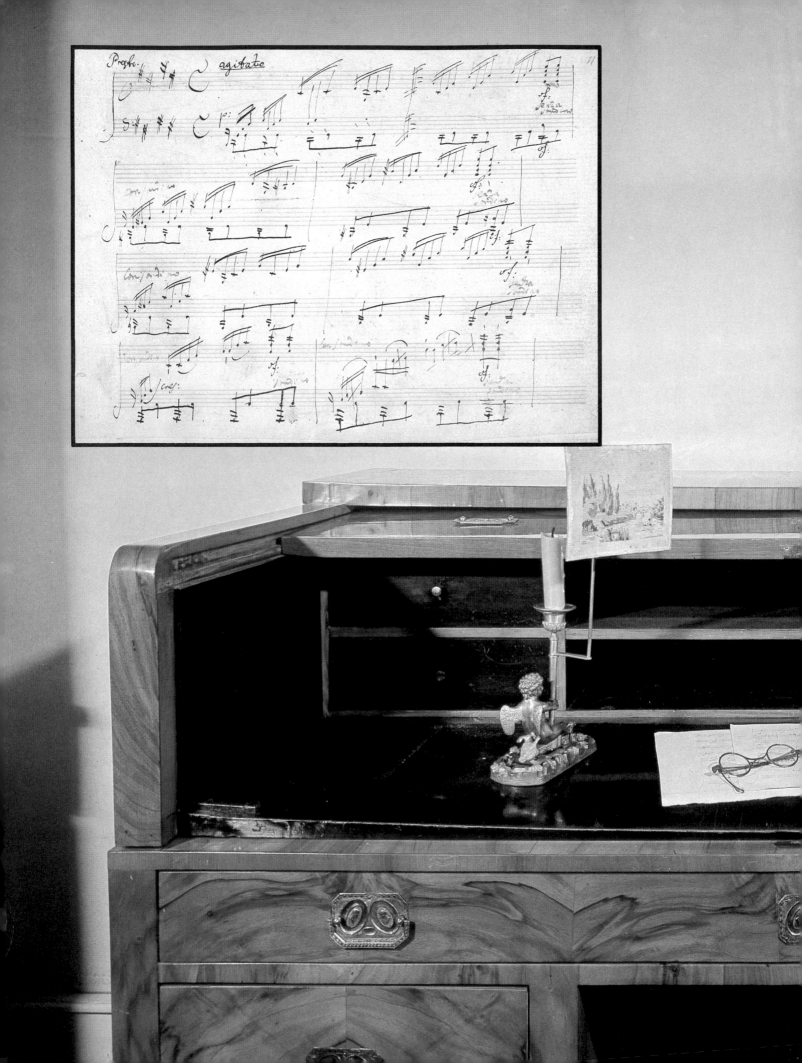

Right: Beethoven's Broadwood piano.
Below: Beethoven's desk, glasses, and writing materials.
Left: Autograph of the first page of the last movement of Beethoven's 'Moonlight' sonata, showing the composer's very precise pedal markings: *con sordino* ('with dampers'), *senza sordino* ('without dampers')—see also p. 110.

CROSSCURRENTS

Schubert, Schumann Mendelssohn, Brahms

Opposite: Franz Schubert: detail of a watercolour by
Wilhelm August Rieder, 1825.
Right: A corner of Schubert's living-room: pen drawing by
Moritz von Schwind, 1821.

Overleaf: A Schubert evening in a Viennese Bürgerhaus:
painting by Julius Schmid.

Schubert

On 25 March 1828, some eight months before Schubert
died, the Viennese newspapers carried an announcement of a concert of his music to be held the following
day. It was the only all-Schubert programme of his
lifetime, and the date on which it took place can hardly
have been chosen fortuitously: March 26 was the
anniversary of Beethoven's death. Schubert (unlike
Brahms) was no neurotic artist, but it is understandable
that he should have hesitated to place himself in direct
competition with the composer he had been too
overawed ever to approach; and it is surely not by
chance that it was the eighteen months following
Beethoven's death that saw the most prolific outpouring
of masterpieces from Schubert, who must have
known—if few others did—that he was now the greatest
living composer.

In his last instrumental works, the three large-scale
piano sonatas completed in September 1828, Schubert
seems deliberately to have invited comparison with
Beethoven. The first work of the group, in C minor, is
clearly influenced by Beethoven's concept of that key,
and it opens with a theme strikingly similar to that of
Beethoven's 32 Variations in C minor. Schubert's finale,
moreover, is based on the *tarantella* rhythm found in the
last movement of Beethoven's E flat major sonata op. 31
no. 3. (Schubert had previously used the rhythm for the
finale of his 'Death and the Maiden' quartet in D minor,
and few would deny that there, as in the sonata, he far
surpassed his model.)

The A major sonata D. 959 has a finale whose
structure follows closely that of the concluding rondo
from the first of Beethoven's op. 31 sonatas, in G major.
Schubert's theme, however, is an improved self-
borrowing, from the middle movement of the A minor
sonata of 1817. As for Schubert's last sonata, the B flat
major D. 960, the theme of its finale begins with the
same oblique approach to the home key that is heard at
the start of the finale Beethoven provided for his B flat
quartet op. 130, as a substitute for the *Grosse Fuge*.

Schubert's last two sonatas are characterized by the
melodic expansiveness that is one of the most original
features of his style. To be sure, Beethoven had written
sonata forms with similarly relaxed material—above all,
in the opening movements of his 'Pastoral' symphony,
'Spring' sonata, and 'Archduke' trio; but such breadth
of melodic conception is not central to Beethoven's art,
as it is to Schubert's, where it springs directly from his
greatness as a song writer.

The opening movement of Schubert's sonata in B flat
major is marked *molto moderato*, and it has a main theme

so broad as to be almost hymn-like. But the tension
necessary for the creation of a large-scale sonata form is
established after only seven bars, with a distantly
menacing trill on the 'foreign' note G flat. The trill
presages first a variant of the theme in G flat major; and
secondly, a new idea in F sharp minor—the aural
equivalent of G flat minor. It is not until the *pianissimo*
coda of the movement (which, if the exposition repeat is
observed, takes the best part of twenty minutes) that the
tonal conflict is resolved.

In the summer of 1828, Schubert's six *Moments
musicaux* appeared in print. The most famous of them,
the F minor *Air russe*, had been written in December
1823, but the majority of the remaining pieces in the
collection were composed in 1827, at around the same
time as the two sets of Impromptus (D. 899 and 935).
The theme of the first of the Impromptus, in C minor, is
distantly related to that of the B flat sonata's opening
movement; but stylistically, the direct forerunner of the
three late sonatas is the sonata in G major, of 1826. It
was the last of Schubert's three sonatas to be published
during his lifetime, and the expansiveness of its opening
movement, marked *molto moderato e cantabile*, is such
that the original edition described the piece as a 'Fantasy',
despite its unambiguous sonata form. The sonata and
the string quartet D. 887, written in the same year, are
Schubert's only important instrumental works in G
major, and both have a third movement in the key of B

minor. The quartet's B minor movement is a scherzo of Mendelssohnian lightness and transparency; while the sonata has instead a minuet (curiously reminiscent of the B minor second theme from the E flat major piano trio of 1827), with a *trio* in *Ländler* style. The minuet's rhythm is carried over into the finale, which finds Schubert at his most profoundly Austrian. It is symptomatic of the serenity of the sonata as a whole that all four of its movements should end *pianissimo*; and that the closing bars of the finale should additionally relax into a slower tempo. This characteristic intimacy does not, however, preclude a violent development section in the first movement, containing the only instance of a *fff* marking in Schubert's piano music. (Indeed, the only earlier occurrence of such a dynamic marking that comes to mind is to be found in the dramatic introduction to Weber's *Grande Polonaise* op. 21.)

The remaining two sonatas that Schubert saw in print are also large-scale works in four movements. The A minor (D. 845), of 1825, is the last of his three sonatas in this key, and the one most palpably influenced by its only great A minor predecessor, Mozart's sonata K. 310. Like Mozart's, Schubert's finale has a *pianissimo* theme in constant quaver motion, and a central episode in A major. Moreover, his concluding cadence reproduces Mozart's almost exactly. The opening of the sonata, with its mysterious theme in bare octaves, is an idea Schubert took over from his own previous A minor sonata, D. 784. The C major slow movement is one of his most original variation structures, with the minor-mode third variation casting its shadow over the remainder of the piece: first, in a variation in A flat major (a far closer relative of C minor than of C major); and second, in the ensuing variation, which hovers continually between C major and C minor, until the resulting tension is resolved in a coda. The scherzo third movement is constructed in irregular five-bar phrases, and the rhythm of its opening anticipates that of the principal theme of the splendid A minor *Allegro* for piano duet (popularly, but misleadingly, known as '*Lebensstürme*'), which Schubert wrote in the last year of his life.

The D major sonata D. 850 was published in 1826, together with the *Divertissement à la hongroise* for four hands. Its grand style was perhaps prompted by the fact that it was written for a virtuoso performer, Carl Maria von Bocklet, but it is nevertheless a work in which Schubert seems ill at ease; and the childlike simplicity of the rondo finale, with its 'tick-tock' accompaniment, sounds oddly at variance with the three preceding movements.

Of Schubert's remaining sonatas, the best known is the A major (D. 664) of 1819. Its fame is well deserved, in view of its freshness and charm, but considerably

Autograph of the first page of the *Andante* of Schubert's G
major sonata D.894.

greater is the A minor D. 784—one of the most intense
and dramatic of all Schubert's piano works. Despite the
subdued tension of its opening, much of the writing in
the first movement is almost orchestral in conception,
and the full-blooded chords that are hurled across the
entire compass of the keyboard in its development
section serve as a reminder that the sonata was written
shortly after the *'Wanderer' Fantasy*. (Only in the
extraordinary middle section of the late A major sonata's
slow movement is the explosive violence of these two
works surpassed.)

Of Schubert's first dozen piano sonatas, no fewer than
half survive in a fragmentary state. In several cases,
entire movements are lacking; but two of the more
interesting examples—in F sharp minor and F minor
respectively—have a first movement that stops short at
the point of recapitulation, which occurs not in the tonic
key, but in the subdominant. This is a procedure that
Schubert followed in not a few of his earlier completed
works, too (the finale of the 'little' A major sonata is a
case in point), and it is one that departs radically from
Classical tradition, where the start of the recapitulation
is always marked by a return to the tonic. (Mozart's
highly original *Sonate facile* K. 545 presents perhaps the
only significant exception to this rule, though Beethoven
made a joke out of beginning his recapitulation in the
'wrong' key in his F major sonata op. 10 no. 2.)
Schubert's was at least in part a labour-saving device: a
subdominant recapitulation ensured that the second
subject would arrive in the tonic without the necessity of
making any alterations to the exposition's course of
events. Schubert more than made amends later in his life
by seizing on the dramatic possibilities of the
recapitulation: the G major quartet, for instance, has a
recapitulation so radically different from its exposition
as to throw into relief the additional background of a
variation form.

The last of Schubert's unfinished sonatas stands apart
from its predecessors. It was written in 1825, and
published posthumously under the title of *'Reliquie'*.
Neither of the last two movements is complete, and
Schubert uncharacteristically wrote the *Andante* in the
tonic minor, as if unconsciously realizing that the first
two movements in themselves formed a satisfying
whole. Since the minuet and finale fall far below them in
inspiration, pianists would do well not to attempt a
completion.

However great the symbolic significance of the date
on which Schubert held his concert in March 1828, from
a practical point of view the occasion was ill-timed:
Paganini made his first Viennese appearances that
spring, and Schubert could not hope to compete. He
went himself to hear the famous violinist, and it is
altogether characteristic that he was struck not so much
by Paganini's virtuosity (as Schumann and Liszt were to
be), as by the purity of his tone. In the slow movement of
Paganini's B minor concerto, Schubert 'heard an angel
sing', and he attempted to reproduce the sound,
complete with *portamento*, in the slow second section of
his *Fantasy* in F minor for piano duet. The *Fantasy*
represents the last, and greatest, example of what had
been a lifelong preoccupation: the compression of the
movements of a symphonic design into a continuous,
unified whole. Among Schubert's earliest efforts at
composition are four incomplete fantasies for piano
duet; and the mature examples include, besides the F
minor duet *Fantasy* and the *'Wanderer'*, the C major
Fantasy for violin and piano.

The F minor *Fantasy* begins with a theme whose
expressive apoggiaturas reflect the influence of
Schubert's two visits to Hungary in the early 1820s. (So,
indeed, does the principal theme of the slow movement
from the great string quintet which Schubert wrote
shortly after completing the *Fantasy*.) The structure of
the work as a whole, with the opening material returning
in a contrapuntally enhanced form near the close, is
modelled on Mozart's *Fantasy* in F minor for mechanical organ, K. 608, which—then as now—circulated in a
piano duet arrangement; and even the thoroughly
Schubertian choice of the Neapolitan key for the two
central sections has its parallel in the sudden plunge into
F sharp minor near the end of Mozart's opening section.

None of Schubert's piano works exerted a greater
influence on succeeding generations of composers than
the *'Wanderer' Fantasy* of 1822. Not only is it the most
strongly unified of all his fantasies, with virtually
everything being derived from the dactylic rhythm of its
opening bar, but its orchestrally-inclined textures
anticipate a style of keyboard writing developed by
Brahms and Liszt. Liszt, whose own B minor sonata
reflects the cyclic structure of the *'Wanderer' Fantasy*,
made a transcription of Schubert's work for piano and
orchestra; and Schubert's transformation of his heroic
opening theme into a triple-time *presto* for his scherzo
foreshadows the similarly parodied use of earlier
material in the 'Mephistopheles' third movement of
Liszt's 'Faust' symphony.

The dactylic rhythm on which the *'Wanderer'*
Fantasy is based is one that haunted Schubert for many
years. It appears also in the B flat major Impromptu of
1827, and the A flat minor variation from the fine set in
A flat major for piano duet. The spiritual forefather of

these pieces—and particularly the last-mentioned of them—is the *allegretto* second movement of Beethoven's seventh symphony.

Schubert is the only instance of a composer who wrote as many piano masterpieces for four hands as for two. In addition to the F minor *Fantasy*, his last year saw the composition of the *Allegro* in A minor (D. 947) and the *Rondo* in A major (D. 951); and the two pieces may well have been intended to form a sonata. The *Allegro* is a dramatic sonata form, whose second subject is initially heard in the very remote key of A flat; while the *Rondo* is one of two pieces Schubert lovingly modelled on the finale of Beethoven's E minor sonata op. 90 (the other being the *Rondo* in E major, D. 506).

Among Schubert's earlier duets are two *Divertissements*, whose seriousness belies their title. The first, written in Zseliz in 1824, is *à la hongroise*, and is the direct forerunner of Liszt's Hungarian Rhapsodies. Liszt made an arrangement of the *Ungarische Melodie* which is Schubert's earlier version, for two hands, of the theme of its finale. The companion work, the *Divertissement sur des motifs originaux français*, suffered the fate of being split up by its publisher into three separate pieces. The opening movement is a *Marche raisonnée* (the adjective refers to the fact that it is in sonata form), and the slow movement is the well known *Andantino varié* in B

minor—perhaps the most perfect of all Schubert's duets. Its model is Mozart's *Andante with Variations* in G major K. 501, and it ends with a similar return to the theme in its original form. But Schubert's reprise is preceded by a variation in the major which offers one of the many examples of a side of his art in which he surpassed even Mozart: the ability to make the change from the minor mode to the major bring with it an enhanced poignancy.

The largest of Schubert's duets is the C major sonata, known as the *Grand Duo*, written in the same Hungarian spring of 1824 that saw the composition of the A flat major Variations and the *Divertissement à la hongroise*. It was Schumann who first voiced the belief that the *Grand Duo* was a symphony in disguise; and in 1855 Joseph Joachim, with more than a little help from Brahms, orchestrated it. Schubert's original is, however, thoroughly pianistic, even at those moments where it deliberately strains against the medium, and musically it shows considerably less affinity with the 'Great' C major symphony than with two more intimate works in the same key: the 'Reliquie' sonata, and the string quintet. Like the sonata, the *Grand Duo* begins with a tranquil theme in bare octaves; and like the quintet, it exploits mediant, or third-related, keys in order to broaden the structure. The second subject of the *Grand Duo*—

Portrait of Schumann as a child.

rhythmically identical with the opening of the first—is initially heard in A flat major, and it breathes the same song-like atmosphere as the E flat major theme played by the two cellos at the parallel juncture in the quintet. But it is in their third movements that the two works show the strongest similarity: in each case, a bright C major scherzo is followed by a sombre and mysterious *trio*. The *Grand Duo*'s finale begins with a dramatic off-tonic held octave—an idea Schubert was to use again in the first of the four Impromptus D. 899, as well as the last movement of the B flat major sonata. It has as powerful a development section as Schubert ever wrote, and its coda contains one of his most startling uses of a Neapolitan key, with the main theme appearing, as if in slow-motion, in C sharp minor.

No discussion of Schubert's piano music would be complete without a mention of his dances. It was above all as a writer of waltzes, Polonaises and Ecossaises that he was known to his Viennese contemporaries, and his most famous single composition was the so-called *Trauerwalzer*, or *Sehnsuchtswalzer*. The titles *Valses nobles* and *Valses sentimentales*, to which Ravel was to pay homage, were not Schubert's own; nor was the selection or ordering of pieces in the various published collections. Several of Schubert's dances appeared in the popular albums that were issued annually for the New Year Carnival; but already before his death, his name as a composer of waltzes was being overshadowed by those of Joseph Lanner and Johann Strauss.

Schumann

As an eighteen-year-old law student at Leipzig, one of Robert Schumann's favourite pastimes was to play Schubert's piano duet Polonaises. Schumann himself wrote a set of eight Polonaises for four hands at this time, and some of its material was to find its way into his *Papillons* op. 2. Two years later, in 1830, he travelled to Frankfurt to hear Paganini, and the experience proved decisive in his resolve to give up law for music. Among his first published works are two sets of Studies, each containing six pieces based on Paganini's *Caprices*. The first set has a lengthy preface which includes preparatory exercises—ironically written at a time when injury to his right hand forced him to abandon all hope of pursuing a career as a concert pianist. Paganini's influence can also be felt in the brilliant Toccata op. 7; and the great violinist is one of the characters portrayed in *Carnaval*, where his *spiccato* playing is recalled. Schumann, however, had little interest in virtuosity *per se*, and the influence of Paganini was short-lived.

Schumann wrote virtually all of his great piano music

between 1830 and 1839, when he was in his twenties. (The following year, in which he finally married Clara Wieck after a protracted legal battle with her father, was marked by a great outpouring of songs.) The series is initiated by the '*Abegg*' Variations op. 1. Its theme provides the earliest instance of what was to be a lifelong fascination with musical cyphers. Abegg was apparently a girl Schumann had met at a ball, and the theme begins with the letters of her name transformed into musical notation.

Five years later, Schumann's fiancée, Ernestine von Fricken, served him as a similar source of inspiration for *Carnaval*. Ernestine's home town was Asch, which in German musical notation yields the motive A-Es-C-H (the 's' being rendered by its aural equivalent 'Es', or E flat; and the 'h' being the German 'H', or B natural). By a coincidence which intrigued Schumann, the same four letters were the only ones in his own name which had a musical parallel. He will have noted, too, the connection with the name Walt Harnisch, the hero of his favourite novel, Jean Paul's *Flegeljahre*. In the 'Piano-Tuning' chapter of the book, three strings break—A-C-H—whereupon it is remarked that they are letters from Harnisch's name.

With the exception of the opening '*Préambule*', all the numbers of *Carnaval* revolve around the same four notes (or a three-note derivative in which Asch is 'spelled' A♭ ([=As] -C-B), and Schumann's original title for the work was *Fasching: Schwänke auf vier Noten* ('Carnival: Jests on Four Notes'). It was eventually published, however, as *Carnaval. Scènes mignonnes sur quatre notes*, and the German title was adapted for the *Faschingsschwank aus Wien* op. 26. The '*Préambule*' actually derives from a projected set of variations on Schubert's *Sehnsuchtswaltzer*, whose harmonic outline can still be traced in Schumann's opening bars.

Towards the end of the '*Abegg*' Variations, the theme is 'verticalized' into a chord whose notes are released one by one, so that the melody emerges, as it were, by subtraction. Schumann used the same diminuendo technique at the conclusion of *Papillons*, where it suggests the final words of Jean Paul's *Flegeljahre*, the acknowledged inspiration behind the work: 'Enchanted, Walt heard the vanishing sounds speak, for he did not realize that with them his brother was vanishing.' (In writing a unified, programmatic chain of dances, Schumann had the example of Weber's *Aufforderung zum Tanz*; but in Weber's case, the verbal 'explanation' was something of an afterthought.) The main impetus for Schumann's piece was the penultimate chapter of Jean Paul's novel, entitled '*Larven-*

tanz'. *'Larve'* signifies both a mask (hence the 'masked ball') and a larva—a double meaning that gave rise to the title of *Papillons*. For Jean Paul, a masked ball was 'perhaps the most elevated way in which life can re-enact playful poetry.' Schumann referred to his *Carnaval* as 'a more elevated kind of *Papillons*', and its autobiographical 'Florestan' movement is twice interrupted by a quotation from the earlier work. Moreover, the seventeenth-century 'Grandfathers' Dance' that initiates the finale of *Papillons* reappears in the concluding 'March of the *Davidsbündler* Against the Philistines' of *Carnaval*, where it symbolizes the stolid, reactionary Philistines. (The *'Davidsbund'* was an imaginary league of musicians invented by Schumann as music critic, to carry the banner for new artistic ideas.)

The protagonists of Jean Paul's *Flegeljahre*, Walt and Vult Harnisch, are twins, and they reflect the two sides of the writer's own personality. A similar duality found its outlet in Schumann in the shape of 'Florestan' and 'Eusebius', representing respectively the passionate and the poetic aspects of his character. Both make an actual appearance in *Carnaval*; and in the first edition of the *Davidsbündlertänze* op. 6, each piece is signed with the initial F or E (or sometimes both together). Schumann's F sharp minor sonata op. 11 was dedicated 'To Clara, from Florestan and Eusebius'. It is more than tempting to regard this split artistic personality as symptomatic of Schumann's long struggle against mental disintegration (and whether his final illness was caused by schizophrenia or—as more recent medical research seems to indicate—syphilis is of little importance).

Jean Paul was one of the two writers closest to Schumann's heart. The other was E. T. A. Hoffmann. From Hoffmann, Schumann borrowed the titles *Kreisleriana*, *Phantasiestücke* and *Nachtstücke*; but also, perhaps, another kind of artistic duality. In Hoffmann's novel *Kater Murr* (which was also the young Brahms's favourite book), a cat scribbles his life story on pages torn from a printed biography of the eccentric musician Johannes Kreisler. Hoffmann explains in his preface that some of the printed pages were accidentally republished, which is why *Kater Murr* consists of two interleaved stories. In a sense, Schumann's *Kreisleriana* can be heard as two similarly interwoven cycles: it is a work of violent contrasts, and it has not one principal key, but two (B flat major and G minor). Even so, it begins impetuously in the 'wrong' key of D minor—an opening that suggests not only the burst of inspiration that gave rise to the work—apparently written in the space of four days—but also the abrupt manner in which so many of Hoffmann's tales begin:

I had death, ice-cold death in my heart—yea, from my innermost being, from my very heart it pierced like sharp icicles into nerves already glowing with heat. I ran wildly, forgetting my hat and coat, out into the dark, stormy night! The weather vanes were creaking: it was as though Time were audibly turning his eternal terrible gear-wheels, and at any moment the old year would roll with a hollow sound into the dark abyss, like a heavy weight.
(*The Adventure on New Year's Eve*)

Schumann's other major piano cycle having more than one tonal centre is the *Davidsbündlertänze*. Although in its choice of keys it ranges considerably wider than does *Kreisleriana*, it is the tonalities of G and B that exert the strongest pull. The true ending of the cycle is the B major seventeenth piece, which recapitulates, 'as if from afar', the theme of no. 2; but Schumann adds a postscript in the distant key of C major—a delicate waltz which (in the first edition) carries the inscription: 'Quite superfluously Eusebius remarked as follows; but much happiness spoke from his eyes withal.' Both the piece and its legend are designed to counterbalance the only other C major number in the cycle, which occurs at its exact mid-point: 'At this, Florestan kept silent, and his lips were quivering with emotion.' Schumann's deliberate weakening of the tonal centre was, incidentally, an experiment carried out with even more boldness by Chopin—notably in his F major Ballade, with its ending in A minor.

Schumann is alone among great composers in that virtually all of his thematic material falls into regular four-bar phrases. (The six-bar phrase that opens *Carnaval* is an exception; and in the Scherzo from the *Four Pieces* op. 32, the pattern is replaced by an equally symmetrical use of five-bar periods.) That his music so triumphantly survives such a self-imposed restriction is a tribute to his melodic genius; that the restriction is there in the first place may perhaps be the result of a deep-rooted psychological reaction to his fear of a mental breakdown. In order to achieve variety within regularity, Schumann frequently resorts to complex syncopation. The melodic lines of *'Des Abends'* from the *Phantasiestücke* op. 12, and *'Fast zu ernst'* from the *Kinderszenen* are entirely written against the bar-line; and the *Humoreske* op. 20 contains a particularly dislocated accompaniment which the pianist is instructed to play 'as if out of tempo'. *Kreisleriana* ends with a ghostly gigue-like piece in which the two hands appear to be curiously out of synchronization. Often, the syncopation is so protracted that the listener ceases to hear the contradiction of metre, and it is only the performer who feels it throughout.

Perhaps the greatest of all Schumann's piano works is

Autograph of the first page of the first movement of Schumann's F minor sonata op. 14.

the C major *Fantasy* of 1836—his response to a suggestion from Liszt that a fund should be set up for the building of a monument to Beethoven at his birthplace of Bonn. The entire first movement gravitates towards its concluding quotation from Beethoven's song-cycle *An die ferne Geliebte*, a title that clearly carried symbolic significance for Robert and Clara. Its opening is one of the most passionate utterances in the Romantic repertoire, with the theme being announced *fortissimo* over a turbulent, yet subdued, accompaniment containing its blurred outline. In this movement, Schumann stands the entire sonata tradition on its head: the piece begins with its moment of maximum tension, and eventually relaxes for a quasi development section ('In the style of a legend'). The recapitulation, which follows the exposition's pattern closely, begins in E flat major; and it is only in the coda, with its Beethoven quotation, that C major is established with any stability. Not until Wagner's Prelude to *Tristan*, and Bruckner's eighth symphony, was the large-scale avoidance of the home key taken a stage further.

Schumann's first title for the *Fantasy* was 'Grand Sonata', and certainly none of his three earlier sonatas approaches it in originality or mastery. All of them have a slow movement using pre-existing material. In the most problematic of them, the F minor sonata op. 14 (published as *Concert sans orchestre*, and first publicly performed by Brahms in 1862), a theme by Clara Wieck forms the basis of a set of variations; while the slow movements of the F sharp minor sonata op. 11 and the G minor op. 22 quote from early settings of poems by Justinus Kerner.

The op. 11 sonata opens with a slow introduction foreshadowing not only the principal theme of the ensuing *Allegro*, but also the song theme—a highly original idea that was to find an echo in the 'Spring' symphony, where the Scherzo's theme is heard in the concluding bars of the slow movement. (The notion of anticipating events from one movement to the next finds its apogee in the fourth symphony of Mahler, in which the climax of the slow movement is formed by a glimpse of the key and main theme of the finale.) The tempo markings of the first movement of the G minor sonata— *as fast as possible*, followed by *faster*, and eventually *still faster*—have been viewed with a certain amusement. Yet the simplification of texture and harmonic pulse at the points of acceleration make it quite feasible to carry out Schumann's directions.

The Little Vegetable Market in Haag: watercolour by Mendelssohn, 1836.

Below: Mendelssohn aged 12: painting by Carl Begas, 1821.

Mendelssohn

Among the forty-three pieces of the *Album für die Jugend* which Schumann wrote in 1848 is one that carries the heading '*Erinnerung (4 November 1847)*'. The date of remembrance is that of the death of Felix Mendelssohn, and the piece attempts deliberately to evoke the atmosphere of some of Mendelssohn's *Songs Without Words*.

As a pianist, Mendelssohn was renowned for the clarity and lightness of his touch—features that express themselves forcibly in his compositions. The violinist Joseph Joachim, who played with Mendelssohn when a boy of twelve, was struck above all by the electrifying quality of his staccato. Mendelssohn transferred his staccato to the orchestra in such pieces as the finale of the E minor violin concerto and the Scherzo from the Incidental Music to *A Midsummer Night's Dream*; to the string octet; to the string quartet, in the scherzos of the E minor and E flat major works from op. 44; and to the piano trio in the two great examples op. 49 and 66.

The transparently textured, fleeting scherzo was, in fact, one of Mendelssohn's most original inventions, and in his piano music he usually favoured the 'crisp' keys of B minor, E minor or F sharp minor for such pieces.

Right: Caricature by Aubrey Beardsley.
Opposite: Prince Albert at the organ, with Queen Victoria and Mendelssohn.

FELIX
MENDELSSOHN
BARTHOLDY.

(The B flat minor *Song Without Words* op. 30 no. 2, and the scherzo in the same key from the B flat piano sonata are notable exceptions.) It is undoubtedly a vein which Mendelssohn overworked, but the well known *Rondo Capriccioso* written at the age of fifteen, and the posthumously published *Scherzo a Capriccio* in F sharp minor are fine examples. Behind these works one can detect the distant influence of Scarlatti, whose shadow can be felt still more strongly in the running passagework of some of the *Seven Character Pieces* op. 7.

Scarlatti was not the only Baroque master whose music Mendelssohn knew and loved. It was his famous Berlin performance of the *St Matthew Passion*, in March 1829, that spearheaded the Romantic revival of interest in Bach. Mendelssohn was the only composer of whom Schumann made an exception when he declared that the successful writing of fugues after Bach, Handel and Beethoven was an impossibility. The best of Mendelssohn's piano fugues are contained in the *Six Preludes and Fugues* op. 35. Their composition was spread over a period of ten years, from 1827 to 1837, and in each case the prelude was written after the fugue. The finest pair of the collection is the first, in Mendelssohn's characteristic E minor. The Prelude, composed fully ten years after the Fugue, clothes its theme very effectively in a continuous swirling of arpeggios. From its calm opening, the Fugue presents a gradual *crescendo* and *accelerando*, until at its climax a chorale melody appears—an idea Mendelssohn was to exploit in the finale of his C minor piano trio.

Of the remaining preludes, the second offers one of Mendelssohn's typical keyboard textures, with an inner-voice accompaniment in constant semiquaver motion, and a 'running' bass in octaves; the third is a staccato scherzo in B minor; the fourth is a duet without words, in the same key—A flat major—as the '*Duetto*' that concludes the third book of *Songs Without Words*; the fifth, in F minor, shows Mendelssohn's melodic invention at its finest, and the sixth at its weakest. None of the later fugues quite matches up to the one in E minor, but Mendelssohn's achievement in combining contrapuntal ingenuity with apparent spontaneity is nevertheless considerable.

The generic title of *Songs Without Words* was not used until the publication of what is now known as Book III, in 1837. Book I appeared in August 1832 under the title of *Original Melodies for the Pianoforte*, while Book II was issued three years later as *Six Romances*. The *Songs Without Words* owe their origin to Mendelssohn's own attitude towards verbal imagery, as expressed in a letter to his friend Marc André Souchay in 1842:

People usually complain that music is so ambiguous; that there's so much doubt as to what they should think of it, while words are understood by everyone. But with me it is exactly the opposite. And not only with entire speeches, also with individual words—even they seem so ambiguous and imprecise to me, so susceptible to misinterpretation in comparison with a good piece of music, which fills one's soul with a thousand better things than words. A piece of music I love conveys to me thoughts not too imprecise to be put into words, but too precise.

The *Songs Without Words* achieved overwhelming popularity during the Victorian era, but they are sadly neglected today. If they are undeniably uneven, many of them show Mendelssohn's invention at its most perfect and original. In their simplest form, they consist of a song-like theme above a smooth accompaniment—as, for instance, in the well-known E major piece that opens Book I, or the 'Venetian Gondola Song' that closes it. Others take a step closer to the German *Lied*, and have an improvisatory prelude and postlude enclosing their song strophe, as in the fourth piece of Book I, or the fifth of Book VI. (Mendelssohn carried out a similar plan on an enlarged scale in the first of the three *Fantasies or Caprices* op. 16.)

Many are far more dramatic: the splendid F sharp minor op. 19 no. 5, which is actually a fully developed sonata form; or the passionate B minor op. 30 no. 4,

which spectacularly demonstrates Mendelssohn's staccato. The C minor op. 38 no. 2, with its continually syncopated accompaniment, exploits one of the composer's favourite devices—the overlapping of the climax of one phrase with the start of the next. Book V, op. 62, was dedicated to Clara Schumann, and it contains three of the most famous pieces. The first, in G major, with its off-tonic beginning, is surely one of the most beautiful melodies Mendelssohn ever conceived; while the E minor funeral march (later to be orchestrated by Moscheles for Mendelssohn's own funeral) left a profound mark on Mahler, who borrowed its opening for the start of his fifth symphony; and the fifth piece is the so-called 'Spring Song', of which Mendelssohn's own performance, with its staccato accompaniment, so electrified Joachim.

It was perhaps in view of his extraordinary melodic fertility that Mendelssohn showed comparatively little interest in variation form. His three sets of piano variations were all written in 1841. Two of them are little more than conventional pieces, and he did not deem them worthy of publication; but the series was initiated by the *Variations sérieuses*—a polemic title that indicates Mendelssohn's intention to avoid the salon style of variations cultivated by such fashionable pianist-composers as Wilhelm Friedrich Kalkbrenner

and Henri Herz. The model behind the work is Beethoven's 32 Variations in C minor, from which Mendelssohn learned the continuity that carries the music with an increase in intensity through the concluding variations. But Mendelssohn's yearningly chromatic theme, with its disguised downbeat, is far more expressive than Beethoven's deliberately neutral subject. It derives, curiously enough, from the variation theme of an otherwise unremarkable sonata for viola and piano which Mendelssohn wrote at the age of fifteen.

Beethoven also served as a model in the last two of Mendelssohn's sonatas. (The first, in G minor, is the work of a precocious twelve-year-old, and need not concern us here, though the sensuous harmonies of the slow movement's initial bars show an astonishing maturity.) The opening movement of the B flat major sonata of 1827 is so closely based on that of Beethoven's 'Hammerklavier' as to sound almost like a parody, and Mendelssohn's cause can hardly have been helped by the well-intentioned editor who published the work posthumously as op. 106! The sonata's single attractive movement is its scherzo, which—as in the string octet written two years earlier—makes a fleeting reappearance during the course of the finale. The sonata in E major op. 6, of 1826, is considerably more successful.

It begins, like Beethoven's A major sonata op. 101, with a song-like *Allegretto* starting as though in mid-argument. But Mendelssohn departs from his model in presenting a complete sonata form (with a second subject derived from the rondo finale of Beethoven's E minor sonata op. 90). The delicate coda, played *una corda*, recurs twice during the course of the sonata, and is eventually used to round the work off. The influence of late Beethoven is also revealed in the use of recitative for the central section of the sonata, though it is nothing if not characteristic of Mendelssohn that he should cast his recitative in the improbable form of a fugue.

The F sharp minor *Fantasy* op. 28 may be considered together with Mendelssohn's three sonatas. Like the sonata op. 6, it plays continuously, though it is not a cyclic work. The strangest of its three movements is the second—a minuet-substitute in duple time, with irregular seven-bar and nine-bar phrases. The finale is a sonata-form *presto* whose agitated instability is enhanced by a recapitulation beginning, like that of the first movement of Beethoven's *'Appassionata'*, over a dissonant dominant pedal.

Brahms

No late nineteenth-century composer was as conscious of the great tradition that lay behind him as Johannes Brahms, who felt so strongly the shadow of Beethoven that he hesitated for a full quarter of a century after the start of his composing career before publishing a first symphony. Yet that career began with three piano sonatas conceived on an altogether symphonic scale; and Brahms significantly chose as his op. 1 the sonata which begins with a rhythmic reminiscence of the opening of Beethoven's *'Hammerklavier'*. It was with his three sonatas that the twenty-year-old Brahms introduced himself to Robert and Clara Schumann, in the autumn of 1853. Schumann hailed him as 'the young eagle', and the orchestral weight of Brahms's piano writing prompted him to describe the sonatas as 'more like veiled symphonies'.

The earliest of the sonatas, in F sharp minor, was published with a dedication to Clara Schumann as Brahms's op. 2. It contains a masterstroke of astonishing originality, and one that he was never again to attempt (though it does anticipate a later fondness for fusing slow movement and scherzo into a single structure): the last of the variations that constitute the slow movement functions at the same time as the sonata's scherzo. To the listener, the fact that the theme's initial eight bars in their scherzoid form are repeated provides only a vague hint that the new

movement has started, and the revelation thus occurs at the beginning of the contrasting *trio*.

Like that of the F sharp minor sonata, the slow movement of the sonata in C major op. 1 is based on a melody of the *Minnesinger* period; and the two pieces provide the earliest instances of a weakness for folksong that was to remain with Brahms throughout his life. In the C major sonata it is the two outer movements that are thematically unified, with the finale's main subject being a variant of the sonata's opening bars. The last sonata of the group, in F minor, presents a solution to cyclic form that is, in a sense, the counterpart of the F sharp minor sonata's amalgam of slow movement and scherzo. The *andante* second movement is a rondo which lacks the final reprise of its theme. Moreover, the piece ends not in the key in which it began (A flat major), but in its subdominant (D flat). Between the ensuing scherzo and the finale, Brahms inserts an Intermezzo entitled *'Rückblick'* ('Retrospect'), which provides the missing reprise—albeit in B flat minor—transformed into a funeral march, complete with an evocation of muffled drums.

At the head of the slow movement from his F minor sonata, Brahms quotes three lines from a love-poem by Sternau. His next piano work, the first of the four Ballades op. 10, is his only instrumental piece actually to follow an extra-musical programme. The inspiration behind it is the Scottish ballad *Edward*, of which Brahms was later to make a vocal duet setting. The third of the Ballades is an Intermezzo in B minor, whose halting first phrases recall the Scherzo in E flat minor of 1851—the earliest of Brahms's published works. The most prophetic of the four pieces is the last, whose intimacy foreshadows the ruminative quality of Brahms's late piano pieces, though without matching their conciseness of expression.

The Ballades mark an interlude between the first two phases of Brahms's output for piano. In the second phase, the emotional—and, indeed, structural—freedom of the early sonatas is counterbalanced by the discipline of variation form. The first of the six sets of variations Brahms wrote between 1854 and 1861 is his tribute to Schumann, whose mental breakdown had occurred less than half a year after the two men had first met. As his theme, Brahms took the first of the five *'Albumblätter'* from Schumann's *Bunte Blätter* op. 99; and in its key—F sharp minor—and overall shape, the work pays homage to Schumann's *Etudes symphoniques*. Furthermore, Brahms takes another variegated leaf out of Schumann's book, and adapts the second of the *'Albumblätter'* for his ninth variation; while the tenth

includes, as an 'inner voice', a fragment from the theme by Clara which Schumann had used as the basis of his Impromptus op. 5. Seven years later, in 1861, Brahms was to cast his finest work for piano duet in the form of variations on a further subject by Schumann. The theme is the last piece of music that Schumann wrote down, convinced that it had been dictated to him by the spirits of Schubert and Mendelssohn (sadly, it was a partly misremembered quotation from his own violin concerto), and Brahms's final variation transforms it into a subdued funeral march.

The first of the two sets of variations op. 21 is Brahms's only such work to be based on an original theme. Its apparent simplicity is belied by a characteristic irregularity which expands the second phrase of each half into five bars. In the concluding variation, the theme unfolds over a long-held trill—an idea clearly modelled on the variation finales of Beethoven's sonatas opp. 109 and 111. Brahms's op. 21 no. 2 takes as its theme a Hungarian song he had probably learned from the violinist Eduard Reményi, with whom he had made a concert tour in 1853. (To Reményi belongs the distinction of having instilled in Brahms an interest in Hungarian gipsy music that found its outlet not only in the famous *Hungarian Dances* for piano duet, but also in the finales of all four of his concertos, the slow movement of the clarinet quintet, and—most spectacularly—the *Rondo alla zingarese* of the G minor piano quartet op. 25.)

In their conception as a series of studies, the two Books of *Variations on a Theme by Paganini* op. 35 again owe something to Schumann's *Etudes symphoniques*. The theme is that of Paganini's well known twenty-fourth *Caprice*, where it also forms the basis of a set of variations. Unlike Schumann in his 'Paganini' Studies, Brahms did not preface his work with suggestions for surmounting its technical difficulties, though as late as 1893 he did publish a set of fifty-one exercises which would serve the purpose well. (With his characteristically wry sense of humour, he gave the exercises a title taken from E. T. A. Hoffmann: *Fantasiestücke in Callots kühnster Manier*—'Fantasy Pieces in Callot's Boldest Manner'.)

The greatest and the most ambitious of Brahms's variation sets is the *Variations and Fugue on a Theme of Handel*, op. 24. It is his most rigorous work of its kind: not only are the theme's shape and proportions maintained throughout the twenty-five variations, but only on one occasion—in the dramatic ninth variation—does Brahms allow himself the luxury of a varied repeat of its second half. (Three further variations have written-out repeats, but the changes affect little more than the music's register.) Still more remarkable is the fact that only one variation forsakes the tonality of B flat, and even this contains a 'hidden' statement of the theme at its original pitch.

In their key and atmosphere, the 'Handel' variations are closely related to the *Variations on a Theme of*

Opposite left: Brahms and Reményi in 1853.
Opposite right: A photograph of Brahms in 1856.
Left and below: Brahms on his way to, and back from, the
'Red Hedgehog', a favourite Viennese restaurant of the
1890s.

Haydn, which in its original scoring for two pianos is Brahms's last large-scale keyboard work. As in the 'Handel' set, there is an elaborate finale—not a fugue, but a passacaglia, as if in preparation for the last movement of the fourth symphony. Brahms's other work for two pianos, the sonata in F minor, also represents an earlier version of a composition more familiar in another guise. Brahms had at first scored it as a string quintet, before lending it greater weight by recasting it for two pianos. The final compromise between the two versions resulted in the well-known piano quintet op. 34, but the sonata has much in its favour, and enables some of the richer textures to sound with a clarity that the quintet cannot match.

Brahms's late piano pieces, composed between 1878 and 1893, are his equivalents to Beethoven's last piano music, the *Bagatelles* opp. 119 and 126. The two largest single pieces are the curiously-titled Rhapsodies op. 79—the first of them in effect a scherzo and *trio*, the second a clear sonata form. They are preceded by the *Eight Piano Pieces* op. 76, and followed by the four collections opp. 116 to 119. The titles most commonly used for individual pieces are Capriccio and Intermezzo (the Ballade and Romance from op. 118, and the Rhapsody that concludes op. 119, are the only exceptions). A few of the pieces recapture the full-blooded writing of the three early sonatas (in particular, the D minor and G minor Capriccios from op. 116, the Ballade op. 118 no. 3 and the Rhapsody op. 119 no. 4), and

two of them—the gipsy-style B minor Capriccio op. 76 no. 2 and the C major Intermezzo op. 119 no. 3—could legitimately be called lighthearted; but this is essentially meditative music, and the economy of means, both thematic and harmonic, is remarkable. The earliest of the pieces, the Capriccio in F sharp minor op. 76 no. 1, is almost entirely based on a four-note motive also used in inversion; the E minor Intermezzo op. 116 no. 5 develops nothing more than a sighing, dissonant two-note phrase; and the bleak opening melody of the E flat minor Intermezzo op. 118 no. 6 is accompanied only by an unchanging diminished seventh chord, rather in the manner of Schubert's visionary setting of Heine's *Die Stadt*. The Intermezzo in B minor op. 119 no. 1, which Brahms described as 'teeming with dissonances', begins with a series of slowly descending thirds, recalling, as if from afar, the principal subject of the slow movement from the F minor piano sonata. The melodic use of falling thirds is an idea that occurs with increasing frequency in the music of Brahms's last years, from the opening bars of the fourth symphony and the F minor clarinet sonata, to the third of the *Four Serious Songs* (where it sets the words '*O Tod, wie bitter bist du*').

Brahms's late piano pieces mark the ultimate refinement of the far-flung gestures of his three early piano sonatas. Unlike the deliberately futuristic late piano works of Liszt, it is music that looks back; but at the same time, it provides a direct link to an Expressionist genre that was to be cultivated in the early years of the twentieth century by Max Reger and Arnold Schoenberg.

THE ROMANTIC PIANO
Chopin to Ravel

Signor Paganini during one of his Performances at the King's
Theatre, June 1831: lithograph, 1831.

Paganini

Paganini was the original Romantic virtuoso. In 1829 Chopin heard him play in Warsaw; in 1830 Schumann, in Frankfurt; in 1831 Liszt, in Paris. Each was much moved, and they responded variously. Schumann produced his Studies after Paganini's *Caprices*, opp. 3 and 10. In one sense they are rather literal transcriptions, in another not: the twenty-four *Caprices* are for unaccompanied violin, and Schumann fills up the middle of his keyboard with notes that spell out Paganini's skeletal harmonies. (Mendelssohn wrote accompaniments for Bach's solo violin sonatas, too.) Liszt's Studies after Paganini re-create the brilliant effects of the violin-writing with inventive freedom. Chopin paid direct homage only with a modest *Souvenir de Paganini* for piano, but set about writing his own op. 10 Studies at once.

These three composers invented Romantic piano music, and it is impossible to leave Paganini out of it. If we think of music as abstract constructions, then Romantic music in general developed continuously out of Classical music, and musicology will find no neat line of demarcation. The thought of Romantic piano music, however, instantly evokes the Romantic Pianist, and his genealogy is much better defined. He is not Czerny, nor Hummel, nor Moscheles, nor even Mendelssohn—though Mendelssohn was only a year older than Chopin (and Schumann and Liszt barely younger). Distinguished performers though they were, they were not Romantic pianists: they were admired for their elegance, dexterity and taste, and their music was designed to display especially those virtues, measured against established standards. Paganini paraded a new persona, that of the artist who exploits unheard-of powers of his instrument to express his own feelings with phenomenal intensity, and must therefore be his own composer.

Schumann's transposition of Paganini's *Caprices* as far as possible to a familiar middle ground, as if trying to show them worthy of educated respect, more than a unique performer's special turns, was a German mistake about the nature of the new beast. (He compounded it in his review of Liszt's versions of the *Caprices*, when he remarked that his own had been intended 'to bring out the more poetic side of the composition' where Liszt aimed rather 'to stress the virtuoso side'. Though Schumann's paraphrases are creditable, one would hardly judge them now more 'poetic' than Liszt's—they go some contrary way toward reducing Paganini to conventional prose.) Schumann perceived well enough that Paganini's powers were musical, not merely acrobatic, but he could not see where to locate them if not within the honoured Austro-German tradition of music-making. He was no pedant, and the new ideal of personal expression in music was wholly sympathetic to him. What he was slow to recognize was the new executive means for achieving it: the constructive possibilities of creative figuration, extreme contrasts of texture and sonority, and harmonies indicated with a bare minimum of notes to leave room for free, non-polyphonic invention.

Somewhere behind most Austro-German music there stands a four-part male chorus. By educated instinct Schumann approached music in the spirit of that model, supposing that whatever resisted accommodation to it must be marginal, mere tricks of presentation and titivation. Through Liszt and Chopin he soon learned better, of course: his great C major *Fantasy* (dedicated to the former) and his *Kreisleriana* (dedicated to the latter) bear eloquent witness to that, without compromising with his own cultivated tradition. We might remark that Schumann, at the time of the Paganini phenomenon, was about to abandon a concert career—the translation of his piano works into performance would be left to his beloved Clara—whereas the young Chopin and Liszt were ambitious professional performers.

Paganini's most vivid pieces were short and formally naïve by the standards of the sonata tradition. Except in orchestral concerts, long pieces were not public fare. If a Beethoven sonata was played, its movements were commonly separated by renditions of irrelevant music, often by another performer. Moscheles claimed to have given the first solo piano recital in Paris, without supporting artists, in 1837 (the institution of the public orchestral concert was only about sixty years older). For a recitalist, especially outside Germany and Austria, the sonata-tradition aim of building up and then resolving long-range tensions was a specialized private interest. Beyond the staple variation-sets and pure improvisations, short, pungent pieces were required—preferably, since much of one's audience played or listened to an instrument at home, pieces that exploited a technique exceeding the domestic norm. Paganini's inventions were sufficiently extraordinary in themselves, and in his hands they revealed an enormous affective power that owed nothing to sophisticated large-scale construction. Furthermore, he appeared on the scene as an exotic alien (with a sulphurous aura about him), thus disarming assessment by established academic criteria. All that made him an ideal Romantic model.

Below: Fryderyk Chopin: drawing by Eliza Radziwill, 1826. Right: Ferencz Liszt in his thirteenth year: lithograph by Leprince, 1824.

Opposite: Group portrait by Kriehuber, 1846: (from left to right) the artist, Berlioz, Czerny, Liszt, Ernst.

Chopin and Liszt

Chopin (1810–49) and Liszt (1811–86) were not really exotic aliens. Any notion of them as respectively impassioned Pole and fantastical Hungarian, descending upon Paris like wild men, would be foolish. Chopin's father was a Frenchman who mysteriously forswore France for Poland at the age of sixteen. After working for a French-owned tobacco factory until it went bankrupt, he became a tutor to well-born children, married a poor but aristocratic lady, and was appointed Professor of French in the Warsaw Lyceum soon after the birth of their only son. Thereafter the family lived comfortably and fashionably. Chopin *père*, himself a flautist and violinist, was quick to detect young Frédéric's gifts; even in provincial Warsaw it was possible to equip him with a good grand piano to study, and a thorough formal education in music.

Liszt's Hungary was only a province of the Austro-Hungarian Empire. His principal languages were French and German (whatever Hungarian he had dwindled with his childhood); his father was a steward in the employ of the noble Esterházy family, Haydn's patrons. 'Liszt' may well have been German 'List', with an added *z* to guide pronunciation in Hungarian, and Liszt's mother was certainly Lower Austrian. Less

materially fortunate than Chopin, young Franz was assiduously promoted as a prodigy by his father, who found him patrons among Hungarian aristocrats. When he was ten the family removed to Vienna, where he had free lessons with Czerny and met Beethoven and possibly Schubert. At twelve he was settled in Paris, though Cherubini refused him admission to the Conservatoire, and he was left to educate himself in music between profitable public appearances. When Chopin reached Paris a dozen years later he had almost immediate *entrée* to aristocratic circles; it took Liszt a long time to shake off the uncomfortable status of performer-as-hired-entertainer.

Liszt made his reputation on the hoof, so to speak. Chopin, thanks to Schumann, was admired before he was heard. Schumann's first published salute to him — 'Hats off, gentlemen—a genius!'—is now folk history, but its context is often ignored. It came in a first review written by an unknown 21-year-old, and it referred to Chopin's virtually forgotten op. 2, the Variations on '*Là ci darem la mano*' from Mozart's *Don Giovanni*. Schumann was perceptive enough to discern the originality of that now faded piece. Meanwhile Chopin was working at the op. 10 Studies, the first ripe fruit of his genius. Liszt had begun the first draft of *his* Studies,

eventually the *Etudes d'exécution transcendante*, in 1826—long before hearing Paganini or Chopin; but they were full of Czerny and Hummel (like the earliest music of Schumann and Chopin), and the later versions were Romantically enriched almost beyond recognition. When Liszt re-composed them, Chopin had intervened. At the end of 1831 Chopin settled in Paris, and he and Liszt at once became friends and colleagues. During the next seven years, while Chopin completed his second book of Studies, op. 25, and much other polished music, Liszt continued to produce transcriptions of other people's music in great profusion, and made new sketches of his own. Finished and distinctively original pieces began to emerge only in 1838; much of his best music appeared long after Chopin's death in 1849.

In short, Chopin arrived in Paris as a self-assured composer, soundly trained in theory and counterpoint, while Liszt—already a seasoned gladiator of the concert platform—still groped after his own style and fattened his repertoire with transcriptions. Liszt was (and remained) generously receptive to fresh musical impulses from any quarter; Chopin admitted to little esteem for any contemporary music, doubtless because his own—in his chosen medium—was so evidently superior. It is singularly difficult to trace any external influence upon Chopin after he left Poland: one might, just possibly, track the odd bit of figuration to Kalkbrenner or Herz.

Other Pianists, and Berlioz
Chopin intended at first to study the piano with Kalkbrenner, one of Liszt's established older rivals. There were several in Paris, which had become the showplace for piano virtuosity: Moscheles (Mendelssohn's teacher), Hiller, Herz, Pixis, later Thalberg. They were pianists who wrote early Romantic piano music, but their art was essentially decorative and conventional; we should not recognize them as Romantic pianists until they began to gather in the wake of Liszt and Chopin. Each had his own finger-specialities, his tricks of bravura for display in endless variations, not much varied. Liszt came to be called 'the Paganini of the piano', less because his technical resources exceeded those of others than because of the unfamiliar emotional power and range of his performances. Transcriptions and fantasies on operatic themes were everyone's stock-in-trade, but Liszt's often recaptured or even intensified the dramatic force of the originals.

Liszt was a magnificent proselytizer for inaccessible

music. Outside the largest European capitals, orchestral performances were infrequent and incompetent. Liszt made fine, resourceful versions (for piano duet as well as solo) of many symphonic works—all the Beethoven symphonies, for example—with and without extraneous bravura; and of Bach's organ music, and of *Lieder*. He found himself devising ways of drawing quasi-orchestral sounds from his modern pianos, and the endeavour of translation was itself creatively fruitful.

There was another Paganini-figure in Paris: Hector Berlioz. Unlike almost every other composer, he was no kind of pianist at all (he had studied only the flute and, like Paganini, the guitar); his instrument was the orchestra. Just before Paganini's revelatory Paris debut came the première of his *Symphonie Fantastique*, which Liszt also attended. Liszt celebrated it in a solo transcription of utterly unprecedented scope and splendour, so faithful to Berlioz that Schumann was able to publish an acute, detailed assessment of the Symphony with reference only to Liszt's version. Nothing like it had ever been written for the piano (nor, of course, for the orchestra). Few pianists braved its hazards in public, and eventually the spread of professional orchestras—and recordings—relieved them of any need to try; but for some decades the transcription was treasured among musicians (notably in Russia, where Liszt and Berlioz were names to conjure with) as a revelation of the possibilities of the instrument. It was a beacon that cast light in many dimensions: on distributing many and variously coloured strands between two hands, on exploiting the different registers of the keyboard, on the expressive weight of different chordal layouts, on varieties of attack. Nobody profited more from its disclosures than Liszt himself. His devoted labour opened the way to his richest later canvases, fixing the Romantic vision of the piano as a universal musical medium. (He proved the point once by playing Berlioz's 'March to the Scaffold' immediately after an orchestral performance of it, and winning.) Years after, he was to place his transcriber's skills at the service of the music of Richard Wagner, his son-in-law and the heir to Berlioz's orchestral kingdom.

Chopin

The faultless grace of Chopin's piano writing, and its inimitably personal stamp, suggest a naturally inspired master, sprung fully-armed. People rarely invoke 'early Chopin' or 'late Chopin'—and he composed virtually nothing, after all, past the age of thirty-six. Still, his precocious maturing was not miraculous. His first teacher, after his mother, was the violinist Adalbert

Zwyny, who instilled him with an abiding love of Bach; lessons with Zwyny ended when Chopin was twelve, and he began harmony and counterpoint with Joseph Elsner, the head of the Warsaw Conservatoire. He soon started to publish his compositions (which included music for flute, cello and piano trio as well as solo piano). He revered Mozart, admired Schubert, was uncomfortable with Beethoven; in town he revelled in Italian opera (but not Bellini, who was not performed in Warsaw before Chopin left), and spent his vacations in the country absorbing folk music. Mazurkas and Polonaises were among his first pieces.

There were also pieces in a weakly Classical mould: rondos, and the unconvincing first sonata (dedicated to Professor Elsner), and even the two concertos—though the charms of the latter outweigh their formal naïvety. Chopin was very ill at ease within the bounds of standard sonata form (unlike, say, Mendelssohn, who was perfectly happy there as long as he could improvise variations on it); and he abandoned it along with

A page from Chopin's pocket diary for 1848 containing the composer's notes of dates of piano lessons given in Britain, accounts of fees, and the names of towns where he stayed and gave concerts, including London, Glasgow and Edinburgh.

Warsaw, once the concertos had been duly premiered there, in 1830. (When the E minor piano concerto—miscalled 'no. 1': it came after the F minor—was published, he dedicated it to Kalkbrenner.) He had begun the seminal op. 10 Studies after Paganini's visit by way of making practice-work for the concertos; completed at last in Paris, they would be dedicated to Liszt, and the subsequent op. 25 set to Liszt's mistress Marie d'Agoult, the mother-to-be of Wagner's wife-to-be. Others had composed *études* that were something more than mechanical exercises, but Chopin transformed the genre, and it became a principal Romantic mode. Beyond Paganini he drew most upon the Bach of the Forty-eight Preludes and Fugues. The first Study is a glorious expansion of Bach's opening C major Prelude, and had he planned opp. 10 and 25 in advance he would surely have imitated Bach in representing every major and minor key, as he did later in the twenty-four Preludes op. 28.

Pursuing his career in the wider world, Chopin went to Vienna with a friend of whom he was passionately fond—Titus Woyciechowski, the dedicatee of the op. 2 Variations which so struck Schumann. Immediately upon their arrival, the abortive Polish revolution against the Russian satrapy broke out; Titus hurried home; Chopin agonized, and at last chose not to interrupt his career. He remained, but the Viennese liked him less than they had done on an earlier visit. He continued to compose—a new vein of bitter defiance entered his music with the first Ballade, the first Scherzo and the 'Revolutionary' Study—and after several months proceeded to Paris. He never again came nearer to Poland than Carlsbad, where just once he met his parents. His Warsaw sweetheart Constantia had written in his album, 'Remember!... In foreign lands they may appreciate and reward you better, but they cannot love you more.' Later, Chopin pencilled in: 'Oh yes, they can!'

The Viennese found him too quiet a pianist for the concert hall, and indeed his Parisian career was centred

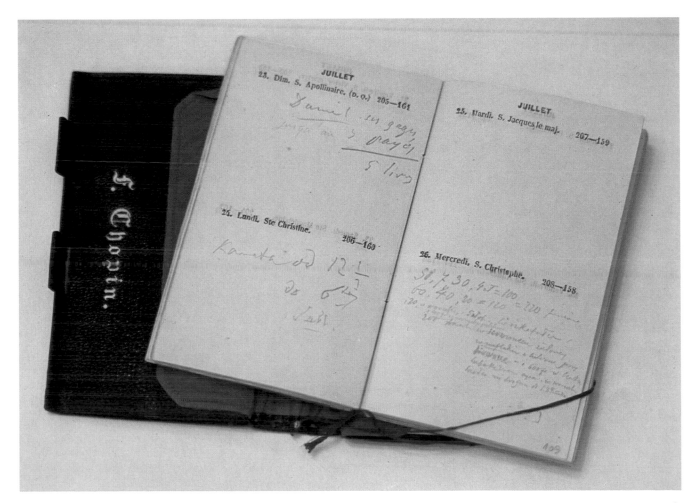

Chopin: daguerrotype made a few months before his death in 1849.

upon the salon *soirée* rather than public concerts, of which he gave very few. In Vienna he had begun work on the half-dozen Nocturnes opp. 9 and 15, in the lyrical-introspective manner that was peculiarly his own. (The genre was certainly created by the Irish pianist John Field (1782–1837), but it is doubtful whether Chopin knew much of his music before Paris, and then he was critical of Field's gentle effusions.) Whether his lack of sheer physical firepower resulted from his frail constitution or from his refined piano-style is an open question. The younger Liszt notoriously broke pianos; Chopin never did. To his pupils he confessed himself unequal to the violence required by some of his own music: at one of his last concerts he took the towering climax of the Barcarolle op. 60 at an exquisite *pianissimo*. But transparent evenness (a Hummel and Kalkbrenner ideal), delicate finesse and a singing legato were the acknowledged hallmarks of Chopin's playing, and they were written into his music. His part-writing, much more fully thought through than Liszt's, allows this or that voice to rise smoothly into the foreground for an expressive aside at any moment. Chopin's tone-palette does not extend to the orchestral and histrionic extremes of Liszt's, and becomes etiolated if exposed to such lurid lights.

The ideal Chopin piano would have the wooden frame of the 1830s, and Liszt's the later cast-metal one. Chopin's has a higher proportion of *thud* to pitched *ping*, its sounds melting together less readily, and for the player a balanced, articulate touch is the precondition for every Chopinesque effect. The essence of the legato is pure phrasing, not boneless fluidity—Chopin was irritated by Englishwomen who constantly exclaimed that his playing was 'laïk oua-tah'. His figuration, even at its most exquisite (as in the late *Berceuse*), remains expressly *figuration*, whereas Liszt's is often aimed at creating quite different effects. The much tauter strings of the new iron-framed pianos made available not only a grander dynamic range, but sonorities which carried farther and lasted longer, and could be graded more suggestively with the pedal—by half-pedalling, for example, where a mere touch of dampers to strings can suppress higher and softer notes while lower and louder notes still resound. Only one or two of Chopin's last pieces suggest anything so *recherché*. Many a Lisztian peroration comes in hammered chords in the middle of the keyboard; the weight of a Chopin peroration is accumulated by many notes running over most of the range, with rich discords clanging in the inner parts.

The famous Chopin *rubato* is not primarily a matter of expressive delays and rushes, but of reconciling such things with a steady underlying pulse. It belongs in the first instance to the Mazurkas and Waltzes: dancers want a reliable beat, but the composer does not want his melody straitjacketed by it. In *rubato*, a bit of time 'robbed' to caress a phrase must soon be paid back—or must at least seem to be—before the basic pulse flags. Furthermore, a sufficiently firm pulse can be subdivided into beats rather flexibly (Meyerbeer swore that Chopin played his Waltzes in *quadruple* time, with a gross Viennese hiatus between the official second and third beats: ONE two . . . three, ONE two . . . three). Judged by his own practice, Chopin's reported assertion that the left hand must be perfectly strict under a free right hand was blatantly over-simple. Dance rhythms are pervasive in Chopin; only some of the Studies stand apart, generating their impetus in toccata-style instead. All four Ballades move to a higher power of waltz-time. Almost every Prelude is by Chopin's canons either an *étude* or a nocturne; and his Nocturnes, when they are not waltzes, are sarabandes or pavanes. The Scherzos are quick waltzes—unlike Mendelssohn's, they have feet.

In seven continuous party-going years in Paris, broken off by his flight with George Sand to Majorca in late 1838 (taking Bach's 'Forty-Eight' with him), Chopin wrote numerous pieces that were beautifully shaped but formally unambitious, and relatively short. He made no new foray into the sonata tradition—and where else could principles of large-scale construction be sought? His music remained sectional, generally in some multiple of A-B-A form, though his codas—sometimes a whole final section—acquired new significance: not mere closing flourishes or afterthoughts, but freshly elaborated statements which could place what went before in another dramatic light. The quasi-narrative form of the first Ballade had already pointed the way. In these years, the second Ballade (unique in having a cyclical recall of its beginning *after* a furious coda, and duly dedicated to Schumann) and especially the second Scherzo stand out as broad edifices. Their sections are successively and purposefully developed, and their key-structures are no longer a matter of contrasting keys for different sections but complete dramatic plans, securing something like the long-range tensions of a good sonata-movement. Yet there is nothing resembling symphonic argument, though there is much *étude*-like play with small rhythmic motives.

The grim winter in Majorca and the summer of recuperation at Nohant, where George Sand had a small château, marked a musical watershed for Chopin, away from performing and from parties. He completed the

85

twenty-four Preludes, and the third Scherzo—and the sonata no. 2 in B flat minor: Schumann declared it to be four astonishing pieces masquerading as a sonata, but its first movement adapts the lessons of the second Scherzo (in the same key) to a version of sonata form. (Its eerie hands-in-unison finale suffers on modern pianos in large halls: where Anton Rubinstein heard 'night winds sweeping over churchyard graves' we are likelier to hear a confused welter, without the drier rattle of Chopin's piano to define it.) There soon followed the F minor *Fantasy* and the third Ballade, the triumphant apotheosis of the salon-piece. The *Fantasy* is anything but wayward, for its pattern is Chopin's most deliberate and self-conscious construction: its impassioned episodes rise by regular modulatory steps (in a sequence announced in the cadenza at the end of the Introduction) to the tiny *lento*, a sort of secret garden, whence the sequence is repeated from a point which guarantees that the last episode will regain the home key.

Finally, between 1842 and 1846 came the B minor sonata (its finale is the apotheosis of the Romantic rondo) and Chopin's single-movement masterpieces: the super-Mendelssohnian last Scherzo, the magnificent last Ballade, the sumptuous Barcarolle and the elusive, visionary Polonaise-Fantaisie, besides the A flat Polonaise and the last Nocturnes and Mazurkas. In Chopin's whole *oeuvre* the Mazurkas supply a subversive undercurrent: only in them did he give free rein to the modal implications of his native music. The harmony of his more ambitious pieces is correctly Western European, though it advanced steadily from the mere surface chromaticism of the earlier Studies (as

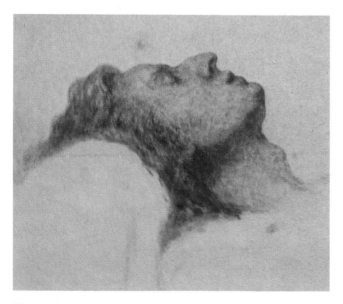

in Liszt's first drafts) to the fraught chord-sequences of the Barcarolle and the fourth Ballade. It remained for Russian and later French composers to explore the special possibilities of modal harmony.

Liszt

Before the advents of Chopin, Paganini and the *Symphonie Fantastique*, Liszt had been on the verge of abandoning his Paris career, bored and dispirited. He was revived not only by those musical revelations, but by the current revolutionary ferment in both politics and literature. The idea of music as popular communication seized him forcibly—in 1830 he planned a Revolutionary Symphony—together with the conviction that new wine needed new bottles; thenceforth he looked out eagerly for radical formal novelties. But he assimilated new methods slowly and cautiously: the next seventeen years were devoted to performing, which meant both developing his own piano-composing and introducing a vast range of other music to his rapt audiences. The year of Chopin's watershed also saw the first mature versions of Liszt's Transcendental *Etudes* (dedicated to Chopin), the Studies after Paganini (dedicated to Clara Schumann) and some of the pieces that would figure in the Italian *Année de pèlerinage*. Not long before Chopin's death, and just before the ambiguous 1848 Revolution, Liszt retired to Weimar and addressed himself seriously to acquiring an orchestral technique. The definitive versions of much of his piano music appeared only later. His voluminous output for the piano therefore does not represent his development fully—the path to his masterly, cyclical B minor sonata (dedicated to Schumann) led through the orchestral poems, in which he worked out the Berliozian principle of 'thematic transformation'.

The same principle is applied in the largest of his other piano works, the concertos and the Sonata Fantasia *'après une lecture de Dante'*. It remains, however, a device for unifying an extended piece, not for determining its progress in any particular way (unlike sonata form); the order of events is really governed by an emotional or theatrical scenario, and needs a sympathetic—as well as brilliantly equipped—performer to bring it to life. The sense of concentrated growth that resides in Chopin's masterpieces is hardly to be found in Liszt's, which may yet convey a musico-dramatic purpose just as compelling. Hence the performer may come to terms with Liszt more easily than the musical analyst. Though the B minor sonata is notable for its economy of means, economy was not in general a virtue that Liszt prized. His ingeniously

Liszt: lithograph by Achille Deveria, 1832.

Announcement of a Liszt recital in Breslau in 1843, including the first performance of *Hexameron*.

unified pieces are therefore no more quintessential Liszt than the Hungarian Rhapsodies, or the Studies, or the songs and sketches of the *Années de pèlerinage*. They are not summations of his piano music as Chopin's last grand canvases are.

Where Chopin cultivated his idiom with almost hermetic consistency, Liszt was open, agglutinative, experimental. Chopin's pieces were perfected in the composing, Liszt's revised repeatedly to make better effects. It was natural that Chopin should retreat from performing, as his compositions more and more spoke for themselves—but Liszt's music is fulfilled only in actual execution. Chopin's first standard was the utterly explicit Bach; Liszt's, whatever would hold and move an audience. Audiences change, and so many passages in Liszt now evoke chiefly their period (except in the hands of master pianists). In the last years of his retirement Liszt was composing for no audience, and the fragmentary pieces of that time give us no bearings at all: one doesn't know what they are *for*, obsessive and strange as they are, and only the rare inspired performance supplies a clue.

Two related features of Liszt's piano music above all account for his imperishable place in the repertoire. One is the sheer practised beauty of his writing for the instrument, his refined instinct for tapping the aural possibilities of piano texture and layout. Rudely energetic modern performances obscure that; the 'pearly' touch which was a salon ideal, an even, unemphatic, translucent flow, is a prerequisite for most of his work, and merely brilliant and melodramatic accounts of the first '*Mephisto*' Waltz or the 'Dante' sonata leave half the music unheard. The other is the incorporation of the performer-conjuror into the music, the musico-dramatic role given to wilful virtuosity, the ironic execution of preternatural feats. That looms large in the Hungarian Rhapsodies, to irresistibly witty effect (Liszt's 'Hungarian' music was not folk stuff but gypsy turns), and many of his passages of 'diabolical' import are precisely the most hazardous ones for the executant. Much of Chopin's music is very difficult, but it contains nothing so viciously chancy as the *presto leggiero* climaxes of the waltz and sonata just mentioned. The pianist who can meet the transcendental technical

The Abbé Liszt in his study and (bottom) a late photograph.

challenge is more than a composer's transmitter, for his relish in his own dexterity contributes vitally to what is heard.

There is much more to Liszt's music, but it runs beyond the scope of this book. As a figure in the history of the piano, he is neatly represented by a curious collective work known as the *Hexameron*. Commissioned for a charitable occasion in 1837, it consists of variations on a March from Bellini's *I Puritani* by Thalberg, Pixis, Herz, Czerny and Chopin, with an introduction, linking passages and a finale by Liszt. The first three composers display their idiosyncratic charm and facility, and Czerny his old-fashioned skill in construction, whereupon Chopin trumps them all with the limpid depth of his simple variation in a remote key; Liszt organizes these diverse idioms into a colourable dramatic sequence, capped by his own concluding survey (the preceding variations are faithfully quoted). The whole became a favourite showpiece of Liszt's own, doubtless with the individual styles brilliantly re-created—Chopin admitted to envying Liszt's way with his own Studies.

The Etude-Principle and Alkan

Piano studies were crucial in the Romantic idiom. Pre-Romantic studies, like Czerny's and the renowned *Gradus ad Parnassum* collection of Clementi, were technical exercises cast in simple musical forms, providing for rudimentary musicianship as well as manual skills. Their object was to perfect the execution of specific manual feats, such as might be required *en passant* in a serious concert piece. Typically, an *étude* was built from a single pattern of notes—a musical figure—incessantly repeated at different degrees of the scale, so that the student might learn to execute it smoothly whatever the distribution of black and white notes might be in its different recurrences. At the lowest level an *étude* might consist merely of some suitably challenging figure reiterated, say, one note higher each time; more gracefully, the figuration might serve as accompaniment to a simple tune, or else be arranged in sequences that made up an orderly little composition.

In Romantic *études* such figuration became vastly elaborated and hand-stretching (small hands became a liability), ripely chromatic, magically evocative. It could be deployed to draw jewelled sonorities from the whole compass of the keyboard at once, with the new sustaining power of the instrument. It could be a glinting filigree, or a thunderous turbulence, or an opalescent wash. It demanded power and great agility as well as dexterity; the heights of the repertoire were increasingly inaccessible to the amateur. For technical reasons, music in this style lies more easily under the hand in keys with many black notes: suddenly the arcane keys of G flat, D flat and B flat minor were ubiquitous, and their fearsome key-signatures daunted casual sight-reading by non-experts. Simple, unfigured piano writing began to acquire the status of a special effect—and when it was native to an older idiom, the Romantic pianist often clothed its nudity with modern jewellery.

The constructive use of *étude*-figuration went far beyond decoration. Its little cells could be treated as significant musical elements themselves, as motives; it could ensure continuity to long passages involving remote harmonic excursions; it could reinforce tension, or heighten dramatic effect. All that had been well known to Bach, but in the music of the Viennese Classical composers such writing had been confined to occasional passage-work and to brilliant rondos—by the standards of proper part-writing it was too inarticulate for the most serious composition. And within the constraints of Classical harmony, it could not but be: the most telling Romantic *étude*-writing carries a harmonic burden too adventurous to lead a well-mapped Classical argument.

The apotheosis of the *étude*-principle is found in the work of Charles-Valentin Alkan (1813–88), a French pianist greatly admired by his neighbour Chopin and by Liszt. Like Chopin he composed chiefly for his own instrument, and he too retired early from a public career. Though he had been a six-year-old prodigy at the Conservatoire, he began to make his strange mark as a composer only when Chopin was already falling silent. His twenty-five Preludes appeared in 1846, and next year the *Grande Sonate* and the twelve Studies in all the major keys—Alkan was making good Chopin's youthful lapse—to be followed, after a decade of silence, by the twelve Studies in the minor keys. The 1847 pieces are massive, and massively difficult, but the minor-key Studies are monumental. They amount to a claim for the capacity of the *étude* to assimilate all the major musical forms: one Study is a grand *Ouverture* a quarter-hour long, four more constitute a full-scale symphony for solo piano, and another three make a whole concerto (with a 35-minute first movement). The concerto is a heroic fantasy indeed, aiming to re-create the epic confrontation of Romantic pianist and orchestra as if on a solo super-instrument.

Much Romantic piano music strains after orchestral colours, but in that sense Alkan's music is not orchestral at all—it is absolute pianism. Alkan was misdescribed by Hans von Bülow (Liszt's sometime son-in-law, before Wagner) as 'the Berlioz of the piano'. Berlioz was an inventor, Alkan a consolidator who sought to capture for the piano the weight and many-levelled sonority of the post-Beethoven orchestra—to put it to post-Beethoven symphonic uses. Alkan's larger forms came directly from the academic end of that tradition, which Chopin and Liszt had abjured. Such 'symphonic' work at the piano was not unusual: many a hopeful symphony had to rest content with performance at the keyboard, and transcriptions of every kind were fed to the omnivorous piano.

The marvel of Alkan's work is his desperately resourceful use of *étude*-technique not only to create piano sonority on a sufficient scale, but to supply—in performance—the tensions needed to sustain long movements, which the academic symphony had ceased to generate. His smaller pieces have original, mostly saturnine qualities, but are not more interesting than hundreds of other Romantic pieces by forgotten composers; it is the monster canvases that compel respect for his uniquely peculiar powers.

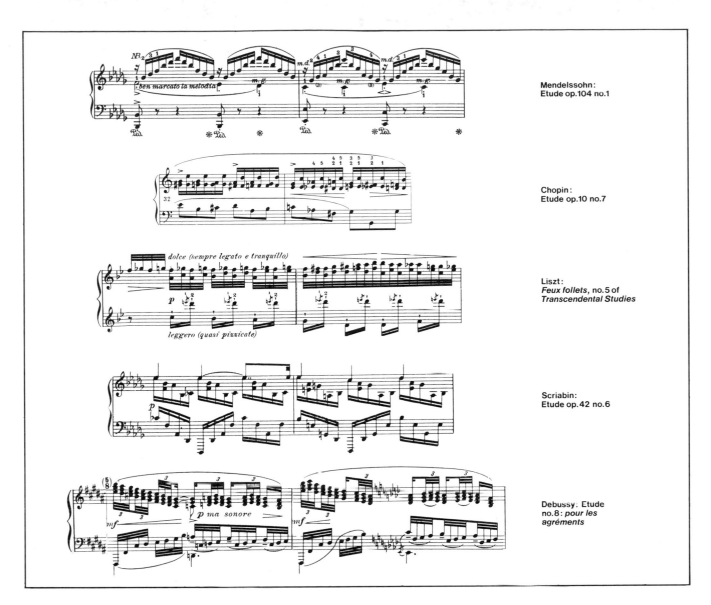

Mendelssohn:
Etude op.104 no.1

Chopin:
Etude op.10 no.7

Liszt:
Feux follets, no.5 of
Transcendental Studies

Scriabin:
Etude op.42 no.6

Debussy: Etude
no.8: *pour les
agréments*

More than Two Hands

Alkan had of course no musical issue. French piano music through Saint-Saëns was rapidly reduced to formulas—sonata-pastiche and salon virtuosity—like the Austro-German tradition (the lonely figure of Brahms standing apart), though in different proportions. Since the piano could now translate everything, it was not heard to have special potentialities; its repertoire became indiscriminately inclusive. Consciously refined piano writing was modelled on Mendelssohn and Schumann, with faint echoes of Chopin. The revolutionary front of music passed on to the opera house and the orchestra with Wagner and Liszt. The freshest and liveliest piano compositions appeared from the margins of Western Europe, where a Grieg or a Smetana might still inherit national turns-of-phrase and dance-rhythms and make something new of them. Such local contributions had small effect upon the established Romantic (or sub-Romantic) piano idiom, which by now was soggy at the centre and all too generously accommodating. The powers of the instrument seemed to have been exhaustively explored.

A seemingly trivial trick of Romantic virtuosity is worth remarking: Thalberg's 'third hand'. From the beginning, piano music has been written specifically for two hands, as its notation on two staves makes clear; there are accompaniment-idioms for the left hand against quite different and freer writing for the right. That is not directly because the right hand is naturally (and etymologically) dexterous; rather, the natural inertia of the bass line in Western harmony made it natural to assign it to the weaker hand. (The keyboard might after all have been the other way round.) From soon after the beginnings of keyboard music, audiences have been delighted by the trick of crossing hands, the right leaping over the left to pick out bass notes, or the left reaching up for a descant phrase. The charm of the trick presupposes their distinct normal roles. Thalberg earned applause by a further twist: sometimes when his left hand was audibly occupied with the bass and his right hand with treble figuration, a melody would be sounded in the middle.

The effect no longer astonishes, and some imaginative effort is needed to understand why Thalberg's audiences crowded round to see how the trick was turned. (He arranged the figuration for the two hands, of course, so that the thumbs could strike melody-notes in alternation.) The assumption that one hand did one thing and the other quite another, except when they did the same thing in unison, was deeply ingrained. Chopin often exchanged material between the hands, but made little use of Thalberg's trick; Liszt employed it often; Alkan was addicted to it. What it dimly presaged was piano music conceived primarily for a whole keyboard, from which the hands would draw whatever was wanted—great blocks of sound, or a bare line, or many overlapping voices, or contrasted rhythms. The interesting possibility was that the musical division of labour between the hands was not, after all, something established by the natural order.

The Classical tradition militated against the recognition of such a possibility. In Bach's keyboard fugues, material is at least passed from hand to hand much more freely than in the piano music of succeeding generations. There the tune-and-accompaniment contrast is greatly sharpened, and with it quite naturally the difference in the treatment of the two hands. Soon there comes a stage when the mere appearance of the tune in the left hand is something of a special event, and from then on, the backstage four-part chorus rules: to the educated ear every theme implies a definite chord-sequence, which ought to consist of voices moving correctly. Sophisticated piano music need not always make that explicit, but the connoisseur expects to be able to divine it behind—and not too far behind—the actual notes. (Thus Schumann and Mendelssohn, civilizing Paganini and Bach for modern consumers.) For these idealized canons to apply, the voices in the harmony must be decently segregated: they must not criss-cross often, and each must remain within a modest quasi-vocal compass. Bach's contrapuntal writing observed those rules, but without the premise that tune and accompaniment are sharply distinct; the result of expecting both a pre-eminent tune *and* an accompaniment of orderly, continuous parts—the very model of the string quartet!—is that in keyboard writing the two hands will take distinct and unequal paths.

Most of Schumann's duller piano music (and some of his best) answers closely to this ideal, and so does Chopin's; Liszt's (and Wagner's) taste for vivid chord-sequences as such, without well-defined component voices, struck conservative ears as vulgar and clumsy. (Schumann deplored the 'incorrectness' of their harmony.) Romantic *étude*-figuration was already a departure from rectitude, insofar as it was used to display

chord-sequences while blurring the question of which voice was which. The device of adding a voice with a Thalbergian 'third hand' could be perfectly proper in itself, as it is in Alkan's writing, an innocent technical ruse. A subversive inclination is felt only when the co-operation of the hands betokens the collapse of their distinct roles, and when the ideal of grammatical harmony in continuous voices is set aside. The new Russian school had a good point of departure for exploring this rude territory.

Balakirev and the Russian Piano

By a curious coincidence, each of the distinguishable piano traditions of the late nineteenth century was overseen by a composer who lived to be a Grand Old Man: Brahms (1833–97), Mili Balakirev (1837–1910) and Gabriel Fauré (1845–1924). Brahms has been discussed earlier, and I shall just observe that his piano writing is unambiguously two-handed up to the 'Paganini' Variations op. 35, less so in the pieces of 1879–80, and decidedly compromised in the music of the 1890s. Fauré is yet to come.

Our Russian piano music is basically Tchaikovsky's first piano concerto, Mussorgsky's *Pictures from an Exhibition*, a good deal of Rachmaninov and perhaps a little Scriabin, together with Balakirev's *Islamey*; and yet we recognize a common character in it. Balakirev was

at the bottom of that; he was the anointed musical heir of the great nationalist Glinka, and for a good half-century Russian music was inseparable from his work. He was born in Nizhny-Novgorod, a market town on the exotic fringe of the Russian Empire, within earshot of Oriental folk music. His formal training consisted of only ten piano lessons with Alexander Dubuque, a pupil of John Field (whose career had fixed him at last in Russia); but he was a precociously brilliant pianist, and he learned practical music with the director of the local theatre orchestra. Already composing, he was sent to St Petersburg by the generosity of a local landowner, an ex-diplomat and keen musical amateur, and won the approval of Glinka. Like Liszt with the Berlioz *Symphonie*, he made an exuberant transcription of Glinka's *Kamarinskaya*—a seminal work, the first big Russian construction with Western musical means. Glinka died abroad (in Berlin) when Balakirev was only twenty (he preserved a relationship with Glinka's sister Ludmilla, as Brahms did with Schumann's widow Clara). Over the next few years, by virtue of superior musical knowledge and force of personality, Balakirev collected about himself other instinctive young musicians including the rest of the 'mighty handful', the Russian Five—Mussorgsky, Cui, Borodin and Rimsky-Korsakov.

When the Berlin-trained Anton Rubinstein founded the St Petersburg Conservatoire in 1862, it already had an aggressively nationalist competitor in Balakirev's 'Free School'. Balakirev's tastes were passionate, exclusive and domineering. He revered Chopin, admired Liszt (with reservations about his gratuitous bravura and overt sentimentality) and despised learned sonata-technique. (Mussorgsky, escorting a friend through the score of a Schumann symphony, stopped at the end of the exposition: 'Now comes the musical mathematics!') He wanted an authentically Russian music, as promised in Glinka's work, and inspired by Chopin's fraternal Polish example. That did not at all mean a rejection of the civilized Western musical language in which he had brought himself up, but he judged the sonata-form tradition to be an excrescence upon it, a damnable temptation to insincere note-spinning. Folksongs and dances—which Balakirev collected on scholarly field-trips, like Bartók and Kodály after him—must be the basis of an honest national music. In working them up into concert-music, their integrity had to be respected; the very concept of a sonata-development involved the distortion and decomposition of themes for the sake of pattern-making.

Balakirev's standards were consistent and exact, arrived at after more critical examination of more music than any of his eager colleagues, all originally amateurs, could boast. He directed their efforts, proposed compositions to them (prescribing appropriate keys and modulations), edited the results sternly and promoted performances of deserving pieces. No special value was attached to individual self-expression: the members of the group continually sent one another promising themes (generally folk tunes, tactfully adjusted). They played far more work-in-progress to each other at the piano than was ever written down. Their Western idols were Berlioz, rapturously welcomed when he visited to conduct his own music, and Liszt, who maintained a keen interest in the new school from a distance, through his Russian pupils. Brahms was anathema, the very model of decadent formalism.

By 1868 Balakirev was a public figure of great authority, almost too laden with responsibilities to compose, but still a fiery catalyst. By 1872 he had forsworn music and was an official in the goods department of the Central Railway Company, on the Warsaw line. He had been seized by a black, peculiarly Russian depression, part religious crisis and part revulsion from the professional hostilities in which he had been embroiled. His friends were suddenly leaderless. Balakirev's teaching had never taken the form of theoretical instruction, for which he was

unprepared, and without his constant practical example and criticism at the keyboard they sought their own ways with difficulty. As professional musical life expanded in Russia, the advantage went to those who had conventional German academic credentials.

Rimsky-Korsakov and Tchaikovsky (another Balakirev *protégé*) hastened to acquire Western defences. (Rubinstein's brother Nikolai, director of the Moscow Conservatoire from its foundation in 1864, rejected Tchaikovsky's piano concerto contemptuously; it was Hans von Bülow who took it up and premiered it in Boston.) Mussorgsky and Borodin died in their forties. At length, little by little, Balakirev was persuaded to return to music, initially to edit Glinka's works. He remained somewhat at the margin of things, addressing himself to raising standards at the Imperial Chapel and enlisting support for a Chopin Memorial; but his Tuesday evenings, convivial sessions of score-playing and analysis in his own parlour, became a legendary institution. He returned to his abandoned orchestral poem *Tamara* (dedicated to Liszt) and a symphony, and completed them. In the last decade of his life, by then virtually a historical figure, he polished and published a considerable piano *oeuvre* (drawing heavily upon fifty years' worth of sketches), besides his second symphony and the 'second' piano concerto (the 'first' is a juvenile single movement), which was left to his pupil Liapunov to complete. Most of his music therefore postdates by a long way the period in which his influence was decisively felt, and it has been duly ignored.

Yet his 'oriental fantasy' *Islamey* of 1869 was heard everywhere, thanks to Liszt's enthusiasm, and it fairly encapsulates Balakirev's style. Its modal tunes—each a folk-borrowing—are brightly two-dimensional, comfortable in two keys at once, implying no basses (there are long pedals instead) and therefore no nicely-voiced harmony. The overall harmonic plan is calculated independently for dramatic effect (the return to the official tonic key at the central climax is a tour de force), and the pianist's two hands co-operate freely from start to finish. Despite all the noise *Islamey* makes, and its torrential energy, the writing is incisively spare and controlled, trading equally upon the percussive, hyper-articulate character of the piano and upon its rich sustaining power.

All that is true of Balakirev's late pieces, and the B flat minor 'sonata' of 1905 outdoes Chopin's by containing no proper sonata movement at all: a sinuous Romantic fugue is followed by a grandly ramified Mazurka, a frail, suspended Intermezzo and a furious Slavic finale with superb *étude*-bravura and a magical coda that melts

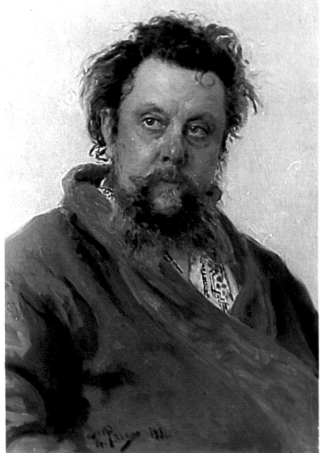

Advertisement and programme for the première of Tchaikovsky's B flat minor piano concerto in Boston in 1875.

away unresolved. It is hard to find any Balakirev piece that ends with the decisive Western *soh*-to-*doh* cadence; the Classical polarity of tonic *doh*-key and dominant *soh*-key is systematically replaced by ambiguous flat-key relationships. There is no continuous part-writing, but even the slow pieces are charged with running toccata-figures—no space is left for *rubato*—and the chord-layout is scrupulously calibrated. (A giant hand-stretch is expected, and the writing is so ambidextrous as to be cruelly exacting for the average left hand.) Except for the sonata, this late music is all salon-pieces, without profundity or developed argument (though Chopin's device of the transforming coda is often powerfully used). It simply represents an original piano idiom of severe, concentrated purity and a seductively non-Western cast—a delight to the pianist lucky enough to come upon it, and a model of the standards Balakirev prescribed to his country's art-music.

None of Balakirev's associates was a pianist of his calibre, and they made no substantial contribution to the solo repertoire. There are engaging little pieces by Borodin and Tchaikovsky; the indiscriminate virtuosity of the latter's only effective piano concerto is not one of its merits, and his G major sonata is a dinosaur. The signal exception is of course the *Pictures from an Exhibition*, less piano-music than splendid Mussorgsky-music which happens to be drafted—very bluntly—for the piano. Until recently it was as unusual to hear the *Pictures* played without discreet improvements as to hear *Boris Godunov* or *Night on the Bare Mountain* as Mussorgsky wrote them. Liapunov dwindled in Balakirev's shadow, but his athletic Transcendental Studies evoke their period (and Liszt's Studies too), and make good practice.

Moscow
Far less culturally self-confident than St Petersburg, Moscow—where Tchaikovsky was more at home than any of the Five—took Western cues with less resistance. It was natural that the first Russian composer to espouse Brahms's music, Nikolai Medtner (1880–1951, of German origin), should have emerged from the Moscow Conservatoire. In his class there were two other composer-pianists from a different preparatory school, and the three of them were to be the last touring Romantic composers. Scriabin (1872–1915) and Rachmaninov (1873–1943) had both studied piano at the 'musical pension' of Nikolai Zveryev, a *louche* figure who was a friend of Tchaikovsky and a one-time pupil of Dubuque (Balakirev's teacher). At his forcing-house for young pianists the menu consisted of all the established

piano literature of the century; the piano-apparatus of Scriabin and Rachmaninov was therefore full-bloodedly Western, and their music Russian chiefly in sentiment.

Sentiment dominates in their earlier music—in tandem with unbridled virtuosity in Rachmaninov's. Economy of notes meant little to Rachmaninov (though his masterly transcription of Mendelssohn's most famous Scherzo is clean as a whistle). He is not less endeared to the public for that, but what is original in his music remains pure personal feeling—the compositional means are knowledgeably eclectic and rather nondescript. He scores some striking hits with them in the smaller, free-form Preludes and *Etudes-Tableaux*; in sonata form he is nervously loquacious. He wrote less and less piano music as his international career blossomed. It is satisfying that his best traditional strengths should appear again in his last concerto, the Rhapsody on a Theme of Paganini—the very *Caprice* that Liszt and Brahms had also taken up. His citations of the '*Dies irae*' plainchant are a reminder that the Russian school took Liszt's astonishing *Totentanz* concerto on that theme very seriously when it was dismissed in Europe as a morbid curiosity.

Scriabin was as sensitive and pampered a child as Chopin, and he was not brought up on Bach: he was brought up on the music of Chopin's time. His mother, who had been a pupil of the great Leschetizky, died when he was a year old, and his diplomat father was perpetually abroad; he was raised by the women of his vaguely aristocratic family. The music of his first period to the turn of the century (including a statutory twelve *Etudes*) is always called 'Chopinesque', though scarcely any two bars could be mistaken for Chopin's. Scriabin had assimilated Chopin's idiom with alarming thoroughness (enriching it with chromatics and some ingenious rhythmic instability), and in detail this music has the extreme finesse of the master himself—but the long-range planning is more tentative. The sensibility it shows is prematurely sophisticated, half ingrown and half shamelessly appealing, pathos-laden to a degree that recalls Liszt more than Chopin.

For four years, until 1903, Scriabin held a professorship at the Moscow Conservatoire, an unproductive time. He resolved to flee abroad with his mistress, and needed money; he made a deal with his paternal publisher Belyaev which resulted in an extraordinary outpouring of music. For three months of the summer of 1903 he composed furiously in a country *dacha*, worshipped by a thirteen-year-old neighbour—Boris Pasternak, who later put him into *Doctor Zhivago* as Uncle Kolya. The music was his opp. 30 through 43 (all for piano but op. 43, the third symphony). Wagner had intervened: each piece is generated from a sharply defined gesture or two, like Wagnerian *Leitmotive*, their melodic and harmonic dimensions quite inseparable. They grow like crystals, not like sonata-subjects, multiplying their facets in symmetrical patterns.

Thereafter the ecstatic single movement became his ideal, pondered over while he wandered in Europe and America and finally returned to Moscow. The notion that his later music depends on one unique 'mystic chord' is a journalistic exaggeration; his method was rather to select a few progressions from the outer reaches of Romantic tonality—a sort of alchemical chord-extract—for each piece, which would be built strictly upon those and from a few gnomic phrases. The pieces tend toward either enigmatic brevity, like fleeting whiffs of a heady scent, or terraced elaboration of musical cells into a visionary procession (the last five sonatas, the *Poème-Nocturne* and *Vers la flamme*). Scriabin produced a fastidious antidote to Rachmaninov's comfortable liberality. The popular image of him as a flailing pyrotechnician is wrong: the risk he ran was not impassioned anarchy, but formalist suffocation, and his best insurance against it was the nerve-end delicacy of his writing. Unlike Rachmaninov and Medtner, he had come to doubt the power of conventional key-based argument to sustain a large work, and intricate, self-conscious mosaic-making was his preferred alternative. In the end, that came closer to the Balakirev tradition, despite appearances, than the unregenerately Romantic music of the other Muscovites.

The French School

In France meanwhile a native academic-musical tradition had been established. Saint-Saëns (1835–1921) was its acknowledged star, like Rimsky-Korsakov in the Russian school: technically facile, indefatigably prolific, innocently prolix. The Belgian organist César Franck (1822–90) popularized an ideal of 'cyclical' form, akin to Liszt's thematic transformation, exemplified in his *Prelude, Chorale & Fugue* for solo piano and more subtly in his little concerto *Variations Symphoniques*. The former piece unrolls, like other Franck piano music, in endless arpeggios and big pedal-held chords—one hears the organist revelling in the special powers of the piano; the latter offers fresher, more varied textures, with obvious inspiration from Chopin—and perhaps also from Fauré's Ballade.

Fauré (1845–1924) had been taught by Saint-Saëns, whose school he attended. His long, distinguished career—first as an organist and then as a pedagogue—

Below: Saint-Saëns at the piano: caricature by Bils.
Bottom: César Franck at the organ of the Basilica of
Sainte-Clotilde.

was never spectacular, and indeed he ripened very slowly. Only his songs were quickly noticed; a merely competent accompanist, he was the first great piano composer who had to rely upon others (sometimes vainly) to introduce his solo works. Not until the arrival of Marguerite Long, prompted toward Fauré by her husband, the critic Joseph de Marliave, did he have a loyal champion. He sent his early Ballade to old Liszt, who returned it with the comment 'Too complicated!' That seems baffling now, for Fauré's writing is scarcely virtuosic; in fact the intricacy of the overlapping inner parts is radically un-Lisztian. (One remembers that Liszt's *Symphonie Fantastique* transcription, for all its sensational resource, shirks the contrapuntal pile-up of the first-movement development, and ignores entirely the superposition of waltz-tune and *idée fixe* in the Ball scene.) Fauré's piano music demanded acute musical intelligence but made thin virtuoso-fodder, an un-marketable combination. The Ballade eventually became a popular success in the piano-and-orchestra version, which relieves the soloist of some of the intricacies while giving him (or more often her) a little extra arpeggio-glitter.

Fauré had been schooled in the old church modes, which may account for the charming modal twists that mark—ever so gently—his other early piano music. Just such twists in the newly imported Russian music were to enchant the younger French generation. With his *Requiem* the 42-year-old Fauré conveyed a broader authority. He wrote no more piano music until after his first glowing song-cycles, and then came his first piano masterpieces without an overt debt to Chopin, impeccably well-made as always and yet formally revolutionary—the fifth Barcarolle and the sixth and seventh Nocturnes. By then Fauré had succeeded to Massenet's chair of composition at the Conservatoire, and Chabrier was dead.

Two Provincials and a Spaniard

Emmanuel Chabrier (1841–94), a civil servant from the Auvergne, made a pilgrimage to Munich for *Tristan und Isolde* at the age of thirty-nine, and promptly resigned from the Ministry of the Interior to become a professional composer. Not that he was a stranger to the arts—his friends included Verlaine and Manet (who died in his arms), and he had been writing music for a long time; but a musical career had not been prescribed for him, and he had not been conventionally educated for it. With that enormous advantage he proceeded to reform French piano music by example (it was only a sideline, but this book is about the piano). When his *10*

Below: Isaac Albéniz and (bottom) Emmanuel Chabrier, after a drawing by Edouard Detaille.

Pièces pittoresques were premiered in 1888, Franck exclaimed, 'We have just heard something extraordinary. This music is a link between our own epoch and that of Couperin and Rameau!'

The remark seems extravagant only if one forgets the relentless smoothness of the academic writing of the period. The utter lack of solemnity in Chabrier's music—he was an incorrigibly jovial man—makes him too easy to patronize. The energetic concision of his writing, the free use of all registers of the keyboard, the sudden contrasts of tone, touch and dynamics, the compacted harmonies and the exuberant rhythms were as original as they were salutary in the prevailing climate. Chabrier explored boldly the range of the piano as a percussive instrument (a robust performer, he left a wake of broken strings everywhere); his quick-witted little masterpiece, the *Bourrée fantasque*, directly recalls Balakirev's *Islamey*—with the Romantic bravura stripped away. His piano *oeuvre*, decisively influential, was all too modest: beyond the works mentioned there were only another ten or twelve small pieces, the two-piano *Valses romantiques*, and the comic quadrille on *Leitmotive* from Wagner (Fauré and André Messager wrote one too)—though Alfred Cortot claimed that the published piano 'transcriptions' of Chabrier's *España* and the *Joyeuse Marche* were in effect the originals.

Chabrier's first piano teachers were Spaniards. So was the other great opener of windows in the French tradition, Isaac Albéniz (1860–1909). Like Liszt he had a father who capitalized on his precocious gifts from early childhood, and he too was refused entry to the Paris Conservatoire (at the age of seven). He decamped at twelve to South America, returned, went back again at fifteen, tried the United States; living from hand to mouth, he gave stunt performances anywhere that would pay. Later he attended the Brussels Conservatoire, solicited advice from Liszt, and spent a frustrating time trying to establish himself back in Spain. Forsaking Spain for London, he composed operas on libretti by his English patron Francis Money-Coutts. All the while he turned out minor piano pieces with negligent facility. At last he settled in Paris, where he was warmly befriended by leading composers—Fauré, Chausson, d'Indy, Dukas (who helped with the orchestration of his *Catalonia*)—and acquainted himself patiently with the new resources of French harmony.

After forty, his health failed and he withdrew from concertizing. While Marguerite Long's chief rival, the redoubtable Blanche Selva, introduced his piquant genre pieces to a delighted public, he had already

Opposite above: From Albéniz's 'Eritaña': for clarity, the composer marks the progress of the melody, shared between the hands, with arrows.
Opposite below: Blanche Selva: drawing by Dalliès.

Below: Déodat de Séverac.

completed the much larger and richer *La Vega*—clouded harmonies brooding over the whole range of the piano—and had begun his masterwork, the *Ibéria* suite. He was a dying man, and knew it; and yet the twelve *Ibéria* pieces, a sequence of three in each of four *Cahiers*, grew ever more fantastical and confidently original, both musically and pianistically. The 1905 *Cahier I* pieces might still be magnified genre studies, Spanishry *à la* Liszt with hiccoughs of undigested Impressionism. *Cahier II* is tauter and more intricately developed (only the extrovert '*Triana*', like Chabrier in Seville, is often heard), and the extent of Albéniz's debt to his beloved Domenico Scarlatti—the great Italian harpsichord master who made his home in Spain—becomes evident. The brittle, dangerous intensity of *Cahier III* comes out in febrile rashes of added-notes, the chords prickly with extra semitones (but strictly logical: the published editions are full of senseless misprints). As in *Cahier IV*, each piece works over a special range of figuration obsessively; but the sonorous breadth of the *Cahier IV* pieces arises from the waiting calm at the heart of each, making itself felt through the teeming surfaces of the music. Strong harmonic plans organize Hispanic modal tags. Not only a Thalbergian 'third' hand but a fourth and a fifth as well crop up again and again (often on three staves—the standard two could not bear the traffic), and a very wide stretch is exploited ruthlessly.

Cahier by *Cahier* Blanche Selva premiered the *Ibéria* pieces, struggling to match their unprecedented demands. The eleventh, '*Jerez*', was finished last, only months before Albéniz died. Debussy loved them (he knew *Cahier I* when he wrote his own orchestral *Ibéria*), and toward the end of his own life played certain ones over and over; Ravel's keen wish to orchestrate them was defeated by legal difficulties over rights. Beyond *Ibéria* there were sketches. *Azulejos*, a fragment of a projected suite, was dubiously completed by Albéniz's younger compatriot Granados (whose own *persona* was more nineteenth-century Romantic); *Navarra*, destined for Marguerite Long, got a conclusion from Déodat de Séverac.

Séverac (1873–1921), a d'Indy pupil from the Languedoc, and a generous personality as widely loved as Chabrier and Albéniz (he dedicated his fantasy *Sous les lauriers roses* to those '*Maîtres aimés*'), deserves special notice for his regional evocations. With hindsight, what is most striking about his piano music—three large suites, a modest one and *Baigneuses au soleil* (written for Cortot)—is its prefiguring of Debussy's later attitude to form: loose, leisurely paragraphs, suggestively isolated phrases and figures, an open

narrative continuity. The 1908 *Baigneuses* pre-echoes Debussy's '*Ondine*' Prelude. Mlle Selva also championed Séverac's music, as later she did Josef Suk's comparably free-form autobiographical cycles (from an independent Czech tradition that runs from Fibich's *Impressions* through Janáček's suites); their common ancestors are surely Liszt's *Années de pèlerinage*. Séverac's homely trail-breaking was the more remarkable, given his academic start at d'Indy's Schola Cantorum.

The Older Generation

D'Indy's folk-inspired 'Symphony on a French Mountain Song' of 1886, the *Symphonie Cévenole*, makes more of its *concertante* piano than his 1907 sonata does of the solo instrument—another dinosaur-sonata, staggering under the deliberate weight of its Franckian formal ideals. The academic tradition ossified rapidly. At the Conservatoire, Paul Dukas (1865–1935) developed a self-critical faculty until it throttled his creative work; after his 1912 *La Péri* he withheld nearly everything he wrote, and destroyed it before his death. He made two impressive contributions to piano literature nonetheless. If his 1900 sonata (dedicated to Saint-Saëns) has

Left: Ravel: painting by Achille Ouvré, 1911.
Opposite: Debussy: painting by R. Forcade.

less seductive surfaces than the old. The sleek ripples had subsided, and altogether there were fewer notes more barely spaced, in less gracious and flexible rhythms.

Certainly the music is toughly compressed, and wears a correspondingly low profile—its main events are not signalled by leisurely preparations. Everything written down has an exact function, and there is no sonorous filling. In fact the greatest change is in the piano writing (Fauré's songs and chamber music acquired the lineaments of his late style much more gradually): it parallels the change in Dukas from his sonata to his Variations—perhaps at similar promptings. Chabrier can be heard in the eighth Barcarolle, and Albéniz's 'Jerez' in the ninth (Fauré had attended Albéniz faithfully in his dying years); they are *not* often heard, of course, for the similarity of diction is outweighed by the huge difference in musical grammar. Still, the manner of address is important. One reason that this potent music has scarcely entered the repertoire is that when played like Chopin or Debussy, it sounds non-committal and diffuse. Fauré indulged no unmarked *rubato* (he made his pupils play against a metronome, and demanded a defence for any departure from tempo), though nuances are all-important; and any pedal-haze obscures the expressively elliptical movement of parts. The introspective range of the laconic op. 103 Preludes is revealed only by exact representation, not by effusive pleading. Cortot prevailed anxiously upon the composer to let him titivate the solo part of the late *Fantaisie* with orchestra. The Romantic pianist can feel more at ease with the last, passionate Nocturnes of 1915 and 1921, where Fauré combines intense concision with the noble declamatory style of his fifties. Even there, the old tune-and-accompaniment model is quite compromised; like Balakirev at his best and the later Brahms, Fauré (who was fully ambidextrous) wrote piano music that is alive in every part.

Ravel and Debussy

Fauré's devoted pupil Ravel (1875–1937) and the anti-Fauréan Debussy (1862–1918) make an uneasy but musicologically inseparable pair. The older Debussy was an established power when Ravel was a novice, and yet his mature piano music made essential use of Ravellian finds; that explains the uneasiness. They are often contrasted by analogy with Chopin and Liszt—the sincere and poetic Debussy against the calculatingly brilliant Ravel—but the analogy is the wrong way round, despite Fauré's worry that the young Ravel was 'trop recherché, trop raffiné', and the general conviction

too solidly Franckian textures to make comfortable listening for its considerable length, his masterpiece of (apparently) only a few months later is bracingly spare: the *Variations, Interlude and Finale* on a theme of Rameau. Here there is no pianistic rodomontade, but only close-focus exploration of isolated aspects of a plain Rameau *Menuet* (Dukas prepared editions of both Rameau and Scarlatti). The pawky black-and-white severity of the manner accommodates pure keyboard invention of the first order, astringent and direct, neither pseudo-harpsichord nor orchestral. The work promises no virtuoso rewards beyond the articulation of a civilized musical intelligence; Cortot, writing about it, was moved to invoke the 'Diabelli' Variations of Beethoven.

There remained Fauré. Soon after his appointment at the Conservatoire the seventh Nocturne appeared, and the Schumannesque op. 73 *Theme and Variations*, tender and gravely ornamental. The next seven years saw no solo music from him but the *8 Pièces brèves*, two of them dating from thirty years earlier (though they are all undiluted Fauré, however modest, and gratefully accessible to the amateur as hardly any other serious piano writing of the period is). In 1905 Fauré began to add new links to his chains of Barcarolles, Nocturnes and Impromptus. His tragic deafness was already setting in; coincidentally or not, the new pieces had far

Satie: drawing by Picasso, 1920.

that Chopin and Debussy were respectively the greater composers.

Ravel's work, like Chopin's, was guided by the aim of being consistently original by the best professional standards. Debussy's most consistent piano writing is his least original, which is to say the earlier music up to the 1901 Suite *Pour le piano*. He had found his distinctive voice as a composer already, but his pianism was still defined by nineteenth-century routine; he could afford without risk to listen and learn, and did so. In fact the two composers were proceeding in quite different directions. Debussy's abandonment of closed musical forms marked his maturity, whereas Ravel's formal patterns grew ever tighter. It is true that Debussy prepared an edition of Chopin—but Ravel edited Mendelssohn.

In the 1890s, Debussy's most fruitful musical contact was with the inspired eccentric Erik Satie, then in his Rosicrucian period: limpid harmonies modally suspended, full of parallel chords, as innocent of progressive impetus as of any pianistic refinements. The chief extra-curricular influence on Ravel, as he candidly acknowledged, was Chabrier, on whose doorstep he and the Spanish pianist Ricardo Viñes appeared as students to play him his *Valses romantiques* by way of homage. (Viñes was to become a great exponent of the new, like Cortot and Mlles Long and Selva: he championed Albéniz, Debussy and the Russians—he commissioned a concert *Valse* from Balakirev—and premiered all Ravel's major piano music up to *Gaspard de la nuit*.) Ravel's first published pieces owed a gross debt to Chabrier. An unpublished but crucial one, the two-piano *Habanera* of 1895, was peculiarly original, capturing echoes of Chabrier's popular *Habanera* in the frieze-like manner of the *Rose + Croix* Satie. A dozen years later it became part of the orchestral *Rapsodie espagnole*; but meanwhile Ravel had shown his manuscript to Debussy. When the latter's 'Soirée dans Grenade' appeared in 1903, in the suite *Estampes*, it contained something very like Ravel's *Habanera*. Embarrassment was compounded by the fact that the piano writing of the other *Estampes*, the pseudo-Balinese 'Pagodes' and 'Jardins sous la pluie', plainly drew upon the devices of Ravel's dazzling *Jeux d'eau* of two years earlier. Relations between the composers never recovered.

Jeux d'eau, first heard when Ravel played it in Fauré's composition class, had an obvious model itself—Liszt's 'Jeux d'eau à la Villa d'Este', freshly translated into a harmonic idiom like Debussy's, and shaped into a self-sufficient formal pattern instead of Liszt's dramatic

sermon. Ravel's sound-fantasy showed how much of conventional piano layout could be jettisoned for Impressionist purposes, and Debussy took the point at once. (It is curious that his 1894 *Prélude à l'après-midi d'un faune*, which had been a revelation for Ravel, should resemble *Jeux d'eau* in having the formal structure of a Fauré nocturne.) Next, after Debussy's first book of *Images* (which owed nothing new to Ravel) Ravel published his first and last free-form Impressionist music, the piano *Miroirs* and the *Histoires naturelles* songs, with heady and pungent chords displayed for their own sake. Debussy duly responded with the second book of *Images*, and eventually the two books of Preludes (one piece in each book takes a cue from Ravel's 'Alborada' to raid Albéniz, too). Yet if

Poissons d'Or: the Japanese lacquer which inspired the last
of Debussy's 1907 *Images*.

Ravel fixed the geography of the new piano sound-world, Debussy introduced his own fauna and flora into it, and they flourished there while Ravel travelled to austerer climes.

Ravel's virtuoso *chef d'oeuvre* for the piano, *Gaspard de la nuit*, found no answer in Debussy's work—though the grandly obsessive 'Le Gibet' of *Gaspard* may represent a (successful) intention to trump the *Image* 'Et la lune descend . . .'. The suite is at once the last masterpiece of Romantic fantasy, and a deliberate, ironic tour de force: Ravel admitted to having been carried away perhaps ('*je m'y suis, peut-être, laissé prendre*') while aiming to caricature Romantic pianism. The haunting lyrical curves of '*Ondine*' are strictly written out, not left to the pianist's whims, and at the climax the right hand actually quotes the rapturous centre of Liszt's 'Dante' sonata. Ravel expressly set out to compose something 'more difficult than *Islamey*'; his '*Scarbo*' accordingly invokes not only *Islamey* but the '*Mephisto*' Waltz. (Debussy and Ravel both loved Russian music, but it was the anti-formal directness of Mussorgsky that most inspired the older composer, whereas Ravel hurried to buy every new, polished piece by Borodin and Balakirev.) Behind the fantastical virtuosity, each *Gaspard* piece is firmly shaped—the alarmingly unpredictable '*Scarbo*' conceals a kind of sonata form.

Therewith Ravel abandoned Romantic bravura, having turned his trick. In the same year (1908) he began the concise and beautiful little *Mother Goose* duets, in the tradition of Fauré's *Dolly* Suite. Only two more solo works followed, the formally elegant suites *Valses nobles et sentimentales* (spirit of Chabrier) and *Le tombeau de Couperin* (mock-archaic *clavecinisme*). He had invented a new genre: mock-pastiche, serious music-making behind the double blind of period-costume and irony. His pieces are, like Chopin's, scrupulously explicit and self-contained, and he increasingly resented 'interpretation', even by Viñes—the première of the *Tombeau* was entrusted to Mlle Long. Ravel addressed himself to the piano again only at the end of his career (1929–31), attracted characteristically by technical challenges: to write a light, 'Mozartean' concerto for himself to play (his executive skills proved to have rusted too much for that, and Mlle Long took it), and another concerto for the one-armed pianist Paul Wittgenstein, brother of the philosopher. The latter project was a perfect excuse to re-create multi-handed Romantic pianism again, for the sake of the paradox (and to double Thalberg's trick!), and it is a noble Lisztian edifice.

The true Lisztian was nevertheless Debussy, an intuitive inventor and a lover of open-ended forms, happy to seek expression through any fresh and interesting means. His pieces are unthinkable without sympathetic 'interpretation'—even his *12 Etudes* (dedicated to the memory of Chopin), his last piano work. The contrast with the original model is remarkable. Executive virtuosity has no real role in Debussy; these are studies in sensibility and lyric invention. They draw *en passant* upon all sorts of piano idioms, held together simply by the personality of the composer. No school or tradition could be founded upon them, for they are wilfully unique. Romantic pianism is playfully enlisted for modern purposes; but in its own communicative terms, it was as good as exhausted.

THE ROMANTIC PEDAL

'The pedal is the soul of the piano' (Anton Rubinstein).

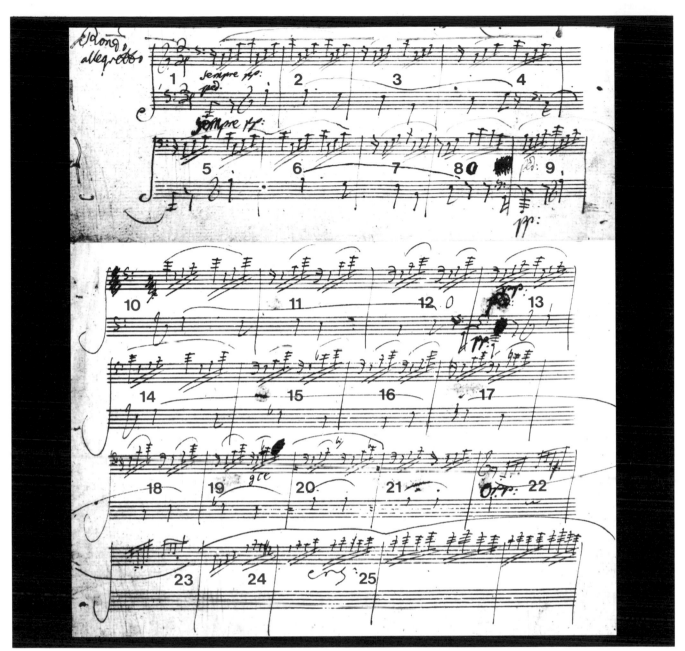

Ex. 1 (In Beethoven's ms. 'ped' = depress sustaining pedal; 'o' = release).

There are few better ways to understand the revolution in piano style accomplished in the nineteenth century than by examining the way composers required the sustaining pedal to be used. It is, in fact, as much by the pedal as by the possibility of gradations of touch that the piano is distinguished from all other instruments. It is by means of the pedal that the pianist is able to control the decay of sound in various ways—gradual release, half-pedal (allowing the dampers just to touch the strings without fully damping the sound), pedalling before or after the attack of the note.

The wrong question to start with is: what did it sound like when the dampers were lifted, and the strings left free to vibrate, on an instrument contemporary with the composer? That is an interesting subject, but a secondary one. The first question, in time as well as importance, is: why did the composer indicate the

pedal? Or more precisely: what is the function of the pedal in a given passage?

The pedal has two different basic functions (as well as some subsidiary ones): it sustains struck notes; and it allows those which are not struck to vibrate in sympathy. Until this distinction is clear, no sensible observations can be made about, for example, the execution of Beethoven's notations for pedalling.

We may start with the notorious indications for the main theme of the rondo-finale of the 'Waldstein' sonata op. 53—Ex. 1. Played thoughtlessly as written, on the modern piano this makes a terrible smudge: Beethoven asks the performer to hold the pedal down steadily through many changes of harmony, releasing it only in bars 8, 12 and 22. Major and minor modes, tonic and dominant harmonies, would all seem to be fused together almost impossibly by this instruction.

Ex. 2

Beethoven is, however, very firm about holding the pedal down; later in the work he writes—Ex. 2. So intent is he on having the pedal held throughout bar 101 of Ex. 2 that he writes *three quaver rests* in place of the more usual and convenient one quaver, one crotchet. He wants the pedal held almost to the end of the bar, released only with the last quaver rest—and we can see from the autograph that, in order to make this absolutely clear, he has actually scratched out the crotchet rests he originally wrote, substituting in each case two quaver rests in their place. (Why does he write the last note of the phrase (bar 101) as a quaver if it is going to be sustained anyway by the pedal?—in order to avoid an accent. The first note of the phrase (bar 98), on the other hand, is written as a quaver in order to *imply* an accent. Such are the vagaries of notation when it comes to delicate matters like phrasing.)

Note that the opening passage of the movement (Ex. 1) performed on an early nineteenth-century piano of the kinds available to Beethoven would also make a disagreeable blur unless played with considerable care. In this passage, the primary function of the pedal for Beethoven is not colouristic but *motivic*.

The theme of the rondo begins with the low C bass note, and not with the repeated treble Gs: the bass note is always an essential and integral part of the theme. The function of the pedal is to sustain every appearance of this note. In order to get this motivic pedal point, Beethoven was evidently willing to countenance a certain amount of light smudging. If the right hand is played as softly as possible (Beethoven marks *sempre pianissimo*), so that the notes just speak without resounding, a delicacy and clarity can be achieved even on the modern concert piano. (An alternative solution would be to sustain the bass notes with the concert piano's middle pedal, but this is less satisfactory, and could compromise the—secondary but important—colouristic effect intended.)

The sustaining of the opening bass notes is absolutely essential to the thematic conception of this rondo. If the opening page is pedalled correctly, the development section (as well as the bars of Ex. 2) take on a new meaning—Ex. 3.

This passage shown in Ex. 3, which continues at great length, is not an arpeggio over a left-hand accompaniment, but a right-hand decoration of a left-hand theme, the opening fragment of the main theme. This movement, therefore, is one of the first in the history of the pianoforte in which the motivic structure of the music rests upon the technical capacities of the instrument. It must be emphasized again, however, that an understanding of the music and an interpretation of it depend on our first asking, not what it *sounded* like, but what the purpose of the notation was. The primary purpose of the pedal here is to sustain the low note: the vibrancy of the open pedal is both a bonus and a liability, a beautiful cloud of sound that threatens to engulf the music.

Ex. 3 ('Ped' = depress sustaining pedal; ✳ = release).

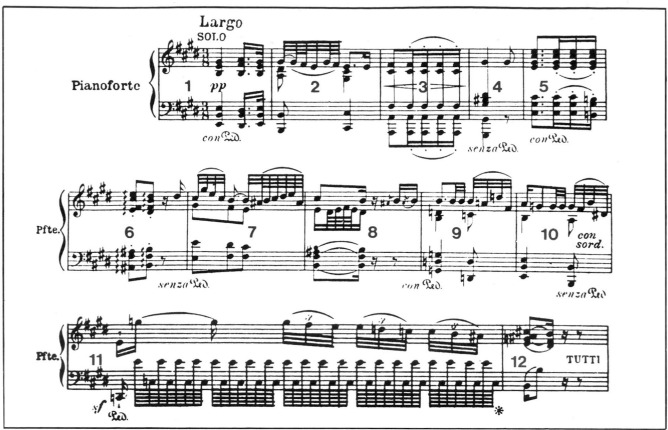

Ex. 4

The function of the equally notorious pedal indication at the opening of the slow movement of Beethoven's piano concerto no. 3 in C minor lies at the opposite pole. On old as well as new pianofortes, an insensitive performance will result in a smudge, although the problem can be solved even on the modern concert grand, if not with ease. What is significant in this passage, however, is not where the pedal is to be held down, but where it is to be released—Ex. 4. The chord in bar 4 is to be played without pedal, as are bars 7 and 8. There is to be a change of pedal at the end of bar 10, but the rest of the passage was evidently intended to swim in pedal. It is, however, not the sustaining power of the pedal that counts in this passage, but the way it makes the piano vibrate.

The withholding of this vibrancy in bar 4 gives this chord a strange effect of distance, after the rich sonority of the opening bars: the sound suddenly withdraws, and the movement towards C sharp minor (in bar 2) becomes graver with the contrast in tone colour. The *senza pedale* of bars 7 and 8 has a similar effect, but here even more deeply expressive. The sound becomes more delicate, the texture thin: all the concentration is focused horizontally on the upper line instead of on the harmony. The return of vibrancy marks the surprising move to G major, and the release of the pedal the turn back to E—although this brief change of pedal must be made almost as much for clarity as for expression.

We must note here the essentially Classical nature of this procedure. The pedal is used here as an extension of dynamics, as a means of characterizing the different succeeding functional and emotional significances of the phrases—bringing out the inward sentiment of bars 7–8 by witholding the pedal, adding the pedal to set in relief the dramatic change to a G major chord in bar 9. The pedal effects work precisely like accents or contrasts of dynamic levels. They can be properly reproduced on a modern concert instrument by what is called half-pedal, i.e., raising the dampers just slightly so that they still remain in contact with the strings, but not enough to cut off all the resonance when the keys are released: this achieves a very delicate blur at the change of harmony, which quickly dies away as the new chord is held. It is an effect, however, difficult to achieve and must be practised carefully on each individual instrument. The essential point, in any case, of Beethoven's indications at the opening of the slow movement is the opposition of pedalled and unpedalled sonorities: and it is this for which the modern pianist must seek to find an equivalent.

In sum, Beethoven's use of the pedal is either for sustaining important structural notes, or as a form of dynamic emphasis. In an early work like the 'Moonlight' sonata, he can also require the pedal as a form of orchestration. Playing the first movement of the 'Moonlight' as Beethoven directed, very delicately (*delicatissimamente*) with full pedal throughout (*senza sordini*—'without dampers') on an early nineteenth-century instrument with little sustaining power, produces a lovely sonority difficult to reproduce with a modern keyboard. But none of these procedures—orchestration, dynamic emphasis or contrast, the

Ex. 5

sustaining of important notes—is essentially at odds with late eighteenth-century style. They are merely expansions of standard procedures of the previous generations: they extend to the pedal what had previously been achieved by phrasing, dynamics and instrumentation.

The generation of Chopin, Schumann and Liszt born around the year 1810, however, had a very different attitude to the sustaining pedal — and indeed the revolution in musical style effected by these composers in particular is intimately linked with their new pedal techniques. We may start with the most normal use, progressing to the most eccentric. The opening of Chopin's Nocturne in E flat major op. 9 no. 2 is a good point of departure—Ex. 5. Here the function of the pedal is both to sustain and to induce sympathetic vibration. The pedal sustains the bass line, which would otherwise be lost; but, above all, it allows the piano to sing.

The first beat of this Nocturne is instructive: by means of both the pedal and the spacing of the chord, it exploits, as few works had done before, the sympathetic

overtones of the piano. The G in the right hand sings because of the E flat four octaves below it: and the two quavers that follow the low E flat continue to reinforce the vibrations of both the E flat and the G, bass and melody. Throughout this passage the spacing is conceived in terms of the vibration of the piano, a vibration made possible by the pedal, which sustains the main notes while others arrive and reactivate their harmonics. Note that the overtones of this passage, like those of all nineteenth-century piano music, are conceived in terms of equal temperament. In just intonation the minor seventh is an important overtone, and therefore an important component of the sonority, while the major seventh is a very distant harmonic and of little weight; in equal temperament this arrangement is reversed. In the first bar, the Ds in the inner voices of the second beat vibrate against the E flat below them, held by the pedal. On the third and fourth beats, it is the pedal that makes the extraordinary dissonance of the parallel ninths between upper and lower voice sound so mellifluously, heard as they are in terms of the vibration created through the inner parts.

Ex. 6 (In Chopin's ms. 'ped' = depress sustaining pedal; ⊕ = release).

Other composers, notably Mozart, had tried by means of spacing to exploit the piano's capacity to make one note sing sympathetically against another. But although Mozart's pianos had pedal mechanisms, he never wrote music which required them for this purpose. The new style of Chopin and the extraordinary sonority he created for the first time depend above all on a new and original conception of pedalling.

Even Chopin's radically new conceptions of polyphony and phrasing depend on the pedal—as an interesting problem in the Ballade no. 3 in A flat major demonstrates. It is reproduced incorrectly in most editions, and the manuscript is instructive—**Ex. 6.** At the second bar of the second system, Chopin started to write a pedal indication and then crossed it out, placing the pedal only in the second half of the bar. Four bars later, when the phrase is repeated, the same indication occurs, now written without hesitation: the first half of the bar is again to be played 'dry', and the pedal introduced only later.

This twice breaks the phrase in two. Notice first that the pedal is systematically placed with the bass line in a way that few pianists pedal today. What is most significant, however, is the insistence on leaving half a bar without pedal—an idea that occurs to Chopin only as he writes, as we can see. This is not how he indicated the pedal for the same theme when it occurred two pages back; and at a later appearance of the theme, he places a break, but at a different point. Not only the phrase is shaped by the pedal: the polyphonic movement in this passage is blended and moves in blocks as the pedal sustains and articulates the harmony.

In the piano writing of the Romantic generation of the 1830s, in fact, a fully pedalled sonority becomes the normal one: the piano is expected to vibrate fairly constantly, and an unpedalled sonority is an exception, almost a special effect. Furthermore, the phrase is now shaped at least partially by changes in this full vibration. The change of pedal is crucial to the conception of rhythmic movement and to the sustaining of the melodic line over the bass.

At this time we arrive close to the modern conception of pedalling. Still to be developed was what might be called 'syncopated' pedalling—that is, depressing the pedal before or after the attack of a note. Moriz Rosenthal believed that this was a development of the later nineteenth century, and that earlier pianists had always pedalled *on* or *with* the note. There are still pianists today who 'beat time' with their right foot; but in general syncopated pedalling is now so inbred that doing it any other way would seem as unnatural to most pianists as playing without vibrato would seem to the modern violinist. (The consistently vibrant sound of the piano required by the Romantic style is, of course, the equivalent of the continuous and unremitting vibrato of the string instrument.)

The importance of these developments was very great. For Beethoven, music was still shape, realized and inflected by instrumental sonority: other realizations may be as absurd as arrangements of the '*Hammerklavier*', for example, always are, but the musical conception takes precedence over its realization in sound. The sonority serves the music. For Chopin, however, as for Schumann and Liszt, the conception was worked out directly within the sonority as a sculptor works directly in clay or marble. The instrumental sound is shaped into music.

Schumann's use of the pedal, very much more adventurous than Chopin's, shows this still more clearly. The indications are, indeed, sometimes vague. 'With pedal' is generally placed at the beginning of most pieces—and its absence is more interesting than its inclusion (an omission often demands at least a consideration of the possibility of oversight).

But at other times, Schumann's pedalling is both precise and remarkable. Schumann invented the idea of playing a melody by *withdrawing* notes from a chord—a melody by absence; so it is fitting that his most famous pedal effect should be a 'withdrawal of sound'. It occurs in *Carnaval* at the end of 'Paganini'—**Ex. 7.**

After playing the four resounding thirds with full pedal, the pianist depresses the keys of the next chord

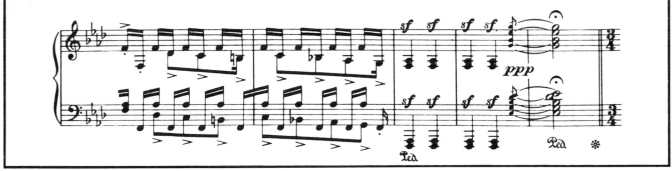

Ex. 7

without allowing the hammers to strike, and then changes the pedal. All the strings of the piano have been resounding with the previous *fortissimo*, and the change of pedal withdraws all the sympathetic vibrations except those in the notes silently held down. As the other sounds die away, there is an extraordinary auditory illusion: the notes of the chord appear with what seems like a *crescendo*. This is probably the first use of piano harmonics by themselves in the history of music—and a device rarely to be used again until the op. 11 of Schoenberg, although after that it was to have a busy future. (There is complex use of harmonics in the piano sonata of Elliott Carter and in *Constellation* by Pierre Boulez, as well as in many works by George Crumb.)

This is an extreme effect in Schumann, but it shows that a musical conception was for him not merely 'realized' in sound, but was identical with the sound: the musical idea *is* the pedal effect. Similarly in the seventeenth piece of Schumann's *Davidsbündlertänze* op. 6—**Ex. 8**.

This is labelled 'As if from a distance', but the words describe the music rather than the other way round.

The passage must swim in pedal, so that the bass and treble notes are sustained against the inner ostinato. This is not merely a price to be paid for a pretty effect, but the whole point of the music: a soft, widely-spaced texture blurring tonic and dominant harmony together in a single mist.

A few bars later the fluid melting together includes full chromatic harmonies (bars 15–18). We do not need to be told how to play the pedal in this passage. To sustain the bass, the dampers must remain raised throughout. On paper this seems impossibly daring, yet in performance the effect is miraculous: no composer could have written such a passage who had not discovered it for himself while improvising at the keyboard. The sonority of the piano has now become a primary element of musical composition, as important as pitch or duration. Not since Couperin and Domenico Scarlatti had the actual sound of a keyboard instrument provided the basic material of music: a revolutionary departure, which represents a fundamentally different approach to music itself from that of the late eighteenth century.

Ex. 8

NOTES ON THE GRAND ROMANTIC VIRTUOSOS AND AFTER...

Galop chromatique: cartoon of Liszt, 'the Devil of
Harmony', at the piano, 1843.

What is a Grand-Romantic virtuoso? Liszt had few
doubts. With characteristic zest he saw the virtuoso as
one:

called upon to make emotion speak, and weep and sing and
sigh—to bring it to life in his consciousness. He creates
passions he will call to light in all their brilliance. He breathes
life into the lethargic body, infuses it with fire, enlivens it with
the pulse of charm and grace. He changes the earthly form
into a living being, penetrating it with the spark which
Prometheous snatched from Jupiter's flesh. He must send the
form he has created soaring into the transparent ether; he
must arm it with a thousand winged weapons; he must call up
scent and blossom, and breathe the breath of life.

The definition is given with authority, for Liszt may
well have been the grandest and most romantic of all
virtuosos.

Later, Leopold Godowsky had much to say concerning virtuosity. Godowsky, whose compositions nonchalantly flaunt near-impossible difficulties, and whose
playing no less nonchalantly dismissed them, equated
virtuosity with an empty, soulless expertise. For
Godowsky:

technique is something entirely different from virtuosity. It
involves everything that makes for artistic piano playing—
good fingering, phrasing, pedalling, dynamics, agogics, time
and rhythm—in a word, the art of musical expression as
distinct from mechanics. I consider it an insult to be called a
virtuoso. Anybody can learn the mechanics of piano playing.

Debussy, on the other hand, thought the virtuoso
neither grand nor romantic but a figure of fun, the stuff
of caricature. For him:

the attraction of the virtuoso is like that of the circus for the
crowd. There is always a hope that something dangerous may
happen. Mr X may play the violin with Mr Y on his
shoulders; or Mr Z may conclude his piece by lifting the piano
with his teeth.

Debussy's compatriot Gabriel Fauré showed a no less
marked distaste, in his 'horror of virtuosity, of *rubato*
and of those effects in performance which send shivers
down the spine of the audience.'

The layman may be less precise, vivacious or
idiosyncratic in his expectations. For him, virtuosity is
often synonymous with speed and noise, and the term
thus becomes one of abuse. The English, with their
natural suspicion of professional accomplishment, have
often deplored what they consider a kind of arrogance,
or mastery for mastery's sake. But virtuosity can never
be reduced to this simple level: a redefinition in
contemporary terms is called for.

Virtuosity may be thought to combine two basic
elements. First, a transcendental expertise that illu-
minates but does not extend beyond a reasonably

scrupulous reading of the text and is therefore kept
subservient to musical and textual considerations; and
second, a phenomenal quality that unashamedly, and
with no other consideration, delights in its own
exuberance—an aesthetic embodied to some degree in
the Italian word *sprezzatura*. This quality is present in
the refined complexities and bejewelled intricacy of
much of Thalberg and Godowsky (the fifty-three *Etudes*
on twenty-six Chopin *Etudes* are an outstanding
example). Such music is not profound: its very task is to
weave ornate and seductive fabrics from the slightest
and most insignificant materials. Can one, such
virtuosity seems to ask, make something momentous out
of a Strauss waltz? Or dare one, on the other hand,
decorate and dazzlingly extend an already flawless
composition such as a Chopin *Etude*?

There is a paradox to the art of performing such
music, for it requires a stylistic ease and assurance which
at once casually denies yet cunningly acknowledges the
existence of seemingly unsurmountable difficulties.

One of Moszkowski's most popular virtuoso works,
La Jongleuse, conjures the image of a juggler and his near
relation, the Grand-Romantic virtuoso. To hear
Rachmaninov or Jorge Bolet, for example, play this
piece is to be made precisely aware of that dual image: of
an ever-widening pattern of glittering clubs and balls as
the pianist continuously refines and widens the scope of
his legerdemain.

The public, of course, does not wish to know
anything of the practical considerations involved—the
performer's gruelling preparatory schedules or nervous
anguish—since it feeds above all on a grand illusion of
the impossible made not only possible but simple. Great
virtuosos are usually artists of striking physical economy
of movement, and an apparent lack of effort is an
essential part of their scintillating trade. The immobility
at the keyboard of Rachmaninov, Horowitz, Michelangeli or Moiseiwitsch is legendary. Arthur Rubinstein's
famous threshing-machine imitation in Falla's *Ritual
Fire Dance*, on the other hand, is surely no more than an
amusing concession to unsophisticated taste. In reality,
virtuosity such as theirs requires split-second timing,
and reflexes that rule out extraneous movements.
Beneath the casual demeanour burns a laser-like
concentration and intensity; a moment's faltering can
shatter into a thousand fragments the public's dearly-
cherished fantasy.

In such a repertoire, then, the public will hardly
warm towards a performer with whom they can easily
identify. In this sense the Grand-Romantic virtuoso is
both solipsist and narcissist, and the composer may be

no more than a springboard for the virtuoso's own self-devotion.

It follows that the virtuoso's shortcomings are only evident when he strays from the narrow path of his Grand-Romantic repertoire to the broader plateau of works requiring a supreme abdication of self. The proposition is, of course, reversible: most of us will know born poets of the keyboard less confident when called on to assert themselves beyond the strict textual indications of the composer.

To turn from the theory of virtuosity to the virtuoso himself is to discover a rare and deified figure, crowned with gifts incomprehensible to lesser mortals, whose life-style and idiosyncratic bearing are objects of wonder and uncritical admiration. Liszt's capacity to faint in wonder at his own charisma, Paderewski's royal train and noble profile (as much admired in its day as Ivor Novello's) or de Pachmann's antics—all these are inseparable from 'the golden age' of the Grand-Romantic virtuoso. That Liszt paid his ladies— some say in sexual currency—to swoon at his recitals, or that Paderewski employed students to start the famous stampedes which concluded his concerts, are only symptoms of an opulent and unapologetic ostentation. Even rudeness had its virtuosity. Liszt, for one, described the playing of Thalberg (his supposed rival) as 'pretentiously empty, supremely monotonous and boring'. Criticism, too, ran riot. Thalberg's Boston recital debut in 1865, for example, received the following review:

Rarely has the omniambient aether pervading the purlieus of the palatial metropolis vibrated resonant to more majestic music, to more soothing strains, than on Saturday morning from the digitals of the gifted Sigismond.

Argument about the real meaning of Beethoven's 'Moonlight' sonata waxed loud and long. Some opted for weeping willows and funeral urns, whilst others favoured more precise interpretation, noting how in the music 'the moon discovers his pale corpse-like face.' Stravinsky's austere pronouncement that musical feeling is unrelated to human emotion was yet to come.

This, then, was the age of the Grand-Romantic virtuoso and the grand lion of the keyboard. A high-born style and manner that had technique as its arrogant *raison d'être* only gradually gave way to less egocentric, and in some ways still more ambitious, aims. In the words of one of today's most celebrated virtuosos: 'I like to think that today we are more the servants of the music than its masters.'

Naturally, many of these pianists lived before the era of recordings, and survive only in the memory of those fortunate enough to have heard them. Others exist in recordings so dim and acoustically dated as to make a true estimate impossible. By the time early recording techniques came into being many of the finer pianists were already past their prime. It may be amusing to hear the ninety-year-old Francis Planté's angry exclamation of '*merde!*' as he ends his performance of Chopin's C major *Etude* op. 10 no. 7 in a cascade of inaccuracies: but one can hardly suppose that this disc offers a fair summary of his art. Paderewski was suffering from chronic arthritis by the time he made most of his recordings: again, they cannot always be considered

He appears with the smile of conscious superiority, tempered by the modesty of his garment (as abbé). Tremendous applause.

Hamlet's broodings; Faust's struggles Deep silence. The very whisper becomes a sigh.

representative of the artist in his prime.

Pianists of the pre-recording age we can only judge by report and in judging them we can hardly ignore the element of indiscriminate public worship, or the often doubtful quality of contemporary reviews, or privately waged vendettas involving either exaggerated praise or curt dismissal. But the actual *quality* of the performances remains a mystery. Was Liszt one of the greatest pianists of all time, or did he perform both his own and others' music in a manner that would seem both vulgar and meretricious today? Liszt had many students, some of whom handed down that most doubtful of Grand-Romantic manners, 'the Liszt tradition', and not all of

the recordings they leave behind them are encouraging. A piano seminar, for example, held during the 1977 Sydney International Piano Contest, presented performances from an extensive collection of piano rolls of such curiosities as Saint-Saëns, Busoni and Raoul Pugno, all playing Chopin's F sharp major Nocturne, and Fanny Blumfeld Zeisler playing the G flat Waltz. All four pianists, whilst not necessarily direct heirs of the Liszt Tradition, came from scarcely less celebrated backgrounds; yet many listeners will have been forgiven for assuming that the much vaunted 'grand manner' of the past often amounted to little beyond a marriage of incompetence and eccentricity.

The first chord — R–r–r–r–rum! —Looking back, as if to say: "Attention,— I now begin!"

With eyes closed, as if playing only to himself. Festive vibration of the strings.

Pianissimo. Saint Assisi Liszt speaks to the birds.—His face brightens with holy light.

Chopin, George Sand, Reminiscence, Sweet youth, Moonlight, Fragrance and Love.

Dante's Inferno. Wailings of the condemned—(among them those of the piano.) Feverish excitement. The tempest closes the gates of Hell.—*Boom!*

He has played; not only *for* us but *with* us. Retiring, he bows with lofty humility. Deafening applause. *Eviva!*

Below: '*Le Grand homme*': Liszt at the piano.

Below: Paderewski: painting by Edward Burne-Jones, 1890.
Bottom: 19th-century cartoon of Paderewski.

LE GRAND HOMME

POLICE PROTECTION FOR PIANISTS!!

MADE NECESSARY BY THE ANTICS OF THE PADDED-ROOMSKI DEVOTEES AT ST. JAMES'S HALL, WHO RUSH AT,
TRY TO EMBRACE, AND DECK WITH ROSES, A CERTAIN MASTER WHENEVER HE APPEARS.

Below: Making a piano recording in the 1890s and (bottom)
a pianist records a punched paper roll for use on a player
piano at the premises of the Perforated Music Co., London,
1909.

Even after the advent of the gramophone, the problem was not always resolved, and the early recordings which survive of, for example, D'Albert, Lamond, Rosenthal, Paderewski, or even Rachmaninov, can be misleading. The piano is a miniature orchestra of infinite resource and subtlety, and recording techniques which fail to capture the vital and individual tone-quality of a performance can offer only the most provisional of impressions. For this reason one is thankful that the rumour of a long lost recording of Liszt himself has not so far proved true, since the antiquated techniques of the time would allow little of the real quality of his playing to emerge.

In general, piano rolls, reproducing machines, and the stream of dubious early recordings which purport to show how this or that pianist played often suggest severe mechanical distortion. Even the much-praised Ampico rolls, now available on LP discs, are not above suspicion: some listeners may find it disconcerting that so large a selection of 'great' pianists thus recorded should sound so interchangeable, united only by their coldly uninflected virtuosity and eccentric mannerism. Lhevinne's legendary performance of *La Campanella*, or Nyiregyhazi's of *Mazeppa*, for example, both give rise to serious doubts. Does the 'infinite subtlety' which Deryck Cooke finds in Levitzky's playing really extend to anything beyond the illumination of elegant trivia? In what sense does Robert Schmidt have 'few if any rivals' in his performance of Debussy's Toccata? Where is the 'deep poetry' in Lhevinne's blandly mechanical, if technically astonishing, *La Campanella*? Lhevinne's response to more inward and searching music, such as Chopin's B major Nocturne op. 9, seems significantly dull and commonplace.

Did Moiseiwitsch ever play the scherzo from Chopin's B minor sonata quite as fast as his Ampico recording suggests? It is said that on hearing the same performance late in his life he remarked: 'Yes, I used to play like that'. But the appeal to his vanity must have been strong, the more so at a time when his technique had largely deserted him. Perhaps it would have taken an unusually honest man to admit, 'No, I never played as well as that'—though he might have added mischievously, being Moiseiwitsch, 'and neither did anyone else!'

The flamboyance of such old-fashioned virtuosity is rare today, although echoes of the same rhetoric can still occasionally be heard. Such performers are born mischief-makers, spurred on by an audience's insatiable demand for fresh novelty and daring. I can recall a performance of Chopin's *Tarantelle* by Samson François which proceeded at a slow *allegretto*, a perversely elegiac and bewitching experience—a *Tarantelle* in slow motion is scarcely less startling than a funeral march taken at a quick step. One could mention the names of Shura Cherkassky, Georges Cziffra and Vladimir Horowitz as notable examples of determined and unashamed romanticism in an often fiercely unromantic age.

To say that the modern school of piano playing commenced with Cortot and Schnabel may be an oversimplification; but they were almost exact contemporaries of Rachmaninov, who was one of the most remarkable 'transitional' figures in the history of piano playing. He was the last of the great composer-pianists, a line which extends from Mozart, Chopin and Liszt to Busoni, and a combination which had seemed until the late nineteenth century both natural and inevitable. Like his predecessors, Rachmaninov wrote with his own pianistic prowess in mind. His compositions, which brought virtuosity of the highest level to the attention of a wide public, were hardly vehicles for an empty expertise. His colleagues Hofmann and Godowsky were, by comparison, authors of brilliant trifles: pianist-composers, rather than composer-pianists.

Rachmaninov's change of style as a composer is significant, and perhaps best illustrated by the contrast between the *fin de siècle* virtuosity of his third piano concerto and the harsher, more skeletal writing of the fourth. The single-note melodies which open the first and second concertos as well as the third give way in the fourth to a theme in block chords—an unprecedented innovation for Rachmaninov, who had previously only used block chords for ostinato, rather than primarily for melodic, effect. The result may sound clumsy and foursquare: yet it suggests an attempt, after a long and depressingly fallow period, to move with the times.

The intimate links between composition and performance meant that this transition, from lyricism to percussiveness, was also reflected in Rachmaninov's playing. The austerity and lack of sentimental indulgence of his later recorded performances, the quick, impulsive, rather than languid *rubato*, are starkly arresting. Today his style sometimes appears extreme, or idiosyncratic; but it was considered puritan and uncompromising in its day.

Prokofiev, Bartók, and Stravinsky all exploited the percussive nature of the piano far more radically than Rachmaninov. Liszt's 'late' or final period, too, is remarkable for its prophetic harmonic and rhythmic experiments and for its increasing use of percussive rather than lyrical effects. The opening of the *Totentanz*, for example, is the very antithesis of conventional

Rachmaninov, *c.* 1935.

Artur Schnabel by Kapp.

Alfred Cortot in 1928.

Romanticism. Oddly enough, it was only when the piano became capable of a full and sustained *cantabile* that it also gained its full percussive character. Alicia de Larrocha has pointed out that as pianos became bigger, and their timbre more strident and brilliant, their action also stiffened and became more unwieldy. She wonders whether Ravel could ever have conceived '*Ondine*', '*Alborada*' or '*Scarbo*' on the piano of today, lacking as it does the older light and fluent action and also the right luminosity of tone. The pianist can only do so much to compensate for the evolution of the instrument.

Cortot could be 'wilful' in his interpretation—yet while he was undoubtedly free (even to the extent of occasional textual tampering), he did not make free; he was liberal, but did not take liberties; his approach was spontaneous without being ill-planned or arbitrary. Arthur Rubinstein's early Chopin playing, now often thought to have been delightfully irresponsible, was actually a determined attempt to erase the sentimental view of Chopin propagated by the Grand-Romantic tradition which had reached its zenith in Paderewski. Great performers are still natural autocrats. But we have come a long way from the comic conceit and flamboyance of the so-called 'Liszt Tradition'. The pianism of Cortot, Schnabel and Rubinstein already heralded a more sober and democratic age which demanded that even the most extrovert gifts were tempered with modesty.

It has already been stressed that true virtuosity is an approach, an attitude of mind, that goes beyond mere mechanical facility, and in this sense Cortot was a supreme virtuoso. It is a popular notion that he was plagued throughout his career by a weak technique; but there is ample evidence to suggest the opposite. True, his playing was often subject to alarming memory-lapses. (Sir Thomas Beecham once told of conducting a concerto performance with Cortot: 'We started with Beethoven, and I kept up with Cortot through the Grieg, Schumann, Bach and Tchaikovsky, but then he hit on one I didn't know, so I stopped dead.') His proverbial inaccuracy could, on the other hand, vanish as if by magic. The Russian pianist Alexander Uninsky recalled Cortot performances in Paris of Saint-Saëns's fourth concerto and the Fauré Ballade (two Cortot specialities) which were woefully haphazard one night and brilliant the next.

Cortot's activities, which included teaching, conducting, editing and writing (to say nothing of a penchant for political intrigue), hardly allowed him time for organized practice—with the result that his well-known philosophy of 'spontaneity above all' would sometimes collapse into confusion. But when we listen to his recording of Franck's *Prelude, Aria and Finale* (to take a supreme example of his art), his mastery is indeed gloriously evident; and in the *Prelude, Chorale and Fugue*, despite one or two muddles, it is fascinating to note how strongly his dare-devil, virtuoso relish contrasts with Richter, a technician of the first order in the established sense, whose performance of the same work sounds tame and cautious by comparison.

Schnabel, on the other hand, made little claim to the pianistic brilliance Cortot achieved at his inspired best. He aimed at different goals, at once admiring some and repudiating other characteristics of the virtuoso temperament. His attitude to the box-office success of his more conventional colleagues was often bitter. He fought fiercely for recognition of the poetic and visionary quality of the Schubert sonatas, for example; but Rachmaninov, to his way of thinking, scored an instant success with instant music.

Schnabel's early doubts about the Grand-Romantic tradition were confirmed when he was told by his teacher, Leschetizky, that he was destined to be 'a musician rather than a pianist.' He wrote later of a fellow student and 'rival':

To him Leschetizky could have said: 'You will never be a musician; you are a pianist.' His name was Mark Hambourg. He really had elemental qualities. His thunderous octaves, incomparable ones, had real fire, were not mechanical. He made a big career, was a very popular virtuoso.

Understandably, Schnabel came to have misgivings about Leschetizky's philosophy, geared as it was to the production of the virtuoso type. Schnabel would not have been interested in playing Chopin's G sharp minor *Etude* in thirds with Cortot's aplomb; and in any case,

Sviatoslav Richter in concert.

Chopin's *Etudes* just failed to qualify for his beloved category of works which are always 'better than they can be performed'.

Cortot swept aside with magnificent disdain what he considered a purely pedantic search for accuracy; his was a different sort of spiritual quest, certainly concerned with virtuoso principles, but never with mastery for mastery's sake. A Cortot performance could storm the heights with irresistible élan, fire and poetry: and in doing so demonstrate a virtuosity far more exciting (and in its own way more exacting) than any grand-romantic Steibelt or Dreyschock circus-act. As teacher and pianist, Cortot was almost exclusively concerned with the re-creation of the spirit of the music—and if the curious came from miles around to hear Cortot's wrong notes, they were, as Yvonne Lefébure put it, the wrong notes of a god.

Dinu Lipatti, whom Cortot greatly admired, attempted to take Cortot's quest a significant stage further. We can only guess how this legendary pianist would have developed had he lived longer than his tragically short thirty-three years, but it is clear from his recordings that he considered spontaneity a less important virtue than did some of his predecessors. Cortot's insistence that one should never play a piece twice the same way ('lose yourself, improvise. . .') would have been alien to the arch-perfectionist Lipatti. The story of Lipatti's unwillingness to record Beethoven's 'Emperor' concerto before five years of preparation, or Tchaikovsky's first concerto before three, is well known. He scrupulously avoided the distractions of Cortot's protean life. Composing was a subsidiary activity, and he taught few students, devoting himself not so much to the attainment of mechanical perfection as to a degree of accuracy and control that he considered worthy of Bach, Mozart or Chopin. Any compromise was an insult to the composer's genius.

Since Lipatti's death in 1950, the number of brilliantly proficient concert pianists of international repute has greatly multiplied. But the view, often expressed, that there has been a dilution of standards is only partly true. Today we can afford to be more discriminating because the choice is so wide. Cooler, more calculating manners have replaced rapture and

rhetoric. A young pianist making his debut in Beethoven's 'Emperor' concerto, for example, must bear in mind that many members of his audience have recently listened to recordings of the same work by Schnabel, Fischer, Gilels or Arrau, and are in no mood to be trifled with. Again, they may have heard it played the previous week by an internationally famous soloist, and close comparison will be unavoidable.

If we live today in a more sober and, arguably, a duller age, we are, perhaps, at the same time more demanding and more sophisticated. Critically, a harsher clarity reigns, and the old, familiar forms of eulogy are laughed to scorn. Listeners, too, are apt to be more informed, more critically aware of the precise notation, say, of Chopin's G minor Ballade, and less inclined to see in it, as James Huneker once did, a 'tender lily which drips in cadenced monotone', or to note 'the most delicate flower-work which the frost-fairies draw upon the window pane in their frolicsome hours of winter moonlight'.

Standards have undoubtedly risen, and there are now more technically and musically able players before the public than at any other time in history. But an ability to 'get around' the keyboard must never be confused with virtuosity: a too rigorous and abstract conception of artistic creation can lead to a deadening of impulse, a freezing up of vital heat.

Today, at best, we tend to expect a young artist's early volatility to settle into something still highly-charged yet composed; we note the progress from brilliant but uncoordinated parts into a serene and integrated whole. The finest pianists remind us of Charles Köchlin's description of Fauré's piano playing, which proved, he said, that 'a controlled manner of playing can still allow scope for a great many shades of emotion'. We can be sure that if the Golden Age of pianism, the age of the Grand-Romantic virtuoso, were reconstructed for our benefit, we should find much of it tarnished. Yet criteria change also—much as they may appear confidently fixed and immutable. And despite talk of an age of gold turned to steel, of Grand-Romantic virtuosity turned to calculating dullness, we should remember that great artistry, and the agility and expertise which form so vital a part of it, are necessarily rare. It is in the nature of things that genius is not commonplace.

THE CHAMBER PIANO

Previous page: *The Grosvenor Family* (detail): painting by
C. R. Leslie, 1833.
Title-page of Haydn's Piano Trio, 1798, op. 80.

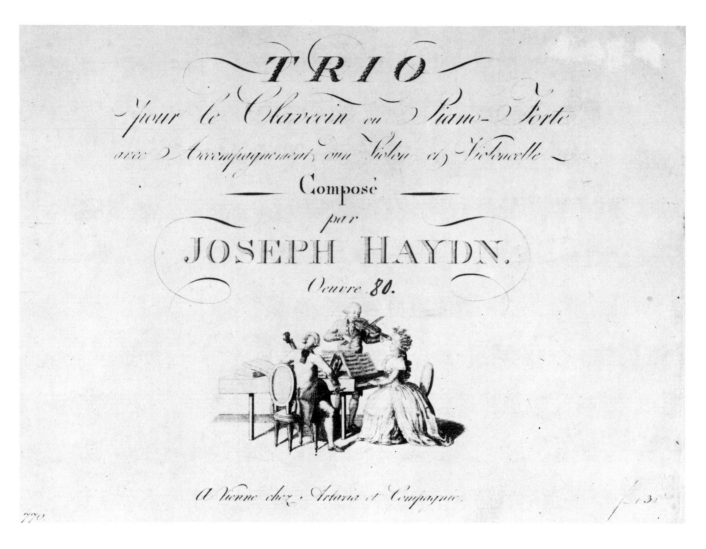

Origins and Distinctions

Of the two instruments that immediately preceded the pianoforte in popular use, the harpsichord was essentially a brilliant public instrument, while the clavichord belonged to the private 'chamber', where its small, pure-toned voice could make itself heard. The hammer-mechanism of the piano emphasizes its descent from the clavichord rather than from the harpsichord, with its plucked mechanism; and as we shall see, the role of the new instrument in 'consort' with strings or wind has varied greatly.

The ousting of both harpsichord and clavichord by the piano was naturally a gradual process, which in fact lasted throughout the second half of the eighteenth century and was by no means complete by 1800. But by the late 1880s (when the piano makers Erard and Pleyel began to make specialized 'modern' harpsichords in Paris to cater for a revival of interest in the instrument)

the harpsichord had become virtually obsolete in the concert hall, and the clavichord almost wholly forgotten.

It is certainly not by chance that the repertory of chamber music with piano centres round the early days of the instrument (1800–50) before the development of the modern grand piano had been exploited by Franz Liszt—or at least before that exploitation had revolutionized the general conception of the piano. In this matter both dates and the received accounts of musical historians are often misleading. The works in which Liszt revolutionized piano technique by imitating Paganini's treatment of the violin were written in the 1830s and 1840s, but their effect was neither immediate nor universal; it was only considerably later, in the seventies and eighties, that the next generation of *Klaviertiger* had so popularized the Lisztian conception of the instrument that it became virtually unfitted for the teamwork essential to chamber music.

The Central European Cradle

Before that Lisztian revolution the piano had known extraordinary changes of fortune, and had revealed itself as equally fitted to play a leading or a subordinate role. All chamber music with piano originates in fact with the trio sonatas of the Baroque period, in which the part of the keyboard instrument (harpsichord) was essentially supporting, filling in, ornamenting, or expanding the top-line melody and the harmonizing bass-line provided by the two other instruments. Here in fact we have the immediate ancestor of the piano trio as we find it in the works written by Haydn, mostly during the 1790s, for performance in the princely household of the Esterházy, or else dedicated to such friends as Magdalene von Kurzböck, who received the excellent trio in E flat minor. There is a great variety of interest in the trios, which often show Haydn at his most inventive, and few of them are beyond the powers of good amateur players—though the only one which has become universally known is no. 25 in G major, with its 'Gypsy' (*rondo all'ungarese*) finale.

Chamber music presupposes a society devoted to music not simply as listeners, but as performers too, however humble. The list of Beethoven's patrons, beginning with the Archduke Rudolf, shows that not only patrons but performers, and even composers, of chamber music were to be found in the highest social class. Friedrich Wilhelm II of Prussia was a more than passable cellist, and Prince Louis Ferdinand an accomplished pianist and composer: it was natural for chamber music to flourish in societies which took their tone from such leaders.

It is arguably a cultivated middle class that in fact determines the artistic character and achievements of any modern society, and Vienna was almost ideally suited to form the nucleus of such a society in the years between the arrival of Beethoven in 1792 and the death of Brahms in 1897. Here there were the positive elements needed for such a musical flowering—a strong tradition, a cultivated court, a swiftly changing number of gifted individuals attracted to the capital of a great cosmopolitan empire, and the intimacy inseparable from the conditions of a comparatively small city. There was also a negative force which acted particularly strongly in favour of chamber music during the years 1798–1848—namely the virtual exclusion of the cultivated bourgeoisie from all careers of a political nature. These were reserved to members of the nobility during the years of reaction against the French Revolution, the two invasions of Austria by Napoleon, and that period of conservative reaction led by Austria and planned by her chief minister, Metternich. Music is the art least open to charges of subversiveness; and music which is performed in private houses and does not even involve large public gatherings must have been, in the eyes of Metternich, an almost ideal pastime for his citizens.

Mozart had died in 1791, before the Austrian government had begun to take serious measures against the influence of the French Revolution; and his chamber music was written for a society shocked awake from the traditions of Maria Theresa's age by the reforming zeal of her son Joseph II. Beethoven's subversive opinions were forgiven him in view of his close association with a member of the royal family and leading members of the aristocracy. It was Schubert who provided the received pattern of the Austrian artist, showing no interest, let alone political interest, outside his music, wholly absorbed in the intellectual and emotional activities of composition and the trivialities of everyday existence. This same pattern was followed, though no doubt unconsciously, by Brahms when he settled in Vienna; so it was for a Central European world of musical amateurs, still very largely debarred from public life, that the main corpus of Classical chamber music was written.

Mozart

The distinction between piano trio and piano or violin sonata was by no means clear in the 1760s when Mozart wrote his first violin sonatas—sixteen of them, composed in Paris, London and The Hague. These sonatas are 'clavier' sonatas with violin *ad libitum*, or '*clavier-duetti mit Violin*'; and it is only with the so-called 'Mannheim' sonatas (K. 301, 296, 302–6) that Mozart really confronts the problems of the combination. Even then his approach varies. Five of the sonatas have only two movements, like those of J.C. Bach. If the A major sonata K. 305 is an untroubled exploration of what the two can achieve working on something like an equal footing, the E minor K. 304 is one of the first works in which Mozart looks clearly forward to the world of drama which Beethoven was to substitute for the well-bred dialogue, diversified by lyrical moments and philosophical reflection, that was the characteristic musical pattern of the eighteenth century. These 'Mannheim' sonatas are often close in spirit as well as date to the four violin concertos written in 1775.

The earliest of Mozart's pianos trios (K. 254) is no more than a piano sonata with obbligato violin, and cello strengthening the bass line. His greatest successes with this combination came much later, though they were

Opposite: The boy Mozart, aged seven, at a French
harpsichord with his father and sister: watercolour by L. C.
de Carmontelle, 1763.
Below: Autograph page of a violin sonata in C major (1782)
by Mozart, dedicated to 'my dear wife' in the first year of
their marriage. The four violin sonatas belonging to 1781
are all very different in character. K. 376 is light-hearted,
whereas the D minor variations in the first movement of

K. 377 look forward to the string quartet K. 421 and the
whole work is more tense in character. The works designed
for his wife in 1782 were not completed: especially fine are
the Introduction and (unfinished) Fugue of K. 402. Of the
three remaining violin sonatas (K. 454, 481 and 526) the last
is outstanding – another A major work to set beside the
piano concerto K. 488, and the clarinet quintet, and in
fact contemporary with the composition of *Don Giovanni*.

ushered in by the trio for piano, clarinet and viola K.
498, a unique and wholly individual exploration of a
particularly fruitful combination. Of the four remaining
piano trios, the two gems are K. 502 (B flat) and K.
542 (E major), this last written just before the last three
symphonies and uniting fabulous ease and grace with
eloquence of feeling and brilliant craftsmanship.

Chamber works were not expected to make serious
demands on their audience, and the piano quartet in G
minor K. 478 met with some opposition simply on
account of the very qualities which we prize in it: the
almost grim seriousness and directness of the first
movement particularly. The second piano quartet K.
493 in E flat, no less skilful in exploiting the possibilities of the combination, is an altogether more light-
hearted work. Mozart himself described the E flat
quintet K.452 for piano, oboe, clarinet, horn and
bassoon as 'the best work I ever composed'; and indeed
no composer ever showed a greater awareness of

instrumental character, a surer sense of effective
combination or a better balance between serious
thought and high spirits than Mozart in this work,
which Beethoven tried in vain to match in his op. 16.

Beethoven and Schubert
Of Beethoven's six piano trios, op. 97 in B flat ranks with
the greatest of his chamber music productions, and the
two of op. 70 show him already at the height of his
powers – especially no. 1 in D major, whose uncanny
tremolandos (possibly connected with ideas for an opera
of *Macbeth*) have earned the work the nickname of
'*Geistertrio*' or 'Ghost trio'. Beethoven dedicated a
considerable number of works to the Archduke Rudolf,
but it is only to op. 97 that the title 'Archduke' has
become attached. The spacious proportions and serene
gait of the two opening movements are replaced in the
trio section by a strange alternation of dance-rhythms
and mysterious chromatic progressions, which in their

Title-page of Beethoven's three piano trios op. 1, published by Artaria in 1795.

turn give way to the sublime meditations of the *Andante cantabile*, some of the richest variations that Beethoven had as yet (1811) composed.

Beethoven's duo sonatas include ten for the violin, five for the cello and one for the horn. In all of these the two instruments enjoy virtual parity, although the three sonatas of op. 12 (1797) are described as for '*clavecin* or pianoforte and violin'. The third of this set (E flat major) has an interesting *Adagio con molta espressione*, whose florid piano part exploits differences of register and texture. In op. 23 (A minor), which opens with a *presto* 6/8 movement, there are already premonitory hints of op. 47, the so-called 'Kreutzer' sonata, while in op. 24 (the 'Spring') it is the *cantabile* character of the violin that is to the fore. The most outstanding of the three sonatas op. 30 (1802) is the second in C minor, whose characteristically stormy first movement, with a fugato and broken-octave passages, is followed by a hymn-like slow movement and an aggressive finale. The A major sonata op. 47 was dedicated to the French violinist Rodolphe Kreutzer, whom Beethoven met in Vienna in 1798, but he is said never to have played the work, which is on a scale, and of an intensity, that makes unique demands on both performers and calls for nothing less than a concert hall to make its full effect. The colossal rhythmic energy of both the first and last movements is only emphasized by the tranquil lyricism of the F major variations that intervene. Entirely different in character, but hardly less concentrated in quality, is the G major sonata op. 96 of 1812.

The two cello sonatas of op. 5 (1796) are dedicated to Frederick William II of Prussia, and it was twelve years before Beethoven wrote his next cello sonata, op. 69 in A. This shows him at his most balanced and comparatively serene, fully mature but not here plagued by the problems and anxieties which beset his last years. The last two cello sonatas (op. 102) belong to the end of his life and each in its different way has the remote, transfigured, self-communing quality characteristic of many of the works written during his last decade.

Schubert completes the small band of composers who, over two generations, made Vienna the central flowering-place of Classical chamber music. After his early death in 1828, a quarter of a century was to elapse before Vienna saw a second flowering of chamber music in the works of Brahms, while in the northern, Bohemian province of the old Austro-Hungarian Empire Dvořák was to take the music of both men, Schubert and Brahms, as basic models for his own chamber works. Schubert wrote only a handful of chamber works with piano, but they include at least

three of his most memorable creations: the two trios in B flat and E flat, and the quintet in A. Although movements of both trios have been criticized for not living up to their opening, and although their beauty and satisfying musical quality lie in a mass of individual felicities rather than in tautness of construction, the two works are so rich in melodic invention and harmonic imagination—and even 'the long way round' which Schubert is always inclined to take on his musical excursions is so diverting and varied—that it is pointless to regret the lack of a conciseness quite foreign to Schubert's nature when writing instrumental music. The circumstances in which the piano quintet was composed—on holiday with friends in the Austrian Alps—go a long way towards explaining the character of the music. The variation movement, based on Schubert's own song '*Die Forelle*' ('The Trout'), has given the work its nickname, and is essentially an entertainment from beginning to end.

An *Adagio and Rondo Concertante* is the only work that Schubert left for piano quartet, and it is well worth performing, though 'not free from the influence of the café and the theatre'—an objection to Schubert's chamber music in general that bears much less weight today than when it was first made by the late Professor Westrup. Pure virtuosity plays a large part in the finest work for violin and piano—the *Fantasy* written in 1827 for the Czech violinist Josef Slavik, which has a superbly imagined opening and contains a Hungarian movement and a set of variations on the composer's song '*Sei mir gegrüsst*'. The Rondo in B minor is brilliant and orchestral in manner, while the four violin sonatas answer more to our idea of chamber music proper, though none has the marked character of the sonata that Schubert wrote for the *arpeggione*—a 'guitar violoncello' invented in 1824 by the Viennese Johann Stauffer and replaced in modern performances by the cello.

The popularity of chamber music with piano during the last years of the eighteenth and the first years of the nineteenth centuries is attested by the productions of a gifted royal amateur, Prince Louis Ferdinand of Prussia, a professional soldier killed at Saalfeld in 1806. Beethoven expressed admiration for the piano playing of the Prince, who left three works for piano trio, two piano quartets and one piano quintet. These show a fluent mastery of the musical language of his day—something between Mozart and early Beethoven—and real professional craftsmanship, though the thematic invention is more variable in quality.

Mendelssohn and Schumann
The generation of musicians born around 1810, and destined to form the nucleus of the Romantic movement, had comparatively little interest in chamber music; and the gradual disappearance of the small cultivated courts of the eighteenth century also reduced the demand for chamber works. Chopin's only chamber composition for more than one instrument is a cello sonata in which the overwhelming interest lies in the piano part, quite beyond the powers of any but professional players. None of Mendelssohn's three piano quartets written in 1822–4 has anything approaching the quality of the famous octet of 1825. Both his best-known chamber pieces, the D minor piano trio of 1839, and the later C minor trio, though vigorous, inventive and most rewarding to play, suffer from the restlessness which the composer confessed overcame him every time his fingers touched a keyboard, and which is reflected in the ceaseless passage-work of scales, arpeggios, broken chords and octaves that fill the keyboard part. They indicate the growing popularity of the piano as a domestic instrument, for both trios are essentially designed for domestic performance.

So indeed is the sextet for piano, string quartet and double bass (1824), with its polka finale and conventional keyboard writing. None of Mendelssohn's duo sonatas (one each for violin, viola and clarinet, and two for cello) rises above his very professional second best; and it is significant that it was not in sonata form, but in the freer form of variations, that Mendelssohn wrote his finest duo, the *Variations concertantes* for cello and piano.

The same is true of Schumann, neither of whose violin sonatas is as interesting as are the *Fantasiestücke*

(clarinet and piano), the *Fünf Stücke im Volkston* (cello and piano) and the *Adagio and Allegro* (horn and piano), where Schumann's acute sense of instrumental character is not overlaid by the richness and impetuosity of his piano writing, or clouded by the nervous instinct to 'double' melodic lines which mars much of his concerted instrumental writing, both orchestral and chamber.

Schumann's piano quartet and even the much more famous piano quintet—both in E flat, and both dating from 1842—suffer in differing degrees from these weaknesses; but the character and quality of their ideas, and their development, make this fault of presentation comparatively unimportant. The material of the quintet especially shows Schumann in his most felicitous vein, at once varied and mercurial, robust and forthright. The combination of piano and string quartet had never been attempted before, and the frequency with which later composers tried to imitate or rival Schumann's quintet during the rest of the century is an eloquent tribute to his achievement.

Brahms and Dvořák
If chamber music was of secondary interest to Mendelssohn and Schumann, it was central in the work of Brahms, much of whose orchestral writing has a chamber-music quality. A great and original pianist himself, he was most successful in chamber works in which the piano plays an important role: these form a large part of his chamber output, and include a number of masterpieces.

Of the five trios, three are for violin, cello and piano, while in op. 40 the horn replaces the cello and in op. 114 the clarinet replaces the violin. The earliest of the trios (1854), op. 8, is an expansive, high-spirited work in B major, which already shows many of what were to be the characteristics of Brahms's chamber music for the rest of his life. The keyboard-writing in particular is heavily chordal, with marked preference for extremes of pitch, passages in thirds and sixths, triple-time scherzos with suggestions of hunting-music and long-drawn lyrical or lamenting slow movements. This pattern is followed again in the horn trio, written for the old natural horn, not the new valved instrument for which Schumann wrote his horn works. Unquestionably the greatest of the piano trios is op. 101 in C minor. Here the diffuseness of Brahms's earlier chamber works has been tempered without any loss of interest or variety.

The clarinet trio, altogether smaller and lighter, was written for the clarinettist Richard Mühlfeld, for whom Brahms also wrote two fine clarinet sonatas in E flat and

Joseph Joachim. Apart from three sonatas for violin and piano (the G major op. 78 of 1879, the A major op. 100 of 1886, and the D minor op. 108 of 1887), only one piece for violin and piano survived the very self-critical appraisal of his work which led Brahms to destroy so many sketched and semi-completed projects. This was a scherzo in C minor for a violin sonata dedicated to Joseph Joachim in 1853 (when Brahms was twenty). The violin sonatas, however, belong to the most fruitful period of his maturity, for between 1877 and 1889 all four symphonies were published, as well as the violin concerto, the double concerto and many of his finest works of chamber music.

Tchaikovsky: painting by Kuznetsov.

Tchaikovsky: painting by Kuznetsov.

Antonín Dvořák (centre), Hanus Wihan, and Ferdinand Lachner (seated) at the time they were touring Bohemia and Moravia playing the 'Dumky' trio.

movements in E major, the *Andante* of the trio consisting of sophisticated variations on a superb *cantabile* theme first given to the cello.

Probably the best known of Brahms's chamber works with piano is the quintet in F minor op. 34, which had two previous existences, first as a string quintet and then as a sonata for two pianos. The first movement is as masterful and powerful as anything that Brahms wrote in any medium, but the second is a gently lilting lullaby, beautifully 'orchestrated' for piano and strings and recalling the song '*Pause*' from Schubert's *Die schöne Müllerin*. The finale is something of an enigma: a passionate introduction leads to what has been described as 'a sauntering cello tune', and it is not until late in the movement, and supremely at the climax of the coda, that there is any hint of the passion that permeated the opening movement.

It was very largely the influence of Brahms's music that brought Antonín Dvořák within the musical world of the Central European Classical tradition. Dvořák's strong and conscious local, Slavonic affiliations give his music a kind of peasant strength, its own very Slavonic sort of tenderness, and a whole repertory of unfamiliar dance-rhythms; but all these were easily accommodated within the capacious world of the Classical tradition. By the second half of the nineteenth century the great masters of the Viennese period were all dead; but the North German Brahms had settled in Vienna, and it was still as a provincial looking towards Vienna, rather than as an independent 'Czech' composer from Prague, that Dvořák took his place in the European tradition.

His chamber music is as copious and almost as rich as Brahms's. He wrote four piano trios, two piano quartets, two piano quintets (the earlier of which, in A major like his op. 81, was published only in 1959), and a sonata and sonatina for violin and piano. Two of the trios stand head and shoulders above the rest. The trio in F minor op. 65 of 1883 opens in a tragic Brahmsian manner, though the lighter lyrical passages and both the inner movements are marked by Dvořák's very personal harmonies and, in the *Allegro grazioso*, by memories of folk music.

The '*Dumky*' trio op. 90 is quite unlike any other chamber work. There are six movements that have no close musical connection, but form variations (not unlike those in Schumann's sets of piano pieces) on a mood rather than on a musical idea. No satisfactory explanation has been given for the title (the word literally means 'thoughts' or 'ponderings')—and though the basic mood of the music is certainly pensive, serenity

F minor. Equally diverse in character and rich in musical and technical interest are the three violin sonatas op. 78 (G major), op. 100 (A major) and op. 108 (D minor), and the cello sonatas in E minor and F major opp. 38 and 99.

Brahms's first two piano quartets are early works, and show him not yet able fully to discipline the torrent of ideas they contain—in the first movement of the G minor quartet op. 25 especially, a torrent of enormous proportions. The A major quartet op. 26 is marked by Brahms's predilection for the contrasting or combining of binary and ternary rhythms. The trio section of the scherzo is a canon, and the finale, though rhythmically vigorous, would have been more effective if compressed, a lesson which had been well learned by the time Brahms wrote his third piano quartet op. 60 in C minor. Here there is a striking parallel with the first symphony— both works are basically in C minor and both have slow

and even cheerfulness alternate with melancholy. The A major piano quintet op. 81 of 1887 rivals the 'Dumky' trio and is probably the most frequently played of all Dvořák's chamber works for its wealth of melody and for the extraordinary felicity with which the medium is handled. The second piano quartet op. 87 in E flat followed very soon after the quintet and has many of the same qualities, although the echoes of Schubert, Brahms and even Italian opera, which gave the quintet its immediate appeal, are less noticeable in the quartet, whose inspiration is entirely local.

Dvořák's older contemporary Bedřich Smetana wrote only three chamber works with piano—of which a trio on the occasion of his small daughter's death, composed in 1855 and seldom heard outside Czechoslovakia, deserves especially to be better known.

Tchaikovsky and the Moscow School

If the proximity of Prague to Vienna, with its German-Austrian musical traditions, does much to explain the flowering of chamber music in Bohemia during the second half of the nineteenth century, there was no corresponding influence on the Russian nationalist composers of the St Petersburg school. The 'Westernizers' in Moscow, on the other hand, were proud of their Germanic musical training, which included at least an acquaintance with Classical chamber music. Tchaikovsky's one chamber work with piano is the trio in A minor op. 50, written in memory of Nicholas Rubinstein (1882). This follows no conventional model, consisting as it does of only two movements, a *Pezzo elegiaco* and a *Theme and variations*. The composer was concerned to make its piano part worthy of the memory of a great virtuoso, and the trio is in fact an exemplary instance of chamber music in which the Lisztian conception of the piano totally disrupts that equable distribution of interest between the instruments that is the essence of the chamber style.

Less distinguished musically (though more satisfactorily balanced) are the chamber works with piano of Anton Arensky—two trios, of which the first, in D minor, was at one time enormously popular, and a quintet. The academic strain in Russian chamber music was continued by Sergey Taneyev, and by Alexander Glazunov—although Glazunov's chamber music is for strings only, except one quartet for saxophones. The traditional chamber forms held no interest for Prokofiev or Stravinsky, although Prokofiev wrote a characteristic and attractive *Overture on Hebrew themes* for clarinet and piano quintet; and of his two violin sonatas the D major, originally written for flute,

has won deserved popularity. The cello sonata op. 119 is one of the composer's later lyrical works, quite innocent of his earlier asperities.

The most significant chamber music written in the Soviet Union has been that of Dmitry Shostakovich. His best-known chamber works are the string quartets, but the composer himself valued very highly the eleven songs *From Hebrew Popular Poetry* op. 79, deeply moving vignettes that include a lament, a lullaby, and family scenes of parting, warning, rejection, and happiness, for three solo voices and piano. The piano quintet op. 57, which contains a fugal movement, and the extremely interesting piano trio op. 67, also with a fugal introduction, are both well worth performing. Even more ambitious are the later *Seven Poems of A. Blok* op. 127 for piano trio and voice. Each poem is set for a different combination of instruments, and treated with a great variety of sonority and texture.

Below: Edvard Grieg: a late photograph.
Bottom: Zoltán Kodály at home on the eve of his eightieth birthday in 1962.

Grieg, Sibelius and Contemporaries

Edvard Grieg's three violin sonatas and one cello sonata used to be more widely performed, but belong more to the historical than to the performing repertory. The same, though for very different reasons, has been thought to be true of Max Reger's chamber music with piano, which includes a pair each of trios, quartets, and quintets. The profuseness of Reger's production is only matched by what often seem to be deliberate complexities of tonality and texture that make his music hard work for the listener, and seldom reward the performer well enough for his pains. The violin sonata op. 21 in C sharp minor of his Hungarian contemporary Ernö (sometimes Ernst von) Dohnányi, on the other hand, is a fine work, not greatly original but excellently written; and the early cello sonata of Zoltán Kodály, though somewhat overshadowed by the sonata for solo cello produced five years later, is likewise rewarding.

All the chamber works with piano of Jean Sibelius — trios, quartets, a quintet and two violin sonatas — are early, mostly student pieces written between 1880–90, and the later works for violin or cello and piano are of small significance. Carl Nielsen, on the other hand, who was also a professional violinist, wrote two admirable violin sonatas. The first, op. 9, is an early work which, like the first symphony, clearly shows the influence of Brahms, though Nielsen's own voice is also unmistakable. The second, op. 35, dates from 1912 and in some instances anticipates the fourth symphony (the 'Inextinguishable'). A tough work, with characteristically stormy key relationships, it deserves to be better known.

France

It was one of the declared objects of César Franck, and the 'school' developed by his pupil Vincent d'Indy, to renew and strengthen that symphonic tradition which the opera had so largely overlaid. Hector Berlioz had already struck a resounding blow on behalf of French orchestral music, but the 'thin red line' of chamber music had been all but obliterated except for the indefatigable production of the Anglo-Frenchman George Onslow, who composed a huge amount of chamber music for strings; mostly quintets.

However, it was not Onslow's already somewhat old-fashioned chamber music that inspired the young Camille Saint-Saëns, who was really the initiator of the chamber music revival in mid-nineteenth-century France, but the example of the Viennese classics and, more recently, Mendelssohn. Saint-Saëns' output of chamber music with piano was eventually as large as it

César Franck (seated centre) surrounded by a group of
musicians; standing immediately to the composer's left is
the Belgian violinist Eugène Ysaÿe.

was in almost every other field, and includes two trios, a
quartet, a quintet and a septet (for trumpet, strings and
piano), and two sonatas each for violin and cello, as well
as one each for oboe, clarinet, and bassoon. All these
works are strongly marked by Saint-Saëns' personal
keyboard style. He himself was a player of extraordinary
facility and brilliance, particularly in the extended scale
passages which figure largely in all his chamber music.
Added to this, a corresponding facility (indeed a fatal
fluency) in fugal writing and a sweet tooth in the matter
of melodic invention combine to make up a somewhat
trivial effect. The harmony is always elegant, occasionally Schumannesque; but though rewarding to play,
these works too often sound faded and insufficiently
demanding for modern taste, important though they
were in their historical context.

Franck and his Pupils
Edouard Lalo, who was the first viola-player in the
Armingaud-Jacquard Quartet founded in 1855, wrote
three piano trios, the last of which (op. 26 in A minor)
dates from 1881, when Franck had already written his
piano quintet. Franck's concern with chamber music,
however, goes back to the outset of his career when his
Trois Trios concertants op. 1 (1841) were admired by
Liszt, who performed them in Germany. At that time
Franck was still unwillingly touring the country as a
piano virtuoso to please his father, and it was only after
thirty-five years that he returned to chamber music.

The qualities most admired in Franck's music during
his lifetime—what the student Debussy called his 'chic'

ideas in the matter of modulation, and his use of the
cyclic forms elaborated by Liszt from hints in
Schubert's music—are those that most irritate the
modern listener. Franck's quintet is a masterpiece of its
kind, as admirable as those of Schumann and Dvořák,
though inferior in musical quality to Brahms's. The
chromatically moving basses (partly no doubt suggested by the composer's organist's feet, just as Saint-
Saëns' scale passages are suggested by his pianist's
fingers) give his music a certain queasy instability, while
the ceaseless chromatic alteration of the melodic line
invites the kind of conscious emotional expressiveness
that easily palls. Some of the writing in the third
movement is frankly orchestral, where the strings are
heard in unison against a hammering figure which
suggests a piano concerto rather than a chamber work,
but Franck sustains the dramatic excitement to the end.

Incomparably Franck's finest chamber work is the
violin sonata, written for the Belgian violinist Eugène
Ysaÿe, and one of the greatest works in the repertory of
the instrument. Planned on a grand scale and rich in
contrast, the four movements include a recitative that
harks, in spirit if not in matter, back to J.S. Bach, a
searching and by no means facile lyricism, and genuine
appassionato writing that owes nothing to mere convention.

None of Franck's pupils achieved anything to
compare with his violin sonata, or indeed with his
quintet. Alexis de Castillon, who died at thirty-five, left
an extremely promising body of chamber works, marked
by an admiration for Beethoven but already sounding an
original, personal note. Vincent d'Indy's chamber
music was spread over his whole life, from the piano
quartet op. 7 of 1878 to five works written in the 1920s,
among them a piano quintet op. 81 and a trio op. 98. If
none of these has won a place in the repertory, it is no
doubt because in d'Indy's case composition was a duty
rather than a necessity—and this lack of spontaneity is
revealed most clearly in his chamber music, where there
is no orchestral colour to distract the listener's attention.

Ernest Chausson's finest chamber works, apart from
the *Chanson perpetuelle* for soprano voice and piano
quintet (or orchestra), are the *Concert*, a kind of concerto
grosso for violin, piano and string quartet; and the piano
quartet in A, published posthumously in 1917. All these
are marked by the melancholy, nostalgic mood familiar
from Chausson's songs; but they also contain passages,
and indeed whole movements, where the composer rises
above his subjective moods and achieves a solider, more
robust music.

Almost certainly the most gifted of the Franck group

was the youngest, Guillaume Lekeu, who died at the age of twenty-four, leaving among his finished compositions two piano trios and a violin sonata; and it is the sonata, like Franck's also dedicated to Ysaÿe, which shows most plainly Lekeu's quality as a composer.

The music of Franck and his pupils has an unmistakable seriousness of manner and a conscious nobility very uncharacteristic of the French, who often emphasize the fact that Franck (like Lekeu) was of Belgian origin. It is from the same sources as those tapped by Saint-Saëns in his chamber music—and particularly from Schumann—that Gabriel Fauré drew the inspiration for his own chamber works. As in d'Indy's case, they were spread over the whole range of a long life; but the chamber works by which Fauré is best remembered are those written at the beginning of his career—the two piano quartets opp. 15 and 45 and the violin sonata op. 13—rather than the two later quintets, the trio op. 120, or the sonatas for violin and cello written between 1917–22. In the early period the workmanship is already assured and the musical language fully formed—a style of keyboard writing derived from Schumann rather than Chopin, and an absolutely personal harmonic idiom with strong modal overtones. The rhythmic impulse is particularly powerful in these early works, and the spontaneity suggested by their varied character has the unthinking and generous quality of youth. This spontaneous, physical quality is often absent, or at least much rarer, in the later period, when reflection largely takes the place of lyrical invention, and textures are often thicker, though the workmanship and characteristic delicacy of detail are still very fine.

The piano trio of Fauré's pupil Maurice Ravel is one of his most robust works, constructed on a grand scale and with many original traits, including the 'pantoum' second movement and the passacaglia in the third (although the composer maintained that he took Saint-Saëns' early F major trio as a model). In a very different style are the two sonatas for violin and cello and violin and piano, and the brilliant *Tzigane* for violin and piano, written during the 1920s, when Stravinsky's influence in French music was paramount. On a much larger, and more grandiose, scale than Ravel's trio is Florent Schmitt's piano quintet of 1908, orchestral in dimensions and feeling. On the other hand Albert Roussel's *Divertissement* for flute, oboe, clarinet, bassoon, horn and piano (1906) is one of the earliest examples of the anti-Romantic, *extra sec* style that Stravinsky was to popularize a decade later in France. Debussy's violin and cello sonatas also represent a parallel, though by no means identical, movement towards clarifying, econ-

omizing and lightening the emotional load of a musical composition, combined with a wholly individual mood and language.

The New Aesthetic

The piano, with its overwhelmingly romantic associations, fared badly in the changed aesthetic climate of the twentieth century, in which the strings were regarded with disfavour compared with the more direct and unambiguous sonorities of wind instruments. It was pointed out that the piano was essentially a percussion instrument, and that only by fraud could it ever suggest a true singing-tone. Rigorists even rejected as essentially unsatisfactory any combination of the piano with voice or strings; and it was no longer customary for young composers to try their hands at the piano trios or piano quintets which figure among the earliest opus numbers of almost all nineteenth-century composers from Beethoven onwards. So, apart from the solo sonata, the piano virtually disappears from chamber music after 1920, except where the new aesthetic met with hostility or incomprehension not only among the public but also among composers. This happened most noticeably in England, where the musical renaissance initiated by Parry and Stanford in the last quarter of the nineteenth century brought with it a protracted autumn in which romantic values and attitudes persisted despite the brisk, wintry weather which had descended elsewhere.

In this climate a number of composers wrote worthy chamber works for instruments, including the piano. Arnold Bax's sonatas for violin, cello and (most notably) viola followed an earlier piano quintet, and John Ireland's second and third piano trios an earlier '*Phantasy*', while his second violin sonata is still played today. A prolific composer of chamber music, much of it including the piano, was Frank Bridge, a fine craftsman and in some substantial ways an original composer. In France the new, basically neo-classical style of Stravinsky was combined with many nineteenth-century elements by Francis Poulenc, among whose chamber works are a trio and a sextet for piano and wind and a number of sonatas for wind instruments and piano, including an admirable oboe sonata. Honegger's chamber music is mostly without piano, but he wrote a number of duo sonatas, and an excellent clarinet sonatina. Perhaps it would be just, as well as apt, to conclude this survey of instrumental chamber music with piano by mentioning Olivier Messiaen's *Quatuor pour la fin du temps* for violin, clarinet, cello and piano, written and performed during 1941 in a German prison camp in Silesia.

Below: A Schubert Evening at Josef von Spaun's house (Schubert at the piano, with the tenor Michael Vogl beside him): drawing by Moritz von Schwind.
Bottom: Schubert and Vogl 'setting out to Fight and Conquer': pencil drawing by Franz von Schober, 1825. In 1825 Schubert made a tour of Upper Austria with his friend Michael Vogl, as he had done six years earlier; but this

time it lasted for five months, the longest and most productive holiday of his life. 'I find my compositions everywhere in Upper Austria', he wrote proudly to his father. Wherever they went, Schubertiads were held; Vogl would give the new songs from Scott's 'Lady of the Lake', and Schubert his latest piano sonata in A minor op. 42, of which the variation movement proved especially popular.

Voice and Piano

In any duo combination it is possible for either one of the partners to play a leading role, with the other subordinate, or for the two to collaborate as equals. The history of the song with piano 'accompaniment' can show instances of all three types of combination, though songs in which the piano plays a dominant role are rare, and rarely successful. Just as the keyboard sonata 'with obbligato violin' was soon superseded as unsatisfactory, so songs for the piano with obbligato voice have generally pleased neither singers nor public.

The German Lied Although Schubert's songs may make demands on the pianist, the primacy of the vocal part is never in doubt. In some of Schubert's happiest inspirations, such as '*Gretchen am Spinnrade*' or '*Die Forelle*', the mood of the song is established and maintained by a single musical figure which remains constant throughout. In both of these songs there is a strong visual suggestion, the motion of the spinning-wheel and the leap and glitter of the trout. In '*Der Musensohn*' the persistent rhythm of the accompaniment is purely musical, the expression of an indefatigable youthful energy; and in many of Schubert's

Illustrations to Goethe's '*Heidenröslein*' (left) and '*Der Junggesell und der Mühlbach*' (right): woodcuts by Ludwig Richter, 1852.

greatest songs the piano sets the scene, not with any manifest 'imitation' of exterior circumstance, as in '*Gretchen am Spinnrade*', but by a figure that corresponds to a remoter musical 'stylization' of some feature in the outside world. The semiquaver figure in the bass of the piano part in '*Im Dorfe*', for example, is a musical stylization of dogs barking and rattling their chains.

Schubert will often open a song with the piano playing the part of accompanist in the humblest sense, and gradually develop the piano part so that it eventually stands on a level with the voice (as in '*Trock'ne Blumen*'). Occasionally voice and piano are absolutely complementary, with the piano if anything predominating (as in '*Der Leiermann*'). A rarer procedure is seen in '*Die liebe Farbe*', where the pianist's left hand follows the vocal line exactly, with simple harmonies, against a persistent pedal in the right hand. More commonly the pianist's right hand is engaged with a persistent figure, harmonized and punctuated by the left, which sketches out a skeleton of the vocal line (e.g. '*Liebesbotschaft*') The truth is that Schubert is endlessly resourceful, and among his six hundred-odd songs examples can be found of almost every kind of technique—from the primitive

accompaniment of '*Heidenröslein*' to the chamber melodrama of '*Die Stadt*' and the miniature symphonic poems of '*Der Wanderer*' and '*Die junge Nonne*'.

Unlike Schubert, Schumann was himself an accomplished pianist. Schumann often makes wonderfully imaginative use of simple repeated chord accompaniments, either slow (as in '*Die Lotosblume*') or faster ('*Er, der herrlichste von allen*') and occasionally really fast, as in '*Frühlingsnacht*' which has more than a hint of virtuosity. The broken-chord figurations of '*In der Fremde*', echoing the vocal line on the weak beat of the bar, is a purely pianistic conception, while the persistent pedal in the right hand, with the left hand harmonizing the vocal line ('*Mondnacht*'), recalls similar songs by Schubert.

In Schumann's *Dichterliebe* cycle there are also songs which recall Schubert, but the piano generally plays a more important role. '*Die Rose, die Lilie*' and '*Ich grolle nicht*' belong to the simplest category of accompaniments, but there are few things in Schubert comparable to the harmonic sophistication of '*Am leuchtenden Sommermorgen*', where the piano part carries on a dialogue with the voice half a beat later. This syncopated effect, also found in '*Hör' ich das Liedchen klingen*', is

Hugo Wolf.

used with exquisite effect in the postlude of the cycle, where the piano takes over from the voice, completing and summing up the interior narrative in a way that the voice cannot do. One of the songs in the *Dichterliebe* is a happy example of the piano actually playing the leading role. In '*Das ist ein Flöten und Geigen*' we are primarily conscious of the wedding-dance in the piano part, which would stand alone without the singer's comments and in fact continues for some twenty bars after the voice ceases. Among the most original of Schumann's devices in the *Dichterliebe* is the separation of voice and instrument, as in '*Ich hab' im Traum geweinet*', where the piano merely punctuates the voice, and the two are not heard together until the third and final stanza. Only the lower range of the instrument is used, and the effect of *pianissimo* staccato chords in a dotted rhythm is uniquely confidential and despairing.

Schumann was a writer as well as a composer and in many ways a more scrupulous and sensitive setter of poetry than Schubert. Brahms showed less discrimination in his choice of poems, and his songwriting was deeply affected by his devotion to German folksong. This often accounts for his treatment of the piano part as accompaniment merely, as in the popular '*Wiegenlied*', '*Der Schmied*' and '*Sonntag*'. Pianistically the finest, as well as the most characteristic, of Brahms's songs are marked by many cross accents, widely spread arpeggio or broken-chord figures, and a decided preference for the lower and darker range of the instrument: '*O wüsst' ich doch den Weg zurück*', '*Wie Melodien zieht es*', '*Der Tod, das ist die kühle Nacht*', '*Waldeinsamkeit*', '*Liebestreu*', '*Alte Liebe*' and '*Botschaft*' show one or more of these characteristics. In contrast to the predominantly dark-hued songs (to which the quasi-orchestral '*Vier Ernste Gesänge*' might be added) are the simple love-songs, frequently retrospective, like '*Wir wandelten*' and '*Schön war, das ich dir weihte*'; and the exquisitely playful '*Das Mädchen spricht*', '*Therese*' or '*Vergebliches Ständchen*', in which the piano plays a part quite as important as that of the voice.

In the songs of Hugo Wolf the piano plays a rather different role, comparable with that of the orchestra in Wagnerian music-drama. Unlike Schumann and Brahms, Wolf was not a concert pianist, and much of his piano-writing is quasi-orchestral. '*Geh', Geliebter, geh' jetzt!*' from the *Spanisches Liederbuch*, shows this well, as does Wolf's use of a vocal line which resembles a recitative against the richer texture of the piano part. Physical motion, as well as character and emotion, is often suggested by the piano in Wolf's songs. An obvious example is '*Zitronenfalter in April*', where the

butterfly's precocious struggles from its chrysalis and its flight, first faltering and then headlong, are depicted with a wonderful sureness of touch underlined by the *sempre pianissimo* marking.

The stock imagery and vocabulary of the German *Lied* is often employed by Wolf with unusual sophistication. Thus he sets Mörike's '*Jägerlied*' in 5/4 metre, and the musician-lover of the *Italienisches Liederbuch* is introduced half comically, while his violin playing in the postlude is shy and tentative. The opening song of the same volume, '*Auch kleine Dinge*', shows another favourite Wolfian device. The charm of 'little things' is, as it were, symbolized by the very close spacing of the score, in which the voice is characteristically given a line between the broken chords of the pianist's right hand and the high-lying left-hand part, almost all in the treble clef. Wolf often divides even the shortest songs into two or three sections without destroying the unity of the whole. The form of '*Schon streckt' ich aus die müden Glieder*', for instance, also from the *Italienisches Liederbuch*, resembles a miniature recitative and aria, though the piano is well to the fore throughout.

When Liszt, many of whose songs deserve to be more widely known, subdivides his songs, the result is sometimes less satisfactory—as in his settings of Herwegh's '*Ich möchte hingehn*' or Schiller's '*Der Hirt*'. He carries it off most successfully in the portraits of Lenau's '*Drei Zigeuner*', whose piano part is a miniature Hungarian Rhapsody—although this is not a common feature with Liszt, whose best songs have comparatively modest piano parts, often brilliantly imaginative

Poulenc: drawing by Jean Cocteau, 1924.

(Hugo's '*Comment disaient-ils?*' with its guitar imitations, Heine's '*Im Rhein, im schönen Strome*' with its rippling wave-accompaniment, the floating syncopations of Geibel's '*Die stille Wasserrose*').

The two composers who complete the history of the nineteenth-century German *Lied*, Gustav Mahler and Richard Strauss, were both masters of the orchestra, and the piano writing in their songs often clearly suggests a much larger ensemble of instruments. In some cases, as in Mahler's *Des Knaben Wunderhorn* settings, we have in fact two versions, both equally valid. Mahler's songs with a military setting ('*Wo die schönen Trompeten blasen*', '*Revelge*', '*Der Tamboursg'sell*') follow an imaginative line first exploited by Wolf, and they demand a pianist who is able to evoke orchestral colours and effects. On the other hand in '*Ich bin der Welt abhanden gekommen*' and '*Ich atmet' einen linden Duft*' (both Rückert) the individuality of the piano is perfectly exploited. The same is true of Strauss's '*Ständchen*' and '*Traum durch die Dämmerung*', and the early '*Morgen,*' which shows Strauss still under Liszt's spell.

French Song It was not until after the middle of the nineteenth century, and under the direct influence of Schubert and Schumann, that French composers started to write solo songs comparable in emotional scope and musical intention with the German *Lied*. Berlioz's orchestral *Nuits d'été* are the only exception; and both Gounod and Bizet continued to write songs which were either drawing-room pieces—and often excellent of their kind, like Gounod's '*Sérénade*'—or

else dramatic vignettes, like Bizet's '*Adieux de l'hôtesse arabe*'. Many of Gabriel Fauré's early songs were essentially salon pieces, with accompaniments that were well within the reach of any amateur ('*Dans les ruines d'une abbaye*', for instance). But Fauré's piano accompaniments become increasingly organic, richer not simply in notes but in harmonic implications. '*Nell*' is an admirable example, and the same opus number includes both '*Automne*' and '*Rencontre*', in which the Schumannesque outline of the piano part clothes unmistakably individual harmonic progressions. Broken and repeated-chord accompaniments recur, though in less obvious forms ('*Au Cimetière*'); and continue in the Verlaine settings of op. 58 ('*En Sourdine*', 'Green') and even in some of *La Bonne Chanson*—though by this time his piano parts are hardly more 'accompaniments' than Wolf's; and in the late song sequences there is all but complete parity between singer and players.

This parity had in fact been foreshadowed in the handful of songs written between 1865 and 1885 by Henri Duparc. The best of these are perhaps the first French *mélodies* to which similar standards may be applied to those established by the German *Lied*; and the absence, or transformation, of conventional accompaniment figures is an integral part of their quality. '*L'Invitation au voyage*' and '*Soupir*' are instances of a convention transformed; '*Lamento*' and '*Le Manoir de Rosamonde*' of convention superseded. Some twenty years later Debussy was to revolutionize not only the setting of French words themselves but the partnership between voice and piano. He recognized that French is a language with no strong tonic accent, and that the piano is not by nature a singing, but a percussive, instrument; and the character of his songs is determined by this double consideration. Many of the finest are fundamentally recitative duos for voice and instrument (*Chansons de Bilitis*, *Fêtes galantes* I and II), and this proved from his point of view an ideal solution. It remained strictly personal, however. Ravel's songs are more traditional in form than Debussy's, and the best of them go back to the form of the dramatic vignette (*Histoires naturelles* and *Chansons madécasses*) or the genre piece (*Cinq mélodies populaires grecques* and *Deux mélodies hébraïques*) with the piano providing what is still essentially accompaniment. The same is true of French song-writers of the next generation, notably Francis Poulenc, whose own personal style of pianism marks all his songs but never aspires to primacy over, or even to equality with, the voice. In the same way Olivier Messiaen's accompaniments, though often formally and texturally elaborate, remain essentially ancillary.

Des Knaben Wunderhorn: painting by Moritz von Schwind, *c*. 1860.

Grieg and his wife: detail of a painting by Peter Severin Kröyer.

Russian and Scandinavian Song In no other European country has folksong played so important a role in musical development as in Russia; and it is not always easy to be certain whether a given melody in a Russian work, even by a composer as recent as Stravinsky, is actually an existing folksong or an original theme composed in the spirit of folksong. The introduction of Italian opera in the middle of the eighteenth century affected the court and court circles only; and even eighty years later, the drawing-room songs of Glinka and Dargomyzhsky were imitated from French models, and were in fact called *romansy*. Like their French counterparts, these Russian songs for the most part have harp-like broken-chord or arpeggio accompaniments, and are designed for amateur players.

The composers of the Nationalist school were naturally not content with such Western models, and they turned to folksong in order to renew their musical language, and to poets whose imagery and subject-matter were drawn from contemporary Russian life. The greatest Russian song-writer, Mussorgsky, wrote his own texts for vignettes of Russian life, starting with *The Nursery* and including 'The Ragamuffin', 'The Orphan', 'The Seminarist', 'Darling Savishna'. In these the keyboard layout, the rhythms, the accents and the dynamic changes are all designed to heighten the miniature drama. The piano part in the ten settings of poems by Golenishchev-Kutuzov (*Sunless* and *Songs and Dances of Death*) is often more formal and more elaborate and enriches and modifies the vocal line rather than merely accompanying it.

Like Mussorgsky, Borodin also wrote the texts of some of his best songs, such as 'The Sleeping Princess', 'The Song of the Dark Forest', 'The Sea Princess' and 'The False Note'. In these the piano plays an important role, though always secondary to the vocal line, which it

enriches and ornaments. Rimsky-Korsakov's songs rely more heavily for their charm on piano accompaniments which are often harmonically rich, though never as pianistically elaborate as in some of Balakirev's, such as the superb 'Song of the Golden Fish' and the 'Song of Georgia', with its elaborate Oriental evocation in the piano part.

Of the Moscow composers, three were prolific song-writers. Tchaikovsky, characteristically, took his models from folksong and street song, from gypsy music, from church music and from the ballroom. Occasionally, as in 'If I'd only known', he combines a folk-lament with the mood of a modern psychological poem. In other Tchaikovsky songs (such as the gypsy 'Reconciliation' and the drawing-room 'At the ball') it is the delicacy or ingenuity of the piano part that makes the charm of the song, though it always remains subordinate to the voice.

This subordination was not always preserved by one of the other Moscow composers, Nicolai Medtner. Both he and the third of the trio, Rachmaninov, were in the first place fine pianists; and Medtner often takes for granted an ability to master, unobtrusively, a complex piano part such as only a concert pianist can hope to achieve. On the other hand his songs also include a considerable number in which the piano part is by no means too demanding, and these are among his best — 'Willow' and 'Whispering Nature', for example, from his op. 24. Both Medtner and Rachmaninov wrote *vocalises* for wordless voice and piano; but they chose their texts in general from rather different sources, Medtner often turning to Goethe and the German Romantic poets, and Rachmaninov mostly preferring the Russian poets of the nineteenth century. Unlike Medtner, Rachmaninov normally kept the piano part in his songs relatively simple, as in the best known ('Before my window', 'Lilacs' and 'To the children'). Even the more elaborate piano-writing in 'Spring Waters' is essentially subordinate to the vocal line.

The Scandinavian repertory of solo song with piano accompaniment is headed by Grieg, many of whose songs were written for his wife. They vary widely from sentimental drawing-room romances to intense, even powerful *Lieder*, like those of the *Haugtussa* cycle. If Grieg's songs are mostly of Norwegian inspiration, those of Sibelius are more general in their appeal, while Kilpinen has a large number of Swedish and German as well as Finnish texts among his seven hundred-odd songs. Scandinavian songs for the most part take after German, and more rarely Russian, models; but except in the case of Kilpinen, the model is Brahms rather than Wolf, and the piano remains secondary to the voice.

Michael Tippett in 1955 (left) and Benjamin Britten in the 1940s (below).
Opposite: Mozart with his sister Nannerl at the piano, and his father Leopold; a portrait of his mother on the wall: engraving after J. N. della Croce, *c.* 1780.

English Song As in France and Russia, the solo song with piano accompaniment only emerged in England from the comparatively primitive form of romance or ballad in the last quarter of the nineteenth century, and under the influence of the German *Lied*. The seventy-four songs which appeared under the title of *English Lyrics* in twelve sets between 1880 and the 1920s (when the last two sets were published posthumously) give Hubert Parry the right to be considered the prime mover in this renaissance of English song. He was seconded, as in more general musical matters, by Charles Villiers Stanford, whose six cycles of Irish songs appeared between 1901–8. The more gifted Edward Elgar and Frank Bridge wrote fewer songs (Elgar's best have orchestral accompaniment); and Delius characteristically alternated English texts (Tennyson and Shelley) with Björnson, Jacobsen, Verlaine and Nietzsche.

None of these composers was revolutionary in his handling of voice and piano; nor do any of them demand virtuosity of the pianist. The consciously plain and straightforward nature of many of their songs seems to denote a certain emotional limitation—certainly a woodenness of expression if we compare them with the best German, French and Russian work. The piano writing in John Ireland's songs is freer and more imaginative, and Ivor Gurney and George Butterworth approach more nearly to the ideal of the unified *Lied*; but it was not until Benjamin Britten wrote his *Seven Sonnets of Michelangelo* in 1940 that England produced songs comparable in both musical and emotional quality with the best of those produced elsewhere in Europe. *The Holy Sonnets of John Donne* and *Winter Words*, which followed, show the same very close relationship between voice and instrument, which together form an indivisible unity.

Equally remarkable are Michael Tippett's two song-cycles, *Boyhood's End* and *The Heart's Assurance*. As his piano sonatas were later to confirm, Tippett's work for the keyboard in these songs was potentially, and often indeed actually, the more original. Britten's relationship to the musical past, always deeper and more pervasive than Tippett's, is nowhere more evident than in his songs, where the choice of texts (Italian, French and German) as well as the music itself reveal him as a conscious heir of the European, not merely the English, tradition. Perhaps it is not too fanciful, at the same time, to see in Tippett's choice of W. H. Hudson's poems, based on a youth spent in South America, a forward-looking, expansive, 'New World' quality matched by the affinity sometimes shown in his earlier music with Aaron Copland.

Duet and Duo

The very conception of two players sitting at one keyboard is social rather than musical; and it belongs essentially to the Vienna of the Biedermeier period, when the Emperor Franz was concerned that his subjects should be good, dull and domestic—*brauchbare Menschen*, as he called them. Domestic music-making had the advantage not only of harmlessly employing any surplus energies that might remain after a proper day's work as a *Staatsbeamter*, but also of avoiding public congregation (inseparable in the official mind from discussion of public events and possibly unfavourable comment on governmental action).

Musically, piano duets—four hands on one keyboard—are wholly delightful for the performers, who can achieve a quite extraordinary unity of taste and perception and, of course, a richness of texture beyond the reach of a single pair of hands; indeed, much of the piano-duet repertory consists of transcriptions of orchestral music. The listener's experience may, unfortunately, be different—exposed as he is to a duplication of the instrument's faults or weaknesses: the mechanical clatter, and the elaboration of figuration intended to disguise the fact that the piano is after all a percussion instrument unable to sustain, let alone swell and diminish, a note without losing volume. At the same time the advantages of the piano as a solo instrument are to a great extent lost, or at least obscured, in piano duets: two minds may come to think alike, and two sensibilities even come to a mutual understanding, but total freedom and independence are impossible. In music for two pianos (piano duo), on the other hand, there is an important spatial element: and the effects to be obtained by antiphonal writing—question and answer, statement and variation, contrast on the one hand and unity in diversity on the other—are not only greater in fact, but seem to the listener greater still.

If most of the four-hand repertory, whether for one or two instruments, is fundamentally domestic and designed for gifted amateurs, there is nonetheless plenty to explore and to admire. Mozart wrote six keyboard sonatas for the combination—K. 19d, K. 357, K. 358, K. 381, K. 497 (in F major, the finest of all) and K. 521—as well as an *Andante* and five variations (K. 501) which distil the very essence of one side of his complex musical personality.

The domestic, Biedermeier character of the medium is shown to greatest advantage in Schubert's dances and marches (echoes of grand public events of the day filtered for the drawing-room); while the best of Schubert's Variations, the *Divertissement à la hongroise*, the *Allegro* called 'Lebensstürme' and above all the *Fantasy* in F minor, transcend the limitations of the medium, while remaining in the drawing-room's realm. There is also a delightful early Chopin *Rondo* for two pianos (originally written for piano solo), and a *Concerto pathétique* by Liszt that lives well up to its name.

Schumann contributed a considerable number of thoroughly Biedermeier dance-pieces, as well as a set of genre-pictures (*Bilder aus Osten*) and a convincing two-piano version of an *Andante and Variations* originally conceived for two pianos, two cellos and horn. Mendelssohn, Saint-Saëns (a set of amusing 'Beethoven' Variations as well as the *Carnaval des animaux*), Bizet, Rachmaninov, Debussy (*En blanc et noir*), Ravel, Poulenc, and in our own time Lutoslawski, have all contributed to this small repertory.

THE PIANO IN THE TWENTIETH CENTURY

Opposite: *Le piano*: painting by Francis Tailleux, 1947.

Even now, well into the last quarter of the twentieth century, much of the music written during the century's early years remains bewilderingly 'new', and the piano music of the period in particular is scarcely more approachable today—except by a minority of mainly professional performers—than it was when it first appeared. This strange state of affairs cannot be due only to the somewhat daunting technical aspect of many recent additions to the keyboard repertoire; for the fact that most of the larger pieces of the later Classical and Romantic eras are still more difficult technically is not in itself a deterrent even to spare-time pianists of only limited skills. The pleasure to be had from having a go at such well-known virtuoso pieces, however haltingly, is both real and intensely rewarding.

If this has ceased to be true of contemporary music, it is obvious that there must have been some radical changes over the last seventy-five years or so—and that these changes have concerned not only the use or mis-use that composers have made of the piano as an instrument, but also the development of an increasingly diverse collection of musical languages or idioms. Nevertheless, once the problems caused by lack of a common language can be put in perspective, many of these changes can be seen as extensions of earlier techniques—in some cases relating to musical styles prevalent long before the invention of the piano.

One of the more alarming results of the stylistic diversity evolved in recent years has been the increasing lack of a written means of communication understood by all; hence the forbidding *look* of much of today's music, which often requires as many words of explanation as there are notes in the score. But this is less the fault of individual composers than of a system of notation not designed to cope with extremes.

Take the question of sharps and flats (accidentals). In the days when every piece of music was composed throughout in a particular key, sharps and flats were needed only to indicate keys shifts, or modulations, to harmonic areas not already defined by an initial key signature. But as key changes became more and more frequent, so too did the number of necessary accidentals, until eventually—as composers began to dispense altogether with any notion of 'key'—they became an essential adjunct to every note. This was of course an inevitable outcome of the curiously inadequate system of Western musical notation, which proposes only seven pitch names (A, B, C, D, E, F, G) for the twelve-note chromatic scale; but of the various attempts made to eliminate its ambiguities, none has proved generally acceptable—though several have been interesting experiments in themselves. One of these—an invention of the Belgian composer, Henri Pousseur (b. 1929)—was a system without sharps, in which all black notes (♩) were 'naturals', and all white notes (♩) flats (see **Ex. 1** from his *Caractères* for piano); the disadvantage of this idea was that it could be used only by composers who did not wish to specify precise rhythmic durations (since traditionally, ♩ means twice the duration of ♩).

Apart from the profusion of accidentals in modern pieces using more conventional notation, many piano scores are additionally complicated by the need to include an increasing amount of unpredictable information—some of it concerning details of expression, some purely practical. An enormous number of instructions of various kinds may be needed to express not only a range of dynamics extending from, say, *pppp* to *ffff*, but also a comparable range of various kinds of touch and accentuation (signs for which are even now not standardized, often needing verbal prefaces to explain them). Add to these the many instructions required to indicate the various uses of two, sometimes three pedals, as well as indications for clusters of notes to be played (or silently depressed) with palm, fist or forearm, and this imaginary score begins to assume an appearance of such complexity as to deter all but the most courageous (or patient) even from starting to decipher it, let alone beginning to discover what kind

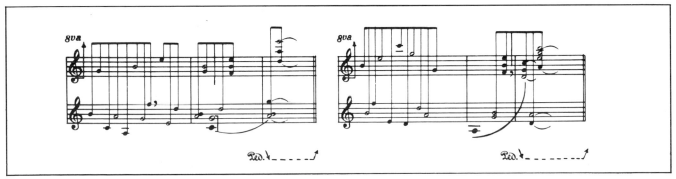

Ex. 1: From *Caractères* by Henri Pousseur.

of music might eventually be coaxed from it. Nor have what might be called extra-keyboard activities yet been taken into account: 'playing' on the frame or the strings of the piano with nails, finger-tips or hands, or with any number of different objects—for which still more symbols must be found.

It was perhaps the complex visual aspect of many contemporary scores that, in 1958, led the visual artist, stage-designer and composer Sylvano Bussotti (b. 1931) to produce some almost wholly pictorial scores—artist's views of the expressive details with the notes left out

near obsolete pastime. It is possible to gain an impression of even the most virtuoso pieces of the nineteenth-century repertoire by picking out the more easily playable sections and skipping over the rest; in the case of music that has ceased to depend on recognizable tunes associated with particular rhythmic shapes, there *are* no readily playable bits. To make matters worse, rhythmic patterns are often not 'countable' in relation to a regular metre—or indeed, to a constant rhythmic unit of any kind—and bar-lines have tended to become indications of phrasing rather than of measurement.

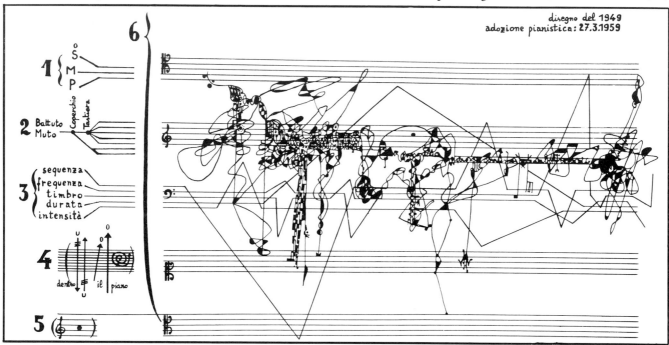

Ex. 2: *Piano piece for David Tudor ♯ 4* from *Pièces de chair II* by Sylvano Bussotti.

(Ex. 2); this exuberant comment on some of the more extreme kinds of over-notated music was in fact an early example of a general trend in the late 1950s which became known as *graphic notation* (see also Exs. 9 and 11). Seeking similar ends but with different means, the American John Cage (b. 1912) and the Englishman Cornelius Cardew (b. 1936) are amongst those who have in certain instances offered only verbal suggestions—the instructions without the music (Ex. 3). But of course such 'pieces', whether presented in the form of pictures or words, are really only starting points for improvisation; they do not of themselves add anything new to developments in instrumental technique.

The seeming unapproachability of much recent piano music is due not only to its novel presentation, but also to the fact that (and the two are certainly related) the pleasurable occupation of sight-reading has become a

The would-be sight-reader is thus deprived of his final refuge—that of striving to keep the continuity of the metrical beat while sketching in whatever possible of the rest.

But all is not yet lost. It is said that history always repeats itself; and while this is a generalization too broad to be more than broadly useful, there are in fact a number of ways in which composers of the present have looked to the past as a starting point for the future. To trace the chosen routes into the past of some of the most influential of them may be one of the best ways to dispel the apparent mystery of the present—and here the pianist has a head start: since there is no composer of importance who has not written at least one work for the piano, a complete survey of twentieth-century trends is literally within reach of his fingers (even though, in some instances, he may wish he had more than ten!).

The End of the Late-Romantic Tradition

At the beginning of the new muscial era, roughly coinciding with the turn of the century, the steady progress of history was as yet scarcely ruffled, and two of the composers who were later to be instrumental in disrupting its continuity—Arnold Schoenberg and Alban Berg—were initially among those least at odds with nineteenth-century tradition. As Viennese, they were after all natural heirs to the music of a century largely dominated by the work of Austro-German composers.

Unlike them, and prompted by a growing distaste for all things German, the Frenchman Claude Debussy had already been forced to find ways to escape this influence if he were not to be swamped by it. And since he was unhampered by any strong national tradition of his own, he was able to develop a keyboard style less imbued with echoes of the Classical past than that of any other composer of his time: in the history of twentieth-century piano music, there was to be nothing so astonishingly 'new' in every respect as Debussy's mature piano pieces until the later keyboard works of Stockhausen appeared in the 1960s.

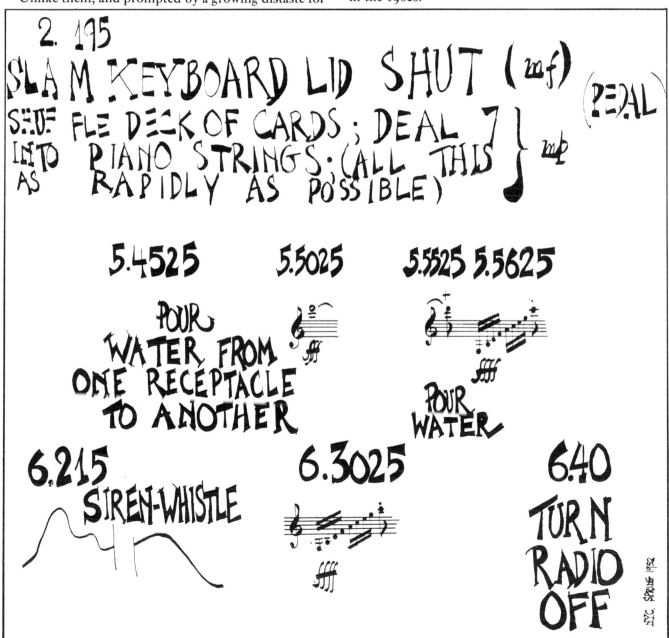

Ex. 3: From *Water Music* by John Cage (1952).

Alban Berg: painting by Arnold Schoenberg, 1910.

Twelve years older than Schoenberg, Debussy had already begun to effect a minor revolution in piano playing before the Viennese wrote their early pieces. His whole-tone harmonies, developed as an antidote to Austro-German chromaticism, enabled him to super-impose sequences of undamped sounds without risking the dissonance of clashing semitones, and his determination to avoid the Wagnerian implications of motivic writing led him to explore a quite unprecedented range of non-percussive (his own playing was said to suggest a 'piano without hammers'), 'impressionistic' colours. Here, for the first time, the sustaining pedal became a *harmonic* implement, essential for the sustaining of widely spaced chords.

But if Debussy in his late piano music owed little to the Classical or early-Romantic past (except, in certain instances of keyboard layout, to Chopin), the young Alban Berg (1885–1935) must surely have been impressed by Debussy's works for the instrument by the time he came to write his op. 1 sonata in B minor, begun when Berg was twenty-one and finished two years later in 1908. Although Berg's sonata is pianistically much closer to the works of Brahms and Liszt than to those of the Frenchman, his use of successions of intervals is obviously influenced by Debussy's whole-tone harmonies—even though Berg's major thirds take the form of melodic motifs for development in the Classical manner. And it is here that the difference between Debussy and his Viennese contemporaries really begins to make itself felt: for it was Berg's effortless acceptance of Classical development techniques that made it possible for him to adapt the pianistic conventions of nineteenth-century virtuoso writing to his new harmonic thinking, and to pursue the tradition of filled-out chordal textures and octave doublings in a manner that would hardly have surprised a composer like Schumann.

At about this time, Berg's teacher Arnold Schoenberg (1874–1951) was writing his *Three Piano Pieces* op. 11—pieces which, in retrospect, can be seen to trace the development of piano music from past, to present, to future. The second piece reflects the past both in its recapitulatory form (now linked to a tonality rather than to a key, strictly speaking) and in its use of extended themes and sequential passage-work—eventually arriving at an emotional climax in the grand manner. The first piece represents the present (of 1908) preoccupation with omnipresent motifs, and there is only the merest hint of an enveloping tonality—although there is still just enough evidence of recapitulation to sustain its link with the past of the second piece.

Arnold Schoenberg (below) with Alban Berg (bottom).

Nevertheless, pianistically speaking, Schoenberg is already stepping into the future. This piece contains the first known use of sympathetic string vibrations (or 'harmonics') in a modern piano work, and it remains the only instance until well after the Second World War of a European composer experimenting with piano sounds not produced as a direct result of hammers striking the strings.

But it is the third piece of Schoenberg's op. 11 which sets the scene for a future still more than thirty years ahead in the first piano sonata of the young Pierre Boulez. Here, all Classical aids to coherent musical development—themes, motifs, recapitulation—are set aside; not only is there no hint of recapitulation (beyond the sequential structure of the opening bars) but scarcely any repetition of any kind. Most drastic of all, perhaps, there is no consistent element: in addition to frequent changes of tempo, the changes of register, texture and dynamics make it seem as if each few bars could have come from a different piece, so that its ideas seem to be held together purely by free association.

Quite apart from its revolutionary compositional design, this piece was to effect changes in piano technique just as radical in their way as those brought about by Debussy. In Schoenberg's case, these changes came about not as a result of any difference in approach so fundamental as Debussy's 'piano without hammers', but because so many different techniques were for the first time pressed into service in quick succession. In this respect, the *Six Little Pieces* op. 19, composed three years later, form an ideal introduction to the third piece of op. 11, since their miniature forms pose similar problems but without similarly excruciating difficulties: they represent a rare example of piano music dating from this period that can be easily read and enjoyed by pianists of no great technical ability.

In spite of the extraordinarily prophetic suggestions they contain, the op. 11 pieces are very much *of* their time. They not only reflect the growing awareness among European artists in general of being on the threshold of a fresh century but, for all their newness, they continue to expand the dramatic intensity so characteristic of the late-Romantic movement. Even in the last piece, the individual musical gestures still clearly belong to this tradition; it is only their juxtaposition that makes them seem so violently destructive of it.

The first two decades of the new century—roughly, up to the end of the First World War—would seem to have been musically characterized by three main trends, two of which are exemplified by Schoenberg's early piano pieces: namely, a continuing use of the grand

Sergei Prokofiev in 1943.

gestures and virtuoso display typical of nineteenth-century piano music, now expressed within the extended tonality of a rapidly expanding harmonic language; and a parallel, if opposite, move to clean up the overladen textures and curb the more overt excesses of this fading Romanticism by restricting it to smaller forms and to the fewest possible number of notes. That these parallel trends were by no means confined to the Viennese can be seen, for instance, in the work of a technically more conventional composer like Prokofiev who, during this period, was using large forms and typically virtuoso keyboard figurations for his sonatas, while exploring more concentrated and often more probingly hard-edged ideas in his small-scale *Sarcasms* and *Visions Fugitives*.

The third trend characteristic of this period would seem to have been that unwittingly initiated by Debussy. At any rate, Debussy's determination to express himself in terms of specifically French musical thought is evidently reflected in the work of composers on the fringes of Europe—composers similarly determined to retrieve their own national identities through drawing upon various aspects of their particular folk cultures. Most notable of these were Albéniz, Granados and Falla in Spain, who collectively succeeded in breathing new life into the Romantic tradition through the freshness of their dance rhythms and brightly coloured, folk-influenced harmonies. And they in turn were to influence Debussy, particularly with their ideas on rhythm, just as his impressionistic harmonies had already begun to affect them. Without a living folk tradition on which to build, other far-flung European composers born during the twenty years or so before the turn of the century were nevertheless similarly preoccupied with finding independent routes into the new era. Although they may have had less influence on mainstream musical developments and were not concerned to expand the bounds of keyboard technique *per se*, such composers as the Norwegian Fartein Valen (1887–1952), the Dutchman Willem Pijper (1894–1947), the composers of the group '*Les Six*' (Auric, Durey, Honegger, Milhaud, Poulenc and Tailleferre) in France, and John Ireland (1879–1962) and Frank Bridge (1879–1941) in England, made significant contributions to the fast-expanding and increasingly varied repertoire of music for piano composed during the prolific early years of the century.

From quite early on in the new century—and certainly by the end of the First World War—it becomes evident that music in general, and piano music in particular, had begun to move outwards like the spokes of a wheel from the hub of mid-nineteenth-century Central-European tradition. Obvious too, having once reached the limits represented by the rim of this imaginary wheel, that new decisions were both inevitable and urgent if future developments were not to be confined to describing an unending path around its circumference. To conclude the metaphor, it then began to seem that there were connecting links between the hub of tradition and the rim of modernity that might profitably be explored as a means of strengthening the exploratory spokes. Once again, it was the tradition-conscious Schoenberg who was to initiate this move towards consolidation—just as, paradoxically, he had been the first and indeed the only composer to anticipate a more distant future in the last of his three op. 11 pieces.

Setting out now to achieve a harmonic coherence which this piece, for all its confidence, had not and could not have envisaged, Schoenberg at first retraced his steps in order to pursue the more controlled motivic writing propounded in the opening piece of the three. As a consequence, the first four of the *Five Pieces* op. 23, composed between 1920 and 1923, are noticeably more

Manuel de Falla: painting by I. Zuloaga, 1921.

conventional in keyboard layout: here the densely packed motivic arguments are shaped alternately into contrapuntal strands with a strong, almost Bachian awareness of voice-leading, and as melodic lines embedded in their own ornate reflections. With the final piece of op. 23, Schoenberg unveils his long-planned method for bringing order to the arbitrary structure of atonal harmony, which had by then ceased even to pay lip-service to the sorts of controls previously exercised by the diatonic system of major and minor keys. But so smooth is the transition between the free motivic organization of the first four pieces and the systematically organized 'composition with twelve notes related only to one another' of the last, that the difference in musical character is scarcely perceptible. From the pianist's point of view, however, this piece had another significance—for with it would have come the final realization that a mastery of predictable chord-shapes based on combinations of major and minor thirds could no longer form the sole basis of technical accomplishment, and that practice of symmetrical patterns alone would not enable him to keep pace with the new age.

The Beginning of Neo-Classicism

By now the die was cast, and as if to compensate for an apparent lack of symmetry on the one hand, Schoenberg fell back on a different kind of predictability on the other: his rhythms, until now fluid and often only loosely attached to unstressed bar lines, are in the final piece of op. 23 pinned to the simplest and best known of all dance metres—that of the waltz. And it is first and foremost through the symmetrically recurring emphases of the waltz rhythm that the seemingly dissonant intervals and asymmetrical chording of its harmonic structure begin to make sense.

That this neo-classical slant was a quite conscious move on Schoenberg's part is confirmed by another set of piano pieces completed a year later. The three dance movements from the *Suite* op. 25 are characterized not only by their unmistakable rhythmic outlines, but also by formal designs established a couple of centuries earlier: thus the *Gavotte* encloses a *Musette*, the *Menuet* a *trio*. Only in the final *Gigue* does the characteristic triple rhythm become blurred with cross accents, presaging the methods of development-by-distortion which are so much in vogue among younger composers today.

But it is not only rhythm and form which link Schoenberg's music of this period with that of a relatively distant past. In spite of a continued use of busy counterpoints and of rich chording, even here more reminiscent of late-Romantic piano music, the noticeably more buoyant textures of the *Suite* are evidently part of a conscious attempt to lighten and aerate the over-dense expressionism of the recent past—just as the invention of the twelve-note system had been prompted by a will to clean up the over-sweet chromaticism of turn-of-the-century harmony.

Arriving at a similar position by a quite different route—in his case initially attracted by the rhythmic precision and vigour of early jazz and, in particular, of ragtime—Igor Stravinsky (1882–1971) was much less restrained in his joyful plunderings from the vocabulary of the early Viennese composers, notably that of Haydn. His 1924 piano sonata avoids pastiche through the sheer zest of an invention that strings together arpeggio figurations based on triadic chords, Alberti bass accompaniments, and singable tunes often embellished with trills and ornamental passage-work—giving the whole piece a poised detachment that would seem to have by-passed any trace of nineteenth-century influence. And even though he widens the compass of the 1925 *Serenade* to allow for more characteristically wide-spaced chords and for octave doublings with a touch of

157

A photograph of Stravinsky in 1929 (below) and a drawing
of him *c.* 1910 (bottom right).
Bottom left: 'Stravinsky plays me *The Rite of Spring*':
drawing by Jean Cocteau.

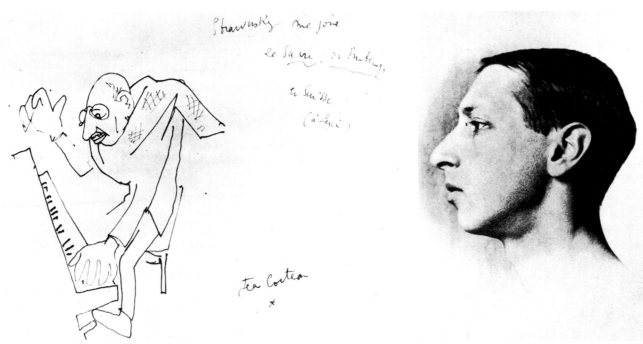

Anton Webern.

the grand manner, the muscial language seems to retreat still further into the remoter reaches of time.

It is fascinating that the two most prominent figures in this neo-classical movement — Schoenberg and Stravinsky — should not only have been such opposites (musically, historically and personally), but that they should have arrived at such similar standpoints, and in each case through the medium of their piano music, at precisely the same time. In spite of the fact that their points of departure were so different, their motivation was of course broadly the same: the need to fine down and to reassess the basic elements of their music in relation to a post-war era no longer overshadowed by the nineteenth century.

Webern and the Pre-Classical Influence

There remains one enormously important figure among the European composers of this generation — important not least in connection with the development of keyboard music. Even though Anton Webern (1883–1945) himself acknowledged only one brief piano piece among his mature works, this one can safely be said to have had a greater influence on music written for the instrument in the second half of the twentieth century than any other single piece by any composer.

Unlike Schoenberg's other famous pupil, Alban Berg, Webern appears to have been distinctly ill at ease with the prevailing musical language of his youth. Two posthumously published pieces, dating from 1906, show him floundering at uncharacteristic length amidst an oddly assorted mixture of diatonic, chromatic and even whole-tone harmonies, leaning heavily on sequential writing and on textures thickened by octave doublings — and this from a composer whose music was so soon, and for the rest of his life, to become notable for the absence of those very traits.

Composers as well able as Schoenberg and Stravinsky to adapt themselves to their turn-of-the-century surroundings had, by the early 1920s, already begun to take stock and to retreat from the large forms and resplendent textures of their previous works; so it is hardly surprising that Webern, the turn-of-the-century misfit, should have been forced to take similar steps both sooner and to a much more radical extent. For it was only when he discovered his inner musical motivation to be entirely unrelated to large-scale gestures of any kind that he was able to find his way out of the impasse represented by the 1906 piano pieces. Indeed, it would seem that he may even have been indirectly responsible for the upsurge of neo-Classicism, although he himself took no part in its development; even as early as 1909 he

was writing music that Schoenberg described as 'a novel expressed in a single sigh' and of which Webern himself later said, 'I had the feeling that when all twelve notes [of the chromatic scale] had been sounded, the piece was over'.

From this moment on, Webern's problem was no longer that of paring down his means of expression, but of how to continue to compose at all within the extreme restrictions of the limits he had set himself. And it was this new and unexpected problem that led him to look back through history towards the early Flemish composers he had studied as a young man, and whose musical outlook now seemed to accord more closely with his own than that of any others during the intervening centuries.

When Webern came to write his Variations op. 27, it was already 1936, and he was nearing the end of his composing career, with only five more works to come before his tragic accidental death nine years later at the hands of an American sentry. By then, the carefully constructed canons and mirror images of his models seem to have become a natural reflection of his own esteem for symmetry. And it is Webern's way of using symmetry as a means of abstract, quasi-architectural expression, striving for the most perfect distribution of the fewest possible number of sounds in relation to the surrounding silences, that makes his late works so startlingly different from anything written by his contemporaries. Only the Italian Luigi Dallapiccola (1904–75), twenty years younger than Webern, was to tread a roughly comparable path into the past — and the canonic forms of his *Quaderno Musicale di Annalibera* clearly owe much to Webern, as do the admitted medieval influences in the music of Peter Maxwell Davies, the English composer born in 1934.

Paul Hindemith.

The Variations are austere even by Webern's standards: in the context of the piano repertoire as a whole, they are unique in their economy and in the quality of musical concentration as well as in the degree of physical dexterity they demand of the player. There is no other piece so pianistic in conception, so unthinkable in any other context, which yet makes so few concessions to the nature of the instrument. For Webern was the first composer since Bach to force a keyboard instrument to overcome its inability to sustain and to differentiate between melodic lines—in Webern's case, lines so wide-ranging in register and so devoid of camouflaging decoration that even to attempt to reconstruct them in performance seems foolhardy. Certainly, in a piece such as this, entirely without surface gloss, virtuosity of the more blustering kind counts for nothing; this music has to be rebuilt from the inside, each tiny two or three-note cell carefully balanced in relation both to the next and to the regular, though often silent, pulse of its metrical background. In spite of the obvious unsingability of Webern's wide-stretched lines, they are as much 'singing' music as the vocal lines of his songs are instrumental: like the works of composers six centuries earlier, Webern's style is essentially the same whether he is writing for voices or for instruments.

Hindemith and the Neo-Bach Movement

Whether influenced by Webern in this respect or not, Paul Hindemith (1895–1963) was another composer whose music came to depend more and more on linear writing towards the latter part of his life—though in his case the model was Bach's chord based part-writing, rather than the weaving of independent lines proposed by the early contrapuntalists.

Hindemith's youthful music tended to be a bit heavy-handed, sometimes rather ponderously humorous in the Germanic manner and, in the less successful works, overweighted with unresolved dissonances. Like others, he was soon prompted to find ways of bringing order into increasing harmonic chaos and, recognizing that the evidence of tonality in his music far outweighed its modernistic chromatic elements, he gradually began to build on the undeniably logical relationships (with octaves, fifths and fourths as the dominant intervals) of the natural harmonic series.

But first, like Stravinsky, he had fallen under the spell of jazz in the 1920s, and then that of the eighteenth-century Viennese composers—in his case Mozart rather than Haydn; it was not until the last and by far the most substantial of his works for piano that he was able to finalize the organization of his new tonality. *Ludus Tonalis: Studies in Counterpoint, Tonal Organisation and Piano Playing* (completed in 1942) proposed a system of harmonic priorities that was to have a profound if not altogether beneficial effect on a whole generation of composers born during the first two decades of the century, particularly in Germany and England. Indeed, for twenty years or so, Hindemith's system of harmonies based on fourths and fifths was to provide the only methodical alternative to the twelve-note chromaticism of the Viennese—perhaps because, apart from its inherent attraction, Hindemith was, after Schoenberg, the only really visionary teacher of our times.

At any rate, he brought back a style of keyboard playing based on athletic rhythms and on voice-leading (*Ludus Tonalis*, as its title suggests, is a series of fugues and interludes, one for each degree of the chromatic scale) which, like that of J. S. Bach, is not specifically dependent on instrumental colour. Shostakovich's *Preludes and Fugues* (1950), composed in memory of Bach, obviously belong to this category, and there are many other examples of clean-lined, quasi-tonal writing in the piano works of composers of such different stylistic persuasions as Michael Tippett (b. 1905), Lennox Berkeley (b. 1903) and Peter Racine Fricker (b. 1920) in England, Boris Blacher (b. 1903) and Wolfgang Fortner (b. 1907) in Germany.

Charles Ives.

The Neo-Folk Influence

At about the same time that Debussy was trying to obliterate all traces of the then prevailing Austro-German influence, Charles Ives (twelve years younger than Debussy and an exact contemporary of Schoenberg) was equally determined to discover what it meant to be a specifically American composer. Like Debussy, Ives (1874–1954) was not burdened by the weight of any national Classical tradition, and in his case there was the added advantage of a slate almost entirely unmarked by any of the European giants of the nineteenth century. So while Debussy's search for a national identity involved a jettisoning of harmonic clichés, clichés of all kinds were the very grist to Ives's mill: he cribbed as freely from the Classical past as from the sounds of the present (hymn tunes, tavern choruses, marching songs, folk music, jazz, and even street noises) to forge his own highly original vision of the future.

Perhaps the most original aspect of this vision was its very inclusiveness: for such diverse elements—imagined simultaneously, at various levels of awareness—produced no coherent harmony, but only strands of different harmonies; no single rhythmical pulse, but layers of many different metres. Ives's task as a composer was then to select from this imagined cacophony, sometimes allowing one element to take control for a time, but more often juggling with mixtures of several elements—keeping each intact with subtle reminders of its continuing presence.

In his efforts to produce a playable (or even not strictly playable) impression of his extraordinary

musical visions, Ives writes for the piano as though there were no limit to the number of notes that can be sounded simultaneously by two hands; only occasionally does he admit defeat by suggesting a second player (Ex. 4). Moreover, because there is not always any consistent metre, his rhythms are often unbarred, counted in

Ex. 4: From the *Three Page Sonata* by Charles Ives.

Béla Bartók and (below) Bartók (in centre of photograph)
on a folksong collecting tour of Anatolia in 1937.

whatever unit happens to dominate at the time—and it
is this continual switching of rhythmic emphasis,
together with the harmonic contrasts obtaining from so
many diverse sources, that makes a lot of his piano music
sound like a stylistic hybrid of sophisticated virtuosity
and bar-pianist vamp.

While Ives was carving out an American tradition
from the 'folk' sounds of urban life, Béla Bartók
(1881–1945) was scouring the Hungarian countryside,
recording for posterity the remnants of an unusually
rich rural musical culture. As a composer, he was to be
amply repaid for his ethnological dedication, since it was
the haunting shapes of these often complex melodies
and, in particular, their asymmetrical metres, that were
later to form the foundation of his own musical vocabulary.

A professional pianist himself, Bartók's contribution
to the piano repertoire is not only larger and more varied
than that of any other twentieth-century composer: it
also develops a use of the instrument that was to lead to
changes in piano technique even more radical in their
way than those brought about by Debussy. In fact,
Bartók was certainly influenced initially by the older
composer's impressionistic harmonies and use of the
sustaining pedal; but while Debussy's keyboard belonged to a piano without hammers, often sounding like the
soft-spoken vibraphone, Bartók used his to emphasize
the percussive nature of an instrument which, in his
hands, seems to have closer affinities with the hard-
edged xylophone or with the jangling tones of the
Hungarian cimbalom.

Bartók wrote a number of piano pieces during his
childhood and early teens, culminating in a sonata
composed at the age of sixteen. The bulk of his output
for the next decade was to be music for or with piano—
including, in 1908, the first of his sets of children's
pieces based on peasant tunes. But it was not until 1911
that he wrote the piece that was first to expose the
startling novelty of his approach—although the full
impact of his *Allegro Barbaro* was not felt until its first
public performance ten years later, by which time
Stravinsky's *The Rite of Spring* (completed in 1913) had
taken some of the sting out of earthy ostinatos of this
kind.

The *Allegro Barbaro* was followed by the *Suite* op. 14,
the *Three Studies* op. 18, and by the 1926 sonata: works
which together show the range and variety of Bartók's
middle-period keyboard virtuosity as well as his
increasingly inventive use of simple diatonic chords
(often with the addition of major seconds) placed in
unusual juxtapositions and stressing the ambivalence of

Olivier Messiaen.

the relationship between major and minor tonalities. But he also wrote a host of shorter, technically much simpler pieces, at a time when composers in general were not greatly concerned to make their music accessible either to children or to performers of limited technical ability; some of his best and most characteristic music is to be found in *Mikrokosmos, 153 progressive pieces for piano*, which he began writing in 1926 for his young son Peter, and to which he continued to add right up to the outbreak of war in 1939. With these pieces, Bartók drew much needed attention to a side of the repertoire neglected since Schumann.

But however great the impact of Bartók's music, his 'linguistic' originality was of a kind not directly applicable to the work of others: because of its national flavour, it was as impossible to adopt Bartók's harmonic

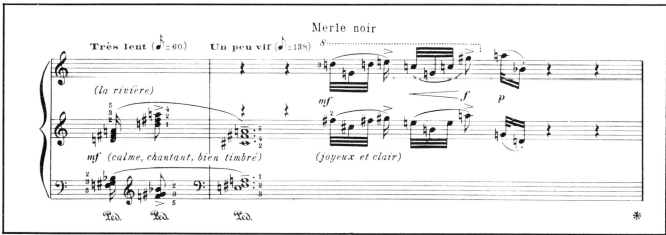

Ex. 5: From Messiaen's *Catalogue d'oiseaux*.

style without being Hungarian-born as it was to follow in the footsteps of Debussy without being French; only Ives, the urban American, has been able to exert a more cosmopolitan influence in this respect. On the other hand, Bartók's technical innovations have had a profound effect — in his piano music, quite as far-reaching as those of Debussy.

The influence of both composers can be seen in the piano music of Olivier Messiaen (b. 1908), much of whose character derives from contrasting the 'hammered' and the 'hammerless' qualities of the instrument. Like Bartók, Messiaen has been a lifelong collector, in his case of birdsong, and his careful cataloguing of bird-melodies gathered from around the world can certainly be compared in scope and endeavour with Bartók's notating of Hungarian folksongs. Just as Ives was fascinated with the man-made mixtures of the sounds of urban life, Messiaen the devout Roman

Catholic takes a similar delight in the interplay of natural, God-created sounds of all kinds — in his case set against the timelessness of light and colour suggested by recurring chord patterns whose harmonic structure often seems to reflect the devotional overtones of the organ (**Ex. 5**).

It is however the more abstract, technical qualities of Messiaen's music that have made him such an important link between the old world and the new — between those composers whose life's work was largely complete before the Second World War, and those whose composing careers began in the late 1940s and after. And this technical influence stems from the evolution of a 'system' for the ordered development of rhythm that was to prove every bit as important in its way as Schoenberg's 'system' for the control of twelve-note harmony.

Like Debussy, who was lastingly affected by his visit

Ex. 6: *The Banshee* by Henry Cowell.

as a young man to the Javanese exhibition in Paris, Messiaen had been deeply impressed early in his career by the music of the Far East—and not only, like Debussy, by its exotic timbres, but also particularly by its complex rhythmic structures. This in turn led him to explore other traditional sources, such as the metrical patterns of Greek verse; and then, noting the connection between repeating rhythmic 'series' of this kind and the recurring twelve-note pitch rows of the contemporary Viennese composers, he began to test the possibility of treating rhythmic patterns in the same way as melodic ones—by expanding or contracting them without altering their relative durations, stating them backwards as well as forwards, and even, at one stage,

experimenting with a 'scale' of twelve durations running parallel with the pitch row. But it was Webern's implicit suggestion that tiny rhythmic motifs could function as independent cells (that is, without being tied to particular melodic shapes) that was to prove the key to the door connecting all these possibilities.

From this moment on, Ives's occasionally chaotic, often vaguely expressed dream of a multiple-layered rhythmic structure would seem to have become a reality: working outwards, as it were by addition and multiplication of the smallest unit, rather than inwards by the division of larger ones, Messiaen has found the means of controlling every detail of his apparently free-ranging rhythms. And it is this underlying control of the

John Cage.

was two American composers—Henry Cowell and John Cage—who were together responsible for setting the young avant garde on a second, parallel course which might have seemed to be the ultimate negation of the first.

Cowell (1897–1965) was an accomplished pianist, and it is through his imaginative explorations of the more peripheral possibilities of the instrument that he made his most memorable contributions as a composer. He not only invented new techniques of piano playing, but also initiated a more general move towards debunking the increasingly intellectual complexity and emotional seriousness of much contemporary European music. In this he was doubtless prompted as much by the deflating mockery of Eric Satie's piano pieces as by the inclusion of everyday sounds in the works of Charles Ives; but his novel approach to the piano as a sounding-board rather than just a keyboard was entirely his own. It was Cowell who first thought of the keyboard 'cluster'—that is, depressing groups of adjacent notes with hands or arms, either to create a quasi-harmonic backing to tunes or to paint impressionistic sound pictures; he also made considerable use of the strings themselves, either in conjunction with the keys or on their own, like a harp (Ex. 6).

A pupil of Cowell—and oddly enough, though much later, of Schoenberg—John Cage (b. 1912) took this move to de-sophisticate the piano several steps further. This he has achieved partly by investigating every possible sound to be coaxed from the huge resonating body of the instrument (the accompaniment to his song, *The Wonderful Widow of Eighteen Springs*, for instance, is 'played' entirely on the piano's wooden casing), and partly by seeking ways to extend the range and even to alter the pitch of sounds produced by the hammers striking the strings in the normal way: this invention, which involves placing objects of all kinds on or between the strings, he calls the 'prepared' piano.

Important as these extensions to the possibilities of the instrument have proved (not least in recent ensemble music with piano), it was Cage's study of the ideas of Eastern philosophy and his attempts to link them with sounds involving the least possible pre-determination on the part of the composer—sometimes none at all, as in *4′33″* of silent non-participation by the pianist—that have been still more influential. There is perhaps no single contemporary composer of any importance who has not been influenced to some degree by the deluge of freedoms unleashed by Cage.

And not only composers. There must be few performers by now who have not at some time been

relationships between changing units of rhythmic pulse that has enabled him so successfully to unify the many disparate sources of his colourful inspiration. Meanwhile, the American composer Elliott Carter (b. 1908) has underlined his kinship with Ives by developing a method of superimposing different rates of rhythmic pulse—a development already hinted at in his early sonata for piano.

The Neo-Primitives

It was Messiaen who gave the composers of the post-war era their first lessons in the techniques of twentieth-century musical organization (literally so in the case of Pierre Boulez and others, since he taught them); but it

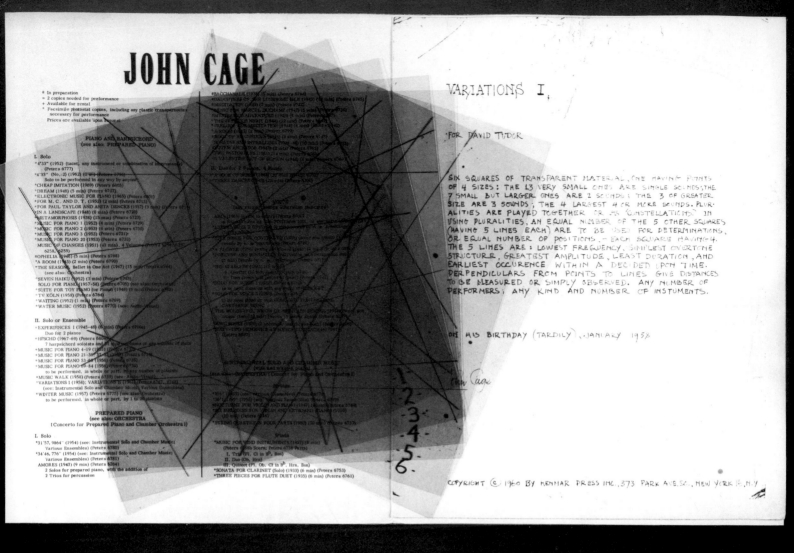

Ex. 7: The complete 'score kit' for John Cage's *Variations I*, 1958.

asked, as it were by Cage, to draw on their own inventive, compositorial powers. As has already been suggested, even a fully composed and conventionally notated piece such as Webern's *Variations* requires the performer to think himself into the mind of the composer if he is to understand the full range of complex relationships hidden beneath its surface. But, post-Cage, the performer has temporarily to 'become' the composer of every piece he plays and, if he is a pianist, to have at his fingertips as many different kinds of technique. Yet in the more extreme instances, it almost begins to seem as if the player most likely to succeed would be the one with the least pretensions to technique of any kind—because such composers seem to be searching back in time towards a rediscovery of sounds that long pre-date the invention of instruments as we know them. Certainly, many of the means needed to reproduce these sounds find the conventional virtuoso no better equipped than the merest beginner—particularly since some of the means used to notate them require a generalized response to visual suggestion rather than a precise interpretation of musical symbols (**Exs. 7, 8 and 9**).

The New Virtuosity

The impact of these New World ideas on the composers of western Europe was necessarily postponed by the hiatus in communication resulting from the Second World War. So by the time John Cage came face to face with the Europeans in the mid 1950s, the musical public had already been stunned by the explosive energy of the so-called avant garde.

For the first time since the beginning of the century, a move was afoot to disregard national boundaries. As if to mirror the growing internationalism within society as a whole, a group of composers born in the 1920s came together (literally, during the annual summer schools at Darmstadt in Germany) with the apparently single-minded aim of creating a new musical language for their common future. And it so happens that the two most influential figures of this generation—Pierre Boulez (b. 1925) and Karlheinz Stockhausen (b. 1928)—are also the two who have done most to take piano music by storm into the second half of the twentieth century from its relatively becalmed state in the 1930s and throughout the war years.

The prevailing mood was now that of ruthless

Ex. 8: *Edges* 'for any number of players, any number of instruments' (1969) by Christian Wolff.

Ex. 9: *Piano Piece* (1963) by Morton Feldman.

Pierre Boulez.

confidence, sustained by a belief that, by sheer force of talent, a new tradition could be forged almost overnight from what were seen as the flickering remnants of the nineteenth century pervading the work of twentieth-century Vienna. Like that of Schoenberg before them, the piano music of both Boulez and Stockhausen reflects all the most important developments that took place over a crucial period in the career of each composer: Boulez's three piano sonatas span the years 1946–58, and Stockhausen's eleven *Piano Pieces* were written between 1952 and 1961.

The earliest of these works date from a time when Webern alone was acknowledged as prophet of the new age, yet only Stockhausen's *Piano Piece III* reveals any obvious indebtedness to Webern; elsewhere, the widely spaced lines of Webern's exquisitely balanced symmetries explode into contrapuntal textures of an almost savage density, closer in expressive kind to those of late Beethoven than to Webern (it is perhaps no accident that the form of Boulez's second sonata was inspired by that of Beethoven's op. 106, the 'Hammerklavier'). In effect, these works employ the age-old techniques of superposing strands of melody and rhythm, but to very different ends: the identity of individual strands is here subservient to the particular type of conjunct or disjunct, ornate or bare, texture on which musical contrasts largely depend now that every other level is characterized by extremes (of register, pulse, dynamics and accentuation). The results in terms of keyboard technique are truly astonishing—and the mere handful of pianists who even today attempt to perform them is witness to the fact that these pieces respond only to the most transcendental virtuosity. For the time being, at least.

This ten-year period beginning in the mid-1940s was in many ways the most musically eventful and exciting of our times; certainly, in terms of its piano music, these two composers set standards of compositional bravura that have not since been equalled—although *Herma* (1960–1) by the Greek composer Iannis Xenakis (b. 1922) must be said to represent the *ne plus ultra* in its purely physical demands.

The Neo-Baroque Trend
However, the intense elation, evidently experienced by all the Darmstadt composers as they succeeded in expanding relatively conventional techniques to a point beyond the wildest dreams of their predecessors was to be short-lived: the limits of the possible in this direction were quickly reached.

It was at this moment that the musical personality of

John Cage first touched on the collective consciousness of the young Europeans, with two immediately noticeable results. First, there was a move to abandon the increasingly vain struggle to find new closed forms to fit essentially open-ended musical ideas; and second, a search began for a less complex and uncompromising

Karlheinz Stockhausen.

means of communicating those ideas. As at other such moments of truth, this search would appear to have led backwards through history, on this occasion to the pre-contrapuntal era of the decorative baroque.

Without the need to ensure musical reference points essential to closed forms like the sonata, the creation of hugely ornate structures could become an end in itself. *Constellation-Miroir*, from Boulez's vast and still partly unpublished third piano sonata, consists entirely of the highly complex and ornate decoration of a series of chords, additionally coloured by the extremely intricate use of all three pedals (**Ex. 10**). Whole stretches of

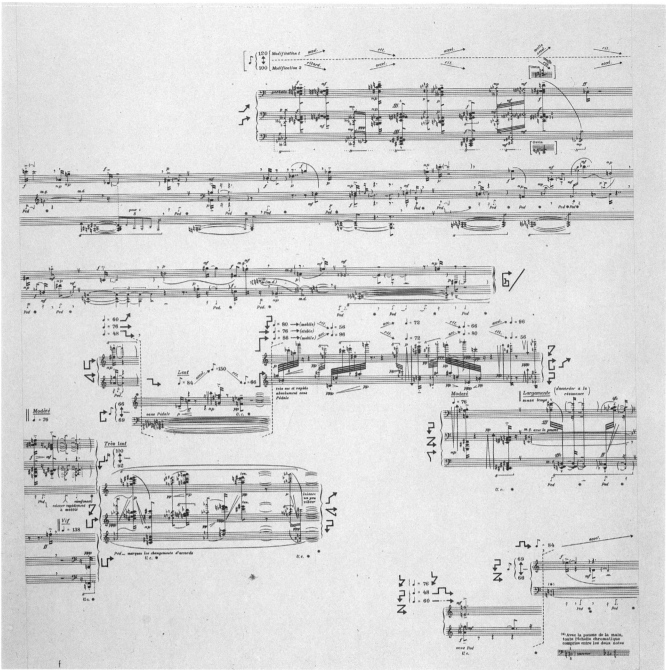

Ex. 10: A page of Boulez's *Constellation-Miroir*.

Stockhausen's glittering *Piano Piece X* (much more original and inventive than the fragments that make up the do-it-yourself form of his notorious *Piano Piece XI*) comprise nothing but decorations of a barely discernible harmonic skeleton (**Ex. 11**); again, all three pedals here play a vital, almost Debussyesque role in effecting alterations in tone quality. But the neo-baroque trend is nowhere more clearly exemplified than in *Sequenza IV* of Luciano Berio (b. 1925), with its sectional form and variation-like approach to the embellishment of both single notes and chords—here sustained mainly by the centre pedal (as found on European grand pianos, a not always reliable but very useful device for lifting the dampers from selected strings; though on many American upright pianos the centre pedal performs a

different function, lifting all together the lower half or third of the bass dampers).

That this move towards the baroque-like decoration of chords has remained an attractive alternative to the wide-ranging and sometimes excessively complex counterpoints of the 1940s and early 1950s can be seen in the works of composers of very different musical inclinations. *Makrokosmos* for amplified piano by George Crumb (b. 1929) obviously belongs to this category; but so too does such a work as Michael Tippett's third piano sonata (1972–3)—in which characteristically clean-limbed ideas are set within extremely ornate surroundings. But of the representative twentieth-century trends observed earlier, this is by no means the only one whose influence continues to

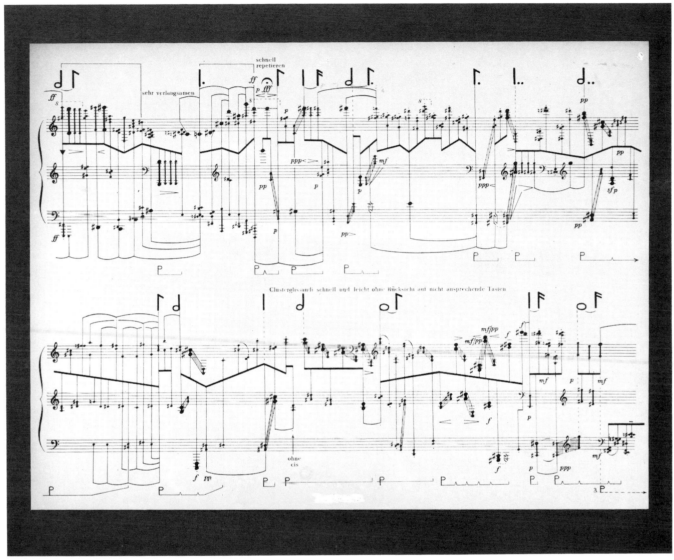

Ex. 11: From Stockhausen's *Piano Piece X*.

be felt in the music of today. In fact, most of the 1960s and 1970s would seem to have been a time of taking stock: in terms of musical form, a period of recapitulation, following the historically based exposition of the first part of the century and the avant-garde development of the post-war years. Much of this stocktaking is currently reflected in collage-like techniques of juxtaposing, and sometimes even superimposing, contrasted fragments of historical evidence, or of weaving threads of past styles into textures characteristic of the present.

However, apart from the publication in the mid-1960s of *Catalogue d'oiseaux*, Messiaen's enormous thirteen-movement work for piano composed between 1956 and 1958, there has been a noticeable decrease in the amount of keyboard music to have appeared since the major works of the 1940s and 1950s. Many of today's most interesting composers are writing little or nothing for solo piano—though the instrument is used more frequently, and often more imaginatively, than ever before in ensemble music of all kinds. Yet in spite of this relative neglect by composers, as pianists we should be grateful for the fact that during the course of the present century there have been more stimulating additions to the repertoire of the keyboard than to the repertoire of any other instrument—and that we have already more than enough contemporary masterpieces to keep us going for some time to come, regardless of what the future may bring.

THE AMERICAN PIANO

Le public de l'exposition, saisit tout à coup de la rage de se faire pianiste à l'audition des admirables pianos américains Steinway.

Opposite: 'The public at the exhibition is suddenly seized with the rage to become pianists on hearing the admirable American Steinway pianos': lithograph by 'Cham' (Amedée de Noé), 1845, inscribed to Theodore Steinway from the pianist Vladimir Horowitz.

Below: Letter from Liszt, 1884: 'When Steinway gets here, I shall have a piano shop-talk with him about the new construction of his grand pianos. F. Liszt'.
Bottom: Benjamin Franklin and his 'glassychord'.

The Crossing

Around the year 1850 the American composer William Henry Fry visited Paris, hoping, among other things, to encourage interest in American music. Introduced to the director of the Opéra, he asked for a trial rehearsal of his own *Leonora*, offering to pay any costs. The director refused: 'In Europe,' he explained, 'we look upon America as an industrial country—excellent for electric telegraphs, but not for art.'

The piano is the most industrial of instruments. Not surprisingly, then, the American piano sounded an early challenge to the parent music cultures of Europe. At the Paris exhibition of 1867, not so long after Fry's dismissal, American instruments swept the awards. Almost unnoticed, the piano had emigrated; by 1900, half the world's instruments would be made in the United States.

The American triumph resulted not from superior skill or materials but from new conceptions of the instrument which reflected America's culture, her politics, and even her geography. The piano and the United States were born about the same time. The new country, proudly independent, severed the young instrument from Europe's keyboard tradition and applied to it the pressures of frontier culture. Rootless and under stress, like many an immigrant, the piano began to change.

America's climate was rigorous, her transportation crude, her housing primitive; new approaches to design and maintenance were required. American industry, modular and mechanized, provided these and made it possible to produce instruments in unprecedented quantities. American composers, more concerned with production than with refinement, made extravagant, innovative demands. Successive waves of populist democracy unseated the colonial aristocrats, and the piano made new friends in low places: it became the first voice of mass culture. Manipulated by inventors, manufacturers, composers, and millions of amateurs, it was continually transformed to satisfy their passion for novelty and display.

First Experiments

From the beginning, American music was as much invention as composition. The gentlemen amateurs of the Revolution were inveterate tinkerers. Ben Franklin (1706–90) applied the keyboard principle to the 'musical glasses,' producing his celebrated 'glassychord' or 'armonica.' Thomas Jefferson (1743–1826) and the poet-politician Francis Hopkinson (1737–91) toyed endlessly with their harpsichords, contriving new

Left: The interior of a 'portable grand' piano by John Isaac Hawkins, 1801. The keyboard folds into the piano, which then becomes a portable cabinet (with carrying handles on each side).
Bottom: Square piano by Alpheus Babcock, c. 1835, constructed with a tubular iron frame cast in one piece.

quilling methods, built-in pendulums, and other esoteric devices.

More prophetic were two little-known experiments of the 1790s. In 1792, the New York piano-makers Dodds & Claus announced new means 'to prepare their wood to stand the effects of our climate, which imported instruments never do, but are sure to suffer from the saline quality of the seas.' And eight years later an English engineer living in Philadelphia, John Isaac Hawkins, patented a 'portable grand' remarkable for its strength and compactness, featuring upright construction, a partial iron frame and a novel system of stringing (see also pp. 32 and 243). Although neither Hawkins' invention nor the firm of Dodds & Claus survived, these products were the first attempts to overcome the two principal difficulties American manufacturers faced: designing instruments strong enough to withstand the American climate, and marketing and distributing them over a vast country on a crude transportation network.

A quarter of a century passed before these difficulties

Chickering concert grand piano, 1840: the first grand made
by Chickering, incorporating the successful cast iron frame
that he patented three years later.

were next confronted, but then three developments
opened the way to a distinctive American industry. First
was the patent for a cast iron frame issued in 1825 to
Alpheus Babcock of Boston (see pp. 32 and 244).
Babcock's design initiated a continuing American invest-
ment in strength, volume and uniformity, even at the
expense of tone and touch. His plans were improved by
Jonas Chickering, the new partner of John Mackay,
Babcock's former associate, and in 1843 Chickering &
Mackay patented a one-piece iron frame for grands. In
1855 the young Steinway company redesigned the frame
for square pianos, adding to it a new system of over-string-
ing which dramatically improved the tone; and when in
1859 they applied a similar design to grand pianos, the
universal adoption of metal-framing was assured.

A second development was sociological rather than
technical. In the 1820s and 1830s Lowell Mason led a
massive, largely successful effort to include the study of
music in America's state schools. Within two decades,
regular instruction had produced a generation of
musically literate amateurs; neglected by a declining

aristocracy, the American piano found refuge in the homes of the emerging middle classes. The democratization of the keyboard created a new and turbulent market, requiring innovative sales techniques. Chickering & Mackay divided their business; Chickering oversaw the workshop, Mackay made sales into a new speciality. Trained agents throughout the States began to create as well as respond to demand. Performers lent their names to the firm; promotional tours were arranged. The durability of Chickering's instruments enabled Mackay to build a distributional network extending to the most remote cities. Geographically as well as sociologically, the piano became available to all.

The new designs and their wide circulation encouraged a third feature of the emerging industry: the division of labour and the dispersion of manufacturing. Firms appeared whose sole function was to supply components to the principal builders. Already in the 1830s the manufacture of wire, action and cases was partly handled by specialists; as design became standardized, subsidiaries proliferated. Although world-wide, this trend was most noticeable in America: specialization suited well the uneven distribution of materials and skills in the States, and made it possible to produce large numbers of instruments at low cost. Thus all three factors—design, demand and the division of labour—were mutually supportive, fuelling an industrial expansion that became explosive in the second half of the century.

Opposite above: 'Steinway and Sons' new piano-forte manufactory, situated on the Fourth Avenue, between 52nd and 53rd Streets, New York' in 1860.
Opposite below: The first permanent Steinway factory building at 82–8 Walker Street, New York City; occupied from 1854 to 1860. The building at no. 82 is still standing. The entire family and staff are assembled in front.

Below: Title page of *The Dawning of Music in Kentucky*.

Anthony Philip Heinrich

In the early years of the republic, most music in America remained securely European in style. But in 1821, anticipating slightly Babcock's landmark patent, there appeared the first keyboard music that seemed peculiarly suited to the new culture: an extraordinary 269-page volume by Anthony Philip Heinrich (1781–1861) modestly entitled *The Dawning of Music in Kentucky*. Everything about this collection reflected its surroundings: the title, self-consciously proclaiming a new beginning; the size, enormous as the land itself; and the style, an astonishing mix of inventiveness and extravagance.

Heinrich's music anticipated many characteristics of later, better-known American composers. Since its beginning, American culture has been compounded from fragments of many others, and American composers have often sought to synthesize these, fabricating a new music from the bits and pieces at hand rather than elaborating an inherited tradition. They have treated the piano similarly, inventing or compounding techniques rather than simply continuing them; the piano, for them, has been simply a machine which produces a wide range of sounds, all potentially useful. Compared with European contemporaries, their work has generally been more extravagant, more technological, more concerned with quantity, diversity and novelty than with logic or tradition.

Heinrich emigrated from Bohemia in about 1810, first to Philadelphia, then inland to the less-cultured Pittsburgh, and finally to Bardstown, Kentucky, an aptly-named village then at the edge of the wilderness. There, nearing forty, he began composing, and three years later had amassed the material for his remarkable debut. Heinrich was utterly devoted to his adopted country; his preferred appellative, taken from an autobiographical song, was 'the Log House composer from Kentucky'. Aware of the nation's artistic limits, he determined to transcend them. 'The many and severe animadversions,' he wrote, 'so long and repeatedly cast on the talent for Music in this Country, has been one of the chief motives of the Author, in the exercise of his abilities; and should he be able, by this effort, to create but one single *Star* in the *West*, no one would ever be more proud than himself, to be called an *American Musician*.'

Untutored and far from Europe, Heinrich invented composition anew to suit American culture, much as piano makers rebuilt the instrument to suit the climate. Retaining a European veneer, he experimented with a wide range of compositional frameworks, using formal

Title-page of Heinrich's *The Log House.*

From Heinrich's *The Chromatic Ramble of the Peregrine Harmonist.*

principles yet untried in Europe. He was capable of simplicity ('Love in Ohio' is a short, strophic, two-part song of great beauty), and could also employ conventional forms, often ingeniously interlocked (the *Marcia di Ballo, Rondo Fanfare* contains a straightforward march, *trio* and rondo, but with a set of variations on 'Yankee Doodle' inserted as the second contrasting section). On the other hand, some works were deliberately chaotic, such as '*The Banjo*' from *A Sylvan Scene in Kentucky, or the Barbecue Divertimento*, in which nearly thirty musical ideas follow without a single recurrence.

Even in traditionally structured pieces, however, quirky detail often obscures the formal logic. *The Hickory, or Last Ideas in America* concludes with another set of variations on 'Yankee Doodle', the measures of which are harmonized alternately in major and minor. In more radical works, phrases and modulations, each of which alone is unremarkable, are

linked into highly unconventional chains.

Heinrich's melodic material ranged from the deliberately mundane to the astonishing. At one extreme, he anticipated Ives by quoting American tunes and by imitating banjos, fiddles, Indian songs and other native musics; at the other, he wrote melodies which were, he said, 'full of strange ideal somersets and capriccios', characterized by sudden displacement and florid, disjunct ornamentation.

The formal daring and melodic extravagance of Heinrich's style led him to colouristic effects not approached again until the twentieth century: unsupported trills in extreme registers, low *sforzandi* triads in closed position, constantly repeated *fortissimo* chords. Moreover, Heinrich wrote for the two hands independently like no one since Scarlatti or before Cage; repeatedly he required the player to perform in an 'unpianistic' manner for structural reasons. These and other extraordinary techniques are perhaps best seen in

the remarkable *Chromatic Ramble of the Peregrine Harmonist.*

Until very recently, those few scholars to discuss Heinrich's music dismissed it as incompetent or hopelessly eccentric. But the many elegant passages of conventional beauty demonstrate Heinrich's competence, and the oddities, heard over a century later, are remarkably convincing. His fragmented, experimental eclecticism resembles the culture he adopted; it is as though European musical ideas had emigrated, as her peoples had, and had been thrown into unexpected arrangements by the turbulent New World. Heinrich's music is a mixture of the cultivated and the primitive, of the acquired and the newly-made; in this it represents fairly the America he knew. His resourcefulness in exploring the sheer sound of the piano through unconventional techniques, and his disregard for traditional artistic values like logic, balance and coherence, reflect the American willingness to start

anew in inventing music for the piano-machine; his interest in quantity and spectacle, his choice of subjects, and his quotation of popular tunes, instruments and idioms manifest his desire to align himself and the instrument with the populace, rather than with an élite.

Louis Moreau Gottschalk

Generally regarded as a charming eccentric, Heinrich received the affection but not the respect of his American audience. At that time, success in the States required European approbation; indeed, to the present day, performers from William Mason to Van Cliburn have found that transatlantic accolades transformed their American careers. Of the many who achieved European successes in the nineteenth century, only Louis Moreau Gottschalk (1829–69) was able to remain strikingly American in style.

Gottschalk's career was the antithesis of Heinrich's. A child prodigy from New Orleans, he was sent to Paris at thirteen and in a few years had become the darling of Europe's salons. He returned eight years later, bearing an unprecedented reputation for virtuosity and virility, and embarked on four years of tours in the States, England and Cuba, featuring his own compositions. In 1857, sated with concerts and amours, he began a self-imposed exile in the West Indies; wandering aimlessly, he played and wrote erratically and began a now-famous journal (*Notes of a Pianist*) that mixed breathless protestations with shrewd cultural insights.

Five years later he surfaced in New York and started an unbelievable series of tours, performing in even the smallest towns by scheduling as many as three concerts a day. In 1865, in San Francisco, he lingered too long with the wrong young lady and had to sneak aboard the boat *Colorado*, headed for Panama. Undaunted, he worked his way south, conquering Central and South America as he had the States—playing, organizing, composing and constantly alert for a receptive smile from the third row. Four years later, in Rio de Janeiro, he contracted yellow fever; ill as he was, he refused to rest, and it killed him.

In some ways, Gottschalk's music was as different from Heinrich's as his life. Many of his pieces were sentimental effusions like *The Last Hope*, or bombastic pastiches like *The Union*, shaped by European moulds and designed to please. Nevertheless, his deepest allegiance was to populist America; like Heinrich, he was devoted to spectacle, extravagance and popular culture. Heinrich tossed European gestures into the tumult of the frontier; Gottschalk injected native materials (Black, Creole, and Latin-American) into

Below: Louis Moreau Gottschalk and (opposite bottom) the title-page of his *The Banjo*.
Opposite above: A satire of Gottschalk's first Argentinian monster concert, performed by fifty-six pianists and two orchestras at the Teatro Lyrico Fluminense, Rio de Janeiro, October 1869.

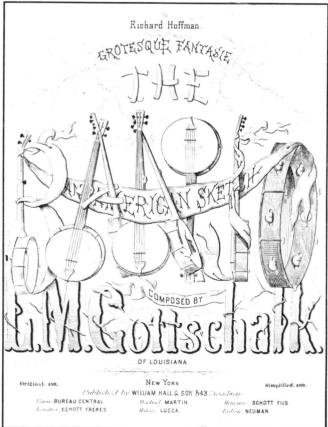

European genres. Gottschalk, too, subverted the directionality of traditional European forms; but whereas Heinrich concealed them behind a thicket of material, Gottschalk reduced them to uniformity by eliminating contrast. *The Banjo*, Gottschalk's most persistently popular piece, contains only motoristic, mechanical elaborations of simple harmonies; in *Le Bananier*, even harmonic movement is discarded.

Rhythm and sonority were fundamental to Gottschalk's sources, his compositions and his playing. Contemporary descriptions repeatedly mention his energetic precision and hard, glittering tone. Like Heinrich, Gottschalk was fond of colouristic effects, and especially of rapid, reiterative figuration in the highest octaves. Played on the iron-framed Chickerings, often criticized for their harshness, these passages would have had a noticeably steely, brittle sound. In part, Gottschalk exploited the very properties of American instruments that others wished to change.

Heinrich reflected America's devotion to quantity in the length and diversity of his pieces. Gottschalk's commitment was less subtle: he simply produced innumerable man-hours of music. Although his journal contains many wry references to listeners who, like General Grant, could recognize only two tunes ('one is "Yankee Doodle" and the other is not'), he played for all, without discrimination. He was music for hire, a

The burning of out-of-date pianos by American piano retailers in 1904. Meeting at their annual congress in New Jersey, they voted to condemn to the flames all models of piano considered 'out-of-date'. The same evening, the sentence was carried out, and the ceremony ended with a banquet at which elegies were spoken to the memory of old pianos, and fiery speeches delivered to the Glory of Progress.

Cowboys in a cattle-town saloon after a long trail drive:
print of the late 1870s.

one-man mass medium, a proto-pianola, a music machine: 'I am a symphonic voltaic pile,' he said, 'a steam engine become man.'

Gottschalk industrialized single concerts as well as tours; in dozens of monster concerts throughout the Americas, he offered a performer's vision of the mass-production future. Multiple-ensemble events had long been popular in Europe, but Gottschalk's approach was distinctive; rather than assembling a team of well-known performers to support his own playing, he submerged himself in local, amateur ensembles. Managing these situations required great ingenuity; in one programme, the impossible playing of one participant was only cured by surreptitiously substituting a dummy piano in the performance. Gottschalk seemed determined to envelop his own virtuosity in the collective, to become one among many, to lose his identity; the last two spectacles, for thirty-one players

on sixteen pianos and for eighteen orchestras totalling six hundred and fifty players, literally killed him.

Such radical democracy was peculiarly American; in Europe, only Berlioz, Gottschalk's friend and supporter, pursued remotely similar aims. Gottschalk was the first pop superstar, an ambivalent virtuoso whose idolization became greater the more he tried to blend. He seems to have been convinced that music, the machine age and American democracy could be reconciled in a kind of manic multiplicity. To a certain extent, he was proved correct.

The Piano in Mass Culture
In the rest of the century the piano became the first machine used to disseminate a mass-music culture. Between 1860 and 1900, piano makers' productivity increased sevenfold. As mechanization and specialization developed, allowing reliable instruments to be

Front and back views of a piano-player: the device is pushed up to a piano, whose keyboard it 'plays' with its felt 'fingers'.

built at moderate cost, the piano became a necessary luxury for the aspiring middle classes. An enormous sheet-music industry arose to supply them with a constantly changing repertoire.

More important still, the piano began to appear in new contexts: it accompanied fiddle players in the country, blues singers in urban ghettos, and replaced expensive orchestras in bars and brothels everywhere. Distinctive playing styles evolved, in which finger slides, tremolandi, and percussive effects imitated the supplanted instruments. Unnotated piano music, leading directly to ragtime and jazz, began to diverge from the written tradition. The piano took on two identities: a pillar of culture in the concert hall, school, and parlour; and a tool of the devil elsewhere.

At the outset, in the 1870s and 1880s, it seemed that the piano boom would finally produce the universal literacy sought by generations of music educators. Music was disseminated by the printed page; the consumer had to play to hear it. Those without the necessary skills had to be satisfied with music boxes. Then, near the end of the century, several inventors and manufacturers combined the music box and the piano into a single device which reproduced keyboard music mechanically: the player-piano. The high-point of amateur performance had been reached; from this time on, music in mass culture would be directed increasingly toward listeners rather than amateurs. Initially an agent of this change, the player-piano eventually succumbed to it, as phonographs and radio made unnecessary even the minimal participation it required.

The history of the automatic piano is a hopeless snarl of patents, mergers, lawsuits and thievery. It seems impossible at present to decide exactly when it was invented, or even what it is. Mechanical keyboard instruments date back to the Renaissance, and their designs were applied to the piano almost as soon as it appeared. The modern player-piano dates from about 1875, although the first devices marketed commercially were piano-players, not player-pianos. The former contained sets of pneumatically-activated levers which fitted over conventional keyboards, striking the keys like fingers; in the latter, a similar pneumatic mechanism, housed inside the piano itself, operated the hammers directly. Various designs competed inconsequentially until about 1898, when the Aeolian Company launched its improved 'Pianola' with an unprecedented advertising campaign. As Chickering & Mackay had found earlier, the combination of better design and overpowering marketing proved irresistible, and the 'Pianola,' produced first as a piano-player, then as a player-piano,

Weber 'Pianola Grand', incorporating the player mechanism within the instrument, and an advertisement extolling the player-piano.

set an accelerating pace for the industry. Within a decade, roll size, speed and other variables had been standardized, enabling new companies to specialize and grow as conventional builders had half a century before.

The player-piano had a considerable vogue in England and on the Continent, but in the United States its impact was phenomenal. Feeding on America's fascination with machinery, multiplicity, novelty and spectacle, player-pianos took over the industry: in 1900 some 6,000 automatic instruments were made, compared with 171,000 conventional ones; by 1925, player-pianos outnumbered the conventional by 169,000 to 137,000. Then came the plunge; improved recordings and network radio were more efficient suppliers of mass music. In 1929, the year before the depression, only 37,000 player-pianos were made; production of conventional pianos, supported by a less fickle élite, declined only to 94,000.

At the beginning of the century, automatic instruments were enthusiastically employed by composers and performers of concert music to preserve their ideas or interpretations. But by the 1920s player-pianos served primarily as a kind of proto-*Muzak*. By then,

Conlon Nancarrow adjusting one of his rolls for playing on an Ampico reproducing player-piano in his Mexico City studio, 1977 (left) and his custom-made hole-punching machine (right).

Opposite: One hundred girls play one hundred pianos in Busby Berkeley's *Gold Diggers of 1935*.

conventional pianos had become the principal medium for background music; hundreds of musicians made a living by playing deferentially in hotels, clubs, restaurants and the like. The best of these gradually evolved an approach to sonority and figuration quite unlike either jazz or art music. Their style declined after the 1930s; today, these gifted professionals, able to freshen any tune imaginable with cascades of unobtrusive dexterity, are unjustly neglected or derided.

For smaller establishments, unable to afford live musicians, the player-piano provided a solution; thousands of movie theatres, in particular, found it the only economical way to accompany silent films. Spurred by the cinemas' need for sound effects and novelties, manufacturers added auxiliary devices to their products; by 1920, automatic instruments might include whistles, bells, drums, even baby cries or crockery crashes. Establishments still more economy-minded could install coin-operated machines; these, too, often had optional effects or devices which applied metal or paper directly to the strings, producing a metallic or rattling timbre.

Composers in the art tradition generally shunned the plebeian player-piano. Only one, Conlon Nancarrow (b. 1912), has pursued the remarkable potential of piano rolls. Nancarrow has spent most of his life in Mexico. Geographically and temperamentally removed from the mainstream, he restricted his music to several generations of player-pianos, personalizing different

instruments by subtle adjustments of the action; for them, beginning in 1948, he composed a series of extraordinary *Studies*. Regulated by complex polyrhythms and punctuated by unperformable sonorities, these brilliantly exploit the mechanical piano's capability for precision and profusion. Nancarrow's rich figuration, his striking registration and his preoccupation with rhythm recall Heinrich and Gottschalk, although his compositions inhabit one of the most peculiar backwaters of music history.

The Twentieth Century

The main stream of twentieth-century experimentalism, however, passed by Nancarrow and the 'Pianola'; instead, American composers reconceived the function of conventional instruments. Earlier, the piano had been a string instrument often used to approximate large instrumental ensembles. Its percussive nature was deliberately obscured; builders, composers and players evolved sophisticated techniques to suggest the sustained tone of the voice or violin. Twentieth-century experimentalists turned this idea on its head. For them, the piano was a percussion instrument, a metallophone; its attraction lay in its forceful attack and in the extraordinary range of noises it could produce.

Of prime importance to this new approach was Henry Cowell (1897–1965). In *The Tides of Manaunaum* (1912) and other early works, Cowell used the keyboard as a massive mallet, producing 'tone-clusters' by playing a

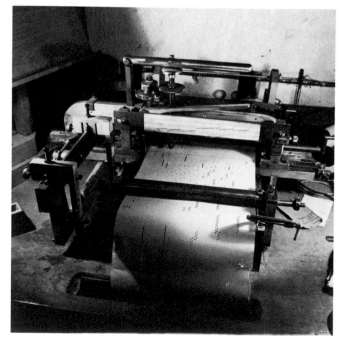

A First National Production Corp. Picture

GOLD DiGGERS of 1935

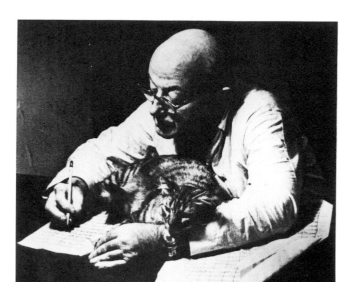

dozen or more adjoining keys with his hands or forearms. In pieces like *The Banshee* (1925) he abandoned the keyboard altogether, plucking, scraping and stroking the strings directly. Cowell's inventiveness may have been stimulated by player-piano novelties or ragtime and jazz, in which clusters and other percussive effects were quite common. In any case, the ideas were in the air; both Charles Ives (1874–1954) and Leo Ornstein (b. 1892) began using clusters independently of Cowell and at approximately the same time.

The piano quickly found a new place in percussion ensembles. In *Ionisation* (1931), the first major work for percussion alone, Edgard Varèse (1883–1965) embedded massive sonorities in a context that made the piano almost unrecognizable. Composers like John Becker (1886–1961) and Lou Harrison (b. 1917), drawing percussion instruments from a variety of cultures, used the piano as a sort of giant cembalo, applying beaters, mutes and metal rods to the strings.

But it was John Cage (b. 1912) who altered the piano most radically. The son of an inventor, and a student of Cowell, he fabricated a new instrument, the 'prepared piano', by inserting screws, coins, bits of rubber and other small objects between the strings. The keyboard then controlled timbre rather than pitch, and new colours could be devised at will: both the type of material and its position on the strings affected the sound. In a score of works, culminating in the elegant *Sonatas and Interludes* (1946–8), Cage refined his gentle noise-machine and clarified his notation. Profoundly influenced by the Orient, he used his instrument as a kind of gamelan, writing simple, subtle rhythms that articulated shifting timbral melodies. Like Cowell, Cage

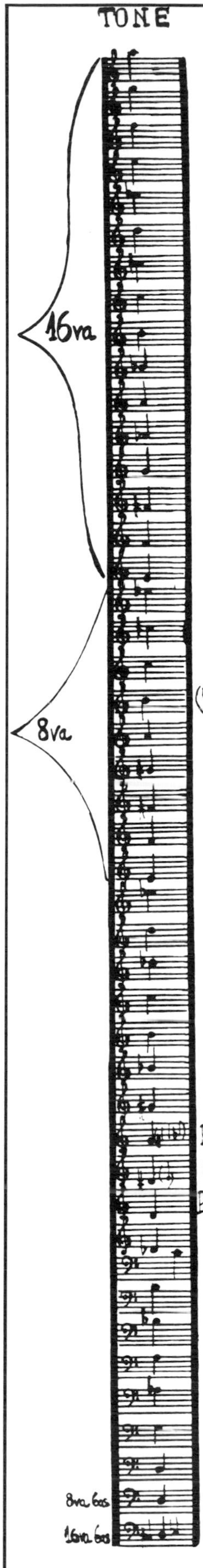

TONE
16va
8va
8va bas
16va bas

MATERIAL	STRINGS LEFT TO RIGHT	DISTANCE FROM DAMPER (INCHES)	MATERIAL	STRINGS LEFT TO RIGHT	DISTANCE FROM DAMPER (INCHES)	MATERIAL	STRINGS LEFT TO RIGHT	DISTANCE FROM DAMPER (INCHES)	TONE
			SCREW	2-3	1¼*				A
			MED. BOLT	2-3	1⅜*				G
			SCREW	2-3	1⅝*				F
			SCREW	2-3	1 13/16*				E
			SCREW	2-3	1¾*				E♭
			SM. BOLT	2-3	2*				D
			SCREW	2-3	1 9/16*				C♯
			FURNITURE BOLT	2-3	2 3/16*				C
			SCREW	2-3	2½*				B
			SCREW	2-3	1⅞*				B♭
			MED. BOLT	2-3	2⅞*				A
			SCREW	2-3	2¼*				A♭
			SCREW	2-3	3¾*				G
			SCREW	2-3	2 15/16*				F♯
SCREW	1-2	¾*	FURN. BOLT + 2 NUTS	2-3	2⅛*	SCREW + 2 NUTS	2-3	3¼*	F
			SCREW	2-3	1 13/16*				E
			FURNITURE BOLT	2-3	1⅞				E♭
			SCREW	2-3	1 15/16				C♯
			SCREW	2-3	1 1/16				C
(DAMPER TO BRIDGE = 4 7/16; ADJUST ACCORDINGLY)			MED. BOLT	2-3	3¾				B
			SCREW	2-3	4 7/16				A
RUBBER	1-2-3	4½	FURNITURE BOLT	2-3	1¼				G♯
			SCREW	2-3	1¾				F♯
			SCREW	2-3	2 5/16				F
RUBBER	1-2-3	5¾							E
RUBBER	1-2-3	6½	FURN. BOLT + NUT	2-3	6⅞				E♭
			FURNITURE BOLT	2-3	2 9/16				D
RUBBER	1-2-3	3⅝							D♭
			BOLT	2-3	7⅛				C
			BOLT	2-3	2				B
SCREW	1-2	10	SCREW	2-3	1	RUBBER	1-2-3	8¼	B♭
(PLASTIC (see G))	1-2-3	2 5/16				RUBBER	1-2-3	4½	G♯
PLASTIC (OVER 1 UNDER 2-3)	1-2-3	2⅞				RUBBER	1-2-3	10⅛	G
(PLASTIC (see D))	1-2-3	4¼				RUBBER	1-2-3	5 7/16	D♯
PLASTIC (OVER 1 - UNDER 2-3)	1-2-3	4⅛				RUBBER	1-2-3	9¾	D
BOLT	1-2	15½	BOLT	2-3	14/16	RUBBER	1-2-3	14⅛	D♭
BOLT	1-2	14½	BOLT	2-3	⅞	RUBBER	1-2-3	6½	C
BOLT	1-2	14¾	BOLT	2-3	9/16	RUBBER	1-2-3	14	B
RUBBER	1-2-3	9½	MED. BOLT	2-3	10⅛				B♭
SCREW	1-2	5⅞	LG. BOLT	2-3	5⅞	SCREW + NUTS	1-2	1	A
BOLT	1-2	7⅛	MED. BOLT	2-3	2¼	RUBBER	1-2-3	4⅛	A♭
LONG BOLT	1-2	8¾	LG. BOLT	2-3	3¼				G
			BOLT	2-3	14/16				D
SCREW + RUBBER	1-2	4 7/16							D
ERASER (OVER D UNDER C♯ + E♭) AM. PENCIL CO. #346	1	6¾							D

*MEASURE FROM BRIDGE.

Oscar Peterson.

combined a highly individualistic inventiveness with a powerful desire to integrate disparate cultures and aesthetics. In this, and in their interest in rhythm and sonority, both extended the work of nineteenth-century innovators like Heinrich and Gottschalk.

Other composers approached the prepared piano differently. Christian Wolff (b. 1934) used each sound almost as though it were a separate instrument, structuring the collection as he would a chamber ensemble. For George Crumb (b. 1929), piano preparations are part of a wider collection of unusual effects used to illustrate texts or programmes impressionistically. The distinction between conventional and prepared pianos has become increasingly vague in recent years, and pianists now must often alter the interior of the instrument during the course of a piece.

When Cage turned to chance procedures around 1950, his interest in novel or unpredictable noises increased. Already in *The Wonderful Widow of Eighteen Springs* (1942) he had asked the pianist to play with knuckles and fingers on the closed keyboard cover. In the 1950s, he and the virtuoso David Tudor (b. 1926) explored every crevice of the instrument, banging, scraping and modifying the action and housing as well as the strings. Their work culminated in the *Concert for Piano and Orchestra* (1958), which, as played by Tudor, is an exhaustive encyclopedia of percussive possibilities. Again, composers of other persuasions used similar effects to different ends: in Ben Johnston's *Knocking Piece* (1965), two percussionists play precise, intricate rhythms on the frame and casing of the instrument, the strings acting only as resonators.

Executing such effects often entailed a sensational theatricality, and it was a small step to works in which theatre predominated. Cage again led the way. In the first performance of Cage's famous *4′33″* (1952), David Tudor sat quietly before the keyboard, producing no sounds; the piano was simply a sign to indicate that the work was being performed. Thereafter it was used as a theatrical signifier in dozens of works by the 'Fluxus' group of composers—George Brecht, Nam Juin Paik and others; LaMonte Young's *Piano Piece for David Tudor ♯1*, a celebrated example, begins: 'Bring a bale of hay and a bucket of water on to the stage for the piano to eat and drink. . . .'

It can be argued that in such works the piano has ceased to be an instrument at all. In other circumstances it has remained an instrument but ceased to be a piano. During the 1950s, the piano took the final step in its physical evolution: from mechanical to electronic device. Cage and Tudor amplified conventional instruments with air and contact microphones, making audible an entirely new repertoire of pianistic noises. Pop musicians devised electronic equivalents to the piano, dividing even more clearly the pop and art traditions. In mutating once again to suit mass culture, the piano began to lose its identity; electric pianos have no strings at all but are rather a species of glockenspiel. In recent years, a wide variety of synthesizers has compounded the confusion; abandoning distinctions, many jazz and rock musicians now call themselves simply 'keyboard' players.

In the late 1960s, on the basis of these and other developments, it was sometimes asserted that the piano in America had reached the end of its history, that the future belonged to other instruments. Recently, however, using a full spectrum of electric and conventional instruments, composers like Steve Reich (b. 1936) and Phil Glass (b. 1937) have inspired a renaissance of American keyboard music. Like their predecessors' music, their pieces emphasize quantity, colour, rhythm and percussion, unconventional forms, and cultural synthesis. Reich has called his *Phase Patterns* (1970) 'literally drumming on the keyboard'. In this and other works, audible, mechanical compositional processes unfold slowly without contrast, producing hypnotic permutations of a limited but rich set of sonorities. Reich and Glass appeal to both concert-goers and rock fans; Reich's synthesis of African and European techniques is perhaps less important than his unification of American musical subcultures. Indeed, a remarkable feature of the new generation of American musicians is their ability to employ without prejudice the vulgar and the refined, the old and the new, the conventional and the unconventional. As never before, the past is present; all that the piano has done is a part of what it is doing now.

In retrospect, it seems possible to discern cycles of innovation in the history of the piano in America: the early experiments of the 1780s, Heinrich in the 1820s, Gottschalk at mid-century, Cowell after 1900, Cage in the 1940s. Each cycle seems to last about forty years; each period of invention is followed by one in which advances are consolidated and traditional values temporarily reasserted. Too much credence is often given to cyclic theories of history, and prediction is a tricky task in any case. Nevertheless, by most measures, the piano in America seems about due for another major change. The keyboard remains a remarkably efficient way for one person to control an intricate machine; the question for the future is what that machine will be capable of doing.

THE JAZZ PIANO

Opposite: The Mississippi Blues.
Below: Slaves for sale: a scene in New Orleans, *c.* 1850–60.

Prelude

Jazz is a phenomenon of the twentieth century, mainly associated with industrial societies. Its roots, however, were in 'darkest' Africa, a world alien to the West. Stravinsky's *The Rite of Spring* and neo-primitive elements in the art of Picasso suggest a reaction against the ego-obsessed values of 'Western' civilization, a reaction that has been pervasive throughout our century; but this is not adequate to explain why the music of a black, persecuted, alienated, dispossessed minority became a mouthpiece for white men too, over the so-called civilized world. Maybe we are all in some ways, if not black and persecuted, at least alien and dispossessed. In any case the black man's music, transmuted in a white world, did two contradictory yet complementary things: it asserted the violence of dispossession (which exploded in the mechanized monstrosities of the Wars); at the same time it reaffirmed man's roots in the earth, in the cycles of Nature. This is why the techniques of a primitive society could be transplanted into a strange land. In the process they served a new purpose, and were themselves transformed.

European musical traditions, stemming from the watershed we call the Renaissance, effect a communication in time. Monophonic melody flows into polyphony; which implies harmonic alternations of tension and relaxation; which involve functional tonality; which creates progression from A to Z. Western man is a pilgrim; through his music, man 'invents himself'. African musics on the other hand are concerned less with man's search for *identity* than with the world he exists in; his musical techniques explore *identification* rather than acts of self-discovery. Forms tend to be circular and repetitive rather than linear; melody is monophonic, often pentatonic; texture is heterophonic rather than polyphonic; harmony, if it exists, is non-developmental. African musics effect magical acts; we live in the music while it lasts. When African solo voices sing or play they are seeking to lose, rather than to assert, personal identity. The African singer is a mouthpiece for his people's culture and history.

In his new, white world the black man, enslaved, inevitably used the techniques he had been reared on. He danced to express solidarity with his oppressed fellows; alone he hollered to the empty fields. His

The Old Plantation: watercolour of the late 18th century, artist unknown, believed to have been painted on a plantation between Charleston and Orangeburg. The stringed instrument is probably a *molo*, the drum a Yoruba instrument called *gudugudu*, and the dance non-secular of Yoruba origin. The significance of the stick and the scarves is unknown.

ululations were virtually unchanged from those he had uttered at home, for although the Afro-American was no longer singing a tribal song, he saw himself as belonging to the downcast tribe of Black Mankind; his immemorially ancient formulae of roulade and 'tumbling strain' were modified only by the fact that he sang in the American, rather than in an African, language.

But the black man's African music was to suffer a sea-change more radical than this: for inevitably it came into contact, and then conflict, with the musical manifestations of the New World, most particularly with the white march and hymn. The hymn offered a substratum of tonic, dominant and subdominant harmony; the march provided also the four-square beat of military discipline; and when the American Negro took over the white man's guitar—relatable to many plucked-stringed instruments in his own country—the blues was born. The early blues is a collision and fusion of the therapy of the black field-holler with formal elements of the white hymn and march, in so far as they can be emulated on an acoustic guitar. For the guitar is a melody instrument that can sing with much of the sensitivity of a human voice; it can also strum harmonically those basic chords of European convention. So hymn and march become a prison against whose bars the black singer or instrumental soloist beats: yet not in vain, for from tension is generated resilience. Against the military thump of the march the flexible rhythms of the African body prance and dance; the rigidity of martial metre induces tension as black and white rhythms interlock. Similarly black melody and white harmony interact in a pain that at once disturbs and heals. The phenomenon of 'blue' notes epitomizes this: for the natural flat sevenths of modal melodies clash with the sharp '*leading* notes' demanded by Western *dominant*-tonic harmony. This repeats a process that had happened in European history, when 'false relations' occurred between the vocal flat sevenths of medieval modality and the sharpened intervals called for by post-Renaissance harmony. Blue notes in Afro-American jazz are exactly comparable, likewise springing from a clash between worlds. They indeed imply *false* relations, which may prove symptomatic of a change no less crucial than that between the Middle Ages and the modern world.

In the Barrelhouse

The guitar, the basic jazz instrument, was intimate and solitary; but the blues also had a communal function most evident in working communities. In mid-west logging camps the workers tended to substitute two guitars for solo guitar, one playing the rhythm-harmony, the other the tune and embroideries thereon. Though a fairly rough sonority could be extracted from two guitars, the plangency of the instrument was not suited to this rawly masculine music; so 'fast western' blues players seized avidly on the broken-down pianos that came their way in shanty-town bars. Most of the players were camp-men; even after barrelhouse piano moved into the cities, players were not often fully professional, but rather taxi-drivers, ball-park or lavatory attendants who performed in their spare time.

The instruments they played were essentially percussive; they had to be noisy enough to be heard over the bar-room babel. So the music played on barrelhouse pianos represented the triumph of the guitar's percussive aspects over the vocal lyricism of the blues. The pianist's left hand is kinetic, creating a chugging of low-spaced triads in crotchets, quavers or the thrusting triplet or dotted rhythm known as boogie-woogie. Against such a relentless bass, dynamically unvaried, the treble line, wide-spaced and often in complex rhythms, pulls against the rhythmic-harmonic drive that apportions two chords to the bar, one on the first beat, the other on, or just before, the third.

Fundamentally barrelhouse piano is a two-voiced music for the player's left and right hands. Rhythmic momentum is everything, though the right hand introduces crushed notes, chromatic slides, repeated notes and tremolandi in an attempt to emulate, however crudely, the expressive devices of the guitar. Pitch distortion was fundamental both to guitar and piano blues, but on the piano was accidental rather than deliberate: the tumble-down instruments were grievously out of tune, and the jangle was approved of since it enhanced the clamour—and perhaps reminded black men of the 'fuzz-buzz' noises prized in African musics. Despite this partiality for extramusical sonority, however, the sustaining pedal was never used, any advantage in volume being outweighed by the blurring of hard-edged line and sharp-marked rhythm.

Barrelhouse piano emerged at the turn of the century and came to fruition in the thirties. Nonetheless it is a primitive style independent of chronology, for oral traditions change only as a life-style changes. It would seem that for Pinetop Burks, recorded in Texas as late as the sixties, there had been no change at all. His *Shake the*

shack[1] is functional music for moving to, with yelled exhortations encouraging strenuous participation. The boogie rhythm stomps in the left hand, the right hand stabs in cross-beat clusters and chatters brittly in the top register. *Aggravatin' Mama*,[1] slightly slower, is a twelve-bar blues with a vocal theme primitive as a tumbling strain; pianistically the piece is hard, yet affecting in its rhythmic hesitancies. Tremolandi and repeated notes are ebulliently employed: as they are by Black Boy Shine in *Back home blues*,[1] which is expressive enough to count not merely as communally functional music, but also as 'personal therapy'. The same is true of the music of Robert Fud Shaw, finest of Texan barrelhouse pianists who, playing *Whores is funky*[2] or *Groceries on the shelf*,[2] slams a hard-hitting bass against right-hand clusters of electrical intensity. At once energetic and relaxed, the music liberates, even as it stabs the listener in the solar plexus.

'When you listen to what I'm playing', Shaw says, 'you got to see all them gals out there swinging their butts and getting the mens excited . . . . That's what this music is for.' Barrelhouse piano is indeed an extremely sexy music, in which the beat and thrust of the boogie rhythm become synonymous with male potency. However confused its etymology may be, there is no doubt that one of the meanings of the phrase 'boogie-woogie' is sexual intercourse; and what happens in Shaw's music is both descriptive and aphrodisiac. Thus the obsessively repeated figurations of the riff adapt a primitive orgiastic technique to the bar-parlour: while both the repetitions and the cross-rhythms of the right hand brace the body against the forward thrust. The deeper implications of coition come in too, because in the relationship between the two voices (or rather hands) there is both a duality of tension and a desperate desire for unity which would, of its nature, make Time stop. From this point of view the significance of the *break* (which Shaw excels in) is interesting. Technically it is a rest for the pianist's hard-stomping left hand; but it becomes, in its explosive cross-rhythms, literally a break in Time—a seizure within the music's momentum. In this sense it is, though never finally resolving, an orgasm.

The twelve-bar blues—fusing the tonic, subdominant, dominant, tonic triads of the white hymn with black melody and rhythm—remains the basic convention of barrelhouse piano; though even after the players moved north to the cities they still exploited a 'pre-blues' style in which continuous drive mattered more than structure. One of the most fascinating of primitive barrelhouse players was a character with the romantic-heroic name of Romeo Nelson. When he plays *Head-Rag Hop*[3] energy surges into the physical activity of his left hand, which generates the familiar thrusting *tum-ti tum-ti*. This rhythm is strictly comparable with the unequal note convention of Classical baroque music. In the seventeenth and early eighteenth centuries it was a celebration of mundane power and glory; boogie-woogie too is a sensual celebration, but its creators, far from being lords of the earth, have nothing to celebrate but their animal vigour. So the difference between Romeo Nelson's boogie and the dotted rhythm in Lully and Purcell lies in the fact that the European rhythm's bounce is marshalled by the will into defined harmonic and tonal periods, with beginning, middle and end: whereas Nelson's energy exists apart from the will and without sequence or consequence. Lully's rhythm makes for order and civilization, which Romeo Nelson's music denies. The insistent thrust, the oscillation of pentatonic figures, the lack of recognizable 'theme' make Nelson's barrelhouse hop a raw, shanty-town form of African ritual music, rather than art in the post-Renaissance sense. It is irrelevant to complain that it goes on too long. 'Time', in this sense, is a European notion. The music is not meant to be listened to in a linear way; it is a context in which to exist.

Romeo's track was recorded in Chicago in 1929. One of the earliest Chicago barrelhouse players to be recorded is Jimmy Blythe, whose *Chicago Stomp*[4] and *Mr Freddie Blues*,[4] recorded in 1924 and 1926, are slightly more sophisticated in that they alternate Nelson-like 'ramblin' sections with passages that have a blues-based harmonic direction. Clarence Pinetop Smith develops the convention not only towards sophistication, but even towards 'art': for although his *Pinetop's Boogie-Woogie*[3] is functional music for dancing it is executed with delicacy as well as with exuberance. Such artistry is off-centre in the early history of barrelhouse style, though it will have consequences later. More typical of the evolution of barrelhouse music from its origins is Montana Taylor's *Indiana Avenue Stomp*.[3] The physicality of the bass here has a viscid texture, over which the right hand tune neither rides will-less and mindless like Romeo Nelson's pentatonic doodlings, nor floats in levitatory elegance like Pinetop Smith's arabesques. Acquiring melodic definition, it has a more positive identity to some degree *opposed* to the bass, the dynamism of which both sustains and threatens the tune's lament or ecstasy. It keeps us going; but it may also obliterate us: which may be literally true, since the more vehemently we live in our bodies (which are all we have), the sooner we are worn out and die. In *Indiana Avenue Stomp* the breaks in the line get more jittery, until the music thins out in chromatically descending thirds. This seems an odd end for so vigorous a piece. It *has* an end, unlike Romeo Nelson's music which might as well go on for ever; nonetheless it stops not by will or choice, but because the clock runs down, as did the nerves and bodies of so many early jazzmen.

There is thus an incipiently tragic quality in this piece: a tragedy which finds fulfilment in the work of the great Chicago pianists Meade Lux Lewis and Jimmy Yancey. We may approach this tragic aspect of piano blues by way of the Negro's obsession with a twentieth-century myth: that of the railway train which, powerful at the head, snake-like in elongation, is readily a phallic image, and which opened up and ravished the American wilderness. The Negro worked on the railroad and rode on it legitimately or as hobo; he was a traveller, living in the mere fact of motion because he had little else to live for; embarking on an endless series of departures, there was always hope that he might arrive somewhere at the end. In Meade Lux Lewis's justly famous *Honky-tonk train blues*,[4,5] the chunky left hand chords create tremendous momentum, which is enhanced by the right hand's fantastically complex, though intuitive, cross-rhythms. Meade's foot stamps a regular four-in-a-bar, which his left hand energizes with a boogie rhythm; while his right hand alternates crotchet triplets with the $3+3+2$ rumba rhythm. The effect— perhaps the closest jazz ever came to the complexities of African polymetre—is possible because all elements are subservient to rhythm; melody is demolished, harmony becomes purely percussive; and we are 'sent' into a trance wherein motion itself is a kind of immobility. Yet although the rhythms are potently sexual, orgasm is again incomplete. The train chuffs to stillness, and fades out on the flat seventh: the black man's denial of the finality which the white man's *dominant* cadence seeks and celebrates.

I have called Lewis's *Honky-tonk* incipiently tragic, but perhaps 'latently' would be a more accurate adverb. For although 'train pieces' become timeless in equating life with motion, it is only when rhythm is experienced in relation to melody and harmony, and therefore to passion and growth, that barrelhouse piano can claim tragic stature. This being so, we can understand why Jimmy Yancey stands supreme among Chicago pianists. Meade Lux Lewis made a train piece—*The Yancey Special*—for and about Jimmy; Yancey's performances of it tend to be slower than Lewis's and to stress the pathetic quality of blue false relations, in parallel sixths

Job applicants outside the Federal Employment Recovery
Act Offices, New Orleans, 1935: photograph by Ben Shahn.

or thirds, over the intrepid beat.[6] A train piece of his
own, *P.L.K. Special*,[7] he also plays at moderate speed,
with nothing approaching Lewis's virtuosity; nonetheless, cross-accents are articulated with such precision
that the piece generates formidable excitement. Though
Yancey's keyboard technique is limited, it cannot be
called inadequate: the music works. Danger is of the
essence: in *Yancey's Bugle Call*[8] the dislocation of the
fastish *habanera* rhythm combines with the thin texture
and the intrusive blue notes to give to the arpeggiated
tune an innocent vulnerability. Here the breaks, in the
technical sense, are perilous, each one poised over a
small abyss.

Yancey is the only barrelhouse pianist to specialize in
slow blues. *Mournful blues*, *Death Letter blues*, *Five
o'clock blues*[8] manage to suggest, on the mechanical and
tempered piano, something of the expressive plangency
of jazz voice, guitar and clarinet. Yancey could play
chromatic slides with such control of timbre that they
sound like true vocal *portamenti*; he could even create
the illusion, by infinitesimal delays in attack, that a blue
note was minutely off-pitch, not merely a minor instead
of major third. In his forlorn version of Leroy Carr's
How long blues[6] the emptiness of texture—the distant
separation of treble and bass—combines with the
limpingly slow tempo to create an aural image of urban
loneliness. This is genuinely tragic pathos, and for his
'lost' state Yancey creates a musical synonym: his
pieces, though formally simple, even elegant, all tail off
on a dominant seventh of E flat, whatever key he is
playing in. He, and we, are left in limbo.

If Yancey is the king of barrelhouse pianists, a few
others stand in his company. Like Yancey, Walter
Davies favoured slowish tempi in vocally derived
modality, though few of his blues remain 'in' one mode
throughout. On the whole he is partial to very flat
transpositions of the mixolydian mode, creating a music
poetically melancholy—and disturbing because tonally

Opposite: Title-page of *Jelly Roll Blues*.
Below: Title-page of Joplin's 'Afro-Intermezzo' *The Chrysanthemum*.

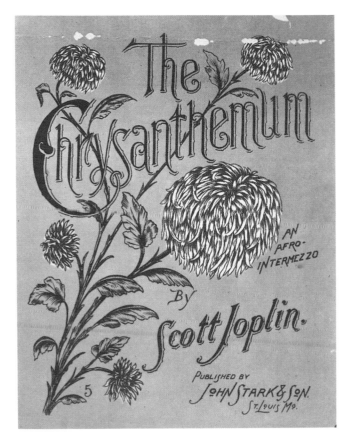

ambiguous. *Why should I be blue?*[9] provides at least musical answers to its question, for although the tonic triad is major, both dominant and subdominant chords are usually minor, with oddly depressive effect. Little Brother Montgomery, whose family came from New Orleans, can drive a fierce Chicago-style bass, but is still more impressive in slow blues such as his own *Vicksburg blues* and *Dangerous blues*,[10] which explore textures alternately skeletal (with octave unisons, wispy glissandi and flickering repeated notes) and fleshy. A corporeal music here becomes also nervously emotive; one might say the same of the playing of Roosevelt Sykes the Honeydripper, whose singing is as powerful as his pianism. He deals in the traditional blues themes of sex, poverty and the two-timing woman, the same 'personal therapy' themes of the early guitar-playing blues men: for blues (as he puts it) 'is a thing that people that can't explain themselves but know what they want to say, can bring out in a song, and it's for real. Blues is a true confession thing.' At the same time Sykes's 'shouting' style and the virility of his playing make him a communal artist too. In his version of Montgomery's *Vicksburg blues* (renamed *44 blues*) or in his own *Security blues*, *Ran the blues out of my window* and *All my money's gone*,[11] the piano's ebullience bolsters the near-desperate tumbling strains of the voice. The effect, for all its savagery, is moving, even poetic. The potency recalls the Texan style of a Robert Shaw, though the emotional charge behind the music—its awareness of passion past and to come—is heavier. There is more personal involvement in the 'archetypal' experience: as there is in the work of Whistlin' Alex Moore, who has spent all his sixty-odd years in the neighbourhood of Dallas. He can play a furious old-fashioned *Boogie in the barrel*[12] with shattering bass, hammered chords and crashing clusters, yet can also, in *West Texan woman*[12] create a slow blues that is no less corporeal in its sultry swing, while being also passion-rent, an overflow of feelings too deep for tears.

Such music manages to be at once balm-dispensing and stark, even menacing. Its tragic qualities endure, and it is timeless in the sense that it might have been created at any time between the twenties and the present. During the forties, however, 'tragic' blues went underground for a while, since the (in more than one sense) most powerful player, Albert Ammons, stressed physical energy and sheer decibel volume, concentrating on a piano music capable of holding its own with big bands; and succeeded—especially in his collaborations on two pianos with Pete Johnson. Launching obstreperously into their 1941 series of barrelhouse boogies,[13] Ammons and Johnson sweep us off our dancing feet, in vastly amplified versions of the old two-guitar lumber-camp sessions.

From Piano Rag to Jazz Piano

Barrelhouse piano was a low-life urban folk art for a low-life society. Yet by the first decade of the twentieth century a different if complementary tradition was evolving: for the Negro wished to create his own 'art' music capable of holding its own with that of the white man. This music came to be called ragtime, and the ragging was what the black man did to his white sources. Basically rags are marches, of the type grandly epitomized in the marches of Sousa; they also absorbed elements direct from Europe—French quadrille and waltz, Polish 'mazooka', Italian opera, English ballad opera and music-hall tune. Of course ragtime and barrelhouse overlapped; rag composers often started as piano thumpers in the red-light districts, while barrelhouse men used published rags as material for improvisation. Nonetheless the difference in approach between the barrelhouse blues pianist and the composer-pianist who created rags is crucial; and it is significant that the most celebrated rag composer, Scott

Joplin, started his career as a bordello pianist but achieved fame through cooperation with a white, small-time music publisher who prospered in an environment pervaded by free enterprise and Methodist Nonconformity. Joplin's equivocal success started, appropriately, at the turn of the century, when he published *Maple leaf rag*.[14] In its sheet-music form this piece created a furore comparable only—given the then inadequate means of mechanical dissemination—with that of an early Beatles number; it is still selling today.

Its success may depend on its emotional ambiguity. Superficially *Maple leaf rag* incarnates the careless optimism and self-confident aggression of the White American March in two-step rhythm. Both the melancholy of the vocal-guitar blues and the earthiness of barrelhouse blues are banished in favour of a deadpan jauntiness, the white-toothed grin in the black or blackened face. At the same time this bouncing self-confidence is modified in the process of re-creation, for the obvious reason that the Negro could embrace it only in wish-fulfilment. So the white march's bonhomie is compromised by the habitual syncopation, the Negro body-rhythm, flexed against the pulse of Time, displacing metrical symmetry; by the chromatic passing notes that may derive from the Negro's *ad hoc* talent for

choral improvisation; and by the dandified elegance of the figuration.

We may recall that the black (as distinct from white) source of ragtime was the cake-walk, a grotesque dance wherein, in the days of slavery, Negroes competed for a prize of cake. Parodistic imitation of the white man, of the white man's image of the Negro, and perhaps of the black man's image of himself co-exist, and lend undercurrents at once satirical and wistful to the merriment of Joplin's music. It may have been this ambiguity that conquered black and white public alike: through his rags the black man yearned for the white man's presumably civilized sophistication, while the white man longed for an Eden-like innocence which, in his world-weariness, he only affected to despise.

Although *Maple leaf* is a prototype from which Joplin did not radically depart, his art did develop. Having acquired conventional training from a German music teacher in his boyhood Texarkana, he worked assiduously at his self-appointed task of creating a literate black music. On the whole he used his technical skills not to broaden his convention, but to realize its limited implications with deeper subtlety. This is evident if one compares *Maple leaf* with the now ubiquitously popular *The Entertainer*, a ragtime two-

Opposite: Albert Ammons (left) with Pete Johnson in boogie-woogie duet, New York, 1941.

Below: Jelly Roll Morton and his Red Hot Peppers.

step composed three years later. In this delightful piece the lingering syncopation on the upward sixth and the oscillations between F major and minor generate a wide-eyed pathos. Five years later the richer textures of *Gladiolus Rag*[15] or *Wall Street Rag*[16] create an equilibrium between passion and the fragile elegance which is the mask the black man—not to mention the white—presents to the world. A few pieces outside the rag convention, the tango *Solace*,[16] with its sumptuous trio, and the concert-waltz *Bethena*,[16] with its naïvely surprising modulatory capers, encouraged Joplin to intensify the ragtime form, and so led to the rags of his last years: notably *Euphonic Sounds*,[14] remarkable for its elliptical modulations in the second strain and for the stop-time syncopations whose beat is merely implicit; and *Magnetic Rag*,[14] distinguished by its resonant disposition on the keyboard, its complex, Spanish-tinged rhythm, and even by a hint of sonata development in its third and fourth strains.

Rag is a minor art form, charming and, in the better pieces of Joplin, Scott and Lamb, subtle in texture and tonal organization. Nonetheless it is an art limited by its nature—by the black man's desire to remake himself in a white image. This may be why Joplin's success story is also a failure. Broken by the disastrous flop of his

operatic venture, he died in a lunatic asylum, of a condition in part syphilitic, in part neurotic. Yet while the parallel Joplin himself drew between his rags and Chopin's mazurkas is invalid, it is true that the best rags have proved musically more durable than most 'concert' music composed contemporaneously by whites; it is also evident historically that rag was essential to the evolution of the blues into jazz. We have already noticed that rag intrudes into the playing of 'instinctive' blues-men like Roosevelt Sykes, or even the more primitive Robert Shaw. The process also works the other way round: ragtime pianists grow in stature when their ragging veers towards improvisation and the bitter-sweet veracity of the blues. The key figure here is Jelly Roll Morton, self-styled 'inventor' of jazz.

Jelly Roll's *Kansas City Stomp*[17] is a superb example of fusion between the rag's artistry, the improvisatory vigour of barrelhouse piano, and the passion of the blues. Tune and structure are those of a ragged military two-step, with a tuning-up introduction, two themes in the tonic and a trio in the subdominant. The complex counter-rhythms, however, are authentic barrelhouse; while the displacements of accent and false relations betray the influence of the blues. *King Porter Stomp*[17] offers a variant of this formula. There is a four-bar introduction, a sixteen-bar tune in A flat, another sixteen-bar section in the relative minor, wherein the offbeat syncopations become the essence of the melodic line. After the trio, conventionally in the subdominant, the tune does not return to A flat, but falls flatter still, to G flat major. The climax brings in the blues, with a riff alternating between E natural and E flat; abruptly the music stops on the dominant seventh. The impact of this piece depends on the paradoxical way it grows more exciting as its tonality *subsides*. The same happens in a Sousa march, in which the triumphant apotheosis of the subdominant trio theme enshrines the Hearth and Home the warriors are fighting for. Jelly Roll makes his apotheosis—in the subdominant of the subdominant!— a trenchant musical image for the Negro's capacity for acceptance, and then for resilience.

The European influence in Jelly Roll's music is chiefly due to the fact that he came from New Orleans, where French, Spanish, Italian and Caribbean infiltrations brought to the black man's music a relatively easy sensuality. Morton was a literate musician proud of the lightness of his skin ('All my folks was white'), and in playing his version of the '*Miserere*'[17] from *Il Trovatore* he demonstrates that Italian opera flirts delightedly with ragtime, rumba and *habanera*. As early as 1902 Jelly Roll had put 'the Spanish tinge' into his *New Orleans Joys*,[17] and remarked that 'if you can't manage to put tinges of Spanish in your tunes, you'll never get the right seasoning for jazz'. Certainly in a splendid piece such as *Spanish Swat*,[17] Morton creates a synthesis of military two-step with tango and *habanera* that has no less punch than mid-West barrelhouse music, though it is warmer and less aggressive.

The tradition of New Orleans piano still survives, for Professor Longhair (born Roy Byrd in 1918) plays crudely forceful barrelhouse blues, both slow (*Professor Longhair blues*),[18] and quick (*Boogie woogie*).[18] His most characteristic numbers are impregnated with the New Orleans Latin-American flavour, sometimes harking back to the *habanera* style of Jimmy Yancey (*Professor Longhair's blues-rumba*), sometimes translating the Spanish tinge into the exuberance of rock (*Tipitina, Mardi Gras in New Orleans*).[18] Piano rag and barrelhouse piano brashly combine in Professor Longhair's heady music, though the melancholy of the vocal blues is less evident. It is potently present, however, in the singing and playing of Cousin Joe of New Orleans (b. 1917), whether in the weary boogie rhythm of *Life's a one-way ticket*,[19] the bare, Yancey-like economy of *Barefoot boy*,[19] or the seductive slow rumba of *Country boy*.[19]

From Honky-Tonk to Night-Club

Though New Orleans was a melting-pot wherein barrelhouse piano and piano rag stewed productively, it was a backwater since, as we have noted, most of the great jazz pianists gravitated north. The transition from barrelhouse music to rag-influenced jazz was in part a change in social status; we can hear how this happened if we listen to Leroy Carr, a country singer who, having settled in Chicago, took up the piano, while still collaborating with an old-style blues guitarist, Scrapper Blackwell. Both in his lyrics and in his comparatively sweet singing Carr sophisticates the blues. This is true of his pianism also, not because it is virtuoso but because he developed into a composer of memorable, affectingly harmonized blues melodies. When he sings *How long blues*[20] (which Yancey plays so poignantly) the effect depends on the disparity between the lightly lyrical voice and mellifluous, almost bland piano, and the pinched, scrawny sound of Scrapper Blackwell's guitar. The primitive blues was usually a chord sequence with vocal ululations improvised over it; Carr's blues have melodies so distinctive that they can acquire the status of jazz 'standards'. Thus Champion Jack Dupree, who can play the meanest barrelhouse in his *Work house blues*,[21] can also create a movingly lyrical *composition* out of Carr's *Blues before sunrise*;[21] while Memphis Slim, who traces his roots in the hard-hitting barrelhouse-rag of Roosevelt Sykes, can reconcile this, in the big-city lonesomeness of *Four o'clock in the morning*,[22] with Carr's (in two senses) 'composed' lyricism.

Lyricism and composition lead from bar and bawdy-house towards the fashionable night club, where blacks play for whites' amusement. James P. Johnson is a key figure who, nurtured in barrelhouse and rag traditions, moved not to Chicago but to New York. In the metropolitan centre he worked in cabaret and in Tin Pan Alley, writing musical comedies and abortive symphonic works. We do not remember him for these, except indirectly since his style of jazz piano was affected by his dabblings in pop song and art music. His playing offers a history of jazz in microcosm. In numbers such as *The mule walk*,[23] he harks back beyond jazz to the country fiddle and banjo tunes of the nineteenth century, emulating the banjo's click with acciaccaturas, yet jazzing the tunes through his cross-rhythmed tenor parts. In *If dreams come true*[23] he unleashes a bouncing stride bass beneath melodies that dance in rhythmic ellipsis. The gaiety of country dance swings into the ebullience of jazz; while the left hand's tenths and the precision of the figuration veer towards the more hedonistic aspects of pop music. In *Lonesome reverie*,[23]

Cousin Joe (Pleasants) in New Orleans.

Fats Waller at the piano: a scene from the film *Stormy Weather*.

on the other hand, Johnson starts from the negative or escapist properties of Tin Pan Alley (consider the parallel sevenths of the opening), but gives them so clean a refurbishing that they too become zestful. Most characteristic of all is *Blueberry Rhyme*,[23] whose charming tune has the simplicity of a country dance, though the slow swing which Johnson gives it is authentic jazz. The cleanness of texture—the ripely spaced tenths, the noodling tenor part, the delicate *fioriture*, the almost airy boogie bass—is highly art-ful, however; not surprisingly, this music appealed strongly to sophisticated players like Art Tatum and Thelonious Monk.

Directly in the tradition of James P. Johnson is Willie the Lion Smith, who also operated in New York and claimed that jazz might as well have been born, not in New Orleans, but 'in Haverstraw, New York, among the Baptists and in the brickyards'. As a pianist he has much

of James P.'s elegance, playing rag-orientated numbers (such as Johnson's *Carolina Shout*[24]) with no less vivacity, though with jazzier abandon in the right hand. Like Johnson, Willie was a composer who took his creation seriously, if without James P.'s symphonic pretentions. His pieces, usually fast in tempo, are a sophistication of rag with a residue of barrelhouse vigour. Listening to his *Echoes of spring*,[24] with its floating boogie bass and flickering treble, or to the more moderate paced *I'm gonna ride the rest of the way*,[25] with its stalking bass and minor-keyed melody, one can understand why Billy Strayhorn (Ellington's arranger)[50] admired the Lion's compositions. Some pieces are rhythmically as well as texturally elaborate. The oddly titled *Relaxin'*[24] is anything but relaxed, being full of rhythmic hiatuses; while in *Zig-zag*[24] an ostinato bass is pierced by a tune that runs zig-zag in the middle range of the keyboard. Sonority is darkly brooding; and there

is a comparable unease behind the relaxation of *Late hours*,[25] since the loping gait is cut and torn by acciaccaturas.

The hint of unease in Willie's music finds an echo in most of the cabaret pianists, even jolly Fats Waller. In the twenties, Fats played authentic blues with men of the calibre of Muggsy Spanier, proving, in their versions of *Dallas blues* and *Royal Garden blues*, that his fleet right-hand technique could be wedded to a stride bass of remarkable potency. When he took up solo playing he often returned to old-fashioned barrelhouse style, as we can hear in *The Minor Drag*,[26] in which he extracts a ribald comedy from the typical cross-rhythms. To the genial Fats tension was less relevant than exuberance; so he developed his jazz in the direction of pop, maintaining the driving bass and vigorous riffs, while his right hand's twittering became increasingly delicate. His version of *Twelfth Street Rag*[25] is high comedy; irresistibly witty is the zest released, in *Truckin'*,[25] by the repeated-note figure in the bass.

Inseparable from the sprightly elegance of his pianism is Fats' gift for the memorable tune. 'You gotta have a melody, Jimmy Johnson taught me that', he remarked: so in becoming a popular entertainer he was fulfilling, not denying his nature. *Ain't Misbehavin'*[26] is a fetching tune which, played with Waller's bounce, sounds at its climax at once happy and (like the words) non-committal. This gives the song a clownish pathos which is perhaps Fats' most characteristic note. In *I'm gonna sit right down and write myself a letter*,[26] he achieves gaiety out of self-depreciation, the precision of his pianism supporting both the words and the throw-away vocal style. It is in this sense that his jollity may be a release from unease; it says much for the quality of Fats' merriment that he can make something at once daft and deft out of a tune as inane as *Tea for two*.[26] Waller's comedy turns, such as the wry anti-love song *Your feet's too big*,[26] are part of his physical well-being; nor is jazz banished from his elaborate 'piano arrangements'—such as his *Honeysuckle rose*,[26] which begins with chromatic sequences in the manner of Gottschalk's parlour pieces, but hots up the charm with boogie rhythms, and ends by laughing at itself, crossing rag with a genteel waltz.

Waller veers from jazz towards pop; Earl 'Fatha' Hines, born a year later in 1905, embraces some elements of pop, and of art music too. Like Louis Armstrong, Hines started as a Chicago jazzman in the twenties, producing with Armstrong in *Weatherbird*[27] perhaps the most celebrated duet in jazz history, the energy and inner tension of his piano playing a perfect

complement to Satchmo's trumpeting. But the blues remains basic to Hines's playing, and the several versions of his *Blues in thirds*[28] (sometimes known as *Caution blues*) are classic jazz statements. The tune, hesitant yet irresistible, is beguiling enough to be a pop standard; the effect of Earl's improvisations is, however, richly equivocal. The tenths of the bass are sensual fulfilment, against which the 'trumpet style' right hand clatters in sharp octaves, prances in pianistic abandon, imitating brass vibrato. The music is tense within its sensuality, melancholy within its vibrancy—as Johnson's and Waller's is not; passages of sharp directness and of dreamy impressionism alternate. In this respect the sadness of the music is similar to that of Ellington, whose numbers Earl frequently plays with a richness of sonority approximating to that of the Ellington band.

In some of the music of Hines's middle years his equivocation between 'classic' jazz and Romantic impressionism offers temptations he cannot entirely resist. In *Diane*,[29] the slow introduction that comes from Chopin and Debussy via Hollywood has no necessary relationship to the swinging dance that follows it; and the mandoline effects become emptily decorative. There are however successes in this manner—notably a very sad *Rosetta*;[30] and we must remember that it is because Hines has more 'art' than a functional barrelhouse player or an instinctive genius like Yancey that he offers more criteria for criticism. Even today, now well into his seventies, he plays with the highly charged electricity typical of his youth: and can even outdo Waller in creating a large-scale, unfailingly inventive variation-set

Earl 'Fatha' Hines conducting his orchestra during a 1940 session.

on the insidious *Tea for two*:[30] He spreads himself, too, in another corny but delectable standard, *Dinah*, exploring a wide range of keyboard textures with tenderness and wit. His athletic two-voiced, two-handed style is starker and leaner than in early days: but still more potent.

It we can claim Hines to be in many ways the supreme figure in the 'classic' era of jazz piano, it is partly because his bluesy folk roots grow into and embrace the related worlds of pop and art music. Some of his disciples— notably Teddy Wilson—rival him in elegant agility while maintaining the momentum of barrelhouse music; yet their world is circumscribed compared with Hines's infinite variety, and their harmonic-textural sophistication seems almost bland. It is relevant to note that Wilson specialized in standards rather than blues, and not surprisingly succeeded most when the tunes were best. His relaxed, swinging version of *Between the devil and the deep blue sea* [31] is enchanting, and he seldom lets us down when playing the tunes of the finest of jazz-pop composers, Gershwin.[32]

But the climax to the sophistication of jazz piano comes with the phenomenal figure of Art Tatum (b. 1910), the Big City's complement to the blind guitar-playing virtuosos of the country blues. We associate him with city-music, especially with the standards of the jazz era, on which he lavishes a piano technique never before encountered in jazz. Playing Carmichael's *Stardust*, Gershwin's *The man I love*, Berlin's *Isn't this a lovely day*, Porter's *Night and Day* [33]—to cite only numbers distinguished in their own right—Tatum weaves textures of orchestral luxuriance, combining poly-rhythms with chromatic harmony and modulatory adventures made possible only by his prodigious technique. Working as soloist in night clubs, Tatum was no less than Ellington a show-biz man, rather than a functional jazz musician who played for dancers. In *Sophisticated lady* [33] he takes an Ellington tune and treats it with a harmonic and figurative resource entirely comparable with Ellington's. Similarly in his ear-boggling version of Cole Porter's *Begin the beguine*,[33] he maintains a furious jazz rhythm (barrelhouse Latin-Americanized) in kaleidoscopic chromatic harmony, pierced by sizzling scales and rip-roaring arpeggios.

Art Tatum.

Significantly, Tatum is greatest of all when he plays blues not by himself but with other musicians, even though his colleagues may pale beside his virtuosity. The simple, improvised *Blues in C* and *Blues in B flat*,[35] which he made with Benny Carter, are archetypal statements; we do not gasp in astonishment at their acrobatics, but accept with wonder their tug at the heart-strings.

Tatum flourished during the Big Band era of the forties and early fifties; he was a band in himself. The function of the piano in the context of the big band was, however, to stimulate by opposition. In the Basie band soloists do not merely oppose, but *fight against* the ensemble; and the Count usually opens the battle himself with a piano solo, sharp as glinting glass, which calls the horn-blowing soloists into action to confront the savage shouts of the ensemble chorus. Basie's soloists are holding their own against the predatory vigour of an industrial technocracy that barks in the brass, crackles in the percussion. The wiriness of Basie's own playing holds on positively, even jauntily, in the face of the City's threat. Though Basie featured himself as initiator rather than soloist, it was the steely precision of his pianism that gave the band wit—and grace—as well as power.

The human spirit will survive as long as someone can play piano with that incorruptible, fraught economy; and we can appreciate Basie's playing the more easily in the eighties since he has recorded, under the title of *Basie Jam*,[36] a number of improvised tracks with only a few distinguished soloists. The long, slow blues *Hanging Out* ends with a Basie solo characteristically chippy yet at the same time powerfully pathetic; and the nervous energy latent in Basie's fast-driving pianism is manifest when he shifts from the very slow (but not relaxed) *Hanging out* into the vivacity of *Red Bank blues*.

This same quality—elegant yet muscularly tensile—distinguishes the playing of another Kansas City pianist of the 'powerhouse' era, Mary Lou Williams. When she plays a barrelhouse number, *The rocks*,[37] her beat is as resilient as Basie's, her right-hand figuration less glassy but no less delicate. She is closer in this respect to the amiable Fats Waller; and like Fats she also betrays 'compositional' tendencies that recall Jelly Roll Morton. In her later career, since her religious conversion, she has created a highly personal improvised-composed music. Gershwin's *It ain't necessarily so*,[38] for example, is played in hesitantly elusive rhythm over an ostinato bass. The effect is sad—as though, being a committed Christian, she wishes it *were* so, even if it ain't. Her fast

Sometimes Tatum's technique and inventiveness get the better of his musical instinct. The harmonic elaboration, interesting in itself, destroys continuity; the breath-taking *fioriture* lose their shock-value through repetition. *Willow weep for me*[33] is a strange example, in which the rhythm's complexity fails to get over because it does not 'carry' the harmonic and modulatory excursions. There is a danger in being a one-man orchestra, for the pianist-composer's clever hands may carry him where his integrity would not want to go. What happens in *Willow weep* could not occur in an Ellington piece, for Ellington must be aware of the band's identity as well as his own. He cannot play himself tipsy. It is thus hardly surprising that Tatum achieves his greatest work when farthest from the show-biz world. Though we do not immediately think of him in this context, he is a magnificent blues pianist, employing in his versions of *Mr Freddie blues*[33] and *Aunt Hagar's blues*[34] traditionally potent barrelhouse basses, chord clusters, tremolos and riffs to produce an untraditional opulence of harmony and figuration; here the exhibitionism is always at the service of the music.

Count Basie.

numbers also are often melancholy, because precarious: a jittery cat bounds through *A grand night for swinging*,[38] over nervously precise chords. Her version of *My blue heaven*,[38] is again wistful, the innocent tune, over a Latin-American ostinato, being displaced both rhythmically and harmonically. The music sounds wanderingly unresolved: as does *A fungus amungus*,[38] a serious-comic piece imitative of a stuttering gospel preacher, combining the instinctive boogie of a Meade Lux Lewis with the ragtime style of Ives and the experimental pianism of Henry Cowell!

We cannot conclude this section on the Big Band era without reference to its supreme representative: for although it is true that Duke Ellington 'has played piano, but his real instrument is the band', he nonetheless became in later years a formidable pianist — especially in his superb 1960 versions[39] of his own numbers with that other grand old man of jazz, Louis Armstrong. The sensuality of the Duke's 'deep-bedded' keyboard technique is related to that of Hines, and seems also to have been influenced by the spare pianism of Count Basie: patently in the incisive tremolos and false relations of *Lucky so and so*, latently in the introverted chromaticism of *Mood Indigo*, in which infinitesimally delayed accents give an interior electrical charge to apparently romantic relaxation. *Duke's place* achieves something comparable in quick tempo; the incantatory riff becomes atmospheric rather than orgiastic, and the hollow echo effect at the end introduces a new dimension, a hint of the Ellington poetry within the powerhouse. Even more impressive is the Duke's 1973 recording with his Big Four, especially in *Prelude to a kiss*.[40] Polychromatic texture could hardly be more sumptuous; yet again the Duke preserves a Basie-like linear incisiveness, so that the music is never self-indulgent but is, in its emotional quality, tough as steel. His integrity was never compromised by his necessary affiliation with a commercialized world; and 'modern' man's need not be either.

From Cabaret to Modern Jazz

During the Big Band era pianists found it difficult to assert themselves in such a large ensemble; this is probably why the forties and early fifties was the great age of solo pianists, culminating in Hines, Tatum and Williams, all improvisers whose approach was 'orchestral' and compositional. We may regard Erroll Garner as an appendix to these players, though unlike them he was a 'natural', academically illiterate. The fresh gaiety of his own *Play, piano, play*[41] shows little trace of Hines' or Mary Lou's dreamy melancholy; even when he plays

sentimental numbers like *Body and soul*[41] he introduces the melody with a stomp of tremendous rhythmic impetus, which does not entirely evaporate when the tune takes over with a slow-swinging lilt. Indeed, the rhythmic animation climbs deviously through the right hand's repeated chords, which spread upwards from the chugging bass. Hammered triads create a curious stuttering effect, so that although the boogie bass is aerated and the right hand frisks, there is a nervous quality to the happiness.

The nervous intensity latent in Basie, Williams and Garner becomes patent when, with the close of the Big Band era, the jazz pianist began to function once more as

an ensemble player; the key figures are Thelonious Monk and Bud Powell. Although Monk habitually worked as an ensemble man, we can most effectively examine his pianism in the impressive disc he made as soloist, without even the support of bass and percussion. He has recorded many group versions of his famous number *'Round midnight*, a mood-piece with Ellingtonian warmth in the haunting tune, but with a late-night queasiness in the stalking bass and gaunt texture. Nonetheless the deepest expression of this fantasy of lonesomeness occurs when Monk plays it by and to himself.[42] The beat is present only by implication; that we sense it at all is a tribute to Monk's art, for the pulse is

Below: Erroll Garner.
Bottom: Bud Powell.

Opposite: Thelonious Monk.

so slow that the music seems about to stand still. Yet the beautifully spaced, sonorously scrunchy added-note chords, the metallic acciaccaturas, the very high and very low tremolos, the self-communing chromaticism of the inner parts, are all extraordinarily tense, reinforced by the hard tone that Monk's rudimentary technique draws from the keyboard—he plays with stiff, splayed-out fingers.

The solo version of *'Round midnight* 'lets in the silence' more than any of the ensemble versions. There is a sense of screwed-up expectancy; the music might at any moment break down, or it might explode into heaven or hell knows what. It owes its impact partly to the frustration it creates, partly to its acceptance, with 'a kind of furious calm', of frustration itself. The effect becomes still odder when Monk improvises on a standard such as *Getting sentimental over you*.[42] The immensely slow pulse and the rhythmic hiatuses are not here ironical in effect, any more than are the sudden (clumsily Tatum-like) spurts of decoration. The music moves like a bird with a broken wing; the pathos is that of a maimed creature. In *I should care*[42] Monk presses down each note as though its disturbance of silence were an agony. Yet if we consider this piece beside the very slow, very moving blues entitled simply *Functional*,[42] we can see how the modern elements complement the traditional ('functional') elements in Monk's playing. Here pulse, however emaciated, still exists, along with boogie rhythm, glinting tremolos, reiterated chords, percussive blue notes and note-clusters. All these traditional features seem, however, separated in space and time, surrounded by silence.

Perhaps Monk's modernity lies in the force he generates from frustration. Bud Powell did not suffer from Monk's technical limitations, but was a distraught character who sought his own pianistic parallels to the melodic invention of the supreme genius of Modern Jazz—the no less anguished alto saxophone player Charlie Parker. Powell's version of Monk's *'Round midnight*[43] is less hesitant, but more percussively painful, than the original. More typically, he exploits brittle right-hand chords and figurations against a nervously 'bopping' bass, as in *Caravan Riffs*.[43] In its jittery fragmentation Powell's music often sounds 'high', and probably was so. Though he possessed a virtuoso technique which even Tatum is said to have admired, the impact of his performances often depends on our realizing that even technique can falter. Jazz 'danger' is always round the corner—especially in one of his most remarkable performances, *Un poco loco*.[44] This is how he differs from his only rival as pianist of the

Horace Silver.

bebop era, Dodo Marmarosa, who started as a disciple of Hines and Williams but then attempted to refine Tatum's opulence into an intensity comparable to that of Parker's sax-playing: a *conjunctio oppositorum* which could hardly have succeeded. There is fine music in *Bopmatism*[45] and *Trade winds*,[45] but he fell back into obscurity as Powell rose into the ascendant.

Monk and Powell represent the nervously wrought, and in that sense 'hot', pole of the bebop era. It is complemented by a 'cool' pole, the representatives of which are often white. Lennie Tristano, a conservatory-trained musician, is most interesting when closest to the blues, as in *Requiem*[46] (after its pretentiously Debussyesque introduction); least convincing when he attempts to subdue Parker-like complexities to composed formalities, as in his version of *These Foolish Things*.[46] More rewarding is Bill Evans, the white pianist who played with Miles Davis during 'the birth of the cool'. When he performs his solo version of Davis's *Blue in Green*,[47] he preserves the Miles-like sonority of his early playing. Both pulse and harmonic movement are slow, the middle register chords sensuous, the texture enveloping; yet through this texture, calm melodic lines soar high in the treble, insinuate in the tenor, occasionally reverberate in the bass. Evans's ability to make piano lines 'speak' is subtle; his harmonic sensuality is not passive but vital. Even when he plays fast numbers like *Autumn leaves*,[47] the rhythmic zest prompts song; he can preserve the adolescent frailty of a Disney tune, *Someday my prince will come*,[47] while giving it lyrical flow as cross-rhythms float in waltz time against the gentle boogie beat.

Evans came to maturity in the fifties and early sixties, establishing a trio with Scott LeFaro and Paul Motian on bass and drums. In recent years his music has become still more introverted; he plays with himself on double-tracked tape, and specializes in his own compositions, such as the exquisite *Song for Helen*.[48] Comparable to Evans is another white, romantically introspective pianist, Al Haig. In his *Lament* the harmony is of Tatumesque ripeness, but the melodic lines spring vernally and sing, like Evans's. His long version of Gershwin's *Summertime*[49] has an introduction recalling Gershwin's own atmospheric scoring.

Horace Silver combines similarly neo-romantic harmony with a more vivacious bounce and sprightly tunefulness. Having gone underground during the sixties, Silver has re-emerged as composer and lyric writer as well as pianist; in *Out of the night*[50] he delightfully fuses his brand of fifties pianism with

elements borrowed from rock. This works better than the widely publicized efforts of Dave Brubeck to mate jazz and 'art'. His *Two-part contention*[51] is supposed to be a jazzed two-part invention, but lacks Bach's tension between linear movement and harmony. Climax is forced by repetition of Brubeck's notorious punch chords: but white will is here no substitute for black ecstasy. The piece seems vastly too long because it does not, as the Indian music it also emulates does, transcend temporality.

A few other black pianists of the fifties must be mentioned, notably the neglected Herbie Nichols, who played as a trio with Al McKibbon and Art Blakey, and whose own compositions have clearly defined character, with simple diatonic melodies that flutter into arabesques. Pieces like *The gig* and *Terpsichore*[52] ring whimsical changes on quite complex chord sequences,

Otis Spann.

though textures are open, harmonies never opaque. Slighter but none the less beguiling is Red Garland, who like Evans once played with Miles Davis. His left hand swings quietly, while his right hand alternates tremulous roulades with sometimes explosive added-note chords. The effect, both wistful and slightly acid, comes over well in nostalgic ballads like Kern's *Long ago*,[53] whose Tatumesque spurts make the music not more brilliant, but more butterfly-frail. Garland complements Garner: whereas the latter reveals romanticism beneath the insouciant gesture, Garland starts with a nostalgic dream but impatiently shrugs it off. Most of his numbers end with a sudden, fierce barrelhouse tremolo, dismissing self-indulgent mooniness. Among pianists of the same generation Ahmad Jamal[54] achieves a similarly satisfying equilibrium between the elegiac and the immediate.

Jazz Piano Today

During the sixties and seventies all the traditions of jazz piano that we have discussed survive, and some of them prosper. Old-style barrelhouse piano has been reborn, along with the electrophonic revival of primitive blues associated with singers like Muddy Waters. Otis Spann stands among the finest players in the tradition: how deeply he is rooted in the past is evident in his *Home to Mississippi*,[55] which begins as a talkin' blues over a fastish beat, intensifies into something like a field-holler, then smashes irresistibly into piano boogie. *Blues is a botheration*[55] and *Someday*[55] are superb slow blues, grandly wailing, with authentically savage barrelhouse roulades. *Twisted snake*[55] recreates fast-western boogie, bristling with tremolos and cross-rhythms, thoroughly traditional except for its abrupt modulations. An old-style pianist like Robert Shaw is reborn in the hurly-burly of today's industrial technocracy: over which the music bravely rides roughshod.

Between barrelhouse revival and the night-club tradition stands Roland Hanna, for his playing preserves barrelhouse violence while jetting Tatum-like figuration into the upper reaches of the keyboard. He often plays Ellington numbers, which places him in the mainstream; his version of *Take the A-train*[56] is hard as sprung steel, with *fioriture* that spill dangerously over the striding bass, as though passion can hardly be contained. Clarity of outline is still manifest in his gently wayward version of *I got it bad*,[56] Tatumesque both in lyrical figuration and in sumptuous harmony. Among Hanna's own numbers *Perugia*[56] unfolds from slow triple-rhythmed expectancy into a hauntingly Spanish-tinged melody; *Time dust gathered*[56] is rhythmically brittle, harmonically luxuriant. Here his relation to Tatum's and perhaps Garner's romanticism is clear, though the music has grown tighter-sinewed, less opulent.

The direct successor to the Hines-Tatum tradition in today's jazz scene is, however, Oscar Peterson, the only pianist whose technical dexterity challenges Tatum on his own ground. Peterson takes his place among the supreme jazz pianists, combining Tatum's pyrotechnic virtuosity with Hines's linear, harmonic and rhythmic sensitivity, and is at its finest with Basie's wiry integrity as catalyst. How this happens is revealed on two magnificent discs of two-piano jazz issued under the title of *Satch and Josh*. In *Roots*,[57] Basie's linearly minimal, rhythmically elastic pianism carries an emotional potential that Peterson rides on in ecstasy; in *Home run*,[57] on the other hand, Peterson's tornado is pinpricked by Basie's discreet interjections. At his best Peterson without Basie achieves this wry, passionate

Cecil Taylor.

maturity; though it is significant that he is often at his best when duetting, if not with Basie, with a horn-blowing musician. His 1974 performances with the trumpeter Harry Edison are particularly impressive. The improvised blues *Basic* and *Signify*[58] are indeed 'breath-taking' in their rhythmic subtlety, and the swirling Tatumesque figurations are real imaginative 'flights'. Nor does Peterson's agility preclude tenderness, evident in the bluely tinkling, then whirling figurations which the pianist weaves in and out of Milt Jackson's vibraphone in Jamal's lovely *Night mist blues*.[58]

The most significant offsprings from the traditions of Modern Jazz are Cecil Taylor and McCoy Tyner. Taylor is an academically trained, black musician whose early work developed extravagantly from Ellington, Monk, Powell, Parker and Mingus. *Nona's blues*[59] is basically a twelve-bar blues on the conventional chord sequence, the tempo furious, the rhythmic drive dynamic. The effect is wild, the melody instruments wailing almost Asiatically over a voodoo-style African rhythm. Sometimes the saxophone's skirls and the piano's percussive note-clusters boil over in a crazy sizzling; but while this piece is positive in total effect, Taylor's violence sometimes becomes destructive. *Mixed*[60] is a mixed-up love song that begins with soupy piano chords, but its pop-style idiom is soon shattered by rhythmic contrarieties and non-harmonic clusters. *Pots*[60] is a piece of voodooism that grows gradually screwier, off-beat, off-key over the remorseless drumming, until it finally disintegrates. This 'return to the womb' has led Taylor in his recent work to the exploration of a jazz-rooted but 'free' music which does not necessarily call on traditional methods of organizing melody and harmony. Significantly several of these pieces—*Nefertiti the beautiful one has come*[61] for example—invoke the black man's ancestral gods, 'the beauty of his wild forebears—a mythology he cannot inherit'. The howling heterophony, the cascading note-clusters are (like Stravinsky's *The Rite of Spring* half a century before) at once negative, in that their violence attacks a world grown moribund, and positive, in that they remind us of deep instinctive springs that modern man has forgotten.

A similar evolution is discernible in the work of McCoy Tyner, who started in the fifties as pianist to John Coltrane. On the disc *Coltrane plays ballads*, both saxophonist and pianist preserve the ballad's nostalgia, with wailing refrain-phrase on sax and added note chords on piano. There is a destruction of the temporal sense; memory and desire dissolve into an ecstatic present. When Coltrane and Tyner turn from ballads to blues, as in *Blues to Elvin*,[62] they build on the traditional

progressions, though their broken rhythms, nagging repetitions and sudden hiatuses sound both nervous and non-Western. Tyner's piano solos have here learned something from Bud Powell while harking back to the barrelhouse by way of Monk and Basie. In *Mr Knight*[62] Coltrane's wailings are Asiatic and flamenco-like, while Tyner's ostinati on empty fifths are intermittently Latin-American and primitively African. By the time Coltrane has entered his 'religious' phase, as in *Out of this world*, Tyner comes as close as he can, on a tempered piano, to Coltrane's *ecstasis*. His chord changes, hypnotic in their repetition, become in effect non-Western ostinati. The reiteration of pattern makes us wait, breathless, for the return of Coltrane's saxophonic yell, which ends the music in the only way possible—with an explosion.

Since Tyner established his own group in 1964, and became his own composer, he has further explored his revocation of an ancient heritage. In *Song for my lady*[63] the piano riff at the opening is harmonically rich but does not behave like 'Western' harmony: its obsessive repetitions prompt savage howls from the melody instrument. The piece has no beginning, middle and end; we live in it while the sound lasts, as in genuine African musics. In Tyner's recent work the 'return to Africa' becomes explicit. The first side of the disc *Asante*[64] employs indigenous instruments (wooden flute, kungas, bells, an African girl's voice) to evoke African gods, while the second side deals in Tyner's recollections of his childhood in the American South. The sound-world of ancient Africa is magically evoked, no less by Tyner's shimmering piano cascades than by the authentic African elements. And listening to the American side, we realize how profound the Afro-American synthesis is. The basic material is American funky; the treatment of it is African; Tyner turns his modern concert grand into a quasi-African percussion instrument when he plucks its strings.

A comparably African element is inherent in much of the music Keith Jarrett has created for ensemble—for instance the sequence *Vision, Common Mama* and *The Magician in you*.[65] The non-Western qualities of this music are, however, less obvious than those of Tyner's; significantly the vision is summoned romantically by a halo of strings. These pieces link with Jarrett's work as improvising solo pianist, in which his romanticism is implicit in chromatic harmony and elaborate figuration. His music is even more introverted than that of Bill Evans, since its beat is so elusive. It would be accurate to describe Jarrett's music as an authentic, if paradoxically disintegrative, evolution within jazz; jazz harmony and

Keith Jarrett.

melody survive, released from the tyranny of beat; and something is gained even if the traditional tension between beat and line is sacrificed. Everything depends, in so introverted a music, on what used to be called inspiration. When Jarrett really takes off, as in his 1975 Cologne sessions,[66] the music can be deeply moving, with basically simple, often modal melodies, fluid textures and coruscating harmonies. On other occasions, Jarrett's improvisations, which go on a long time, seem self-indulgent; either way their retreat into the inner life relates to the preoccupation of recent jazz with an 'eternal return' to origins. The solo improvisations of Chick Corea—*Noon Song*,[67] for instance, and *Sometime ago*[67]—come into the same category: childlike in melodic modality to start with, luxuriantly turning inwards as harmony and texture flower, while rhythm meanders, seeking a home that might be Eden.

And Eden, we have seen, may also be a legendary Africa whose strong gods are reinvoked—by lost white men as well as by deracinated blacks. The story of jazz piano comes full circle in the music of the Cape

Coloured pianist Dollar Brand, who was born in 1934 of mixed origins, African, Afrikaans, European and Malaysian. His father was a Basuto tribesman, his mother a trained European-style musician, a pianist, leader of a Christian church choir. Dollar's musical start was thus in native musics, in missionary church music, and in the *marabi* bands on city streets. In the fifties he was mainly a band leader, playing innocently eupeptic forms of jazz-tinged African pop. His talent as pianist was, however, so remarkable that Duke Ellington, hearing him while on tour, invited him to New York. There Dollar worked with the Duke himself, and came under the influence of Thelonious Monk. The disc that made Dollar famous, in 1964, *Anatomy of a South African Village*,[68] includes a version of Monk's '*Round midnight* which, although subject to Monk-like frustrations, yet creates its own momentum; the arabesques, though spasmodic, are a kind of release. The midnight he is prowling in is not just New York's, but also that dark time of the year from which, in seasonal cycle, life may burgeon.

As it does indeed in Dollar's most typical music. Starting from barrelhouse blues, tautened by Monk's fragmented pianism, Dollar hands the music back to his ancestors; as the barrelhouse train honky-tonks into the jungle or desert, a tribal world is restored. Interestingly enough, Dollar's most positive pieces are those which most abruptly juxtapose opposites: snatches of African tribal music and of British missionary hymn, pounding African drums and sanctimonious-sounding European chordal sequences. *Tintinyana*[68] is a superb example, in which African ostinati interact with British evangelical harmony and flower into American jazz.

Dollar has now settled permanently in New York, partly because he there has the freedom to develop his music—a freedom denied him in his own country. Not surprisingly, however, the most recent phase of his music tends to be the most African, and also the most 'universal', as we can hear in *Sathima*,[69] in which Dollar becomes a one-man band. He plays a prelude on bamboo flute (assisted by the vocal chords), mysteriously evoking ancient Africa. Clanging bells on piano seem to banish the dark continent, but really renew it, since white-hymn is turned into pastoral pentatonics— what Dollar calls 'rural lament'. The tune is hesitant, lifting up a tone, groping towards the light, over a pedal. Gradually rhythm solidifies, and flute and piano arabesques flow into rippling waters of life. The climax comes in a piano cadenza, no longer a dream, complex both in rhythm and (Ellingtonian) harmony. When the pastoral melody returns it is resolved lyrically, and fades into thin air; and the African flute melody re-emerges, heard with new ears, because the new Africa—that of the City *and* of the pastoral dream—seems to be contained within it. The Edenic dream exists, while the old Africa persists, a fusion of African circular form with European linear structure—enacting in this piece the very process of African history. Maybe the ragbag of races and conventions that go to make up a global village may ultimately embrace the disparities of straight line and circle, and forge new life from an act of praise.

I have described jazz piano in its barrelhouse origins as a very sexy music; its sexuality was a celebration of life within the minimal conditions allowed to the Negro. It is interesting that the playing of the remarkable Arizona Dranes – a black Texan woman who thumped piano to God's glory in the twenties[70]—reveals that there were deep currents connecting the religious enthusiasm of black gospel music with the secular enthusiasm of the barrelhouse. The sounds made by Arizona and by Dollar Brand (who now wishes to be known as Abdullah Ibrahim) are sometimes startlingly similar. Her Christian worship became a corporeal celebration; his bodily ecstasy becomes also Christian-Moslem worship. In going 'back' to Africa, jazz was rediscovering its religious heart; and Dollar's music, not merely in emergent Africa, but in the divided and distracted world we all live in, is balanced on a razor's edge between hazard and hope. That is why the jazz experience is crucial.

Jazz Piano Discography

This discography covers only records referred to in the text; I have kept the list to a minimum, even though this means the choice of examples is sometimes less complete than it could be. I have also restricted records and commentary to Afro-American material, since piano jazz is an Afro-American phenomenon. It is a pity to omit pianists of other nationalities; but to have included them would have opened the floodgates to jazz as a 'global' experience. As it is, I have omitted with regret a number of pianists who could have been included in a longer study—at random I think of Cripple Clarence Lofton, Nat King Cole, Phineas Newborn, Tommy Flanagan and Herbie Hancock.

1 Texas Piano Blues/TBP 001
2 Texas Barrelhouse Piano: Robert Shaw/Arhoolie F 1010
3 Piano Jazz Vol. 1/Vogue LA 9069
4 Cuttin' the Boogie/New World 259
5 The Jazz Piano/JP 5003
6 The Immortal Jimmy Yancey/OL 2802
7 Yancey's Getaway/RLP 12 124
8 Low Down Dirty Blues/Atlantic 590 018
9 Cripple Clarence Lofton and Walter Davies/Yazoo L 1025
10 Little Brother Montgomery: Faro Street Jive/Xtra 1115
11 Blues: Roosevelt (the Honeydripper) Sykes/Folkways FS 3827
12 Alex Moore/Arhoolie F 1008
13 Albert Ammons and Pete Johnson/RCA 730 561
14 Scott Joplin; piano rags/RLP 8815 and Nonesuch H 71257
15 Heliotrope Bouquet/Nonesuch H 71248
16 Piano rags/Nonesuch H 71264
17 Jelly Roll Morton: the Library of Congress tapes/RLP 9001- 9012
18 New Orleans Piano: Professor Longhair/Atlantic SD 7225
19 Cousin Joe of New Orleans/BLS 6078
20 Leroy Carr blues/CC50
21 The Piano Blues/Storyville 671 187
22 Memphis Slim/Xtra 1008
23 James P. Johnson/Col. 1780
24 Willie the Lion Smith/VJD 501/1
25 Fats Waller and his Rhythm/Col. 6127
26 Ain't misbehavin'/LPM 1246
27 Louis Armstrong's Vintage Years/Odeon 2C 152 05 166
28 Quintessential Recording Session: Earl Hines/CR 101
29 The Real Earl Hines/ATL 5031
30 Classic Jazz Piano/RD 7915
31 Teddy Wilson/BBL 7511
32 Mr Wilson and Mr Gershwin/BBL 7344
33 The Complete Art Tatum Piano Discoveries/TCF 102-2
34 The Art Tatum Piano Masterpieces/Pablo 2310 789
35 Art Tatum/Benny Carter/Pablo 2310 732
36 Basie Jam/Pablo 2310 718
37 Women in jazz: pianists/Stash ST 112
38 Mary Lou Williams/Mary FJ 2843
39 Echoes of an Era: Duke Ellington-Louis Armstrong/RE 108
40 Duke's Big Four/Pablo 2310 703
41 Erroll Garner/Col. CL 6173
42 Thelonious Monk himself/RLP 235
43 Bud Powell: Ups'n downs/MSL 1007
44 Bebop/NWR 271
45 Dodo Marmarosa/Spotlite 128
46 Lennie Tristano: Lines/Atlantic 590 031
47 Portrait in Jazz: Bill Evans Trio/Riverside RLP 1 315
48 Bill Evans: New conversations/WD BSK 3177
49 Al Haig: Solitaire/Spotlite SPJLP14
50 Horace Silver: Silver n' Voices/Blue note BN LA 708 G
51 Dave Brubeck Quartet/Col. CL 1609
52 Herbie Nichols: the Third World/Blue Note BN LA 485 H2
53 Red Garland: the Nearness of You/Jazzland JLP 62
54 Ahmad Jamal at the Blackhawk/NJL 48
55 Otis Spann: Cryin' Time/VSD 6514
56 Roland Hanna: Perugia/AF AL 1010
57 Satch and Josh again/Pablo 2310 802
58 Oscar Peterson and Harry Edison/Pablo 2310 741
59 Cecil Taylor Quartet/Ver. 8238
60 Cecil Taylor Septet/Imp A 9
61 Nefertiti the beautiful one has come/FLP 41095/2
62 Coltrane plays the blues/HA K 8017
63 Song for my lady/MSP 9044
64 Asante/Blue Note EN LA 223 G
65 Expectations: Keith Jarrett/CBS 6782
66 Keith Jarrett: the Koln Concert/ECM 1064/66 ST
67 Chick Corea: Piano improvisations/ECM 1014 ST
68 Dollar Brand: Anatomy of a South African Village/Fontana 688 314 ZL
69 Sathima for piano, cello and flute/South African Broadcasting Co. LT 15 498
70 Arizona Dranes: Barrelhouse Piano with Sanctified Singing/Herwin 210

Dollar Brand Speaks . . .

As far back as I can remember I was surrounded by music, at home and in the community. I was born in Cape Town; my father was a Basuto tribesman and my mother's family were Bushmen. On the female side my people were Christians, and my grandmother and mother both played piano in the local church and on social occasions. They played by ear; but sent me to have lessons with a local school teacher who taught me to read European music when I was seven; those local teachers ought to have a song composed in their honour.

But music wasn't basically something I learned from teachers—it was everything I soaked up from the world I lived in. The kids I went around with played any instruments they could lay their hands on—all kinds of bottles, pots and pans, flutes, saxes, drums, guitars, banjos, violins, piano and harmonium; and the music we made was partly traditional African, partly white missionary, mixed up with Cape Malay music (originally introduced by Malaysian slaves), and with snatches of European folk musics and of Afrikaans music which was only a little Dutch and about eighty per cent traditional Bushman. The Bushmen, that my mother came from, were the oldest inhabitants of southern Africa; but there was a big Moslem population too, and we heard a lot of Islamic music . . . . Then of course on radio and records we heard much American and European pop music too.

We never thought about where the different aspects of our music came from; we just picked them up from the air around us. As a kid I played the flute and sax and drums and piano and harmonium, mostly in bands for dancing to. There were lots of pianos around in Cape Town—about one to every home; there were many piano players too, some of them good. We played real African music, as well as missionary music and ragtime, on the pianos; and we played African music on harmoniums too, holding down drone notes, usually in fourths, with match-sticks. The street bands were called *marabi* bands and what we played was a mixture of traditional African music and hymns, ragtime, paso-dobles, quadrilles, lancers, square dances, anything that set us moving. The name of the bands changed with the generations—today they're appropriately called 'Now-now' bands—but they remain the same in essence.

I started playing boogie-woogie piano after I'd heard records of Jimmy Yancey, Meade Lux Lewis and Albert Ammons; I got hold of some notated versions of their music too. I immediately recognized the music as basically African—the left-hand piano style is like African drumming. We didn't regard boogie-woogie as American music, distinct from our own. And a lot of American horn playing sounded African to us also. I remember when we first heard Ornette Coleman it didn't sound at all strange to us; we recognized it because we'd been making that kind of noise for years. We called it 'Squeak Music'; and a friend explained its origins by remarking that, well, there was this woman, a very beautiful woman, and when she came into the dance-hall, wow, I just didn't know where those sounds came from! Then I began to form little groups, playing with the finest horn players in South Africa, like Kippie Moketsi, Basil Coetzee and Hugh Masekela. We took this more seriously, more musically, than the things I'd done as a kid in the community. But I still didn't think of myself as a 'pianist', and maybe I don't to this day.

I was however growing up, getting more aware; and perhaps because of that, my wife and I decided to get out of South Africa, at least for a while. This was in 1962. She came as singer with a piano-drums-bass trio; we played in Zurich, at a club called Africana. It happened that the Duke Ellington band was performing in Zurich at the same time. I'd known the Duke's music for some time from discs, and he was my god. Sathima, my wife, went to the Ellington concert, which was happening while we were doing a gig. By some miracle she managed to persuade the Duke and his entourage to come along, when his concert was over, to hear us play. We seemed to recognize a kinship. Ellington liked my music and took us to Paris, where he arranged for us to record, both as a trio and with Sathima. The trio record, issued under the title of *Duke Ellington presents the Dollar Brand Trio*, was my start in the international jazz field.

After that the Duke got us to New York and found work for us. Perhaps the most wonderful thing that's ever happened to me was when I deputized as pianist for Ellington in the band, on a tour of the West Coast. He asked me to take over because he was working on a film-score, against a deadline. I was too scared to play many notes, but learned and lived in being there—in particular I learned how important is the right piano introduction to an Ellington composition, if the music is to get going. Listening to that music on records is one marvellous thing, like floating on a still lake; listening to that music live in performance is another and more marvellous thing, like flowing down a great river; but being inside that music, making it, is a third and most marvellous thing, like plunging into the sea itself. I still play Ellington's music more than any other except my own. It seems to me deeply African—more so than that of many more obviously 'primitive' players.

In New York I also met Thelonious Monk a few times. I'm supposed to have been influenced by him, but I think it was more like just a spontaneous recognition of an affinity—we play the same, in some ways, because we feel the same. Contrary to report, I found him easy to talk to. When I thanked him for the inspiration of his music he opened his eyes wide and said 'Thank *you*! You know, you're the first *piano player* that ever said anything like that to me'. His technique, of course, is supposed to be limited—both he and Ellington said that, as a pianist, I was much more accomplished. But I've never thought about being technically expert. Of course I have to keep my fingers flexible and my body healthy and all that; but fingers and body and instrument concern me only as the medium through which spirit speaks.

For the last twelve years I've been studying *Bushido*, and the relation of me to the piano is like that of the Zen swordsman to his sword—which is a symbol of the invisible spirit keeping the mind, body and limbs in full activity. 'When the sword is lifted high', the Zen master says, 'there is hell to make you tremble; but go ahead. The fastest sword is never drawn'. It takes years and years of practice to stop thinking about the sword and to identify the sword with the act. That's how it is with me and a piano, when I'm really functioning. The piano is an extension. I don't need to think of technique, because the means have become the end and the end the means: a state of *mushin*, which literally means 'no mind'—a trance wherein everything is nothing and nothing everything.

This may happen with the sword or with the piano or flute or sax or drum; or for that matter with a broom sweeping the street or a rag polishing the floor. In this sense swordsmanship—in our case music—is life, and always was in traditional societies. Musical talent, in traditional societies, never exists in itself, but always in association with medicine, physiological or psychological—or both. I, who come from Africa, know this; but John Coltrane, who lived and worked in New York, knew it too. It applies both to the old tribal village and to the 'global village' of today's big cities, where it's still more necessary for musicians to heal souls and bodies. Our function is still to master the sword which encompasses everything and restores the Whole. Of course our sword-music is also Allah's way of providing us with bodily sustenance.

When I go into a concert I've usually only a vague idea of what I'm going to play. But seated in front of the piano, I soon know, since it's communicated to me from the source and from my response to the audience. The piano is merely intermediary: which is why its quality, as a musical instrument, is not all that important. Of course I'm pleased if it turns out to be a beautiful Bösendorfer—the finest instrument I've ever played. But there's no guarantee that the music made out of the Bösendorfer will be better than that produced from an old honkytonk upright; everything depends on the favourable or unfavourable circumstances. This may apply to most jazz pianists, though perhaps more to an African than to one born and bred in the States. I can't say much about this because I seldom listen to music, not even my own, except in the process of making it. Ellington and Monk, the two musicians who have meant most to me, are not supposed to be particularly brilliant as pianists; among those regarded as top virtuosi I prefer Earl Hines, whose fantastic technique is always the servant of the music, to Art Tatum or Oscar Peterson, who sometimes get drunk on their own acrobatics. I'm not saying they ought not, or that it's wrong for folk to enjoy their terrific performances: only that it's not the way I work.

After our spell in New York in the sixties, we returned to Europe for the Newport Jazz Festival; played and recorded a good deal in Germany; and returned to South Africa, living first in Swaziland, then back in Cape Town. I made a lot of records both solo and with first-class South African musicians; but eventually we decided we couldn't stay there, partly for the children's sake, partly for the sake of my music— what a crazy situation that I should be granted a licence to give a big outdoor concert, using black African musicians, only on condition that there were no black Africans in the audience! We're 'settled' in New York now, in the sense that we have a 'permanent' apartment, and the kids go to school here: though I still spend a high proportion of time touring in Europe, Australia and so on. Despite the much-advertised violence and brutality, I find New York, after South Africa, kind of peaceful. It's fine for the kids, there are excellent musicians to work with, good audiences to play to; basically the American people are good. As for South Africa, we just have to be vigilant, the same mode of thinking as the samurai. But when I talk about my piano as a sword, I'm not really thinking politically. My interest in Zen, in herbalism, in homeopathic medicine, is a force identical with my music. Ultimately it's a human question—the struggle of humanity against inhumanity, anywhere and everywhere. And that's what music has always been about.

Note: What Dollar Brand (Abdullah Ibrahim) means by his references to the Sword perhaps needs a little explanation. A quotation from Suzuki on 'Zen and Swordsmanship' may be helpful:

The sword is the soul of the samurai; therefore, when the samurai is the subject, the sword inevitably comes with him . . . The sword has a double office to perform: to destroy anything that opposes the will of its owner and to sacrifice all the impulses that arise from the instinct of self-preservation . . . In the case of the former, very frequently the sword may mean destruction pure and simple, and then it is the symbol of force, sometimes devilish force. It must, therefore, be controlled and consecrated by the second function. Its conscientious owner is always mindful of this truth. For then destruction is turned against the evil spirit. The sword comes to be identified with the annihilation of things that lie in the way of peace, justice, progress and humanity. It stands for all that is desirable for the spiritual welfare of the world at large. It is now the embodiment of life and not of death; it represents the force of intuitive or instinctive directness, which unlike the intellect does not divide itself, blocking its own pathway.

221

THE POPULAR PIANO

Le Bal blanc: painting by J. M. Avy, 1903.

Connoisseurs and Amateurs

It is not by accident that the piano was invented at a time when a separation between art and entertainment was first discernible: a separation related to the evolution of what we now call democracy, and of the industrialism that made democracy feasible. In the days of the High Baroque, J. S. Bach had composed music for organ, clavichord and harpsichord in which there was little differentiation between religious and secular genres, between functions devotional and social, or between environments aristocratic and bourgeois. His son Carl composed sonatas for harpsichord, clavichord and fortepiano which had no religious or public function but were intended for an élite qualified not by titular right but by sensibility: *Kenner und Liebhaber*, 'connoisseurs and amateurs'—those who know and those who love.

Another of Bach's sons, Johann Christian, said of his own C minor sonata: 'That is the way J. C. Bach would compose if he did not have to address himself to the children': which must be the first instance of a composer admitting that the style he adopted for commercial reasons was distinct from that in which he would honestly express himself. Division between a Style of Sensibility and a Popular Style is implicit in the Classical sonata, which was an external manifestation of inner dualities. Not for nothing was eighteenth-century Vienna a melting pot of Europe, at once a bastion of aristocratic privilege and a nursery of revolutionary fervour. The Viennese masters maintained a tense equilibrium between tradition and revolution, as between entertainment and art, although as the years passed, the breach gradually widened: Mozart's G minor quintet differs in degree but not in kind from his divertimenti, whereas Beethoven's last quartets and sonatas are a kind of music entirely distinct from *The Battle of Victoria* which, to the composer's chagrin, was his greatest popular success.

Only with Schubert, however, do the implications of the split between the Style of Sensibility and the Popular Style become fully manifest. For although Schubert wrote music for the Church, he no longer believed in the institution, which he equated with political oppression, so that his church music is not devotional in spirit. Similarly, although he wrote operas, he no longer believed in the State which heroic opera had been designed to celebrate, so his operas remained unsuccessful or unperformed. All his finest music he wrote for himself and his friends: he was a composer of Friendship as Bach had been a composer of the Church, and Handel a composer of the State. Nonetheless, Schubert was not able to support himself by composing

his friendly music. As a freelance musician he had to produce entertainment music for a degenerate aristocracy and a sentimental bourgeoisie whose tastes he could not fully share. That he would have preferred to spend more time, during the last years of his brief life, composing sonatas and symphonies is suggested by the fact that he disguised large-scale works as sequences of *morceaux* for piano solo or duet, publishable along with 'light' pieces unambiguously intended to amuse. It is evident all the same that he enjoyed writing his waltzes, marches and Ecossaises; and that, although his occasional music is beginning to differ from his 'serious' music in kind as well as (like Mozart's) in degree, he subtly invests it with the power to hit back.

It is clearly desirable that popular music should enliven as well as lull and amuse; if it enlivens too much, however, it will also disturb, and its function as social reassurance will be compromised. *Mere* entertainment must be a denial of the integrity of art. A balance between outward-going entertainment and inward-turning art is difficult to achieve, and is most likely to occur in transitional periods of civilization—such as the emergent democracy of Schubert's Vienna. The virtues of the piano as a democratic instrument are patent. It could serve the needs of democratic man in that it is a one-man band, capable of playing *cantabile* melody, elaborate polyphony and rich harmony. Compared to the harpsichord, it could efface itself to create a poetically 'orchestral' background to song; at the same time, compared to the clavichord, it could make enough noise to encourage social junketing. Its public sociability was thus inseparable from its personal sensibility. This is evident in the chains of dances that Schubert improvised or composed for pianoforte, from his teens to the end of his life. In the *Trauer-oder Sehnsuchts-Walzer* of 1816 we already find sensuous inner chromatics, languishing appoggiaturas and mysterious enharmonic modulations that might have perturbed dancers, had they stopped to listen; by the time of the *Grätzer Walzer* of 1827, there must have been many who preferred to listen rather than dance. These pieces are still bifunctional: exquisite art which also technically and imaginatively measures up to the 'occasion'. The salon pieces of Schubert's last two years, however, have become personal confessions, as romantically lonely as the dances of Chopin.

A piece like Schubert's C sharp minor *Moment musical*—or any of Beethoven's op. 126 *Bagatelles*—is obviously not concert music in the nineteenth-century sense, designed to be projected from a platform towards large audiences. But if such music is domestic, it

Below: Josef Gelinek: engraving, after Louis René Letronne.
Centre: Saint-Saëns in 1910.
Right: Title-page of an *opéra bouffe* by Jacques Offenbach.

presupposes performers who are gifted with uncommon sensibility and intelligence. There were a few such around then, as at any time; but common men, undistinguished by these attributes, were naturally in the majority and, in an emergent democracy, were becoming increasingly powerful. Their appetite for entertainment was insatiable: so there was need for a repertory of sociable music that was 'effective' precisely because it evaded Schubertian and Beethovian equivocation. One of the most obvious outlets was in piano variations on well-known tunes. These might be folksongs, which appealed to the Rousseauesque cult of the 'natural'—as is evident in Beethoven's folksong arrangements; more commonly they were urban tunes from operas and operettas, usually in four-bar periods that lent themselves to decoration.

Haydn, Mozart, Beethoven and Schubert all composed variation sets, mostly for home use. Great composers did not consider it beneath their dignity to produce such pot-boilers, for, given skill and sensibility, fine music could be cooked within the pot's confines. Nonetheless, distinctively original composers were not the safest boilers, and it is significant that at this time a generation of composers appeared for whom music was unambiguously a commodity. Josef Gelinek must be one of the earliest examples of a composing music-

factory, for having hit on a formula for variations that he knew he could sell, he composed virtually nothing else. The catchy tunes were always well known to his public, the treatment of them predictable. His variation sets, instantly acceptable and instantly forgettable, ran into four figures, and made him a substantial fortune.

Genre pieces about battles and tempests also sold well. But it was to the dance as a social act that the greater proportion of the new demotic music was dedicated. The most powerful affirmation of the new spirit was, indeed, the waltz, a call to action through bacchanalian movement, which took over as the aristocratic minuet 'degenerated' into the peasant *Ländler*. In the new society the minuet was 'out' and the waltz 'in'. To be in, it had to become socially amenable; it is no accident that the Viennese Waltz Kings, Lanner and the Strausses, were professional composers who deliberately devoted themselves to Entertainment rather than to Art. All their work was designed to fulfil a democratic social function and was originally conceived in orchestral form, as music for dancing or eating or talking to. Published as piano music, however, Viennese waltzes were copiously purchased for domestic use, and in their keyboard versions remain physical and communal, rather than personal, since they inculcate bonhomie within the group, usually at the expense of

personal feeling. Thus a Strauss waltz is inseparable from its rhythmic impetus and introduces few harmonic subtleties. The genius comes, if it comes at all, in the combination of communal abandon with domestic sentiment, chiefly in the lyrical episodes and *trios*. Both the sentiment and the sensuality are an idealized common experience, which is also the listener's as *l'homme moyen sensuel*.

The Popular Piano and the Theatre

We have suggested that Austria was the nursing-ground of the Popular Piano both because musical traditions were deeply rooted and because revolution was incipient; to a degree traditions could be taken for granted, even while they were being undermined—as Mozart's simultaneous presentation of aristocratic minuet and popular waltz in *Don Giovanni* demonstrates. Professional composers such as the Strausses turned themselves into a small-scale music industry; at the same time conventions derived from popular music invaded 'serious' art, not merely in Austria, but throughout Europe. In France the bifurcation between the Style of Sensibility and the Popular Style was, and has remained, less acute. The dances of Lully, Couperin and Rameau derived from the court masque, preserving their aristocratic finesse when translated into terms of the harpsichord. They gradually degenerated into commoner forms in the work of post-revolutionary opera composers like Grétry, and thence into the ballet dances of Gounod, serving as relaxation for tired businessmen. The 'grand' opera of Gounod, glorifying Empire from a comfortable *fauteuil*, could be guyed by the effervescent *opéra bouffe* of Offenbach without denying the integrity of either. Offenbach's galops and quadrilles, extracted from his theatre-pieces, became immensely popular in sheet-music arrangements for piano; and there was no reason why the people who revelled in them should not also enjoy much of the music of a leading academic, such as Saint-Saëns.

The once-popular G minor piano concerto displays Saint-Saëns' limitations and virtues alike. The last movement reduces the Classical conflict-sonata to a formality, letting loose an engaging clatter in *tarantella* rhythm: sheer Offenbachian folly. The first movement disciplines the panache of the Romantic concerto with Hummel-like operatic cantilena, dissipated by the sweetly sensuous world of the French salon. But the froth of the middle movement is, paradoxically, the concerto's insubstantial core. Beginning as a scherzo with a hunting-call theme, it introduces a second tune that has the animality of a Neapolitan street-song, with a Parisian *gaminerie* which is the closest Saint-Saëns

A charade, 'Adam and Eve in Paradise', at a Schubert
evening in Atzenbrugg: watercolour by Leopold
Kupelwieser, 1821. Among the spectators is Schubert,
seated at the piano, having evidently provided introductory
music. The charade-scene is contemporary with the six
lovely dances that Schubert composed at Atzenbrugg,
known as the *Atzenbrugger Deutsche*, D. 728.

A Russian musical evening, *c.* 1858.

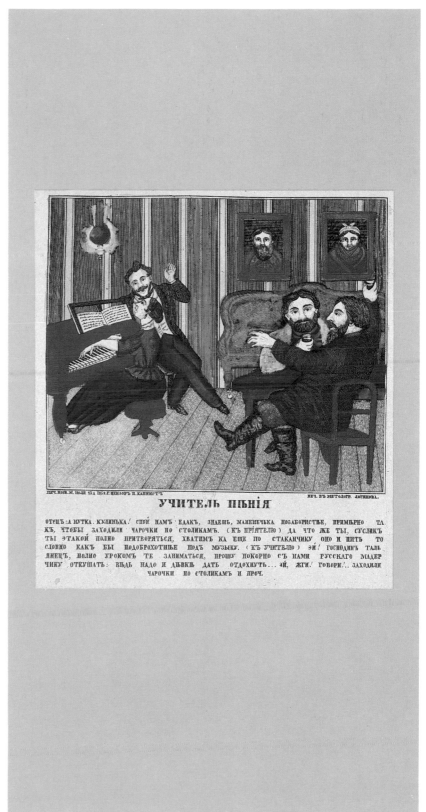

comes to a personal voice. Only in France could a noted academic have created music so beguilingly impudent: 'cheerful, sociable, and lively as a child' was Busoni's description of Saint-Saëns at the age of seventy.

Saint-Saëns' concerto is 'concert' music in a sense that carries it beyond this chapter's scope. Yet it is certainly piano music of grateful vintage; and if it is too difficult to be negotiated by amateurs, it is popular enough to be listened to with half an ear. Much of it would sound happier in a bar or café than in the sanctified atmosphere of the concert hall. Saint-Saëns himself, and most of the composers of nineteenth-century France, from Bizet and Fauré to Reynaldo Hahn, Chaminade and Satie in his role as café pianist, composed music for solo piano or duet, intended for amateurs, yet revealing a sensitivity, as well as vivacity, that does not belie professional expertise. The relatively civilized nature of popular music in France may be due in part to the dominance of the dance and theatre throughout French music from the Renaissance onwards; and in part to the comparative sophistication of taste among the middle class. Whatever the reason, it is a phenomenon not paralleled elsewhere; and significantly 'pop' is most radically segregated from 'art' music in countries least dominated by cultural traditions and most rapidly taken over by industrialism.

What was spawned in Vienna hatched out in London and New York, where the next significant developments in piano manufacture emerged. The Parisian firm of Erard introduced technical sophistications such as the *sourdine*, and perfected the double escapement action, which made possible greater agility and a more brilliant tone. But it was Broadwood in London and Steinway in New York who revolutionized piano manufacture by developing the iron frame. This enabled concert grands to sustain the assaults of the Romantic virtuosos, thereby allowing for a development in piano music beyond the reach of amateurs; by way of compensation it also made possible the mass production of domestic pianos on a scale commensurate with the demand. In industrialized Britain and America democratic man, although or because he was divorced from cultural traditions, developed a voracious appetite for entertainment—which the piano could satisfy if it could be produced in sufficient numbers, at a price appropriate to common pockets, and in a size suitable to the average parlour. The development of the various types of 'square' (really oblong) and upright piano fulfilled this need; between 1850 and 1910 the number of pianos manufactured in Britain rose from 25,000 to 75,000, while in America during the same period the number

increased from a mere 900 to a colossal peak of 360,000.

The piano had become an article of furniture both useful and ornamental, a status symbol, an altar dedicated to the domestic proprieties. No Good Home could be without one, even if it were never played. Of course most people did play their pianos, and played fine music by Classical and Romantic composers whose work was originally domestic in that it was meant to be played in homes rather than in concert halls. Nonetheless Beethoven's and Schubert's sonatas, Schumann's genre pieces, Chopin's Ballades and Nocturnes, and even Brahms's waltzes, can hardly be called popular since they call for skill in execution and for uncommon attention from the listening ear and responsive mind. The authentic literature of 'popular', as distinct from unpopular, piano music would seem to be a product of industrialized democracy. It emerged in Britain and America, countries which had lost, or had never possessed, an awareness of musical tradition.

Hearts and Flowers

England's musical traditions had lapsed in the late seventeenth century, to be taken over by foreign invaders. During the years of our Teutonic-descended monarchy, it was a German composer, Handel, who made so great an impression on our wilted music, creating from his High Baroque heritage a music that could symbolize both the Roast Beef of Old England and our expanding material prosperity. A little later J. C. Bach came to live in London and to entertain, with his Italianate-German composition and his elegant pianism, the prosperous middle class. Around the same time an Italian, Clementi, settled in England and established a piano-making business, specializing in small instruments capable of dissemination among the middle classes. He composed for the instrument not only sonatas worthily comparable with those of Mozart and Beethoven but also studies and mood-pieces inventive enough to tickle the aural fancy without being technically or emotionally exhausting. The Irishman John Field worked for a time in Clementi's London warehouse, demonstrating pianos and piano music, and composing his wistfully melancholic, pre-Chopinesque Nocturnes. But if the Nocturnes represented the real, romantically subjective Field, they were not the main, and certainly not the most popular, aspect of his output. The butterfly frailty of his innumerable short pieces may have worn thin but, as a complement to the poetry of Field's (also consumptive) contemporary Winthrop Praed, it undoubtedly captivated ears and senses in Regency salons.

An English family concert, *c.* 1840.

In the age of Victoria, Mendelssohn was another foreign import whose impact was as pervasive, if not as powerful, as that exerted by Handel on Augustan England. His piously ethical post-Handelian oratorios are still performed, though they seem increasingly anachronistic. His piano music played in Victorian drawing-rooms survives more convincingly, conditioned, though not emasculated, by its environment. Chopin's short piano pieces are explorations of piano technique which are also emotional discoveries; Schumann's domesticities, being personal rather than social, ideal rather than real, imply a new approach to the keyboard. In Mendelssohn's *Songs Without Words*, on the other hand, there is no pianistic feature that suggests the pressure of new experience. Melodically they compromise. The tunes tend to be neither fast nor slow, neither operatic nor folk-like. The gracious melody of the first piece domesticates the stepwise contours of operatic lyricism far more thoroughly than do Schumann's *Lied*-like themes: the arpeggiated accompaniment purrs on the hearth; the tune sinks in the sweet contentment of its feminine endings.

Modest in their technical demands, Mendelssohn's drawing-room piano pieces were widely played: and deserved to be, for they are beautifully written and inventive enough to stimulate our fancy. It is a pity that there was so little in the new demotic piano repertory of Victorian England that could rival them in distinction. Mendelssohn's disciple Sterndale Bennett composed piano music of comparable charm; and in the Edwardian era, the Paris-based composer Moritz Moszkowski produced quantities of expertly fashioned salon pieces that became immensely popular in British parlours. His Spanish Dances in particular demonstrate the characteristics of entertainment music *per se* — for although lively and delightful to play, they are only superficially exotic; the glamour of Spain is in discreet technicolour, any Moorish grit or grime being rigorously excluded.

For the most part, however, the parlour piano had, by the end of the nineteenth century and during the first decade of the twentieth, become dedicated to the accompaniment of lachrymose or inane ballads, or, as solo instrument, to pieces by composers such as the ubiquitous Sidney Smith. If the function of entertain-

Opposite: *Songs Without Words* in the home: 19th-century postcard.

Below: Title-page of Macdowell's *Sea Pieces*.

ment as opposed to art is to reassure at the expense of the veracities of experience, Smith's music is Entertainment in Essentia. His tarnished tinklings—'brilliant but not difficult' was the phrase bandied around in publishers' blurbs—contain a deceit even in their technique, for the twinkling scales and cascading arpeggios sound demanding, but are not. Generously, one might concede that they are 'gratefully' written. More realistically, one recognizes that their musical substance actually offers little cause for gratitude.

A few pieces within this sea of mediocrity achieved a lasting appeal difficult to explain on musical grounds. Moses-Tobani's *Hearts and Flowers*, first published in 1893 but figuring in every album of parlour piano pieces until the First World War, is a case in point. Though the tune is not entirely vacuous, there seems to be no reason for its fanatically enthusiastic reception; can it be that the winning title was more important than the music?

The Music Industry: Hedonism and Escape

Moses-Tobani's *Hearts and Flowers* was a household word, or rather hum, in the homes of my parents and grandparents and must have been pervasive in most middle-class families. Yet the composer was a New York theatre musician, thereby demonstrating how, during the nineteenth century, 'popular piano' became an international language. It was hardly surprising that the Popular Piano should reach its apotheosis in the New World, since man confronting a wilderness had little except his toughly democratic zeal to rely on. As early as 1800 Benjamin Carr composed *Six Imitations*: synthetic English, Scots, Irish, Welsh, Spanish and German airs harmonized in hymn-book gentility, but with indigenously 'characteristic' features in melody and rhythm—a drone for the Irish pipes, a strumming guitar for the Spanish number, and so on. This is a technically raw Americanization of the Exotick character-pieces popular in Europe from Mozart's 'Turkish' *Rondo* onwards. By the middle of the nineteenth century the United States had thrown up a number of quirkily pioneering figures in some ways prophetic of the great Charles Ives. Most remarkable was Anthony Heinrich, who emigrated from Hamburg in 1810, and was dubbed by his contemporaries 'the American Beethoven' (see also pp. 177–9). In a wildly empirical piece such as 'The Banjo' he incorporates quotations from national songs and fiddle tunes, as well as 'God save the King' and some self-regarding self-quotations, creating a circular, non-directed, harmonically non-functional style, so crazy in modulatory licence that Beethoven's tonal disturbances seem supremely civilized by com-

parison: as indeed they are. Heinrich's work is 'popular' in the sense that it is the ultimate in musical democracy, but unpopular in the sense that it does nothing to confirm us in our prejudices!

The very rawness of the American scene helped to safeguard composers from the emotional sloth and intellectual stultification typical of their British contemporaries. Nonetheless America's breath-taking expansion inevitably produced its crop of composing industrialists, most prolific among whom stands Charles Grobe, who emigrated from Weimar in 1839. Described by Robert Offergeld as 'the most productive piano-piece factory that ever existed', Grobe churned out potpourris and operatic transcriptions, piano arrangements of missonary hymns and military marches, along with (dubiously) original compositions that extend to opus 1995. Instantly dispensable, his music is an early example of planned obsolescence. Musical quality, within the conventions of Popular Piano, was more

Eddie Duchin.

likely to be attained when the poles of European traditionalism and American empiricism meet and ignite: as they do in the work of Louis Moreau Gottschalk and Edward Macdowell, composers who epitomize the 'escapism' of popular music, the one in the direction of hedonism, the other in that of nostalgia.

Not surprisingly the hedonist, Gottschalk, comes in the first half of the century, when American optimism was still in the ascendant (see also pp. 179–83). Born in 1829 of mixed (German/Jewish/French/Creole) paren-

tage, Gottschalk was a child prodigy who was sent to study piano and composition in Paris, where he met and was admired by Liszt, Chopin and Berlioz. He returned to his native land to become a backwoods Liszt, travelling the length of the continent as propagandist for himself, his music, and the American piano. Drawing on his New Orleans origins he incorporated elements from Negro rag, French quadrille and Spanish *habanera*, often using authentic Creole or Negro melodies—*La Bamboula, La Savane*—for his elegantly pianistic

Charlie Kunz.

pieces delight by their skill, enliven by their wit, charm with their pathos, while never radically disturbing emotional equilibrium. True, he often disturbs our *physical* equilibrium, especially in the big barnstorming pieces like *The Union, concert paraphrase on National Airs.* In a sense Gottschalk means us to take these cannonading octaves seriously; yet a demotic hilarity breaks in, tempering portentousness, and this latent irony itself effects a kind of equilibrium. In less audience-conscious works this could become a perfect recipe for a popular piano music, in which cliché and creative invention weigh even in the scales.

In *Souvenir de Puerto Rico* Gottschalk hits the balance exactly. The piece is a variation set in the convention of the arriving and departing procession; as the band moves nearer, the 'chromatic grapeshot and deadly octaves' that Gottschalk proudly noted release from us the childish wonder occasioned by a pyrotechnic display. But we know that the fireworks are a game, not an authentic conflagration; and although they remind us of the vanity of human wishes we know, as the procession fades in its *habanera* rhythm, that our lives will go on when the fireworks are spent. This is comforting, but not merely comfortable, for the $3 + 3 + 2$ rhythm still gives a sexy lurch, and also a stasis, to the quaver pulse.

Gottschalk, though a professional, was an entertainer whose entertainment embraced art. Macdowell, born in 1861 to New English respectability rather than in glamorous New France, had the thorough European training of an eastern American composer of the second half of the nineteenth century, yet survives mainly through art which acquires the qualities of entertainment. Though he composed piano sonatas and concertos in the full flush of German Romanticism, he is remembered for his short piano pieces, which are a boy's view of the American past, looked back at from a premature middle age. His *Sea Pieces* attain a New-World freshness in recognizing that they are a 'Dream of Long Ago'; his *New England Sketches* express Hawthorne's sentiment without the blackness at its heart's core. The best pieces are the simplest and sweetest, such as *To a wild rose*, in which the two-bar sequences and trance-inducing pedal notes preserve an innocence that is not belied by the tenderly stabbing appoggiaturas or by the nostalgic haze of added notes. The parallel between Macdowell's mood-pictures and Grieg's *Lyric Pieces* is close: and the similarity in technique suggests that Grieg must have intuitively known that *his* pastoral paradise was doomed no less than the boyhood Eden Macdowell knew he had lost.

pieces. Even his obligatory contributions to the sentimental parlour genre have musical substance to support their delicate filigree. His smash hit, *The Last Hope*, treats a Presbyterian hymn tune with the same seductive yet disciplined luxuriance. Published in 1835, it sold 35,000 copies in a few years, and has gone through more than thirty editions. It is certainly splendid piano music, and no less certainly democratically popular, for it allows us to have a pianistically Good Time, while simultaneously feeling good morally. Gottschalk's

Title-page of Mayerl's *Marigold*.   Opposite bottom: *Pianistes*: painting by Beryl Cook.

From Parlour to Cocktail Lounge

Looking back, it would seem that the best popular piano music has been that which does not cease to stimulate while admitting to its function as escape. Until Mozart's day there was no fundamental separation of 'art' from 'entertainment'. When Mozart civilizes the barbarian in his 'Turkish' *Rondo*, and Haydn dresses up the savage Scot in powdered peruke, they are cultivating the Exotick and the Rousseauesque Naïf; but they are not merely joking, since they believe sufficiently in what they *are* to accommodate their dreams to the real world. Throughout the nineteenth century, however, dreams increasingly become a substitute *for* reality; and once this opposition is admitted to, the breach between art as experience and entertainment as escape can only widen, until, as industrialism takes over, we encounter the phenomenon we now call *Muzak*: the use of music deliberately to efface feeling, and ultimately to efface itself, since it is no longer meant to be listened to.

There is a basic irony in the fact that cocktail-lounge piano, in the first three decades of this century, was closely involved in the evolution of piano jazz, which had become a folk music of the urban metropolis. Jazz—especially black jazz—reminds us of the forgotten physicality of our bodies, and springs at the same time from the pain of stretched nerves and oppressed psyches. Cocktail-lounge piano aims at a goal at the furthest possible remove from jazz reality, for its purpose is not even to reassure, but rather to induce amnesia. It therefore eschews the blue-black elements of jazz, and takes over merely the persistent beat and unremittent boogie rhythm to effect a mechanized hypnosis. In so far as there is any direct relation to jazz it is to ragtime, the black man's attempt to create a literate music derived from the white march. Rag was, even for the black man, a game of Let's Pretend: so is the white man's cocktail-lounge piano, with the distinction that he no longer thinks his dream is worth listening to, and usually it is not.

The cocktail-lounge pianist who allowed the blackness of jazz to intrude into his music would soon lose his job. The desirable norm—desired, that is, by hotel managers—was represented rather, in the twenties and thirties, by Zez Confrey, whose *Kitten on the Keys* sounds as mindless as the small feline herself, tinklingly titillating in perkily emasculated boogie rhythm. Perhaps the immense popularity of the piece was due precisely to its capacity for defusion: elements that are dangerous in real jazz are rendered as pretty as a (clawless) kitty on a chocolate box. The least harmful manifestations of this aural pap are represented by Eddie Duchin in the thirties and Cy Walters in the forties, both of whom concentrated on sentimental standards, animating sensuous chromatic harmony with a gentle swing. While one should not be priggish about the daydreams they fostered, total capitulation to nostalgia may leave one emotionally as well as intellectually bereft. A classic case is Charlie Kunz, whose *sotto voce* pianism proclaimed, from the thirties to the fifties, that Anaesthesia Rules. Later the sophistications of the media came to create myths that belong to the history of publicity rather than that of music. Liberace, with his mum and candelabra, his gold suits and gold-plated pianos, is an extreme instance, for since his pianistic talents are minimal, his charismatic appeal is difficult to explain. Music, in any case, plays a minor role in the projection of the Liberace image.

Popular piano in an increasingly mechanized society had become an international phenomenon. At least it pervaded the English-speaking world; one cannot distinguish between a Zez Confrey in Chicago and a Billy Mayerl in London. Mayerl's piano numbers are prettily written: his *Marigold* is an up-dated, faintly

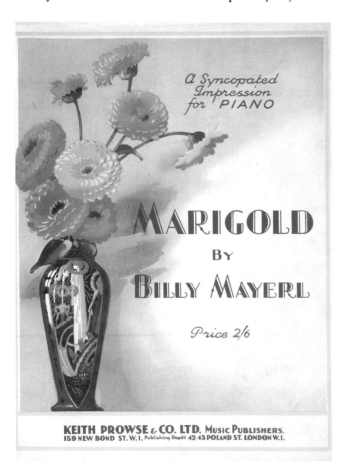

A Syncopated Impression for PIANO

MARIGOLD

BY

BILLY MAYERL

Price 2/6

KEITH PROWSE & CO. LTD. MUSIC PUBLISHERS.
159 NEW BOND ST. W.I. Publishing Depôt 42-43 POLAND ST. LONDON W.I.

ragged successor to the celebrated *Narcissus* of America's Ethelbert Nevin. Neither of these escape pieces could be escaped *from* in my youth, any more than countless others of the period—perfumed sachets of melodic mignonette and harmonic corn, without any trace, of course, of rag, let alone jazz. What these pieces had in common with one another and with Kunz's pianism was their cult of vacuity: which is not an adequate diet for any music, even the most demotic.

The Popular Piano was wobbling on its last legs from the twenties to the forties, and became obsolete when radio and record-player took over, and *Muzak* reigned inexorable, if not supreme. Though the sale of pianos is again on the increase, presumably because more people know more 'classical' music, the Popular Piano belongs to the past, and to an era which ended not with a bang, but with a valedictory whimper. The piano is the most complicated *machine* in musical history; logically enough, its heyday coincided with the emergence of industrial democracy. The instrument has left a legacy of relishable music with which uncommon men and women will continue to refresh themselves, and with which others will pass time agreeably. What will survive of the common round depends on qualities not radically distinct from those that ensure the survival of uncommon music; for Time and Tarnish go their own sweet way, pruning off the cheaper fruits without regard to category.

THE PIANO MAKERS

The Eighteenth-Century Pioneers

Since the first pianos evolved principally out of the harpsichord and clavichord, it was natural enough that the first 'piano maker' should have begun his career making and repairing harpsichords. About 1709, Bartolommeo Cristofori produced his *Clavicembalo* (or *Gravicembalo*) *col piano e forte*. It differed from the harpsichord in having leather-covered hammers to replace the quills, and in having an escapement action that allowed the hammer to fall away from the string after striking, and dampers to stop the string sounding as soon as the key was raised (see p. 20).

Cristofori's essential achievement was to invent an instrument that allowed control of dynamics; he borrowed the shape of a harpsichord, but his *Clavicembalo* is usually regarded as the first step in the evolution of the piano as we know it. Yet the history of keyboard-instrument making in the sixteenth and seventeenth centuries is littered with 'missing links', oddities and innovations (such as Pantaleon Hebenstreit's improved dulcimer, which first alerted makers to the tonal capabilities of a string struck by hammers) that did not survive intact, but which nevertheless were to influence and encourage later designers.

Cristofori achieved little success or fame from his invention. His chief occupation remained making harpsichords, and in the last two decades of his life he went on to produce another twenty pianos, three of which survive today. In later models he strengthened the case to accommodate higher-tension strings, and in 1720 modified the escapement and introduced the *una corda* principle that in essence is used on pianos today. Cristofori established a line of development that was to be carried into the nineteenth century, but within a decade of his first model two other inventors had developed parallel solutions to the set of problems current in keyboard design at the beginning of the eighteenth century. In Paris in 1716, Jean Marius exhibited four model actions for a *clavecin à maillets*, though it is not known whether any instruments were built using the actions; and in the following year, Christoph Gottlieb Schröter, impressed by hearing Pantaleon's dulcimer, set about designing a keyboard instrument that could play loud and soft by using hammers. In 1721, apparently independently of Cristofori, he presented two models of piano actions to the Elector of Saxony in the hope that he would be given the funds to make a fully operative instrument. He was to be disappointed; neither Schröter nor Marius was any more successful than Cristofori in making a fortune out of his inventions.

Ironically it was Gottfried Silbermann (1683–1753), whose name has survived more as an organ builder than piano maker, who was the first to exploit the new instrument successfully. Gottfried Silbermann's instruments were to a large extent based on Cristofori's *Clavicembalo* (see pp. 20–1). But the German instrument was heavy and unresponsive of touch; Johann Sebastian Bach was unimpressed when invited to try out one of Silbermann's early models in 1726. Yet Frederick the Great bought seven of the instruments, and in his treatise on keyboard playing, C. P. E. Bach, keyboard player to Frederick's court, pronounced the piano essential as a solo and accompanying instrument. Silbermann's business was carried on by two of his apprentices, both of whom continued to experiment with the Cristofori action. Johann Heinrich (1727–99) continued Silbermann's business and developed it into a firm widely recognized for its organs and pianos; Christian Ernst Friederici (1709–80) capitalized on the piano action by marrying it to the dimension of the clavichord. Friederici's *fortbien* was the first 'square' piano, a relatively cheap instrument that set out to replace the ubiquitous clavichord in the German domestic market.

The English Piano

While Germany and Austria went on improving Silbermann's design, the first generation of pianos was introduced to England in the 1750s. A copy of Cristofori's design, built in Rome by one Father Wood, was exhibited in London and created quite a sensation, though its shortcomings were readily apparent. London-based harpsichord makers took up the challenge of improvement, but an influx of Saxon instrument makers to London in the early 1760s caused the centre of the piano-making world to switch to England.

Most notable of the expatriates was Johann Zumpe, another apprentice of Silbermann, who joined the London harpsichord maker Burkat (or Burkhard) Shudi in 1761. Zumpe was quick to realize the potential of the square piano, and set up on his own in 1766, turning out square pianos based very closely on Friederici's design. One of these 'Piano Fortes' was used for a performance of the *Beggar's Opera* in London in 1767; a year later Johann Christian Bach gave his seal of approval to Zumpe's instruments with a much noticed recital attended by notables including Dr Johnson and Dr Burney. When in 1770 Muzio Clementi set himself up in London as a pianist and teacher, and three years later began to publish music written expressly for the piano, the instrument was fully established.

Opposite: J. H. Silbermann piano, 1776; nephew of Gottfried Silbermann, Johann Heinrich continued making this pattern of piano until late in the 18th century.

Below: *George, third Earl Cowper and the Gore family*: painting by Johann Zoffany, 1775. Mr Gore is playing the cello held between the knees in the manner of a viola da gamba. The piano is most likely by Zumpe.

But the decisive breakthrough in English piano design came with the work of the Scottish cabinet-maker John Broadwood (1732–1812). Broadwood had been apprenticed to Shudi at the time that Zumpe was working there; after Zumpe's departure, however, Broadwood established himself by marrying Shudi's daughter Barbara in 1769 and becoming his partner a year later. It marked the beginning of the firm of Shudi-Broadwood, later to become John Broadwood & Sons. Once established, Broadwood set about reworking the design of the square piano, improving the stringing to produce a fuller bass, and replacing Zumpe's handstops with sustaining pedals. And with the aid of the new 'English' action developed by Broadwood, Backers and Broadwood's apprentice Robert Stodart, Broadwood turned his attention in the 1780s to the 'grand'—that is,

horizontal—piano. The English action brought power and resonance to the grand, but at some cost to its clarity and lightness of touch.

By the end of the century Broadwood had become the world's largest manufacturer of pianos and, although the industrial revolution had not yet brought machinery into the piano workshop, he had taken the first step along the path from the individually fashioned, craftsman-built piano towards the factory production of the following century. Broadwood shrewdly recognized that the piano could become a symbol of respectability for the rising middle class; and between 1782 and 1802 his workshop turned out some 7,000 square pianos and 2,000 grands. In the last quarter of the eighteenth century ambitious London piano makers proliferated. Zumpe, unable to cope with the demand for his square

pianos, transferred some of his business to Pohlman, and Schoene took over Zumpe's company until 1793; other English makers—John Geib (who made instruments for Longman and Broderip), Pether, Walton, Crang Hancock, Ball, Landreth, Ganer, Beck—all patented their own improvements to both grand and square pianos.

The Austro-German Piano

While Broadwood and his fellows dominated the piano market in London, a very different-sounding instrument was in vogue in Austria and Germany. The pianos produced by Johann Andreas Stein (1728–92) had found favour with Mozart, who wrote to his father in 1777:

When I strike hard, I can keep my finger on the note or raise it, but the sound ceases the moment I have produced it. In whatever way I touch the keys, the sound is always even. It never jars, it is never stronger or weaker or entirely absent . . .

It was such lightness and responsiveness of touch that characterized Stein's pianos and was to set the standard for the Viennese piano well into the nineteenth century.

Johann Andreas Stein.

Stein, originally from Augsburg, had been an apprentice of Silbermann, but his pianos used an action of his own invention, essentially different from that used by Broadwood and Stodart, which in turn was in direct line of descent from Silbermann and Cristofori. Stein's 'Viennese' action, as it came to be called, coupled with small, leather-covered hammers, gave the fortepiano an extraordinary lightness of touch, approximately one third of the weight required for a modern piano. It encouraged an entire style of keyboard writing in the music of Haydn, Mozart and Hummel—a style that laid emphasis on fleetness and cleanly articulated passage-work, and allowed the rapid repetition of pitches, often impossible on the English pianos.

After Stein's death in 1792, the business was carried on by his son Andreas, his daughter Nanette (a gifted pianist whom Mozart heard), and her husband Johann Andreas Streicher. The Viennese piano survived well into the nineteenth century, natural Viennese conservatism maintaining the basic principles of Stein's design with some modifications. The number of makers in the city grew rapidly in the first decades: Brodmann (later to become the firm of Bösendorfer), Moser, Müller, Pohack, Schantz (favoured by Haydn), Seuffert, Graf (later to furnish Beethoven with a forceful quadruple-string instrument to combat the composer's deafness), Wachtl and Walter.

Nineteenth-Century Refinements
The eighteenth century ended with the developing piano clearly polarized into two complementary types: the English piano, robust, resonant of tone yet heavy and slow of touch, and the Viennese piano, fragile, clear and thin of tone, light and responsive to play. The problem confronting piano makers was now to evolve a design that united the virtues of the two instruments into a single, sturdy, flexible instrument. By 1808 Broadwood had applied tension bars to at least the treble regions of his grands. But the first maker to incorporate iron bars systematically into the frames of his pianos was Sébastien Erard (1752–1831).

Erard has been called the inventor of the modern piano: he began constructing pianos in 1777 in the château of the Maréchale de Villeroi, then, as his reputation prospered, brought his brother Jean-Baptiste to Paris to assist him. The first instruments they produced were five-octave square pianos. For Marie Antoinette, Erard built a piano and organ combined, a single instrument with two keyboards. Such royal patronage was the key to success; the Paris lutenists felt their businesses to be so threatened by the

Erard pianos that they petitioned Louis XVI, unsuccessfully, to have the firm closed down. After the outbreak of the French Revolution the brothers moved to London and established another business there; in 1796 Sébastien returned to Paris, leaving his brother Pierre in charge of the London company.

Erard's experience of the London makers was put to good use, and allowed him to produce a formidable range of pianos and innovations. Soon after his return to Paris he made his first grand pianos, using the English action, and transferred the Broadwood 'production-line' methods to his own factory. As early as 1795 Erard had begun experiments with an escapement based on the principle of Cristofori, the 'simple escapement', which reached its final form in 1816. But his most decisive innovation was finally perfected in 1822. The 'double escapement' allowed the rapid repetition of a single note and lent itself to the utmost virtuosity. The first version was fragile and quickly wore out, a disadvantage to which Erard's more conservative rivals were quick to draw attention; but Erard refined the

system, and eventually found his major competitors—Pleyel, Kriegelstein, Blüthner—evolving their own versions from his invention.

In Paris itself, Erard's pianos were usually pitted against those of Pape and Pleyel. Henri Pape, a German emigré, arrived in Paris in 1811 to work in the workshop of Ignace Pleyel (1757–1831); he went on to patent innumerable inventions, but one of his most important contributions was to use, for the first time, felt-covered hammers in 1826. Pape began making square pianos with English actions, later progressing to grands; Pleyel began making pianos in 1807, and quickly established himself as Erard's main rival. Erard's wares were favoured by Dussek, Steibelt and Thalberg; Pleyel's by Moscheles, Kalkbrenner, Cramer and Field. Pleyel's greatest accolade followed Ignace Pleyel's death, after the business had been taken over by his son Camille, when the young Chopin pronounced the Pleyel piano the most suitable to convey his own special 'singing' tone.

Another of Henri Pape's innovations, overstringing, was to have profound effects on the development of both the grand and the upright. The more the grand piano's tonal resources were improved and refined, the greater became the disparity between it and its square, domestic cousin. From the end of the eighteenth century, makers had endeavoured to furnish a compact, portable piano with something approaching the qualities of a grand. In

Opposite above: A workshop of the Pleyel factory in Paris.
Opposite below: Ignace Pleyel.

Below left: Southwell's piano of 1798.
Below right: Piano by Robert Wornum, *c.* 1815.
Bottom: Stodart 'upright grand' piano of 1806.

1795, William Stodart (nephew of Robert) published a patent for an 'upright grand'; the keyboard remained at the bottom of the strings, and the instrument ran to some eight or nine feet high; essentially it was a grand piano turned through ninety degrees. Three years later William Southwell of Dublin did the same thing to the square piano to produce the 'square piano on its side'; but the first upright as we now understand the term, whose strings passed behind the keyboard down to the floor, was produced in 1800 by Matthias Müller in Vienna (a remarkable instrument given the name of *Ditanklasis*), and by John Isaac Hawkins (later of Philadelphia) in London. Further upright models followed from Thomas Loud in London, Pfeiffer et Cie in Paris, Collard, and Wornum. Robert Wornum went so far as to set himself up in business as an 'Upright and Horizontal Pianoforte Maker', emphasizing for the first time the special qualities of his uprights, and endeavouring to corner the one section of the London piano market ignored by the larger manufacturers such as Broadwood.

The Advent of the Modern Piano

In London the Great Exhibition of 1851 provided a focus for the achievements of the piano industry in the first half of the century. The leading makers all exhibited their innovations, emphasizing, as the terms of the exhibition required, the application of new

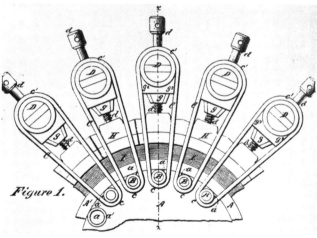

ments could compete numerically with those imported from Europe. Boston was the centre of the industry in the early days and there, in 1825, Alpheus Babcock cast the first one-piece iron frame, for a square piano. Babcock's one-piece frame encouraged a number of similar designs in Europe (by Petzold and Pape in Paris particularly), and in the United States he was followed by Conrad Meyer and Isaac Clark. But the most significant American maker before Steinway was Jonas Chickering, who in 1840 patented an all-metal frame, initially for the square (the square piano was to remain popular in the New World long after it had been superseded in Europe), and later for the grand.

Steinway and Sons, however, rapidly overtook Chickering as the leading American manufacturer. In

technological skills. The increasing popularity of the piano in Victorian homes had encouraged a great number of new makers, but most significant of the unfamiliar names in the exhibition catalogue was that of Steinway, whose square piano, made in the United States, was widely admired. Heinrich Steinweg had made his first piano in Seesen, Germany, in 1836, and established himself in a small way in the years before the revolution of 1848. After the revolution, Heinrich emigrated to New York, leaving behind him his eldest son Theodore, who continued the German business as Grotrian-Steinweg. Within three years of arriving in the United States, Steinweg had changed his name to Steinway, and Henry Steinway and Sons had opened a piano workshop that was to make a thousand pianos in the next three years.

Piano making became established in the United States at the beginning of the nineteenth century, but it was not until the 1830s that American-made instru-

Advertisement for the 'Pianola'.

1859 Henry Steinway Jr introduced overstringing to the cast iron frame of the grand while lengthening the bridge to give it more curvature; in the 1870s Theodore—having sold the German company to Grotrian, Heifferich and Schulz, and joined his father—increased the stress on the frame to the tension employed today; the double escapement was also modified to improve the touch, and in 1874 the sustaining pedal was perfected. The Steinway firm's innovations vastly improved the power and tonal quality of the grand, while its overstrung upright, first produced in 1863, at last provided the domestic market with a piano of acceptable quality. When Steinway exhibited its models at European trade fairs in the 1860s and 1870s and carried off many awards, the established makers

The Return to Home and the Pianola Piano.

Home-coming after holidays happily spent may hold its regrets. Stronger, however, than all regret, is the agreeable sensation of being once more amongst the familiar objects and recreative resources of the home.

The Pianola Piano provides a recreation of which you can never tire, and to which you gladly return again and again.

If you are returning to a home that has no music—where the pleasant diversion of playing your favourite music is unknown to you—it is now, of all times, that you require a Pianola Piano.

The Pianola Piano is a combination of the genuine Pianola with the famous Steinway, Weber, or Steck Piano. Play it at Æolian Hall, or write for Catalogue "H."

The Orchestrelle Co.
ÆOLIAN HALL,
135-6-7. New Bond Street. London. W.

were convinced that to compete they would need to adopt some of the American innovations.

From the beginnings of the industrial revolution the piano makers had absorbed those elements of the developing technology that they required. The process of assimilation was gradual at first, with makers such as Erard and Steinway introducing small improvements as knowledge of industrial techniques increased. But in the latter half of the nineteenth century the prodigious rise of Germany as an industrial power encouraged her piano makers to reap the benefits. The more forward-looking of the established companies, Bösendorfer, Ibach, Schiedmayer and Irmler, were quick to take advantage of the technology; the more recent makers, led by Bechstein and Blüthner, followed suit. Bechstein and Blüthner quickly emerged as the leading makers, and their pianos came to be preferred on concert platforms throughout Europe, not to be supplanted by Steinway until the beginning of the First World War. They offered contrasting kinds of instrument, each with its band of adherents; the Blüthner, using lighter hammers and felts, was thinner, clearer of tone than the more sumptuous Bechstein. By 1884 it was estimated that there were more than 400 piano-making factories in Germany employing some 8,000 workers all over the country, in contrast to the English industry, which was centred in London.

The explosion of piano making in Germany was not confined to the domestic market. Before the outbreak of the First World War, one in six of the pianos bought in Britain was German—a significant proportion, since the German instruments were generally of a higher quality and cost than the British pianos. And as new markets opened up, in Australia for example, it was the German makers' more streamlined production and sales methods that gained them a major share. For a price mid way between that of cheaply produced British instruments and top-quality, expensive grands, German piano makers, led by Ibach, offered a solid, reliable product. But in Britain it was in the lower price ranges that the bulk of the pianos were sold. The massive popularity of the instrument in the last twenty years of the nineteenth century—when any home with claims to respectability could not afford to be without a piano—coincided with the makers' ability to mass-produce instruments. Many of the British piano makers active today began at this time: Bentley, Kemble and Zender, for example. In the Edwardian years a piano could be bought for as little as £20 from a maker such as Cons or Hicks; but when one moved up-market, the German instruments predominated. An upright Bechstein, as good an instrument

Various stages of piano construction in the factory:
Below: Assembly of the keyboard.
Centre: Trimming the hammer shanks to length.
Bottom: Regulation of the finished action.

as could be bought for the home, could be had for £50.

In the United States at the turn of the century, the player-piano, or 'Pianola', also began to enjoy a vogue (see also pp. 184–6). The principles on which the automatic piano operated had been established well before 1850—the movement of the keys by pneumatic action and the control of the mechanism by a roll of perforated paper—but it was not until 1898 that the Aeolian Company produced its first 'Pianola'. In the next six years another forty or more brands of automatic piano were marketed, of which three systems, Welte-Mignon, Duo-Art and Ampico, became established as the most successful, offering the most exact reproduction of expressive nuance. British makers were rather less successful in producing their own versions of the 'Pianola' action.

The First World War almost ended the heyday of the piano. Many of the smaller makers lost their craftsmen and could not continue production; even the more famous companies found raw materials difficult to obtain. The period between the two World Wars then saw the piano industry in a period of retrenchment, threatened by the advent of the gramophone as a cheaper, more passive form of home entertainment. The player-piano reached a peak of popularity in the immediate post-war years, when over half of the American companies' output was devoted to the instrument; another surge of popularity in the 1920s was dashed by the Depression, and throughout the 1930s the major companies tried to revive a waning market with 'miniature' pianos. The Second World War had a less disruptive effect on the industry than the First simply because there was less to disrupt. Production ceased altogether in Britain and Germany from 1939–45, and shortages immediately after the war did nothing to encourage re-expansion. In the 1950s there were eighteen piano makers in Britain; now there are ten, only two of which, Welmar and Danemann, produce a full-length concert grand. In West Germany also, the industry has been reduced to its bare bones.

If the European and American industries recovered only slowly to a position of precarious health, the last thirty years have seen a remarkable expansion in the making of pianos in Japan. The leading Japanese companies, Yamaha and Kawai, were founded in 1887 and 1925 respectively, but they did not come to dominate world piano making until the 1970s, when the output of Yamaha alone exceeded 200,000 instruments per year, much of it intended for home consumption. With highly organized production methods and an enormous output, costs can be kept much lower than in

Below: A stage in the assembly of the soundboard.
Centre: Fitting the guide pins to the bridge.
Bottom: Stringing the piano.

Western companies, while quality is maintained. Throughout the range Japanese instruments now offer a real alternative to the established European and American makes, some pianists even preferring the brighter, lighter tone of the Yamaha concert grand to that of its more famous rivals.

The modern piano has become a product of high technology. Processes that were once the province of skilled craftsmen are now performed automatically; the cutting of soundboards may now be carried out with a digitally controlled machine, and the application of these and similar techniques has enabled the companies to increase dramatically the number of instruments produced per employee. Grover quotes the present-day Bentley factory as producing twenty-five pianos per employee per year; in the middle of the last century the annual rate was more like four.

The use of synthetic resin glues, provided they are sufficiently elastic, today allows a piano to withstand greater extremes of humidity in centrally-heated American and European homes; and the use of laminated boards, with grains opposed, replacing the beech wood that was traditionally employed in the making of tuning planks, can reduce shrinkage. But the need to streamline operations to produce maximum productivity has its less fortunate consequences. It has long been thought desirable for all the wood needed for a single soundboard to come from the same tree, grown slowly, in cool conditions, to produce a fine, even grain. Nowadays it is impracticable for all but the most exclusive makers to choose the timber for their pianos so carefully; of necessity faster grown, less uniform wood must be used. West German manufacturers now use Bavarian pine, and English makers Alaskan or Sitka spruce. Some American companies have gone so far as to attempt to construct laminated soundboards with consequent loss of sound quality.

Specialization too has overtaken the industry. Few companies today can afford the automated machinery necessary to make, as they once did, every component of a piano in their own factories. Frames, wire, pins and actions may be bought in complete from a number of specialized suppliers; opportunities for innovation have devolved from the piano makers to their subsidiaries. Plastics, glass-fibres and carbon-fibres have been incorporated more cautiously into the construction processes—though a plastic-and-wood action is now the standard for many pianos in Europe, America and Japan; but the finish of the case, traditionally a high-gloss French Polish, has given way generally to a variety of polyurethane and other synthetic surfaces.

Bottom: 'The patent Dolce Campana pedal pianoforte' by Boardman and Gray, New York, *c.* 1850: attached to the soundboard of an ordinary piano is a series of pressing hammers, or weights, 'arranged by a lever pedal to fall, at the will of the player, when required, upon an equal number of screws, and which, altering the vibration, affects and produces novel sounds ... as the title Dolce Campana imports, the results of the action of these hammers are a prolongation of the sound, and the production of the tonality of sweet bells, or the harp'.

ECCENTRIC PIANOS

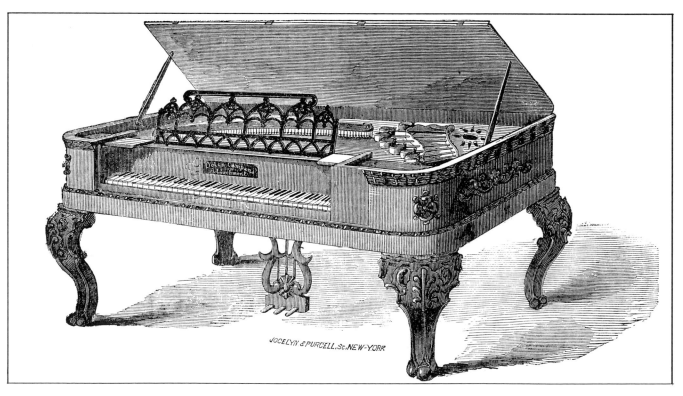

JOCELYN & PURCELL, Sc. NEW-YORK

Opposite above: Table piano by Jean-Henri Pape, mid-19th century (left) and a Chappell *pianino* (right).

Almost as soon as the piano was accepted as a valid instrument of music rather than regarded as a mere experimental curiosity, it became a natural showcase for the ingenuity and imagination of its makers. Keyboard instruments provided their makers with the opportunity to give free rein to their craftsmanship and creativity; the piano, in its rapidly established role as an essential part of the furniture of any well-to-do home, was the most suitable of all. Painters could be invited to decorate its case, sculptors could provide it with elaborate, wooden mouldings. And as its popularity grew, this exploitation did not stop at decoration. The more important the piano became as a symbol of social respectability, the more it could be adulterated to serve the manufactured needs of the burgeoning *nouveaux riches*: if one's neighbour had a piano, what more incentive to acquire one bigger, better and brasher? Why not go further still, and let the instrument become the focal point of the parlour, doubling as a writing desk or a closet perhaps, or including drawers or a looking-glass? By comparison with some of its predecessors, then, the contemporary upright or concert grand seems a very austere object indeed.

Even by the end of the eighteenth century, makers and composers were hard at work trying to broaden the piano's range of colour. The popularity of 'programme' music, and in particular the 'Turkish' music given respectability by Mozart in the last movement of his A major sonata K. 331, made certain pedalled effects *de rigueur* in the smartest circles. For the 'Bassoon' stop a strip of wood covered in paper or parchment was pressed against the strings in the lowest octaves to yield a nasal, reedy tone; the 'Dolce Campana' put pressure on the soundboard, altering the string tension and hence the pitch: operated rapidly it could produce a vibrato. The 'Drum' pedal, usually including the 'Triangle' and 'Cymbal' as well, caused the soundboard to be struck with a drumstick and the lowest strings by brass strips; bells inside the case imitated the sound of the triangle. It is interesting that at this time the *una corda* principle was no more or no less than another special effect. Beethoven is said to have played regularly on a highly decorated instrument with six pedals; Napoleon owned a piano made by Erard in 1801 with five. These attempts to combine the piano with other instruments persisted well into the nineteenth century. In 1841 Paul-Joseph Sormani of Paris invented his 'Piano-Basque' in which the strings were replaced by a series of tuned tambourines whose beaters were operated from a keyboard, and in 1847 in New York a 'Melodicon with drums' was patented; a series of kettle drums was so arranged that

the strings of the piano and the membranes of the drums were struck simultaneously (see also p. 27).

Other inventions were less fanciful, and were earnestly intended to make the instrument more portable and convenient, not to say more attractive. Posterity has established the vast majority of them as evolutionary *culs de sac* rather than as important phases in the development of the modern piano. Shelves were soon added to the upper part of the case of William Stodart's upright grand (patented in 1795) to form the 'Bookcase piano' (see p. 28), and the 'giraffe' and its close cousin the 'lyre grand' became very popular in the first half of the nineteenth century. The lyre grand provided the satisfying symmetry that the giraffe lacked; both designs allowed the maximum of ornamentation. Nearly eight feet high, a shelf above the treble strings could accommodate statues or figurines; the feet could be fashioned as caryatids or, during the craze for Turkish music, plumed Eastern boys.

At the other end of the spectrum Isaac Hawkins produced a 'Portable Grand Pianoforte' in 1800. Barely four feet six inches high, its keyboard folded away; it has been suggested that it was designed to stow away in ships' cabins. When space was at a premium, the potential buyer at the beginning of the nineteenth century could buy a triangular piano made by Pfeiffer and Petzold designed to fit into the corner of a drawing room; Pape, among others, made oval, round and hexagonal instruments designed to be used as tables. Jules Massenet owned a piano that doubled as a writing table, so that a composer could play while retaining his manuscript on the top.

But the summit (or nadir, depending on the point of view) of adaptable design is surely this one patented by Millward in 1866 and described by its builder in every ingenious detail:

The piano instead of being supported by legs in the ordinary manner, is supported by a frame which again rests upon a hollow base; inside such hollow base is placed a couch, which is mounted upon rollers and can be drawn out in front of the piano . . . A hollow space is formed in the middle of the frame for rendering the pedals accessible to the performer's feet, and on one side of such a space is formed a closet, having doors opening in front of the piano, and which is designed to contain the bed clothes. On the other side of the space so formed, firstly a bureau with drawers, and secondly, another closet for containing a wash-hand basin, jug, towels and other articles of toilet . . . A music stool is so arranged that in addition it also contains a work-box, a looking glass, a writing desk or table, and a small set of drawers.

During the Crimean War, grand pianos with especially shortened legs were exported to Turkish

Opposite: Graf 'Pyramid piano', 1829.

Below: Oval piano by William Southwell, c. 1785.

harems, allowing the player to recline elegantly on cushions while still being able to reach the keyboard. In 1835 Broadwood produced an upright with a dip in the middle of the case so that the player could be seen and his voice project more easily. At the Great Exhibition of 1851 John Champion Jones displayed his 'double or twin semi-cottage piano' with 'two fronts and sets of keys, one on either side, suitable for any number of performers from one to six', and William Jenkin and Son brought their 'expanding and collapsing piano for gentlemen's yachts, the saloons of steam ships, ladies' cabins etc, only 13½ inches from front to back when collapsed'.

The catalogue for the Great Exhibition also lists a transposing piano made by Robert Addison. Transpos-

ing pianos had been in existence then for some fifty years, designed specifically with the unproficient amateur in mind to enable him easily to transpose songs to accompany singers, or adjust the pitch of his instrument to accommodate temperature-sensitive wind instruments. A number of systems of transposition had been invented; the change of pitch (in itself impossible before equal temperament was fully accepted) could be effected by moving the keyboard of the frame, by interpolating an extra keyboard on top of the usual one or, more intricately, by having each key split into two, the rear portion being moved sideways to engage the action at a higher or lower pitch. Broadwood put the first transposing piano into production in 1808, using the principle of the movable keyboard; Erard patented a

Below: 'Harp piano', probably by Kuhn and Ridgeway, Baltimore, 1857: an experimental instrument that had a very short life.
Inset: John Champion Jones's 'Twin Semi-cottage Pianoforte', *c.* 1850.

Below: Pedal grand piano by Joseph Brodmann, Vienna, 1815.

Bottom left: Moór seated at a Schmidt-Flohr double-keyboard—a prototype of 1921, somewhat difficult to play because of its parallel keyboards, which preceded Moór's invention of sloping keyboards.
Bottom right: Upright piano with Jankó keyboard by Decker, New York, c. 1890.

Opposite: The Empress Eugenie piano: one of the most ornate pianos ever manufactured, by Bösendorfer of Vienna to the order of the Emperor Louis Philippe, Napoleon III, as a birthday gift for his wife the Empress Eugenie. The wood is principally mahogany, inlaid with kingwood in a Greek key design. The legs and the angels at each end of the keyboard (below) are of hollow-cast brass, crafted in remarkable detail, with an ormolu finish.

transposing piano in 1812, in which the soundboard was circular and could be rotated to obtain the correct transposition.

The Pedal Piano, however, attracted rather more attention from serious musicians. Liszt and Mendelssohn both owned one; Schumann went so far as to write studies and *Sketches* for the *Pedal-Flügel*. To the church organist it was a valuable aid to home practice. The pedal board was either coupled to the bass notes of the main keyboard, or had its own set of accessory strings; Pfeiffer produced a set of pedals that could be attached to any grand piano.

From the beginning, piano inventors also worried away at the design of the keyboard. A concave keyboard was produced in Vienna in the 1780s, and the concept has been revived periodically ever since: a concave shape, so the theory runs, would lessen the problems of reaching the furthest treble and bass regions, particularly for children. The quarter-tone piano also put in an appearance in the early part of this century; in Czechoslovakia, Alois Haba's quarter-tone compositions encouraged the Prague Conservatory to set up a class to teach the quarter-tone piano. In one system a second keyboard was set above the first to operate a set of strings a quarter of a tone higher than usual; in another, made experimentally by Grotrian-Steinweg, two soundboards and two actions were operated by a

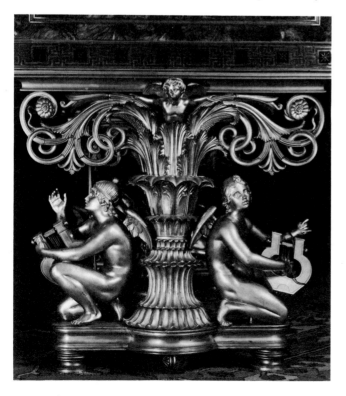

single keyboard including black, white and brown keys.

More ingenious, and intended to facilitate the performance of the standard repertory, were the Jankó and Moór keyboards, both invented by Hungarians. Paul van Jankó patented his in 1882; the keys were banked, and allowed the twelve major scales to be played with only two different hand positions. Spans of a twelfth became child's play; enormous block chords and Lisztian 'skips' were put within the compass of mere mortals. Jankó persuaded several leading makers to produce grands with his keyboard, and toured through Western Europe himself with a modified Ibach grand. But both Jankó's and Moór's designs eventually fell out of favour because of their heavy, unresponsive touch, and because of the need to learn a completely new technique. Emanuel Moór's double keyboard, introduced in 1921, used conventional stringing but the second rank of keys provided pitches an octave higher, and the two sets were positioned so that one hand could play notes on both simultaneously—Donald Tovey declared optimistically that the Moór keyboard could become 'the exhaustive modern concert room translator of Bach's harpsichord'.

But only very few of these historical oddities survive today—although the hugely ornate 'art piano', egocentric rather than eccentric perhaps, lives on, enshrined in museums and collections. The decorated harpsichord was easily translated to the early piano, and by the second half of the nineteenth century Broadwood could offer a variety of styles: Sheraton, Jacobean, Tudor Gothic, Louis XIII, XIV, XV and XVI, Flemish Renaissance, Elizabethan *cinquecento*, Queen Anne, First Empire, Moorish.

Most extraordinary of all, perhaps, was the instrument Broadwood produced for the painter Alma Tadema; the piano and the room in which it was to be housed were designed as a unity. The case was made of oak, inlaid with ebony, tortoise-shell, mother-of-pearl, mahogany, gilt, brass and ivory; a Byzantine frieze decorated the edge. The inside of the lid, surprisingly, was left blank; there Tadema could pin sheets of parchment, on which visitors to his masterpiece could sign their names. The pre-Raphaelite Edward Burne-Jones was commissioned by Henry Broadwood to design a new case shaped more like the traditional harpsichord; and as a young man the architect Edwin Lutyens designed a piano to be placed in his own house. But the artist-designed piano could only prosper while the instrument remained a handbuilt craft object; increasing mechanization of the production processes spelt doom for most eccentricities.

Below: 'Perpendicular pianoforte' by William Henry Percival, 1878: 'the novelty and advantage of this instrument is that it is very small and light and can be played by the performer in a most natural and convenient manner with one hand on either side, on the right for the treble and on the left for the bass, and the performer can sing to its accompaniment facing the audience'.

Below: The Byzantine Broadwood grand piano designed in 1878, with its accompanying bench, by G. E. Fox for Sir Lawrence Alma Tadema. Made to order for Alma Tadema's Regent's Park home, with a room to match, the piano was destroyed during an air raid in the 1939–45 war.
Bottom: An upright piano made by Erard for the Paris Exhibition, 1851.

Below: Broadwood grand piano designed by Edwin Lutyens, 1901.
Bottom: A Broadwood 'William Morris piano' of 1883, with decorations designed and executed in gesso-work by Kate Faulkner of William Morris's firm Morris and Co.

Below: Pop-art upright piano by Eavestaff, *c*. 1960.

EPILOGUE

Unter allen unbeschreiblichen Dingen ist das
unbeschreiblichste die Schönheit und ihr Effect (Schiller)
Amongst all things which cannot be described, the most
indescribable is Beauty and its effect

Clifford Curzon Extemporizes . . .

I've known people who, at about the age of three, just toddled off to the piano, and never left it, so to speak; but with me it didn't happen like that.

In my childhood we had a visiting piano teacher; and until I was about eight or nine, I and my brother and sister, who were not noticeably musical, used to go in together for these Associated Board exams, and not infrequently they got higher marks than I did. I think the only suggestion, the only inkling at all, that one could have had then about my future was that I felt, quite distinctly, that I reacted to everything differently from the way others around me did. I was an acutely shy and non-violent child, and I couldn't communicate this feeling: I just knew that all around me the emotional reactions of my family—a normally happy one—seemed to be quite different from my own. It must have been very trying indeed for them to have such a diffident and uncommunicative outsider around. But I think—mind you, one mustn't deceive or flatter oneself—but looking back, it does seem that I had the sort of temperament which was most likely to express itself in some artistic fashion sooner or later; there were too many pent-up emotions which demanded irresistibly to be let out. And isn't going out and playing music in public, after all, a pretty powerful way of doing just that? It ought to be.

Of course it could have gone any way. I don't think I am exactly the 'born pianist' in the popular sense. But I know exactly how music was awakened in me, because as you may know, I am the nephew of a composer who was, in his time, one of the best known and one of the most widely played English composers of the century. The name is less well known today: Albert W. Ketèlbey (he added the accent to avoid the mispronunciation 'Kettleby'). He was married to my aunt Charlotte; and his Immortal Melodies—*In a Persian Market*, *In a Monastery Garden*, *The Phantom Melody*, *Bells Across the Meadows*, and many more—were the constant background music to my childhood. Almost every Sunday evening Uncle Albert would come to the house to play, and try out some of his latest compositions; my father adored them. And I can remember how, after being put to bed, I used to creep out and sit on the topmost landing in the dark on the cold oilcloth—freezing cold, I'm surprised I didn't catch my death—listening to those immortal melodies wafting up from downstairs; and I can remember the inexpressible longing they filled me with.

Being a businessman—all my family were antique dealers—my father naturally hoped that little Clifford would follow in Uncle Albert's footsteps. So I continued with my piano lessons; but I really don't think I showed many signs, looking back now, of being particularly musical—just particularly aware, maybe, of beauty in the kind of vague, intense way that children can be. All the same, I liked my piano—a lonely child's retreat from a happy family—and I persevered. And I must have shown signs of a certain musical talent, because I was sent to the Royal Academy of Music at an unusually early age.

My career really started there. I didn't fully realize the cause at the time, but after the First World War and the jubilations of victory, an atmosphere of never to be forgotten loss settled over the land. There were men and students everywhere who didn't return; many sons who had fallen, including the elder son of my piano teacher at the Academy, who never recovered from his loss. But I was a post-war adolescent, and I felt somehow removed from it all; and perhaps as a result kept myself very much to myself. A typical lesson was: 'Just play it through again; now bring me something else for next week.' That was the lesson. But at least no one stood in my way: I was left alone to get on with it, grow and explore, and do what I wanted.

But I did leave the Academy with the strangest repertoire—without one single piece by Mozart, but with two and a half sonatas by Arnold Bax. Mind you, I got scholarships with those: probably because nobody knew how they ought to be played. But incredibly enough, hardly a note of Beethoven, Schumann, Chopin or Bach—just the G minor sonata of Schumann, which was a very ill-advised piece to give to a young student: a wonderful work, but very, very hard. No Mozart. The odd Beethoven *Rondo*; the *Andante favori*; perhaps an early Beethoven sonata—I suppose I had a go at the early C major. Not a bar of Schubert, not even the schoolgirls' A flat Impromptu. Nothing. My goodness, what did I play in those four years? The major works were all of them concertos—the Weber *Konzertstück*, the Delius, Beethoven no. 1—which I wouldn't have a chance to play in public for years.

Repertoire planning, of course, should be the principal job of any school of music. A new student, say of seventeen or eighteen, should have a course of study mapped out for him, covering the related fields of his individual programme. A teacher's first instinct should be to say, 'Aha, you play the Beethoven sonata op. 22 in B flat. Now what do you know about the *others*? Where does op. 22 fit into the scheme, have you looked at them all, do you know where it belongs? And what about Beethoven's contemporaries, and precursors?' Busoni

Clifford Curzon, aged five.

always used to say: 'If you play one piece by Liszt, why don't you play the lot?—because they all pose very similar, and related, problems.' In her famous Wednesday classes, Nadia Boulanger used to cover week by week a whole genre of a composer's output—Bach's Cantatas, Schubert's piano sonatas, Beethoven's string quartets, and so on—and expected every one of her students to have a working knowledge of all of them.

But teaching is a tricky subject indeed. I don't really believe that anything can be *taught* directly about piano playing, beyond a certain elementary level. I don't think it can be done, except perhaps by example. If somebody comes to me and asks, 'How? Why? What is the best way, the best method?' there really aren't any clear-cut answers. And this, perhaps, is a sadness of our time, because when I was at a teachable age—I hope I'm still at a teachable age!—but when I was at a really teachable age, I could have gone to any one of ten great pedagogues in Europe and studied with them, lived in the presence of their hands and their minds. Now this is no longer possible. The most a young pianist can hope for, these days, is an occasional master class, to sit at the feet of a master. I'm a great believer in sitting at the feet of great pianists, and watching their hands, and seeing how they produce what they produce: but not merely in order to copy them; perhaps rather to absorb something from them, their spirit, their approach, and if one is very lucky—*very* lucky—catch a tiny spark from them, and fan it into flame with one's own hands. Ravel understood this paradox so well when he said: 'Choose a model; imitate him. If you have nothing to say, then all you can do is copy. If you have something to say, your personality will appear at its best in your *unconscious infidelity* . . .'

All kinds of pianists and teachers have noted down helpful maxims from time to time. Sometimes they are interesting, and sometimes amusing: some are even both. But do any of them *really* tell you anything about the piano? Leschetizky said, 'Always say good morning and good night to your piano'. Busoni said the same thing in another way: 'Never let a single day go by without playing your piano'. Schnabel too: asked about his weekends, he said, 'I happen to belong to a profession where there are only Holy-Days, and no weekends'. Now those little sayings are very useful, as general rules: a pianist must be like a lover to his instrument. They give a measure of the commitment. They say everything: and at the same time nothing at all.

To come under the influence of Wanda Landowska was one of the two apocalyptic experiences of my early twenties. I was with her as a student for about two years,

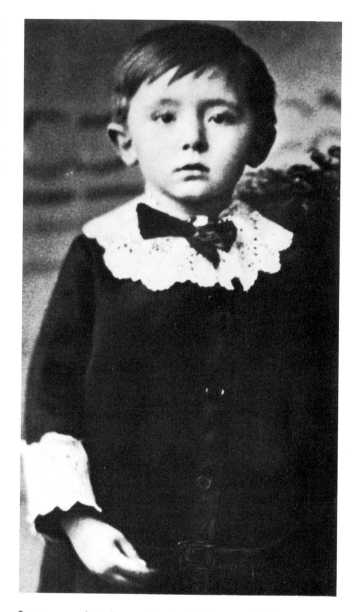

I suppose; but I was also 'with' her until the year she died. I've always felt that being a student, being a teacher, isn't just something you do for a while, and then stop. I hear people nowadays say, for instance, 'Oh yes, I was a pupil of Schnabel's', and they write a long dissertation on Schnabel's teaching, and it turns out that they might have had two lessons with Schnabel and no more. They are not really pupils at all. To be a real pupil, you must be so much more than a pupil. I don't know what it is exactly, but the real teacher-pupil relationship is more like a kind of life-companionship.

The other apocalypse was Schnabel. He was a sturdy young man nearing fifty when I first went to him, and in a sense I also stayed with him until he died. I couldn't imagine that this was a relationship that ended when I paid for my last lesson. I wonder if there could be anything of that kind for an eager young pianist these days? Life is so differently organized.

My own feelings about teaching are very ambivalent—chiefly because I find that it drains me of precisely those things from which I build my own performances. I mean that in some strange way it takes a certain strength from me; so that after teaching, and for some time afterwards, I feel as if I have been drained of a vital emanation which should go out from an artist to his audience. Isn't it true that some conjurors who reveal the secret of their tricks can no longer perform them freely, feel somehow inhibited?

Schnabel had one pupil who copied him so closely that if the door was closed when you came to join the class—you always waited for a pause before you dared to sneak in—you could never tell which one was playing. The pianos were alike, identical Bechsteins, so you couldn't tell tonally; there was no way of knowing till you got into the room. Now this young pianist made a perfectly good reputation, but he never reached the top.

What makes a public performer? The answer is both very simple and very complex. I once heard Schnabel dispose of the question with characteristic directness. Asked about a certain highly cultivated and in general exceptionally civilized pupil whom he really liked and respected a great deal, Schnabel replied, 'Poor boy—he just hasn't enough talent'.

And that was enough reason for him: you might have everything, but you might not have enough talent—whatever that might be. I saw this time and time again: men and women who had so much in them to express that was fine and interesting, who were highly intelligent and highly articulate, and in every way lovely people, but who simply didn't have the strange, special, peculiar *talent* to be a pianist.

On the other hand, even the most glaring physical defects may not matter if the talent is there: a tendency to arthritis, for example, or an unstable memory, or even a seemingly inadequate pair of hands. Towards the end of his career, Paderewski always started his concerts late; it was a great irritation, and the audience would start clapping—a quarter of an hour, twenty minutes. And he was offstage with his hands in hot water because of an arthritic condition! Then he'd come on and play like an angel. And Cortot, of course, hardly ever played a programme without forgetting something: he had a most unreliable memory. A seemingly inadequate pair of hands—well, quite a few have those, and some are great artists all the same!

Schnabel once said to me, 'You know, in my time I've known just two players of genius.' They were a very strange pair of bedfellows, really; one was Busoni—quite incompatible, one would have thought, with a very *Deutscher* Schnabel: for though Schnabel was born a Pole, he was completely Austro-German by background and outlook. And the other was Rachmaninov.

Great geniuses may even seem to be almost of underdeveloped intelligence, or certainly lack a number of so-called 'intelligent' faculties. There was once a very great woman pianist who was unable to read musical leger lines with ease—she had to help herself read the music by writing the alphabet letters above each note like a child. And yet she was quite clairvoyant in her understanding of music, of what is necessary for its communication, and had a marvellous ability to create that aura of conviction and beauty which is so fundamental to it. You know, incidentally, that the greatest performers are often far from being the greatest sight-readers—and vice versa. No, it's not 'intelligence', nor any one easily definable gift. When you have talked about everything, the technique, the fingerings, the agility, the strength, the cunning at the keyboard, there's something else still, something absolutely vital, which defies definition. Perhaps 'magic' is the word for it; or 'charm', that favourite word of the older generation. But whatever it is, it's something that lies quite beyond words.

There's a very amusing story of Ellen Terry, who must have been the essence of feminine radiance, being directed in the theatre by a rather unsympathetic young man, who told her where to stand, at what moment to raise her voice, at what moment to push her chair back, and so on. She didn't agree with a lot of it, but she was very professional, and he was, after all, there to tell her what to do. So she did it all; and at the end, when he had finished with her, she turned to him and she said, 'Now, if you don't mind, I'll just do that little extra something for which I am paid my enormous fee.' That's nice, isn't it? Because in the end what an artist is paid for is not just to produce the notes, but for some small extra something which you cannot describe, but without which the performance is lifeless, flavourless. Magic?—if you like.

I remember once going to a recital of Cortot in his later days. The playing did perhaps show certain weaknesses; but a young pupil of Schnabel's came up to me afterwards in the foyer—he was I should think a good ten years younger than I, and I was quite young then myself—and I said to him, 'Oh, my goodness, that touch! what magic! what poetry!' He said, rather coolly, 'Did you think so?' 'Oh yes', I said, 'I see the other

things of course, but he's such a wonderful artist.' And
he replied — I've never forgotten the expression — 'Well,
I'm afraid I have very high ideals in piano playing.' I
simply turned around and walked away. He was quite a
well-known young player at that time — though, as it
turned out, his high ideals didn't get him very far.

What astonishes me sometimes is that people can't
recognize outright, regardless of the day or the
programme, that a genius is a genius. Richter, for
example, I consider to be a genius. There is something,
an indefinable, invisible *fluidum*, that reaches out from
him to the audience. All right, sometimes he does
strange things; he can play a piece almost unbelievably
slowly, for example, so slowly that it's obviously
'wrong'. But that's irrelevant, entirely irrelevant. He has
the power, a power of inner conviction that goes far
beyond whether the piece is twice too slow, or twice too
fast. Even at his most 'doctrinaire'-sounding, he is an
absolute original, not like anyone else, anyone else at all.
And if he plays a work one day more slowly, even more
slowly than it 'ought' to be played (whatever that may
mean), it doesn't matter, does it? Have people really lost
the ability to have divinities, to be roused to a passion, to
be moved to tears? All they can say is, 'Oh, I play it
much faster than that!' or 'Oh, just look what he did!'

There is another nice story, apropos, about Ilona
Derenburg (*née* Eibenschutz), a pupil of Clara Schumann, who went one day to a recital of Anton
Rubinstein. By all accounts he was badly off form.
Rubinstein had already met Ilona at Clara Schumann's
house, so he knew her face; and on his way off the stage
at the end of the recital, he recognized her as he passed,
and whispered, 'Now don't *you* ever play the piano like
that!'

So Ilona went to Clara Schumann the next day,
absolutely thrilled, and told her what had happened.
And Clara Schumann looked at her very seriously, and
replied, 'We all have our days, good and bad — but you
should never forget that he is *always* a great artist.' That
sums up a lot. First of all it says a great deal for Clara
Schumann. We know that she didn't care particularly
for Rubinstein's playing — it was not of her school. But
she would never permit a young student to make such a
point of a great artist's lapses. In my fashion, neither
would I permit a young pianist to sit down in front of me
and start to dissect or dismiss, let's say, Richter. I would
be delighted to discuss, or analyze: I would say, yes, I
think he does sometimes use very eccentric tempi, and
he does strange things; but you know, all *you* have to do
is learn, go and hear what is startling and beautiful in his
playing. That alone is important; because whatever he

does, he is a great and extraordinary artist.

Schnabel, too, was extremely generous about other
pianists, when they were artists whose qualities he
admired. Somebody would come in and mention, say,
Cortot's having broken down in the last movement of a
concerto, or that some other great pianist of the day had
done something they considered outrageous, and
Schnabel would say, very simply and quietly, 'Yes? I
never heard him when he didn't play extremely well.'
Just like that.

And he would also say, 'Whatever you may think
about Landowska's approach to Bach, or that, or the
other, you have to admire' — and he always used this
word for some reason, because I don't think it's a word
that's used in German very much, and certainly not in
English — 'you have to admire her enormous *maîtrise*.'
And really that is just the right word for Landowska, for
her authority and command. It is somehow the very size
and authority of a master's playing, not just the
'correctness' or otherwise of its detail, that makes it
unique.

I cannot really approve of competitions — I really
can't. Ultimately, they can be damaging; and paradoxically they are sometimes most damaging of all to the
winners. I had one (not a first prize winner) visit me not
too long ago, just before he was to give his American
debut recital in Carnegie Hall. I said — as you see, I've

got a terribly mean streak—I said, 'Are you playing your *first* concert in Carnegie Hall? Well, you know, Busoni always played in the Wigmore Hall in London, because there were things of such delicacy in his playing, and of such subtlety, which he felt were lost in a larger place.' I looked at this young man, and I thought, how can he walk on and give his first American recital at Carnegie Hall? Relatively well-known artists would never have done that in the old days even at the Queen's Hall in London, which was the ideal hall acoustically for a piano recital—it was only when you were very high up in your profession that you began to play there. But this youngster had won a few prizes, and had already been persuaded to live quite beyond his musical means.

As far as pure 'technique' is concerned, I think I went through all the hoops in my fashion. I never did methodical hours and hours of Czerny or Hanon, but I got through. I was actually pretty lazy about exercises, but I always did the things I heard great pianists did—I knew that Liszt, for example, used to practise all the scales with the C major fingering, which is a very good exercise indeed. Nevertheless, when you come down to it, beyond a certain point every pianist is his own master; every pianist is self-taught.

Busoni's remarks in his preface to Breithaupt's book on piano technique make just this point: every artist forms his own technique. That is absolutely true. Beyond a certain point, there is nothing where technique is concerned, that you can learn from another. You can copy, you can watch, you can become impregnated with another's ideas; but to be a real musician, a real artist, you will ultimately have to form your own technique—something which for yourself covers the whole range of music.

I remember Landowska telling me in her later years that she felt she had progressed—because when, as a young artist, she had sometimes failed, she hadn't known why. Now, in her later life, she still failed: but at least she knew why! And that is very true: when I fail, now I know why, and I can work it out of my system. But when I was young, and I failed, I was very much less clear about why, and how, and as a result, of course, about what to do to put it right.

One of the great precepts of Schnabel's teaching was that there was a right movement and a right fingering for every sound and phrase. He returned again and again to that: he was very insistent on the physical side, as well as the spiritual side, of piano playing. That's why he sat so much at the piano, experimenting with so many different ways of playing a phrase, starting the phrase on the first note, starting the phrase on the second note,

going to the fourth note, or the fifth note, here, there, and everywhere—he spent hours experimenting, getting the physical details just right. Without them, there was no basis on which to build.

I wonder if many people—non-pianists, of course, but even some pianists too—realize the crucial importance of fingering? You've got only ten fingers, and you've got nearly one hundred keys. And it's the arrangement of those ten fingers, and the way each follows the other, that not only allows you to play the right notes, but lets you shape the music, and make it speak.

Schnabel never automatically took the easiest fingering. When I was young, one was taught a conventional and fairly rigid style of fingering that usually vetoed, for example, the use of the thumb on a black note. In a way that makes sense, because black notes are certainly awkward for the thumb; but if Schnabel ever felt the phrase demanded it—if, for example, he wanted more weight or attack on a black note—he would never hesitate to go up on to that note with his thumb. Paradoxically—but then music is full of paradoxes—he might also suggest using the thumb in a trill: but this time to give extra lightness.

Landowska was more concerned, in the matter of phrasing, with what put you most at your ease—for since the harpsichord has no sustaining pedal, everything is more exposed than on the piano, frighteningly exposed. But both of these great keyboard players were obsessed by fingering. Schnabel always wanted to achieve a 'second simplicity', that second naïvety you arrive at after having gone through all the difficulties, having come through all the tests, and out the other side. And he would try to do this by looking for the most natural way to play every bar of music: he would go through everything, every phrase, to see how he could play it best *without* practice—which did not mean simply going over and over different patterns and different fingerings, but rather, as it were, throwing his hand on the piano and seeing which way made the phrase speak most beautifully; it might even be the most eccentric fingering, but it was the fingering which most naturally suited a particular phrase.

Now, of course, in a way, the last thing you learn—I know people laugh at me for this, but there is some sense in this madness—the last things you learn are the notes. You've got to learn first what the phrasing is about, the structure, where every phrase belongs, the whole shape of the music: because if you start by learning the notes, and consequently also fingering them, you may have to undo most of those fingerings once you realize better what the phrase is about—and the most difficult thing of all is to *unlearn*. Once you get out there in public and there's a moment's hesitation between the old and the new, maybe between the thumb and the fourth finger, it's fatal—just as fatal as it would be for a dancer who hesitated between the left and right foot in the middle of a complicated routine.

I suspect many people have a quite wrong idea of the role of fingering. They think—well, if you've run out of fingers, you just put the thumb under and continue as before. And many pianists actually play that way: apparently a lot of them do—they just play 'The Fingering'. A very famous pianist once even asked me, almost conspiratorially, 'You know, I don't always do the fingering in the copy, do you?' Well, good heavens!—which fingering, which copy? Fingering indications in the printed music are often pretty dubious, put there by editors and suchlike; but even if their suggestions are perfectly intelligent, it's a matter that each individual performer must study for himself. The indications are just that: suggestions. You need only look at Schnabel's edition of the Beethoven sonatas, and on numerous occasions you will see not just one fingering given for a phrase, but two or three.

But then, Schnabel had this extraordinary ability to get right to the heart of a phrase through the fingering (and through thought-out groups of fingerings, for which he invented the term 'handings')—and as often as not where he makes only one suggestion in his edition, he makes his point exactly. A distinguished colleague said to me once, 'Isn't it odd about Schnabel's fingerings of Beethoven? You go through a sonata slowly trying his fingerings, and you think the man's mad. You like your own, which are so much simpler; and then you get a little dissatisfied, and then you change it, and then perhaps you change it again, which means you are very far from playing it in public; and then in desperation you return to the Schnabel edition, and you see that after all his fingering is the one you've been trying all that time to arrive at.'

Traditionally, most pianists used to start practising a work slowly, and then work it up to tempo; but that wasn't the way with either Schnabel or Landowska. They had so many points of similarity in these things, it's quite extraordinary really. What they did was take small sections of a work at a time and play them up to tempo straight away. Find out what the tempo is; hear the music inwardly; study it; feel what its life and pulse must be.

There is little point in fingering, let's say, a fast movement very slowly to start with. If you do that, when you begin to play it fast, you'll most likely have to take a different fingering: slow and fast fingerings are not necessarily the same. We know slow and fast music; we know slow and fast tempi; but how many students are taught to think in terms of slow and fast fingerings? One should finger a fast piece first at speed, then practise it slowly before working it back to tempo—but always with the first, fast fingering.

Tovey always said that the final, fast speed should never be the goal of a performance, but just a bonus.

In my early days, if the great pianist Katharine Goodson—Leschetizky included her in his pantheon of 'genius players'—thought one was getting careless in any way at all, she would say, 'Do remember, there's one little old lady, in the last seat of the last row of the balcony, who knows the work as well as you do.' And that's perfectly true. Sir Henry Wood would admonish careless players at rehearsal by calling out, 'The audience won't *say* anything; but they'll notice!' And that's perfectly true, too: they may not say anything; they might not even be able to pinpoint a lack or a lapse precisely; but of course they'll notice.

All the same, there are some things I feel audiences don't always notice. They may not realize, for example—because they don't hear all his different performances, or because they forget—how much a real artist's performance of the same work changes: constantly, it changes constantly! This is another thing that Landowska and Schnabel had in common, and something they emphasized every day of their lives. Schnabel always said that he intended to retire from the concert platform at fifty, because by that age he either felt it would be undignified to continue as a public performer, or he imagined that he would have played himself out. But of course he didn't—either retire, or play himself out. It was a constant process of renewal: he was always going out and beginning again—a motto which I think should be engraved above the door of every little room where students work. Begin again, begin again!

The Mozart K. 595 that I am playing now is not the K. 595 of last week, and by next week I will again have changed so many things—there is no end to the changing. I am sure that I have never repeated a programme or a work in my life that hasn't been in some aspect fundamentally re-worked in the light of the previous performance.

Another thing, it seems to me, that a great many people don't realize about piano playing is the great difference between individual instruments. They don't realize that, quite apart from who touches them, all

Below: Clifford Curzon: drawing by Milein Cosman.

Opposite: A page from Curzon's working score of Mozart's piano concerto in D minor K. 466.

pianos are intrinsically dissimilar in character: minute differences of regulation and action can give an entirely different sensation to the pianist when he plays, and either work for or against the tonal reflexes in his hand. And so much of the mechanics of piano playing is reflex—the ten thousand times that you've jumped through the hoop, like an animal in a circus, through the fiery hoop!

Strange to say, many people don't seem to understand, either, that there are such important differences between an upright and a grand piano: the sound is produced by very different actions. It's really not advisable for a pianist to practise on an upright piano if he's going to perform on a grand. On an upright you're *throwing* hammers at the strings, not levering them up from below, and the physical sensations of these two actions are so entirely different that working on one before playing on the other can confuse the reflexes of sensitive fingers. And what does nearly every concert hall in the world have in the Green Room backstage?—well, of course, an upright piano.

And another thing about concert halls today—do you know that practically nowhere in the world can I find a piano stool low enough? They have either to cut the legs off, or go and get one out of the ladies' room. They send a special one when I play at the Festival Hall. And I

don't sit unduly low: it's just that the style has changed. Piano playing has generally become much more percussive, more attacked from above—and so everybody is expected to enjoy sitting up high. And in many places you wind the seat right down at rehearsal, so it's perfect; then you go on at night to give the performance, only to find the dear piano tuner has wound it up again! That's how he has to have it in order to tune properly, but it's no good for me.

Back to performing, though. Picasso said that every picture he painted was the result of a horde of destructions; and that also applies very well to piano playing. You play, and it sounds nice, because you're musical, and you're in love with the music. Then you begin to fuss, and you change something. And then you change it again. And you change it about twenty times, until as often as not you discover something that's very close to the way you first played it—but it's different now, because you've lived through those other nineteen times. And that really is it: all the time, you have to destroy. And that's what I mean by fingerings, and change, and feeling that your reflexes are going to let you down, because—ah, let's start that Mozart concerto on a thumb—well, yes, do: but you'll fall in the soup, you know! Danger, yes, live dangerously! There is nothing more perilous, or more fundamental, or more exciting in music than change—especially on the day of a concert. It may be dangerous, but however late it comes, it is irresistible, and it is a life force—that sudden thumb, that sudden illumination of a phrase.

Stories, advice—where do they lead? I think it was Mozart who said that a real performer should give the impression in public that he has composed the piece himself, almost that he is composing it as he plays. Not so difficult for Mozart, naturally, because he often had, and did. But for others, that's a sublime, unachievable goal. And the paradox is that you can only give that impression of being an original, spontaneous creator when you have been through so many different ways of performing the work—when you've destroyed your hundred ways, like Picasso.

Performers, after all, are free; but we are only free when we are enslaved—and that is an extremely difficult thing to describe. We go through all the disciplines in order to achieve all the freedoms. What we are doing all the time, every minute of the day, is setting up oppositions to be overcome, destroying and changing, until we arrive (if we're lucky) at something nearer to the unattainable ideal. Then for a moment we are happy—until the next day, when the time has come to change again.

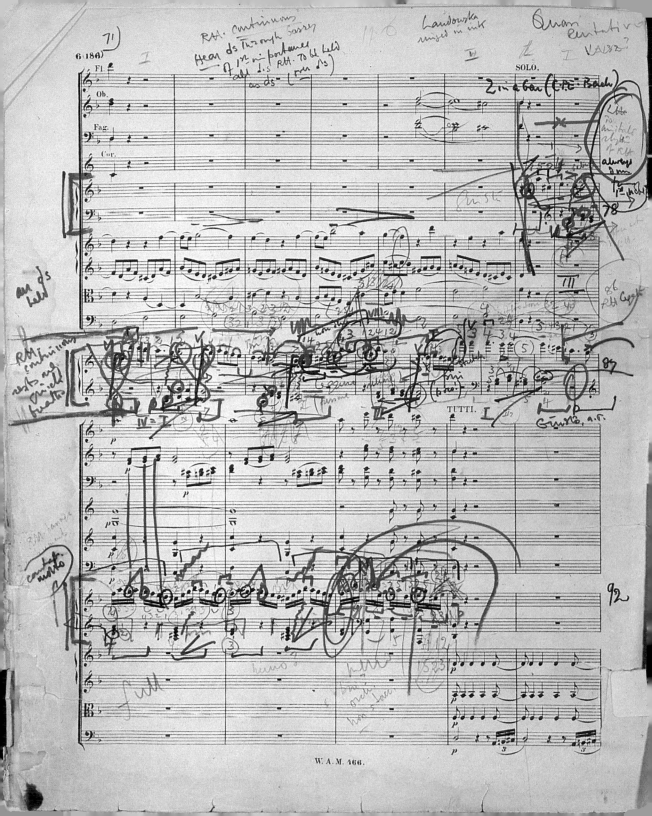

A Chronology of Pianists

Anton Rubinstein Russian, b. Vykhvatinets, Volhynia, 1829; d. Peterhof, Germany, 1894. Studied first with his mother, then, at the age of eight, in Moscow with Alexandre Villoing, who subsequently took him to Paris where he received initial encouragement from Chopin and Liszt (though Liszt later came to regard him as a dangerous rival). After some years of disappointment and poverty, and much travel, he set out once more from Russia to western Europe in 1854, and from there finally launched on a long and brilliantly successful international career. Von Bülow called him 'The Michelangelo of Music': contemporary accounts note a grandeur, loftiness, and passionate, spontaneous quality in his playing that Liszt himself could not match. Famous for his inaccuracy and memory-lapses, often covered by brilliant improvising: perhaps no great pianist ever missed more notes and yet so profoundly moved his listeners. Rachmaninov felt that 'for every possible mistake he may have made, he gave in return ideas and tone-pictures that would have made up for a million mistakes. When Rubinstein was over-exact, his playing lost something of its wonderful charm.' Huge hands, to match a stature that earned him the nickname of 'The Russian Bear', and exceptionally broad fingers, may have contributed to his difficulty with the 'right' notes—Rubinstein himself confessed to having 'paws, not hands'. Recital programmes often of enormous length, and tours of astonishing rigour: on his first journey to America he gave 215 concerts in 239 days. A master of broad and passionate effect, rather than of subtle poetry, he was heard at the height of his career in 1885 by Hanslick, who wrote: 'One seldom finds in contemporary pianists that genuine, spontaneous inward fervour which in the heat of passion dares all things, even to indiscretion, rather than pause to reason and reflect. Rubinstein's temperament is of such compelling force that exhausted Europe yields submissive to his will.' Unrelated to Arthur Rubinstein.

Vladimir de Pachmann Russian, b. Odessa, 1848; d. Rome, 1933. Studied in Vienna with Joseph Dachs, but essentially self-taught. Became famous for his eccentric, picturesque behaviour and bewildering series of appearances and disappearances in Odessa, Paris, Vienna, London and New York. Awarded the Royal Philharmonic Society's Beethoven Medal in London in 1916. Known as the 'pianissimist' and 'Chopinzee'. Chattered whilst he played and commented, often offensively, on the personal appearances of his audience. Dipped fingers in brandy before recitals, wore a curious collection of clothes (socks and underwear) claiming

they were Chopin's, and recommended the milking of cows as obligatory for a good technique. Considered Godowsky 'the second greatest' pianist, while hiding his own (evident) deficiencies behind verbal smokes screen and elaborate pantomine. Said to have played Chopin's smaller works with delicacy, although the few recordings which survive are both perfunctory and inaccurate (e.g. Chopin's Impromptu in F sharp).

Ignacy Jan Paderewski Polish, b. Kurylówka, 1860; d. New York, 1941. After early lack of success he studied in 1884 with Leschetizky, who despaired of his student's lack of natural pianistic reflexes and resource. Debut and first real success in Vienna, then Paris (1888) and London (1890). American debut in 1891 followed by 117 U.S. concerts. A personification of Romantic Polish patriotism, he gave over 300 speeches in America on behalf of his country after the outbreak of the First World War. In 1919 he became the first Premier and Minister of Foreign Affairs of the Polish Republic, and fought tirelessly for an independent Poland. Relinquished these posts a year later and retired to Switzerland; then, in 1921, to California. Resumed tours (1922–3) in America and Europe. He gave much of his considerable wealth to charities, to young artists, and to the cause of his beloved Poland. During 1936–8 he produced his complete Chopin edition, and in subsequent years received nine Honorary Doctorates from universities in many countries. The name of Paderewski is legendary: but his great pianistic days were brief, and his playing in later years marked by an erratic sense of rhythm and uneasy technical command. Few recordings available today give indication of his convincing stature (Liszt's 'La Leggierezza' Etude, enchantingly elaborated by Leschetizky, is perhaps an exception).

Moriz Rosenthal Polish, b. Lemberg, 1862; d. New York, 1946. Studied with Mikuli, Joseffy and Liszt. Detour to study philosophy in Vienna from 1880–6. Tour of America, 1888; England, 1895. Famed for his colossal technique and command of 'the grand manner', and at times also for the violence and excess of his interpretations; found by some critics to be 'lacking in poetry'. Notorious for scabrous attacks on colleagues. On hearing that Schnabel had been rejected for military service he remarked, 'What do you expect? No fingers!' Recordings (especially piano roll) numerous, often brilliant, occasionally suspect.

Ferrucio Busoni Italian, b. Empoli, 1866; d. Berlin, 1924. A self-taught and lofty idealist who bitterly concluded, 'Schumann is of no use to me any more;

268

Beethoven only with an effort and strict selection. Chopin has attracted and repelled me all my life; I have *heard* his music too often—prostituted, profaned, vulgarised . . .' Controversial style, apt to deliver even the smallest Chopin Prelude with an air of monumental grandeur. His New York debut in 1911 included Chopin's four Ballades and A flat Polonaise, and Liszt's *'Robert le Diable' Fantasy*. Much given to doubtful aphorisms such as 'Bach is the foundation of piano playing, Liszt is the summit. The two make Beethoven possible.' His recordings are flawed, idiosyncratic, and certainly unrepresentative: according to one writer who heard him often, 'one might as well confine the Atlantic Ocean in a milk bottle as confine Busoni to records.'

Leopold Godowsky   Polish, b. Vilna, 1870; d. New York, 1938. Studied with Rudorff and Saint-Saëns, but otherwise largely self-taught. U.S. tours commenced in 1884, and in 1894 he was appointed Director of the piano department of Chicago Conservatory. An indefatigable arranger and paraphraser, his most notable composition is a collection of 53 *Etudes* on 26 Chopin *Etudes*, elaborations of the most indulgent and *phantastisch* complexity. Unlike de Pachmann, Godowsky was taken very seriously by his colleagues, who marvelled at such a streamlined keyboard mechanism. He was nonetheless apparently inhibited by public appearance, and performed his most legendary feats in private. Available recordings (notably of Chopin's second sonata) are unrepresentative, oddly tame and diffident.

Sergei Rachmaninov   Russian, b. Oneg, Novgorod, 1873; d. California, 1943. Studied with Nikolai Zveryev, who is said to have vitalized Rachmaninov's initially lethargic, happy-go-lucky approach, and laid the foundations of a unique pianistic skill. Early success with his second concerto and C sharp minor Prelude (referred to as 'it' by Ernest Newman). Left Russia in 1917 for unhappy exile in America. Neurotically indecisive about the priorities of composing, conducting or piano playing: but excelled in all three. As a performer, Rachmaninov was the first and perhaps also in many ways the greatest of 'modern' pianists, and his recorded performances of such works as Schumann's *Carnaval* and Chopin's B flat minor sonata are numbered today amongst the greatest classics of the piano archive. RCA's reissues are an indispensable part of any serious record collection: the same company's refusal in the 1930s to act upon Rachmaninov's suggestion that he record for them a substantial additional series of recital programmes can now be seen as one of the great *gaffes* of recording history.

Joseph Lhevinne   Russian, b. Orel, 1874; d. New York, 1944. Studied with Safonov at Moscow Conservatory. A specialist in the Romantic piano and a famous virtuoso, he was also (like his wife Rosina) one of America's most celebrated teachers and a prominent member of the Juilliard School. Though he made few records, he was much admired for his remarkable technical facility and ravishing tonal palette. His book *Basic Principles of Pianoforte Playing* (1924) is an invaluable guide to the student, and expounds in a strictly empirical and non-scientific manner the tradition of the Russian school, with its emphasis on basic technique, and 'thinking moods into the fingers and arms'.

Walter Gieseking   German, b. Lyon, 1875; d. London, 1956. Studied with Karl Leimer; and although at one time suspected of Nazi sympathies (which led to the cancellation of an American tour in 1949), enjoyed an enormous success in America and world-wide. The French have never found it easy to forgive Gieseking, a German, for poaching so successfully on their own, jealously guarded territory. His performances of Debussy have acquired the status of legend: an exceptionally subtle pedal technique, and an acute ear for texture and colour, play a major part in his exquisitely phrased, flawlessly voiced performances on record of the 24 Preludes, *Images*, *Estampes* and, perhaps most memorable of all, of 15 short pieces. Gieseking mastered an extensive repertoire with the greatest of ease, memorizing all of Beethoven's 32 sonatas before he was twenty, and Grieg's demanding Ballade on a short train journey. Such facility is not without its dangers, and occasionally resulted in performances, for all their pointillist, elegantly-turned detail, under-scale and lacking in robustness. It is not generally known that Gieseking was also an ardent champion of the Russian Romantics, and played Tchaikovsky's first and Rachmaninov's second and third concertos to mixed critical response late in his career.

Joseph Hofmann   Polish, b. Cracow, 1876; d. California, 1957. Studied with Anton Rubinstein; American debut in 1887. Hofmann was a prodigy, and the Society for the Prevention of Cruelty to Children, disturbed by the pace of his schedules, interrupted his early career. He played principally in America and, a greatly celebrated teacher, directed the Curtis Institute from 1925–38. A daunting legend—for Anton Rubinstein, 'a musical phenomenon'; the inaccuracies in his performance were for Godowsky mere 'spots on the sun'. A player of astonishing facility who could learn and perform works of the greatest complexity by ear alone, without the score. Recordings of the finest examples of his art are elusive: Beethoven's 'Waldstein' sonata, Schumann's *Kreisleriana* and Chopin's fourth Ballade (recorded at his Casimir Hall recital of 1938) are, presumably, unrepresentative. More telling, though poorly recorded, are performances from his Golden Jubilee recital, reissued on LP.

Alfred Cortot   French, b. Nyon, 1877; d. Lausanne, 1962. Trained at the Paris Conservatoire with Louis Diémer, and conducted the first performance of *Götterdämmerung* in Paris. Founded the *Société des Concerts Cortot* in 1903, where many important French and German works received their first performances. The same year also saw the founding of the Cortot-Thibaud-Casals Trio. In 1917 he succeeded Raoul Pugno as chief professor of piano at the Paris Conservatoire, and in 1919 founded the *Ecole Normale de Musique*, later famous for its courses in interpretation. Amongst his publications are two volumes of musical essays, a biography of Chopin and a four-volume edition of Chopin's works. In 1944 he was arrested on charges of Nazi collaboration, and although he was later released, there was at the time strong popular feeling against him. Cortot was an artist of protean range and unique personality. Teacher, writer, editor, conductor and pianist were only a few of his tireless roles (see also p. 123). His recordings (mainly of Chopin) are erratic but stylistically vital and brilliant, the nuances magically sprung, the tone-quality hauntingly elusive. His account of Schumann's *Davidsbündlertänze* is as poetic and powerfully drawn as it is inaccurate—a remarkable instance of how *real* 'technique' and instinctive poetry can survive even the most haphazard presentation.

Egon Petri   Dutch, b. Hanover, 1881; d. California, 1962. Studied with Teresa Carreno and Busoni and became a celebrated exponent of Busoni's works. A Liszt specialist (and also a champion of Alkan), he was famous for his performances of such warhorses as Beethoven's '*Hammerklavier*' sonata and Brahms's 'Paganini' Variations—and his recordings of these two works are powerful examples of his characteristically cool, but monumental, style.

Artur Schnabel   Austrian, b. Lipnik, 1882; d. Axenstein, Switzerland, 1951. Studied with Leschetizky. Edited the complete Beethoven piano sonatas and became one of the most admired Beethoven pianists of his time (see also p. 123). His legendary performances of the Viennese classics (a great number preserved on disc) represented for many a new seriousness and a departure long overdue from the charlatanism and tinsel glitter of a previous generation. Whilst others wooed the public with Arabesques on *The Blue Danube*, Schnabel ignored the box office (and his manager's advice) to give stubbornly 'unpopular' all-Schubert programmes. A wry, witty and cultivated man, Schnabel was also deeply reserved; but his self-effacement in the service of music 'which is always better than it can be played' should not persuade listeners to ignore his accomplishments, equally great, in a remarkably wide range of familiar nineteenth-century Romantic works. He was also a celebrated teacher, and a composer (of high seriousness, though of less distinction).

Wilhelm Backhaus   German, b. Leipzig, 1884; d. Villach, Austria, 1969. Studied with Eugene d'Albert, and during his early years established a reputation as an outstanding virtuoso in such works as Brahms's 'Paganini' Variations and the Chopin *Etudes*. Later, as his style mellowed, Backhaus came to be most highly regarded as a Beethovenian—at his finest, a pianist of imperturbable command and rugged strength. His recordings are sometimes disappointing, and do not always provide an accurate image of his greatness in the concert hall—although admirers acknowledge his performance of the Brahms second concerto as a notable exception, and cherish it as one of the pianist's most warm-hearted as well as vigorous interpretations.

Edwin Fischer   Swiss, b. Basel, 1886; d. Zurich, 1960. Student of Huber and Krauss, Fischer formed his own chamber orchestra, with which he played concertos conducting from the keyboard in an 'authentic' fashion later followed by such modern virtuosi as Anda, Barenboim and Perahia. Edited Bach's keyboard works, and published a study of the Beethoven sonatas. Fischer demonstrated in his recordings, especially of Bach, Beethoven, Mozart, Brahms and Schubert, a deep humanity and a luminous sense of polyphony which, for many, speak of an age of poetry and musicianship regrettably past. His performance of Bach's *Chromatic Fantasy and Fugue* is a notable example of his imaginatively free approach to Baroque interpretation, though many of today's younger pianists find the style 'impressionistic' and 'unauthentic', lacking in 'proper' severity.

Arthur Rubinstein   Polish, b. Lodz, 1886. Studied with Heinrich Barth in Berlin (where he made his formal debut at the age of 11) and later, briefly, with

Paderewski in Switzerland. American debut in 1906, giving 75 concerts in 3 months, but waited until 1937 for his first real American success. Lived for some time in Paris (his present home), where he 'shed his immaturity', and in London working as an interpreter (he speaks eight languages fluently), before moving to America after the Second World War. After an early triumph in Spain (1916), he gave a series of remarkable marathons in London, Paris and New York, and in 1961, at the age of 75, celebrated 55 years before the American public with ten concerts in ten consecutive days at Carnegie Hall. For more than half a century, Rubinstein was the international *grand seigneur* of the piano, although at the beginning of his career many audiences found the clarity and simple poetry of his Chopin especially an unacceptable alternative to the then current vogue for sentimentality and grand-romantic hysteria. But his lyrical, uncluttered style soon won their allegiance, and his unpretentious ardour their hearts. Thousands of concerts and recordings streamed from his fingers in the years that followed, each one a lively mirror of the pianist who was, as he often proclaimed, 'the happiest man I know'. He gave his last public recital in May 1976 at the Wigmore Hall, London (where he had first appeared 64 years previously)—the coda of a legendary career, which is said to have taken him to every country of the world except Tibet. Unrelated to Anton Rubinstein.

Myra Hess English, b. London, 1890; d. London, 1965. Worked with Tobias Matthay for five years, and created CBE in 1936, DBE in 1941. One of the piano's household names, and an artist of the highest distinction. Dame Myra's performances were marked by a quiet force and regality, and though her recordings are regrettably few, her disc of Beethoven's opp. 109 and 110 in particular offers substantial compensation. Her series of National Gallery Concerts, given during the Second World War, began as an experiment and became a legend. One thousand people, rather than the expected 50, attended the opening concert. The bombs fell and (for political reasons) Schubert's *'Wohin?'* became *'Pourquoi?'*: but the venture continued. And 1,698 concerts later the pianist was able to exclaim, 'Never have I played more and practised less!' Dame Myra's greatest success, however, was in America, where her quietly-spoken authority and poetical delicacy struck an unfamiliar chord: Virgil Thomson's 'She is not memorable, like a love affair; she is satisfactory, like a good tailor' was one of the rare harsher (though not entirely unperceptive) American judgements.

Benno Moiseiwitsch Russian, b. Odessa, 1890; d. London, 1963. A student of Leschetizky, who made his London debut in 1908, and later settled in London to become one of the piano's household names. A great artist, whose refined manner and quicksilver dexterity were not always fully appreciated during his lifetime. A Romantic specialist, Moiseiwitsch was greatly admired by Rachmaninov, whose works he interpreted with aristocratic distinction; but for many concert-goers Chopin's 24 Preludes or Schumann's *Carnaval*, Beethoven's 'Waldstein' sonata or Prokofiev's third sonata were only a few of the works indelibly linked with his name. In later years Moiseiwitsch's powers declined, and truly representative recordings are hard to find. Admirers will, however, seek out the Mendelssohn-Rachmaninov *Midsummer Night's Dream* Scherzo, Weber's *Moto Perpetuo* or even John Vallier's delightful *Toccatina* as notable examples of pianism as fleet and stylish as it is enchanting.

Wilhelm Kempff German, b. Jüterborn, 1895. A no less subtle and imaginative artist than Cortot—although when the gods are not with him, like Cortot he can topple into confusion. The number of his recordings suggests his remarkable range, and in his Beethoven sonata-cycles (which he has recorded three times) some of the earliest-recorded early opus numbers are memorable examples of a wit, delicacy and pianistic sophistication quite beyond the reach of younger, more earnest practitioners. Kempff's genius, indeed, has never taken wing more stylishly than in early Beethoven (try sonatas 1, 2, 3, 4, 5, 7, 11, 12 or 15); and his first Decca record of Liszt's two *Légendes* is among the most distinguished of all Liszt recordings. His discs also include a wayward, idiosyncratic Chopin series, a more conventional Schumann cycle, and a remarkable set of the Schubert sonatas.

Robert Casadesus French, b. Paris, 1899; d. 1972. Distinguished musical lineage. Studied, together with Cortot and Yves Nat, with Louis Diémer, but stayed only nine months after winning the first prize in his first year at the age of fourteen. Later confessed that his 'real teacher' was his aunt, Mlle Simon, with whom he studied for many years. U.S. debut in 1953; immediately invited to appear with Toscanini. Enjoyed international career and recorded extensively. His fluency and elegance were proverbial, as were also the grandeur and warmth of his playing (not, sadly, captured by many recordings), which made him a notable interpreter of such works as the Schumann

C major *Fantasy* and the Chopin Ballades. One of the great interpreters of the French masters (both ancient and modern), whom he played with subtle yet finely objective clarity. Performed frequently with Ravel (*Ma Mère l'oye*), and formed memorable partnerships with the violinist Zino Francescatti, and in piano duet with his wife Gaby (for which team Milhaud wrote *The Ball at Martinique*).

Solomon (full name, Solomon Cutner)   English, b. London, 1902. A child prodigy who advanced to the highest artistic maturity only to have his career tragically terminated by paralysis in 1955. His repertoire was wide, and his performances of Chopin, Brahms, Schumann and Liszt were greatly loved for their warmth, clarity and refinement—although Beethoven and Mozart were the natural focus for his serene and magisterial temperament. Reissues of his records, notably of twelve Beethoven sonatas, are a powerful testimony to the pure and timeless quality of his art.

Claudio Arrau   Chilean, b. Santiago, Chile, 1903. Trained in Berlin under Martin Krauss. Berlin debut in 1914; major London success in 1922 before American debut in Boston and Chicago. Has been described as 'Emperor, King and Prince' of the keyboard: epithets which convey the awe with which he is regarded by his numerous admirers. His early complete cycles of Bach, Beethoven, Mozart, Schubert, Chopin and Weber quickly established him not only as the doyen of South American pianists, but as a figure of the highest international repute. Arrau's style has broadened over the years, and has embraced an ever more original, human and complex vision. At its best live in recital, his very individual quality can be difficult to capture in the clinical atmosphere of the recording studio—but a disc of Liszt's *Aida: paraphrase de concert* is one of his most notable successes.

Rudolf Serkin   Russian parentage, b. Eger, Bohemia, 1903: naturalized American. Began solo career in 1920; also celebrated for his chamber-music appearances with Adolf Busch (later his father-in-law). Joined the faculty of the Curtis Institute in 1939, and became its Director in 1968; co-founder, with others, of the Marlboro Festival. Serkin has long been considered among the world's foremost musicians, and his performances of the Viennese classics are justly famous for their scrupulous perception and deep humanity. Reger's massive piano concerto, and no less massive *Variations on a theme by Bach*, are also familiar Serkin repertoire. He has also played much Chopin, Schumann and Debussy (rarely Liszt); but it is his Bach, Mozart, Beethoven, Schubert and Brahms that future generations will recall.

Vladimir Horowitz   Russian, b. Kiev, 1904. Studied at Kiev Conservatory with Felix Blumenfeld, and early in his career gave a series of 25 recitals in Leningrad of more than 200 different works. His American debut in 1928 under Beecham in Tchaikovsky's first concerto caused a sensation: Beecham's fears that his own American debut might pass unnoticed on account of his volatile soloist were nearly confirmed; and the following years saw the emergence of one of the most formidable virtuosos in the history of the piano. But the insatiable demands of his audience ('*Un peu de Tosca, s'il vous plaît!*' shouted an admirer after Horowitz had already exhausted himself with his famous '*Carmen*' *Fantasy*) eventually created an intolerable strain and he retired from concert-giving—only to return triumphantly once more in 1965. Appearances and disappearances followed, but have finally led to a glorious Indian summer, a new era in which Horowitz is once more unique and undisputed master. His first concerto performance for 25 years was captured by RCA in 1978 and ranks among the most exciting of all concerto recordings; the same company's 22-volume reissue of most of Horowitz's work is a monument to one of the great pianists of the century. He has been called a master of 'musical distortion rather than poetic truth'; yet even at his most provocative and controversial, he compels his critics to suspend judgement, listen, and marvel.

Vlado Perlemuter   Lithuanian, later French citizen, b. Kaunas, Lithuania, 1904. Admitted to Cortot's class at the Paris Conservatoire in 1917, and after winning important prizes there met Ravel, with whom he studied all the composer's works. He was later one of the first to give a complete Ravel cycle in public. The war interrupted his career for several years, but he returned to the recital stage in Paris in 1950, and has since made regular concert and recital appearances world-wide; since 1951, also a professor at the Paris Conservatoire. As a performer, he is a vividly communicative artist (famous also for dramatic memory-lapses in public), and a noted interpreter of Chopin, Liszt and Debussy, as well as Ravel. Few discs fully capture the refinement and subtlety of his best playing in the concert hall—although some later records (especially those for Nimbus) come closer than most.

Jeanne-Marie Darré   French, b. Givet, 1905. Studied with Marguerite Long and Isidore Philipp. Made debut when still a child playing all five Saint-

Saëns concertos in a single programme. A peerless interpreter of those works and a brilliantly agile and stylish performer of Chopin and Liszt. One of the most exciting of all French pianists: a familiar figure in America, athough her appearances and recordings in Europe have been regrettably less frequent. Especially sought after are her superb recordings of the rarely played first and third Saint-Saëns concertos.

Clifford Curzon   English, b. London, 1907. Studied with Matthay, Schnabel, Landowska and Nadia Boulanger. Beyond argument the greatest living English pianist (and some would declare the national adjective redundant). A perfectionist, and his own severest critic. Public appearances are not frequent: but Londoners have been lucky to hear more often his matchless reading of Mozart's B flat concerto K. 595, and in recent years some memorable recitals. At its finest and most relaxed, Curzon's playing of Mozart and Schubert is without compare: shot through with the deepest poetry, alive with the subtlest, most magical inflection. For a pianist of his stature, he has made comparatively few recordings: a matter of regret not for Curzon himself (who finds the medium difficult and ungrateful), but for the many thousands who will never hear him live. He was awarded the CBE in 1958, and has since been knighted for his services to music.

Shura Cherkassky   Russian, b. Odessa, 1911. Studied with Josef Hofmann at the Curtis Institute. An eccentric genius who specializes in piquant and outrageous surprises. Few pianists offer a more teasing, sophisticated pianism, and in such elegant confectionery as Godowsky's *Alt Wien*, the Albéniz-Godowsky *Tango* and Rachmaninov's *Polka* Cherkassky has few peers. His repertoire is remarkably wide, and caught at his most serious and concentrated, he can also offer thrillingly personal, powerfully coherent readings of such Classical landmarks as Schubert's A major sonata D. 959 or Beethoven's op. 111. At its most self-indulgent, Cherkasskian whimsy can be maddening; but on his great days (and they are frequent), his pianistic sorcery can delight even the most jaded listener with its daring insights and its arsenal of brilliant colours and effects.

Jorge Bolet   Cuban, b. Havana, 1914. Trained at the Curtis Institute, where he studied with Godowsky, David Saperton (Godowsky's son-in-law), Moritz Rosenthal and Josef Hofmann. Assistant Military Attaché to the Cuban Embassy in Washington DC 1943–5, and in 1946 directed the first performance in Japan of *The Mikado*! Winner of the 1937 Naumberg Prize, and now Principal of the Piano Department of the Curtis Institute, a post previously held by Josef Hofmann. A grand-romantic pianist of formidable lineage, whose performances of such virtuoso works as the Chopin-Godowsky *Etudes*, Reger's *Variations and Fugue on a Theme of Telemann*, Liszt's *'Don Giovanni' Fantasy* and Transcendental Studies are notable for their grandeur of scale. A pirated 'live' recording of Franck's *Prelude, Aria and Finale* and Chopin's fourth Ballade shows Bolet at his most assured, and is a supreme example of his communicative warmth and directness.

Annie Fisher   Hungarian, b. Budapest, 1914. Trained at the Franz Liszt Academy under Arnold Szekely and Dohnányi; first public appearance at the age of eight in Beethoven's first concerto. After winning the 1933 International Liszt Competition, her international career commenced in 1936, and she has since focused principally on the Classical repertoire. Her recordings of the piano concertos K. 467 in C and K. 482 in E flat illustrate well the characteristic concentration and refinement of her Mozart playing in particular (even if her choice of Busoni's cadenza in the former caused some raised eyebrows in scholarly circles). A fiery and romantic temperament, ranking among the finest pianists of her generation, though appearances have become disappointingly infrequent.

Sviatoslav Richter   Russian, b. Zhitomer, 1914. Trained first in Odessa by his father, and then at the Moscow Conservatory with Neuhaus. Following a widely praised record of Rachmaninov's first concerto, he burst upon the Western musical scene in 1961, and was acclaimed at once as one of the great pianists of the day. His first recitals (of Haydn, Prokofiev, Chopin, Debussy, Schubert and Schumann) demonstrated the remarkable force and range of his playing, and for all their incomparable quality also suggested a volatile and unstable performer who could as easily lose himself in uncommunicative reverie as unleash the most heaven-storming bravura. But since those nervous early days, Richter's concert manner has become less unpredictable, and his repertoire has broadened still further to embrace a vast body of music from Bach's 'Forty-Eight' to Gershwin's *Rhapsody in Blue*. Inevitably, some admirers find him a more convincing interpreter of certain composers than of others. All who have heard him play, however, acknowledge the force of his insight and musical presence, and (in the most complete sense) his technical mastery.

Rosalyn Tureck   American, b. Chicago, 1914. Studied with Olga Samaroff at the Juilliard School and soon acquired the reputation of 'high priestess of Bach'. Recorded most of Bach's major keyboard works on the piano, including a set of the 48 Preludes and Fugues remarkable for its clarity and expressive command. She has also played Bach on other keyboard instruments, but reaffirms her belief that performance on the modern piano is entirely valid, and 'authenticity' a matter of style and spirit, not of instrumental type. She arrived at her speciality by way of the familiar concert repertoire, and frequently appeared as soloist in such works as Tchaikovsky's first and Brahms's second concertos before devoting herself wholly to Bach.

Emil Gilels   Russian, b. Odessa, 1916. Studied with Yakov Tkatch and Bertha Ringold at the Odessa Institute of Music and Drama, and after a promising public debut in 1929 transferred to the Odessa Conservatory. Won the Concours Ysaÿe (now the Queen Elisabeth Competition) in Brussels in 1938, and made a famous American debut with Tchaikovsky's first concerto in 1955. One of the world's great pianists, whose blazing youthful panache can still be heard on recordings of Liszt's *Carnaval de Pesth* and of Chopin's first Ballade (included in *The Young Gilels*). Later, he greatly modified and deepened his approach: comparison of the early and later recordings of, for example, the Tchaikovsky first and Brahms second concertos is revealing. A Russian MK 'live' recording of the Liszt sonata is among the finest of that masterpiece, and a two-disc American RCA album offers unparalleled accounts of Ravel's *Jeux d'eau* and *Pavane*.

Dinu Lipatti   Rumanian, b. Bucharest, 1917; d. Geneva, 1950. Studied with Floria Musicescu and later with Cortot, Munch, Dukas, and Nadia Boulanger. Cortot resigned from the jury of the International Competition of Vienna when Lipatti was awarded second, rather than first, prize. The few recordings he made before his tragically premature death confirm a magisterial command and artistry. His last public recital at the Besançon Festival, played and recorded two months before his death, is a poignant testimony to his genius. Lipatti's range was greater than is commonly supposed: projected performances of Beethoven's fifth and Tchaikovsky's first concertos, and many other major works, were cancelled during his last years because of illness. No pianist has ever given Ravel's *Alborada del gracioso* with greater zest or a more patrician command; and recordings of Chopin's first concerto, B minor sonata and Barcarolle are justly celebrated. Poulenc called him 'an artist of divine spirituality'; and in a broadcast tribute, Walter Legge declared 'God lent the world his chosen instrument, whom we called Dinu Lipatti, for too brief a space'.

Arturo Benedetti Michelangeli   Italian, b. Brescia, 1920. Studied at the Brescia Institute and Milan Conservatory, and won first prize in the 1939 Geneva Competition. One of music's most shadowy, yet potent, figures and a legend in his lifetime. Michelangeli has never taken kindly to the exigencies of concert life. Long disappearances, and frequent last-minute cancellations, have created a fund of anecdotes. His aristocratic bearing and aloofness are as proverbial as Arthur Rubinstein's genial warmth; the playing is scrupulously modern in its directness and fine-cut precision. His 78s of the Bach-Busoni Chaconne and Brahms's 'Paganini' Variations (perversely rearranged) are eagerly sought, and his recordings of Ravel's first concerto and Rachmaninov's fourth rank him firmly among the immortals. His private repertoire is said to be considerable, although the range of his public offering is tantalizingly small.

Geza Anda   Hungarian, b. Budapest, 1921; d. Zurich, 1976. Studied at the Franz Liszt Academy with Dohnányi, and early in his career commenced a long and happy EMI recording contract under Walter Legge's supervision. The fourteen or so LPs made during this period have rapidly become collectors' items and all, whether of Beethoven, Brahms, Chopin, Liszt or Rachmaninov, reveal an original and highly sophisticated artist. Among the finest of all Bartók pianists (though he disliked Bartók's sonata), his recorded performances of the three piano concertos, which he occasionally played in a single concert, are among his most impressive triumphs.

George Cziffra   Hungarian, b. Budapest, 1921; now French citizen. Studied with Dohnányi; made his first public appearance in a circus, aged five, improvising on popular tunes. After a dramatic escape to Vienna in 1956 (a previous attempt resulted in imprisonment and work in a stone-breaking gang), he launched with immediate success on an international career. His frenzied style, and an octave technique which prompted comparison with Horowitz, were found exciting by some, less satisfying by others. He also composed many paraphrases, brilliantly vulgar confections, spun off with phenomenal agility. Cziffra's first series of EMI recordings confirmed his stature as one of the piano's oddest legends, although by the time he had begun to record for Philips his style had coarsened considerably; but anyone anxious to know what is possible in terms of sheer high-octane bravura should hear his disc of the Chopin *Etudes*. Like a meteor, Cziffra has vanished from the international scene as quickly as he appeared.

Alicia de Larrocha   Spanish, b. Barcelona, 1923. A child prodigy who, at the age of eight, astonished Arthur Rubinstein with her performance of Chopin's B major Nocturne, op. 26 no. 1. A small stretch and diminutive stature somehow accentuate rather than lessen the impact of a formidably articulate virtuosity, most notably in the Spanish repertoire. Her recordings of Albéniz's *La Vega* and *Azulejos* are supreme instances of 'real' piano technique, of seductively inflected melodic lines, and of the most delicate nuances of texture and colour. Her record of Granados's *Goyescas* is no less remarkable: enthusiasts should also search out those of the *Allegro di Concierto* and *Valses Poeticas*.

Julius Katchen   American, b. New Jersey, 1926; d. 1969. Early appearances confirmed an exceptional talent, though Katchen decided to broaden his outlook by specializing in philosophy at Haverford College. Concert appearances later followed under virtually every major conductor and at every major festival (including Prades); and he gave his cycle of the complete piano music of Brahms in Berlin, London, New York, Amsterdam, Vienna and Paris. Not long before his tragically early death, Katchen played both the Brahms concertos in one concert in New York to unanimous critical acclaim. He was nonetheless most successful in the recording studio, and his remarkable range of discs includes the complete Beethoven concertos, the complete piano music of Brahms, and as well as the cornerstones of the repertoire (Beethoven's '*Appassionata*' and Chopin's second sonata), also regularly explores less predictable territory (Gershwin's *Rhapsody in Blue* with Mantovani, and Ned Rorem's second sonata). His performances were occasionally marked by an exuberance and luxuriance that could seem over-indulgent; but his early recording of Prokofiev's third concerto, for example, remains one of the most sensitive and poetically convincing of a work too often mechanically and woodenly dismissed.

Lazar Berman   Russian, b. Leningrad, 1930. Studied with Alexander Goldenweiser, but also worked with Richter and Sofronitski. An early reputation outside Russia was supported by occasional and hotly debated appearances on the 'competition circuit', and by recordings (notably of Liszt's twelve Transcendental Studies and Rachmaninov's six *Moments musicaux*). His sudden emergence in the West after years of obscurity caused a sensation in America. Berman's virtuosity was never in doubt, and there were occasions indeed when his chief ambition appeared to be to claim the title of Mohammed Ali of the keyboard. A subsequent shift of emphasis to more intimate and thoughtful interpretation, however, led to a series of recordings many of which are as remarkable for their reflective quality and insight as for their brilliance—among them a remarkable account of Liszt's austere third book of *Années de pèlerinage*.

Alfred Brendel   Austrian, b. Wiessenberg, Czechoslovakia, 1931. Studied in Vienna with Paul Baumgartner, Edward Steuermann and Edwin Fischer. A comparatively late success, the turning-point of his career came in 1969 after a London performance of Beethoven's 'Diabelli' Variations, and the start of a long-term recording contract; and he has since made a brilliant international career. Brendel's repertoire is centred on the Viennese classics, but he is also a superb Liszt pianist—a speciality scorned in the early years by conservative audiences, notably in Vienna, Stockholm and Amsterdam, where Liszt was not yet a fashionable composer. Has great love for Chopin (especially the concertos), but does not feel ready yet to play the works extensively. The French repertoire, too, he considers a separate field. Yet the range of his recordings and concert schedules is exceptional, and his performances at their best are marked by the greatest seriousness and a wholly musical virtuosity. A fervent admirer of Busoni, he dislikes Rachmaninov and Prokofiev (ironically he was asked to play Prokofiev's fifth concerto for his first record).

Glenn Gould   Canadian, b. Toronto, 1932. After graduating with the highest honours from the Toronto Conservatory at the age of twelve, commenced a brilliant international career only to retire from the public stage at the age of thirty-five: a withdrawal explained on Gould's record *Concert Drop Out*, and described in Geoffrey Payzant's *Glenn Gould: Music and Mind*. In the studio in private, however, Gould has continued to record an unusual, eclectic repertoire (Bach, Mozart, Beethoven, Byrd, Gibbons, Bizet, Sibelius) avoiding composers such as Chopin and Liszt, whom he feels to be 'too much in love' with their chosen instrument to compose music of universal significance. Gould's highly individual style and the light, luminous sonority of his specially prepared piano are instantly recognizable; his performances of Beethoven's first four piano concertos especially, and his recording of Bach's 'Goldberg' Variations, are dazzling testimonies of an eccentric genius. The vocal descant which often accompanies his playing, and the heady Mandarin prose of his sleeve-notes, are (for aficionados) no more than added bonuses.

Van Cliburn American, b. Shreveport, Louisiana, 1934. Won a Levintritt Award in 1954 but only achieved international recognition after triumph in the first Tchaikovsky Competition in Moscow, 1957. Returned to New York to a film-star's welcome, and continued his early career to an acclaim unequalled since Paderewski. After a few years, however, Cliburn's rich, golden tone and free-wheeling romanticism began to lose its appeal; a victim of his own success, his star declined. His finest recording is of Rachmaninov's second sonata, taken at a 'live' Moscow performance and played, as it should be, in the first 1913 version. His first and only London recital, too, suggested an exceptional talent; but commercial recordings, such as *The Debussy I Love*, will not appeal to those who consider stylistic purity a virtue, or who find serious textual misreadings (as in '*Jardins sous la pluie*') difficult to accept.

Cécile Ousset French, b. Tarbes, 1936. Studied at the Paris Conservatoire with Marcel Ciampi. Has had notable competition successes in Brussels and Texas, but until recently concerts and records have been disappointingly rare—although London audiences have heard exceptional performances of Brahms's 'Paganini' Variations, Chopin's B flat minor sonata and Ravel's *Gaspard de la nuit*. Not unexpectedly, she is a powerful and stylish exponent of Fauré, Debussy, Ravel, Saint-Saëns, Chabrier and Satie; more surprisingly, also of Brahms's second concerto and Beethoven's 'Diabelli' Variations.

Vladimir Ashkenazy Russian, b. Gorky, 1937. Studied with Sambatian at Moscow's Central Music School and later with Lev Oborin. He won second prize in the Warsaw Chopin Competition in 1955, first prize in the 1956 Queen Elizabeth Competition in Brussels, and first prize in the Tchaikovsky Competition in 1962. Ashkenazy's brilliant but somewhat superficial youthful facility (shown, for example, by an early Columbia recording of Chopin's F minor concerto) has broadened over the years to embrace a much greater range of character and feeling. Comparison between his first and second (and sometimes third) recordings of the same work is revealing—Rachmaninov's 'Corelli' Variations and Prokofiev's seventh sonata are interesting examples.

Restless, enquiring, sharply if modestly aware of his talent, Ashkenazy is one of music's marathon men. With complete cycles of the Beethoven, Rachmaninov and Prokofiev concertos behind him, he moves to still more ambitious projects including the complete works of Chopin, the 32 Beethoven sonatas, the major works of Scriabin and Rachmaninov, and further recordings of Mozart and Bartók concertos. He has also established partnerships with the violinist Itzhak Perlman and Elisabeth Söderström (with whom he has recorded the complete Rachmaninov songs).

Stephen Bishop-Kovacevich American, b. 1940. Completed his studies with Myra Hess. Early appearances in London (under his first professional name, Stephen Bishop), notably with Beethoven's 'Diabelli' Variations, established him as a formidably serious and talented artist; and his recordings of both this work and the Beethoven *Bagatelles* are instances of scrupulous taste and sensitivity. He performed the complete Mozart concertos in London between 1969–71, and although his Classical leanings are clear, he has also played Schumann and Chopin and made a special study of Bartók's second concerto.

Martha Argerich Argentinian, b. Buenos Aires, 1941. Studied with Scaramuzza, Gulda, Michelangeli, Madeleine Lipatti and Magaloff. A born winner of first prizes, with early triumphs (at the age of sixteen) in the Busoni and Geneva Competitions followed by the Chopin Prize in Warsaw in 1965. A zig-zag career of sudden appearances and disappearances has revealed a player of phenomenal natural talent. Though unpredictable, at her fiery and concentrated best she is one of the most exciting and poetical pianists of her generation.

Daniel Barenboim Israeli, b. Buenos Aires, 1942. Studied with Enrique Barenboim (his father), Edwin Fischer, Nadia Boulanger and Igor Markevitch. In 1954 appeared at the Salzburg Festival and also made London debut (offering at the last minute Beethoven's '*Hammerklavier*' to replace the '*Appassionata*' sonata). In 1957 began a long association with the English Chamber Orchestra, often as soloist-conductor; in 1967 performed the complete cycle of Beethoven sonatas in London. One of the most remarkable pianists of his generation, whose range of accomplishment has reminded many of Arthur Rubinstein's early years. Complete recordings of the Beethoven piano sonatas and Mozart concertos at a very early stage of his career were characteristic of an unusual youthful determination and self-confidence—'Later', said Barenboim, 'I will play them differently'. The range of his work is too extensive to detail, but already embraces a vast repertoire. As a chamber-music player, accompanist, duo partner, as well as conductor, he also enjoys the highest reputation.

Maurizio Pollini Italian, b. Milan, 1942. Studied at the Verdi Conservatory, and later with Michelangeli. Winner of the Warsaw Chopin Competition in 1960, at which Arthur Rubinstein ruffled his fellow jurors by exclaiming 'Technically, he plays better than any of us!' After this triumph, however, Pollini was nonetheless somewhat coolly received in public, and it was not until the early 1970s that his career took wing. He has since emerged as one of the most remarkable pianists of his generation, endowed with a flawless technique and apparently tireless physical strength and concentration. In recent years he has greatly extended his repertoire, always large, which now ranges from Beethoven and Schubert to Boulez and the avant garde. His recitals are usually crowded with fellow performers anxious to observe at first hand an already legendary technical command. The emotional force of the performances is less predictable: sometimes electrifying, sometimes suave and formidably distanced. But at his finest, Pollini has few peers: a 1979 recital of Schubert's last three sonatas, and a recording of Chopin's 24 Preludes, are both supreme examples of impeccable musical taste combined with intimidating technical resource.

Radu Lupu Rumanian, b. 1945. Trained with Neuhaus at the Moscow Conservatory. Won the Van Cliburn Competition in 1966, and continued further study before winning the Leeds Piano Competition in 1969. Lupu's exceptional sensitivity and dislike of the commercial aspects of a public career have not prevented him taking his chances on the toughest concert circuits; but he quickly left the gladiatorial arena to explore, with rapt intensity and intimate poetry, the composers (Schubert, Beethoven, Mozart, Brahms, Schumann) he loved best. Moody and unpredictable, aloof yet confiding, his London cycle of the complete Schubert sonatas (1979) was a memorable occasion; and admirers can be grateful that this mercurial artist has come to terms with recording. The studio may still seem to him to resemble Schnabel's 'torture chamber': but he has produced there nonetheless some of his finest work, notably discs of Brahms's opp. 118 and 119.

Murray Perahia American, b. New York, 1947. Studied with Janette Haien and became closely associated with the Marlboro Festival. Appearances with the New York Philharmonic in 1971–2 suggested a rare artistic potential later confirmed when he was unanimously declared winner of 1972 Leeds Piano Competition. Perahia has since established an enviable reputation, and a world-wide career. An admirer of Cortot and Edwin Fischer, his elegance, precision and tonal finesse in Scarlatti and Mozart are exceptional, and he has made a speciality of Mendelssohn's music.

Peter Serkin American, b. New York, 1947. Studied with Rudolf Serkin, his father, at the Curtis Institute from 1958–64. New York debut in 1959. Repertoire of standard and modern works, but public appearances comparatively rare. Concerts and records have included exceptional performances of Beethoven's 'Diabelli' Variations, Chopin's four Ballades, Bach's 'Goldberg' Variations, Mozart's middle-period concertos, Bartók's first and second concertos, and Messiaen's *Vingt regards sur l'enfant Jésus*.

Krystian Zimerman Polish, b. Zabrze, 1956. Studied with Andrzej Jasinski at the Katowice Academy. Outright winner of the Warsaw Chopin Competition in 1975, where at 18 he won not only the first prize overall but that of all four separate categories (Polonaise, Mazurka, sonata and concerto). A formidable young artist, whose subsequent concerts and records have suggested the highest potential.

Glossary

Accidentals The signs by which notes are *chromatically* moved upwards or downwards by a *semitone* — e.g. the sharp (♯) raises the note by a semitone, the flat (♭) lowers it by a semitone, the double-flat (♭♭) lowers it by two semitones (one tone), and the double-sharp (×) raises it by two semitones. The natural sign (♮) contradicts a previous ♯ or ♭, restoring the note to its 'natural' condition.

Alberti bass A fast, semi-arpeggiated accompaniment figure for the left hand, usually describing a *triad* chord, named after the Italian composer Domenico Alberti (1710–40).

Arpeggio Italian, *arpeggiare* meaning 'to play the harp'. The notes of a chord played in rapid succession, either in regular time or freely.

Atonality, atonal A modern term for music not written in a specific *key*.

Bar The space between two 'bar-lines' drawn through the musical *stave* to indicate the metrical divisions of the music; also called 'measure', especially in USA.

Blue notes Especially in jazz; notes of the scale, especially the third and seventh, played deliberately out of tune to produce a clash, or an ambiguity, between major and minor (see also *false relation*).

Chromatic From the Greek *chromatikos* meaning coloured. The harmony or scale which uses all the semitones of the scale — i.e. all the notes available in traditional Western music, as opposed to *diatonic*.

Clef The sign (e.g. 𝄞 or 𝄢 :) in front of the key and time signatures at the beginning of each composition, repeated on each *stave* to show the position of notes on each stave. The 'G clef', 𝄞 , placed on the third line of the stave, for example, indicates that the note on that line is G.

Concord The sounding together of notes in harmony, satisfying the ear as being 'final in itself.' No following chord is required to give the impression of resolution.

Consonance The purely intoned sounding together of notes capable of producing *concord*.

Counterpoint, contrapuntal The art of combining two or more independent melodic lines. The general practice of counterpoint as a mode of composition is called *polyphony*.

Diatonic The harmony or scale (as opposed to *chromatic*) that uses the notes proper to the major or minor keys or scales only, without deviation.

Discord The opposite of *concord*: the sounding together of notes which does not satify the ear as being 'final in itself', or requires a following chord to give the impression of resolution.

Dissonance The sounding together of notes producing *discord*; the opposite of *consonance*.

Dominant See *tonic*

Dynamic The relative volume of musical notes or combinations of notes; the gradations of softness and loudness in music.

Equal temperament The system of tuning, especially the piano or organ, which divides the octave into 12 *semitones* all divided into exactly the same ratio of vibrations — as distinct from *just intonation*, where the intervals vary slightly, and the sharps and flats (e.g. C sharp and D flat, in equal temperament the same note) are not precisely the same pitch. Also called '*well-tempered*'.

False relation This phenomenon first occurred early in the harmonic era of European music when composers, trained to think vocally and modally (see *modes*), became obsessed with harmonic euphony; clashes between major thirds, favoured for their concordance, and the 'natural' minor thirds of vocal modality became common, and the relation was dubbed 'false'. *Blue notes* in Afro-American music are precisely comparable: white harmony implies the sharp major third, while the Negro spontaneously sings in modal (especially pentatonic) minor thirds; the collision, or 'false relation', is the source of much of the blues' intensity.

Fioriture Italian word, literally 'flowering, flourishes, decorations'. Ornamental figures elaborating a plainer or simpler melody, often improvised.

Gefühlsduselei German word, without English equivalent. Describes roughly: extremes of sentiment, 'breast-beating', sentimental indulgence.

Heterophonic Literally, 'made up of a number of voices or parts'. In non-Western music, the simultaneous performance of a melody and of variants or decorations of it, without regard to 'Western' harmonic sense.

Intonation The tuning of notes, and the way that they are played or sung according to the ear's perception of what is, or is not, 'in tune'.

Just intonation See *equal temperament*

Key The *tonality* of a piece of music that is based on particular major or minor scale, and accepts harmonic relationships deriving from the notes of those scales. The first note of the scale gives its name to the key — i.e. 'the key of G major', 'the key of B flat minor'.

Key signature The arrangement of sharps or flats at the beginning of each line of music indicating which notes are to be consistently sharpened and flattened, and also showing the key (e.g. one sharp, F sharp = G major or E minor; four flats, B, E, A, D flat = A flat major or F minor).

Leading note See *tonic*

Measure See *bar*

Mediant See *tonic*

Metre The rhythmic patterns produced in music by notes of varying length combined with strong and weak beats — similar to the metrical 'feet' (spondees, dactyls, trochees etc.) in poetry.

Mixolydian mode The sequence of white notes on the piano, beginning on G. This mode thus has a sharp third and sixth, but a flat seventh. See also *modes*

Modes The scales, made up of various groupings of the

'white notes' of the keyboard, which became established in the Middle Ages and were accepted, at least in theory, as the basis of Western music until the sixteenth century. They were given Greek names, such as 'Dorian', 'Phrygian', 'Lydian', *Mixolydian*', 'Ionian'.

Monophonic   Single-voiced, one melodic part only.

Motive, motif, motiv   A brief melodic or rhythmic figure, too short to be called a theme or a tune.

Neapolitan key   The distant key of the flattened supertonic (e.g. B flat in the key of A minor), which came into vogue in the seventeenth century especially as part of a closing cadence; later used for more elaborate and dramatic effect, especially by Schubert.

Pentatonic   The various forms of five-note *modes*—one of which is represented on the piano by the black notes of the keyboard. Any 'gapped' scale that omits two of the normal seven notes of the ordinary *diatonic* scales. Of all scalic formulae the pentatonic are those mostly derived from the acoustical facts of the harmonic series; that is why they form the basis of primitive music everywhere, and of most sophisticated music that is melodically conceived. Even today children brought up on equal-tempered music (see *equal temperament*) still improvise pentatonically.

Pitch   The 'height' or 'depth' of a musical sound according to the number of vibrations that produces it; also the standard by which notes (usually in relation to the A above middle-C) are to be tuned in relation to each other. It is not an absolute: the pitch of A, for example, has varied over the centuries and from country to country—although today, by international agreement, it is generally standardized at 440 cycles per second.

Polyphony   Literally 'many voices': two or more melodic parts co-existing (see also *counterpoint*).

Portamento   The effect of carrying on from one note to another with a slight slide; also called scooping.

Register   A set of pipes (organ) or strings (harpsichord) brought into action to produce a particular *tone* (2) or *dynamic*; also the different parts of the range of the human voice, e.g. 'head register' or 'chest register'.

Rubato   Italian word, literally 'robbed'—thus *tempo rubato*, 'robbed time': playing out of strict tempo for expressive purposes, covering a very broad range of manners and styles.

Semitone   The smallest interval normally used in Western music—i.e. the interval between a black note and an adjacent white note (or the intervals between the four white notes with no black note between them, B/C and E/F, on the piano).

Serial music   See *twelve-tone music*

Stave   The five horizontal lines on which music is written.

Sub-dominant   See *tonic*

Sub-mediant   See *tonic*

Supertonic   See *tonic*

Tonality, tonal   Strictly speaking, tonality is the relationship between tones that are inherent in acoustical facts, so that the term covers all scale formulae, from the *pentatonic* to the *chromatic*. In practice, however, tonality has become associated with the tempered major and minor scales of the eighteenth and nineteenth centuries, and their 'functional' behaviour to one another The word is virtually synonymous with *key*, but also means more specifically the feeling of a definite key suggested by a piece or passage of music (see also *atonality*).

Tone   (1) The term used for pure musical notes not containing harmonics, each harmonic being itself a tone; (2) the quality and timbre of a musical sound; (3) the interval between the first and second, second and third, fourth and fifth, fifth and sixth, sixth and seventh notes of the *diatonic* major scale: i.e. two *semitones*.

Tone-row   A translation of the German word *Tonreihe*, to designate the 'rows' of twelve notes on which twelve-note or *twelve-tone* compositions are based; also known as series.

Tonic, dominant, sub-dominant   The main or first note of a *key* (or first 'degree of a scale'), and the fifth and fourth notes respectively above it. Tonic, dominant and sub-dominant *triads* condition the basic *tonal* relationships of Western music in its most rudimentarily harmonic form. The other degrees of the scale are the *supertonic* (second), *mediant* (third), *sub-mediant* (sixth) and *leading note* (seventh).

Triad   A chord of three notes composed of two superimposed thirds—e.g. C-E-G, G-B-D, F-A♭-C, B-D-F♯.

Tumbling strain   A term invented by the ethnomusicologist Curt Sachs to describe a frequent procedure in primitive music whereby a vocal phrase starts at a relatively high, strained pitch and then tumbles wildly downwards with an effect of uncontrolled libido.

Twelve-tone music, twelve-tone harmony   The system of composing on which the later works of Schoenberg, and other subsequent composers, are based, that abolishes *keys* and with them the predominance of certain notes of the scale (especially *tonic*, *sub-dominant*, *dominant* and *mediant*)—using instead the twelve notes of the chromatic scale, each of which has exactly the same importance as any other. In order to ensure that no note assumes even temporary predominance, a 'series' of all twelve notes in any chosen sequence is employed, in which each note must appear only once—thus *serial* composition and *serial* music.

Whole-tone scale   A musical scale progressing by nothing but whole *tones*, without *semitones*—e.g. C-D-E-F♯-G♯-A♯, or D♭-E♭-F-G-A-B.

Well-tempered   See *equal temperament*

Bibliography

GENERAL

1860 **Rimbault, E.**, *The Pianoforte: Its Origin, Progress and Construction*, London, Cocks; reissued 1974, New York, AMS Press

1911 **Dolge, A.**, *Pianos and their Makers: A Comprehensive History of the Development of the Piano*, new edn. 1972, New York, Dover Publications

1933 **Harding, Rosamond**, *The Piano-Forte: its History Traced to the Great Exhibition of 1851*, reprinted 1973, New York, Da Capo Press; 1978, London, Gresham Books

1944 **Closson, E.**, *History of the Piano*, revised 1978, London, Elek Books

1954 **Loesser, A.**, *Men, Women and Pianos: A Social History*, New York; 1955, London, Gollancz

1955 **Hirt, Franz Josef**, *Meisterwerke des Klavier*, Olten, Switzerland, Urs Garf-Verlag; in English translation as *Stringed Keyboard Instruments*, 1968, Boston, Boston Book and Art Shop

1956 **Grove's Dictionary of Music and Musicians**, 'The Pianoforte', London, Macmillan

1961 **Clutton, C.**, 'The Pianoforte' in *Musical Instruments through the Ages*, ed. Baines, A., London, Penguin

1966 **Katalog der Sammlung Alter Musik Instrumente, Saiten Klaviere**, Vienna, Kunsthistorisches Museum

1966 **Sumner, W. L.**, *The Pianoforte*, revised 1971, London, Macdonald

1973 **Buckton, David** and **Barthold, Kenneth Van**, *The Piano: A Short History*, London, BBC Publications

1975 **Hollis, Helen**, *The Piano: A Pictorial Account of its Ancestry and Development*, London, David and Charles

1975 **Wainwright, D.**, *The Piano Makers*, London, Hutchinson

1976 **Ehrlich, C.**, *The Piano: A History*, London, Dent

1976 **Grover, D.**, *The Piano: Its Story from Zither to Grand*, London, Hale

THE CLASSICAL PIANO

1963 **Newman, W.**, The Sonata in the Classic Era, University of Carolina Press

1965 **Hutchings, A.**, 'Mozart's Keyboard Music' in *The Mozart Companion*, ed. Landon, H. C. Robbins and Mitchell, D., London, Faber

1968 **Matthews, Denis**, *Beethoven's Piano Sonatas*, BBC Music Guide, London, BBC Publications

1969 **Mellers, W.**, 'The Sonata Principle' in *Man and his Music*, Vol. III, London, Barrie and Jenkins

1971 **Rosen, C.**, *The Classical Style: Haydn, Mozart and Beethoven*, London, Faber

1971 **Truscott, H.** and **Barford, P.**, 'Beethoven's Piano Music' in *The Beethoven Companion*, ed. Arnold, D. and Fortune, N., London, Faber

1977 **Solomon, M.**, *Beethoven*, New York, Schirmer; 1978, London, Cassell

1977/8 **Landon, H. C. Robbins**, *Haydn: Chronicle and Works*, Vols. II and III, London, Thames and Hudson; Bloomington, Ind., Indiana University Press

CROSSCURRENTS: SCHUBERT, SCHUMANN, MENDELSSOHN, BRAHMS

O. E. Deutsch's *Schubert: A Documentary Biography* (London, 1946) remains the most valuable source of general information on the composer. Alfred Einstein's *Schubert* (London, Cassell, 1951) is a useful biography, but needs to be treated with caution.

For an insight into Schumann's creative mind, one could do no better than recommend a reading of his two favourite authors: E. T. A. Hoffmann and Jean Paul. There have been several collected editions of their works in German; *The Best Tales of Hoffmann* (ed. E. F. Bleyler, New York, Dover Publications, 1967) offers a representative selection in English translation.

As for Mendelssohn and Brahms, readers might be best advised to turn to the composers' letters. In the case of Brahms, the most important addressees are Clara Schumann and Elisabeth von Herzogenberg.

THE ROMANTIC PIANO: CHOPIN TO RAVEL

1939 **Abraham, G.**, *On Russian Music*, London, W. Reeves

1946 **Suckling, N.**, *Fauré*, London, Dent, new edn. 1951, revised 1952, New York, Dutton

1956 **Laplane, G.**, *Albeniz*, Paris, Editions du Milieu du Monde

1959 **Demuth, N.**, *French Piano Music*, London, Museum Press

1962 **Lockspeiser, E.**, *Debussy: His Life and Mind*, London, Cassell

1966 **Searle, H.**, *The Music of Liszt*, New York, Dover Publications

1966 **Walker, A.** (ed.) *Frédéric Chopin*, London, Barrie and Rockcliff

1973 **Vallas, L.** (trans. O'Brien, M. and G.), *Claude Debussy*, New York, Dover Publications

1976 **Norris, G.**, *Rakhmaninov*, London, Dent

1976 **Smith, R.**, *Alkan: The Enigma*, London, Kahn and Averill

1978 **Macdonald, H.**, *Skryabin*, London, Oxford University Press

THE PIANO IN THE TWENTIETH CENTURY

1961 **Cage, John**, *Silence*, Middletown, Conn., Wesleyan University Press; 1968, London, Calder

1968 **Cage, John**, *A Year from Monday*, Middletown, Conn., Wesleyan University Press; London, Calder

1974 **Nyman, M.**, *Experimental Music: Cage and Beyond*, London, Studio Vista

Discography

1978 **Griffiths, P.**, *A Concise History of Modern Music*, London, Thames and Hudson

THE AMERICAN PIANO

1821 **Heinrich, Anthony Philip**, *The Dawning of Music in Kentucky*, new edn. 1972, New York, Da Capo Press
1881 **Gottschalk, Louis Moreau**, *Notes of a Pianist*, Lippincott, Pa.; new edn. 1964 New York, Knopf
1890 **Spillane, D.**, *History of the American Pianoforte: Its Technical Development, and the Trade*, new edn. 1969, New York, Da Capo Press
1939 **Upton, W. T.**, *Anthony Philip Heinrich: A Nineteenth-Century Composer in America*, New York, Columbia University Press
1969 **Gottschalk, Louis Moreau**, *The Piano Works of Louis Moreau Gottschalk*, New York, Arno Press and The New York Times
1969 **Hitchcock, H. Wiley**, *Music in the United States: A Historical Introduction*, new edn. 1974, Englewood Cliffs, N.J., Prentice-Hall
1970 **Ord-Hume, Arthur W. J. G.**, *Player Piano*, Cranbury, N.J., A. S. Barnes and Co.; London, Allen and Unwin
1973 **Bunger, R.**, *The Well-Prepared Piano*, Colorado Springs, Colo., Colorado College Music Press
1973 **Roehl, Harvey**, *Player Piano Treasury*, New York, Vestal Press
1977 **Nancarrow, Conlon**, 'Selected Studies' in *Soundings*, Book 4, Berkeley, Calif.

THE JAZZ PIANO

1950 **Blesh, Rudi** and **Janis, Harriet**, *They All Played Ragtime*, New York, Knopf; revised 1966 New York, Music Sales; 1958, London, Sidgwick and Jackson
1950 **Lomax, Alan**, *Mister Jelly Roll*, New York, Duell; 1952, London, Cassell; new edn. 1973, Berkeley, Calif., University of California Press
1960 **Fox, C.**, *Fats Waller*, London, Cassell
1960 **Williams, Martin** (ed.), *The Art of Jazz*, London, Cassell; new edn. 1971, New York, Oxford University Press
1965 **Willie the Lion Smith**, *Music on my Mind*, London, MacGibbon
1970 **Zur Heide, K.**, *Deep South Piano: The Story of Little Brother Montgomery*, London, Studio Vista
1973 **Kriss, E.**, *Six Blues-Roots Pianists*, New York, Quick Fox
1975 **Gammond, P.**, *Scott Joplin and the Ragtim Era*, London, Angus and Robertson; 1977, New York, St Martin's Press
1975 **Kriss, E.**, *Barrelhouse and Boogie Piano*, London, Oak Publications

This discography does not set out to be in any sense a 'complete' or 'definitive' list of piano records. It is, on the contrary, a very personal selection of around two hundred discs from among many thousands of fine recordings: neither capricious nor arbitrary, but intentionally and unavoidably idiosyncratic. Rather than a reference-point, it should be considered as a starting-point: the heart of a collection, neither 'right' nor 'wrong'.

In many cases, artists have made several recordings of a particular work, and this discography, as a matter of personal preference, chooses one: Kempff's first (mono) set of Beethoven sonatas, for example, rather than his second or third; Radu Lupu's performance of Schubert's A minor sonata D. 784 on the earlier BBC record rather than the later one for Decca. Rubinstein's 78s of the Chopin Mazurkas for HMV were the first of three different versions, and his set of the Nocturnes for RCA the last of three. Geza Anda's early Columbia performances of Schumann's *Kreisleriana* and *Études symphoniques* are preferred to the later ones for DG. Exceptionally, both of Alicia de Larrocha's versions of the Granados *Goyescas* are included, since the one casts precious light on the other, and each in its way is indispensable; but the version chosen of her *Ibéria* is the earlier Erato recording, not the later Decca. The two collections listed separately at the end contain the major part of the collected works of two of the greatest pianists of this century, Rachmaninov and Horowitz: no serious music library can afford to be without them.

A few of the records listed are already collector's items, deleted or out of print. The diligent may search and the lucky find: better still, reissues (often short-lived) appear from time to time.

Albéniz *Ibéria*. Alicia de Larrocha. Erato DUE 20236 (2 records)
Albéniz *La Vega* and *Azulejos*. Alicia de Larrocha. Hispavox hh 10–86
Bach Forty-eight Preludes and Fugues. Rosalyn Tureck. Brunswick AXTL 1036–41 (6 records)
Bach Forty-eight Preludes and Fugues. Edwin Fischer. HMV DB 2079–3239.
Bach Forty-eight Preludes and Fugues. Glenn Gould. CBS 77225, 78277 (2 × 2 records)
Bach 'Goldberg' Variations. Glenn Gould. Philips SBL 5211
Bach Partita no. 1 in B flat. Dinu Lipatti (in concert). Columbia 33CX 1499
Bach Chromatic Fantasia and Fugue. Edwin Fischer. Seraphim 1C 6045 (USA)
Bach-Busoni Chaconne in D minor. Arturo Benedetti Michelangeli. HMV DB 21005
Balakirev *Islamey*. Andrei Gavrilov. EMI ASD 3600
Beethoven Thirty-two sonatas. Artur Schnabel. EMI COLH 51–63 (13 records)
Beethoven Thirty-two sonatas. Wilhelm Kempff. DGG KL 42–51 (10 records)
Beethoven Eighteen sonatas, nos. 1, 3, 7, 8, 13, 14, 17, 18,

21, 22, 23, 26, 27, 28, 29, 30, 31, 32. Solomon. EMI RLS 722 (7 records)

Beethoven Sonatas in E major op. 109 and A flat op. 110. Myra Hess. HMV ALP 1169

Beethoven Sonata no. 8 in C minor ('*Pathétique*'), op. 13. Benno Moiseiwitsch. HMV C. 3246–7 (78s)

Beethoven 'Diabelli' Variations. Artur Schnabel. EMI HQM 1197

Beethoven 'Diabelli' Variations. Stephen Bishop-Kovacevich. Philips SAL 3676

Beethoven 'Diabelli' Variations. Alfred Brendel (in concert). Philips 9500 381

Beethoven *Bagatelles* opp. 33, 119 and 126. Stephen Bishop-Kovacevich. Philips 6500 930

Bizet-Horowitz Variations on a Theme from Carmen. Vladimir Horowitz. CBS 72720

Boulez Sonata no. 2. Maurizio Pollini. DG 2530 803

Brahms Sonata no. 3 in F minor. Clifford Curzon. Decca SDD 498

Brahms 'Paganini' Variations. Arturo Benedetti Michelangeli. EMI C 06100656

Brahms 'Paganini' Variations. Geza Anda. Columbia 33CX 1072

Brahms Rhapsody no. 2 in G minor op. 79. Wilhelm Kempff. Turnabout TV S34386 (USA)

Chopin Twenty-four *Etudes*. Alfred Cortot. Pathé-Marconi C D61–00858 (France)

Chopin Twenty-four *Etudes*. Vladimir Ashkenazy. Melodiya. 06307–10 (USSR)

Chopin Four Impromptus. Alfred Cortot. HMV DB 2021–2022 (78s)

Chopin Fifty-two Mazurkas. Arthur Rubinstein. HMV DB 302–8 and 3839–45 (78s)

Chopin Ten Mazurkas, *Andante Spianato & Grande Polonaise Brillante* and Polonaise-Fantaisie. Arthur Rubinstein. RCA LM 2059 (USA)

Chopin Nineteen Nocturnes. Arthur Rubinstein. RCA SB 6731–32

Chopin Six Polonaises. Arthur Rubinstein. HMV ALP 1136

Chopin *Andante Spianato & Grande Polonaise Brillante*, Polonaise-Fantaisie, Fourth Scherzo etc. Emanuel Ax. RCA ARL 1569

Chopin Polonaise in F sharp minor op. 44. Vladimir Horowitz. CBS 72720

Chopin Twenty-four Preludes. Alfred Cortot. HMV DB 2012–8 (78s)

Chopin Twenty-four Preludes. Maurizio Pollini. DG 2530 550

Chopin Four Scherzos. Sviatoslav Richter. United Artists Cadenza UACL 10016

Chopin Four Scherzos. Arthur Rubinstein. HMV ALP 1136

Chopin Sonata no. 2 in B flat minor. Alfred Cortot. HMV DB 2019–20 (78s)

Chopin Sonata no. 2 in B flat minor. Emil Gilels. Melodiya 011277–8 (USSR)

Chopin Sonata no. 2 in B flat minor. Arthur Rubinstein. HMV ALP 1477

Chopin Sonata no. 3 in B minor. Dinu Lipatti. EMI HQM 1163

Chopin Fourteen Waltzes. Dinu Lipatti. EMI HLM 7075

Chopin Fourteen Waltzes. Krystian Zimerman. DG 2530 965

Chopin Fantasy in F minor. Shura Cherkassky. HMV DB 9598–99 (78s)

Chopin Polonaise in A, etc. Vladimir Horowitz. DBS 76307

Chopin Introduction and Rondo in E flat, etc. Vladimir Horowitz. CBS 72969

Chopin-Godowsky Eight *Etudes* and Six Waltzes. Jorge Bolet. L'Oiseau Lyre DSLO 26

Debussy Twenty-four Preludes. Walter Gieseking. Columbia 33CX 1089 and Columbia FCX 186 (France)

Debussy *Images* (Books 1 and 2), *Estampes* and *Pour le piano*. Walter Gieseking. Columbia 33CX 1137

Debussy Children's Corner Suite. Alfred Cortot. HMV DB 6725–6 (78s)

Debussy *Estampes*. Sviatoslav Richter (in concert). DG LPM 18849

Debussy *Jardins sous la pluie* (no. 3 of *Estampes*). Benno Moiseiwitsch. EMI HQM 1153

Debussy Fifteen short pieces. Walter Gieseking. Columbia 33CX 1149

Delibes-Dohnányi *Valse lente*. Geza Anda. Columbia SEL 1516 (45)

Fauré Complete Piano Works. Germainne Thyssen-Valentin. Ducretet Thomson 300 C 022 85–6 and 225 C 122 (6 records)

Fauré Impromptu no. 2 in F minor. Eileen Joyce. Parlophone E 11372 (78)

Franck *Prelude, Aria and Finale*. Alfred Cortot. EMI 2C61–1354 (France)

Franck *Prelude, Aria and Finale*. Jorge Bolet (in concert). Opus 81A (USA)

Gershwin Solo Piano Works. André Watts. CBS 75608

Godowsky *Alt Wien*. Shura Cherkassky. Oiseau-Lyre DSL 07

Gottschalk Recital. Ivan Davis. Decca SXL 6725

Granados *Goyescas*. Alicia de Larrocha. Erato SYU 70344–5

Granados *Goyescas*. Alicia de Larrocha. Decca SXL 6785

Granados *Escenas Romanticas*. Alicia de Larrocha. Erato STU 70344–5

Granados *Valses Poéticos*, *Danza Lenta* and *Allegro de Concierto*. Alicia de Larrocha. Epic BC 1310 (USA)

Granados Spanish Dances. Alicia de Larrocha. Erato EFM 8059

Grieg Lyric Pieces (selection). Emil Gilels. DG 2530 476

Liszt Christmas Tree Suite. Alfred Brendel. Delta DEL 12004

Liszt *Weinen Klagen* Variations, 'Bach' Fantasia, etc. Alfred Brendel. Philips 9500 286

Liszt *Années de pèlerinage* (Book 3). Lazar Berman. DG 2709 076

Liszt A recital of late works. Sergio Fiorentino. Delta SDEL 18021

Liszt Two Legends. Wilhelm Kempff. Decca LXT 2572

Liszt Sonata in B minor. Vladimir Horowitz. RCA 12548

Liszt Sonata in B minor. Emil Gilels (in concert). Melodiya 011279–80 (USSR)

Liszt Sonata in B minor. Sviatoslav Richter (in concert). Private Edition (USA)

Liszt Hungarian Rhapsody no. 9. Emil Gilels. Melodiya 027069

Liszt Hungarian Rhapsodies nos. 16 to 19. Edith Farnadi. Westminster XWN 18338 (USA)

Liszt *Rapsodie Espagnole*. György Cziffra. HMV ALP 1534

Liszt *Rapsodie Espagnole*. Lazar Berman. EMI SLS 5040

Liszt *Rapsodie Espagnole*. Jorge Bolet (in concert). Opus 81 (USA)

Liszt '*Mephisto*' Waltz no. 1. György Cziffra. HMV ALP 1534

Liszt '*Mephisto*' Polka. Earl Wild. Vanguard VCS 10041 (USA)

Liszt Concert Paraphrase on Themes from *Aida*. Claudio Arrau. Philips SAL 6500 368

Liszt *Les Patineurs scherzo*. Louis Kentner. Columbia DX 923 (78)

Liszt *Csárdás obstiné*. Alfred Brendel. Vanguard VCS 10035

Liszt *Valse-Impromptu*. Edith Farnadi. Westminster WLP 5366

Liszt 'Paganini' *Etude* no. 3 ('*La Campanella*'). Andrei Gavrilov. EMI ASD 3600

Liszt *Etude de concert* no. 3 in D flat ('*Un Sospiro*'). Geza Anda. Columbia SEL 1516 (45)

Liszt *Etude de concert* no. 2 in F minor ('*La Leggierezza*'). Louis Kentner. Columbia DX 960 (78)

Mendelssohn-Rachmaninov Scherzo. Benno Moiseiwitsch. EMI HQM 1153

Moszkowski Waltz in E. Eileen Joyce. Parlophone E. 11239 (78)

Messiaen *Vingt regards sur l'enfant Jésus*. Michel Beroff. EMI SLS 793–2 (2 records)

Messiaen *Vingt regards sur l'enfant Jésus* and *La Rousserolle Effarvatte*. Peter Serkin. RCA ARLS 3–0759 (2 records)

Mozart Sonata in A minor. Dinu Lipatti (in concert). Columbia 33CX 1499

Mozart Sonatas in A major K. 331 and D major K. 576, etc. Solomon. EMI RLS 726

Prokofiev Sonata no. 8. Sviatoslav Richter. DG SLPM 138766

Prokofiev Sonata no. 8. Emil Gilels. Columbia Melodyia M 33824 (USA)

Prokofiev *Suggestion Diabolique*. Andrei Gavrilow. EMI ASD 3600

Rachmaninov Sonata no. 2 in B flat minor (original version; Van Cliburn in concert). Van Cliburn. RCA ARL 1–6352 (USA)

Rachmaninov Sonata no. 2 in B flat minor (Horowitz in concert, playing his own version). Vladimir Horowitz. CBS 72940

Rachmaninov Variations on a Theme by Corelli. Vladimir

Ashkenazy. Columbia 33CX 1813

Rachmaninov *Etudes-tableaux* op. 39 and Variations on a Theme by Corelli op. Vladimir Ashkenazy. Decca SXL 6604

Rachmaninov Six *Moments musicaux*. Lazar Berman. MK k577 (USSR)

Rachmaninov Prelude in B minor op. 32 no. 10. Benno Moiseiwitsch. EMI HQM 1153

Rachmaninov Prelude in G major op. 32 no. 5. Geza Anda. Columbia 33 CX 1143

Rachmaninov *Moment Musical* in E minor op. 16 no. 4. Benno Moiseiwitsch. HMV 7 EP 7055 (45)

Rachmaninov Polka. Shura Cherkassky (in concert). L'Oiseau Lyre DSLO 24

Ravel *Gaspard de la nuit*. Andrei Gavrilov. EMI ASD 3600

Ravel *Gaspard de la nuit*. Vladimir Ashkenazy. Decca SXL 6215

Ravel *Le Tombeau de Couperin*. Robert Casadesus. Philips ABL 3062

Ravel *Pavane pour une infante défunte*. Emil Gilels. Melodia Angel SRBO 4110 (USA)

Ravel *Pavane pour une infante défunte*. Andrei Gavrilov. EMI ASD 3571

Ravel '*Alborada del gracioso*' (no. 4 of *Miroirs*). Dinu Lipatti. EMI HQM 1163

Saint-Saëns Prelude and Fugue (*Etude* no. 3, op. 111). Shura Cherkassky HMV DB 9599 (78)

Scarlatti Twelve Sonatas. Vladimir Horowitz. CBS 848 002 VKY

Schoenberg Piano Works. Maurizio Pollini. DG 2530 531

Shostakovich Sonata no. 2. Emil Gilels. RCA LSC 2868

Shostakovich Six Preludes and Fugues. Sviatoslav Richter. Philips 6580 095

Schubert The Sonatas. Wilhelm Kempff. DG 2720 024 (9 records)

Schubert Sonata in B flat D. 960. Artur Schnabel. EMI COLH 33

Schubert Sonata in D major D. 850. Clifford Curzon. Decca SXL 6135

Schubert Sonata in D major D. 850. Emil Gilels. RCA LM 2493 (USA)

Schubert Sonata in C major (unfinished) and recital. Sviatoslav Richter. Monitor MCS 2057 (USA)

Schubert Sonata in A minor D. 845. Maurizio Pollini. DG 2530 473

Schubert Sonata in A minor D. 784. Radu Lupu. BBC REB 57S

Schubert Sonata in A major D. 664. Sviatoslav Richter. EMI ALP 2011

Schubert Piano Works 1822–1829. Alfred Brendel. Philips 6747 175 (8 records)

Schubert *Moments musicaux*. Edwin Fischer. HMV ALP 1103

Schubert Impromptus. Edwin Fischer. HMV DB 3484–9 (78s)

Schubert Impromptus. Wilhelm Kempff. DG 139 149

Schumann *Kreisleriana*. Vladimir Horowitz. Columbia

Acknowledgements

MS 7264 (USA)

Schumann *Kreisleriana*. Geza Anda. Columbia 33CX 1283

Schumann *Etudes symphoniques*. Geza Anda. Columbia 33CX 1072

Schumann *Fantasy* in C, etc. Sviatoslav Richter. EMI Electrola IC 187 50 340–41 (2 records)

Schumann *Fantasy* in C, *Kinderscenen*. Clifford Curzon. Decca Eclipse ECS 568

Schumann *Fantasy* in C and *Fantasiestücke*, op. 12. Martha Argerich. CBS 76713

Schumann *Davidsbündlertänze*. Alfred Cortot. Pathé COLH 86 (France)

Schumann *Davidsbündlertänze*. Wilhelm Kempff. DG SLPM 139316

Schumann *Waldscenen*. Sviatoslav Richter. DG DGM 18355

Schumann Sonata no. 1 in F sharp minor. Emil Gilels. Monitor MC 2048 (USA)

Scriabin Sonatas nos. 2, 7, 10 and recital. Vladimir Ashkenazy. Decca SXL 6868

Scriabin Sonatas nos. 3, 4, 5, and 9. Vladimir Ashkenazy. Decca SXL 6705

Scriabin Sonata no. 10, 6 *Etudes* and recital. Vladimir Horowitz. Columbia M 31620 (USA)

Scriabin Sonata no. 6 and 8 *Etudes*. Sviatoslav Richter (in concert). Melodia 010011–12 (USSR)

Scriabin Sonata no. 9. Vladimir Horowitz (in concert). CBS 2002

Scriabin Sonata no. 5. Vladimir Horowitz (in concert). RCA ARLI 1766

Scriabin Sonata no. 5. Sviatoslav Richter (in concert). DG LPM 18849

Stockhausen Piano Piece 10. Frederic Rzewski. Wergo 2549 016

Strauss-Godowsky Symphonic Metamorphosis on Themes from Johann Strauss's *Künsterleben*. Earl Wild. Vanguard VSD 71119 (USA)

Strauss-Schultz Evler The Blue Danube, etc. Jorge Bolet in concert at Carnegie Hall. RCA ARL2–0512 (2 records)

Stravinsky Three Movements from Petrushka. Maurizio Pollini. DG 2530 225

Tchaikovsky Six Pieces op. 19. Emil Gilels. Melodia 005891–92

Thalberg 'Don Pasquale' Fantasy op. 67. Earl Wilde. Vanguard VSD 71119 (USA)

Weber *Moto Perpetuo* (finale from Sonata no. 1 in C). Benno Moiseiwitsch. HMV DB 4101

The Horowitz Collection Volumes 1–20. RCA VH 001–020 (20 records)

The Complete Rachmaninov His recorded performances in 5 volumes. RCA AVM 3–0260 (15 records)

The publishers wish to thank all private owners, museums, galleries, libraries, and other institutions for permission to reproduce works in their collections. Further acknowledgment is made to the following (the illustrations are identified by page reference, *t* representing top, *b* bottom, *r* right, *l* left, *c* centre):

Agencja Autorska, Warsaw 83, 86; Charles Amirkhanian 186*l*; Archiv für Kunst und Geschichte, Berlin 39, 66; Associated Music Publishers, New York © 1959: reprinted by kind permission of G. Schirmer Ltd.; BBC Hulton Picture Library 88*r*, 89*b*, 99*l*, 119*b*, 141*t*, 144, 147, 148*t*, *b*, 193, 229, 243; Beethoven-Haus, Bonn 57, 58–9, 59*tl*; Bettmann Archive 161*t*, 180, 206, 209, 232; Bibliothèque Nationale, Paris 80*r*, 89*t*, 242*b*; Bibliothèque Nationale/Hachette/Ziolo 140*b*; Bibliothèque Nationale/Trela/Ziolo 98*b*; Bildarchiv Preussischer Kulturbesitz 75; Bildarchiv Preussischer Kulturbesitz/Institut für Musikforschung, Berlin 238; Bodleian Library 71*t*, *b*; Bösendorfer 33*tl*, 255; Boston Public Library 95*t*, *b*; Bowes Museum 243*b*; British Library 52, 53, 64, 70, 128, 177; Reproduced by Courtesy of the Trustees of the British Museum 69*bl*, *tr*, 88*l*, 97*tr*, 130, 134, 138*t*, 143*l*, *r*, 149, 240*t*; John Broadwood and Sons Ltd. 56; Bulloz/Musée Carnavalet 87; R. Burnett 243*r*; CBS/Clive Barda 168; Courtesy of Frédéric Chopin Society, Warsaw 112; Corvina Archivum, Budapest 58*tr* Hungarian National Museum, Budapest; Culver Pictures Inc. 121, 155*t*, 158*t*, 160, 176*t*, 185*l*, 200, 204, 205, 230; Fritz Curzon 122, 258, 262; René Dazy, Paris, 101; Decca Record Company Ltd. 233; Antonin Dvořák Society of Prague 136; ; Elektra/Chris Callis 218; Mary Evans Picture Library 8, 10, 76*r*, 116–17, 118*b*, 119*t*, 182, 235*t*, 242*t*; Fond National d'Art Contemporain, Paris/Jacqueline Hyde 150; Fotomas Index 13*b*, 48, 49*l*, 126–7, 132, 225; Courtesy of the Franklin Institute, Philadelphia 173*b*; Germanisches Nationalmuseum, Nuremberg 26*t*, *b*, 29*b*, 241; Gesellschaft der Musikfreunde, Vienna 55, 76*l*, 77*l*, *r*; Giraudon 69*tl*, 142*t*; Giraudon/SPADEM 104; Giraudon/Bibliothèque Espagnole, Paris/SPADEM 157; Giraudon/Musée Carnavalet 99*b*; Giraudon/Musée de l'Opéra 114; Giraudon/Museu Nacional de Arte Antiga, Lisbon (Frontispiece); R. Gorringe 14–15, 25, 27*r*, 29*t*, 30–1, 36, 37*r*; Collections of Greenfield Village and the Henry Ford Museum 175; Haags Gemeentemuseum 250; Ellin Hare 35*br*; Harvard Theatre Collection 178*l*; Historic New Orleans Collection 197; Historisches Museum der Stadt Wien 60, 61, 62–3, 142*b*, 154, 226; Horniman Museum, London 16*t*; Hungarian Embassy, London 162*t*, *b*; Import Music Service 216; Max Jones Collection 201, 207, 210*t*, *b*; Kobal Collection/Warner Bros. 187; Kunsthistorisches Museum, Vienna 253*t*; Editions Larousse 131, 139; Lauros-Giraudon/Bibliothèque Nationale 227; Lauros-Giraudon/Musée Carnavalet 118*tl*; Lauros-Giraudon/Musée du Petit Palais 222; Carol Law/Charles Amirkhanian 186*r*; Editions Alphonse Leduc 163*t*, *b*; Library of Congress, Washington 44, 46, 181*b*; Liceo Musicale, Bologna 47 (Scala); Louvre 50*b* (Scala), 51; Mansell Collection 12, 40, 49*r*, 54, 69*br*, 72, 73, 80*l*, 82, 85, 141*b*, 224–5, 245, 252 (inset), 262*b*; Metropolitan Museum of Art, The Crosby Brown Collection of Musical Instruments, 1889, 19*t*; A. Meyer Collection/Ziolo 100*b*, 103, 145, 158*bl*, 188*b*; A. Meyer Collection/Trela/Ziolo 98*t*; K. W. Mobbs/R. Burnett 23; Robert Morley and Co. 24*t*, 33*tr*, 240*b* (Photos R. L. Mitchell); 248*tr*; Mozarteum, Salzburg 50*l*, *r*; John Murray (Publishers) Ltd. 235*b*; Museo di Strumenti Musicali, Castello Sforzesco, Milan 18 (Scala), 248*tl*; Museo Teatrale alla Scala/Nimatallah/Ziolo 102; National Library, Rio de Janeiro 181*t*; National Musical Museum, Brentford 185*r*, 256*tl*; National Trust, Fenton House/John Bethell 19*b*; Peter Newark's Historical Pictures 248*b*; Peter Newark's Americana Picture Library 183; Novosti Press Agency 92, 93, 94*b*, 97*tl*, 124–5, 135, 137, 138*b*, 156, 158*br*; Performing Artservices Inc. 188*r*; Peters Edition 153, 165, 166, 167*t*, *b*, 188*l*, 189; Piano Publicity Association 27*l*, 246–7, 254, 256*tr*, 257*tl*, *tr*; Polydor Ltd. 169; Theodore Presser Company 161*b*; Private Collections 7, 105 (SPADEM); David Redfern 191, 211, 221; Redferns/A. Putler 214; Ricordi 152; Abby Aldrich Rockefeller Folk Art Collection 194; Royal College of Music 41, 43, 78, 81, 118*tr*, 224; Russell Collection, University of Edinburgh 16*c*, 22*br*; Schack Gallery/Verlag Joachim Blauel 146; Herbert Shead 253*bl*; Ronald Sheridan's Photo Library 11; G. Sirot/Ziolo 123; Smithsonian Institution 16*b* (56–341D), 28 (56–403A), 35*t* (77–15076A), *c* (78–12539), *bl* (76–19238) 37*l* (76–19240A); 174*t* (56–414A), *b* (56–445); 252*l* (56–385); 253*br* (56378B); Sotheby Parke Bernet and Co. 22*t*, 34*l*, *r*, 251; Staatliche Schlösser und Garten Potsdam-Sanssouci 21; Steinway and Sons 172, 173*t*, 176*b*, 236*b*, 244*t*, *l*, *r*; Trela/Ziolo 106, 140*t*; Universal Edition 151, 155*b*, 159, 170, 171; Victoria and Albert Museum 22*t*, *bl*, 256*b*, 257*b*; Valerie Wilmer 192, 203, 208, 209*b*, 212, 213; Worcester Art Museum, Mass. 13*t*; Yale Center for British Art, Paul Mellon Collection 239.

Index

Note: page numbers in *italics* refer to illustrations and/or captions; those in **bold type** to main entries. Where confusion might arise between page numbers and, for example, opus numbers, the page numbers are prefaced by 'p.' or 'pp.'